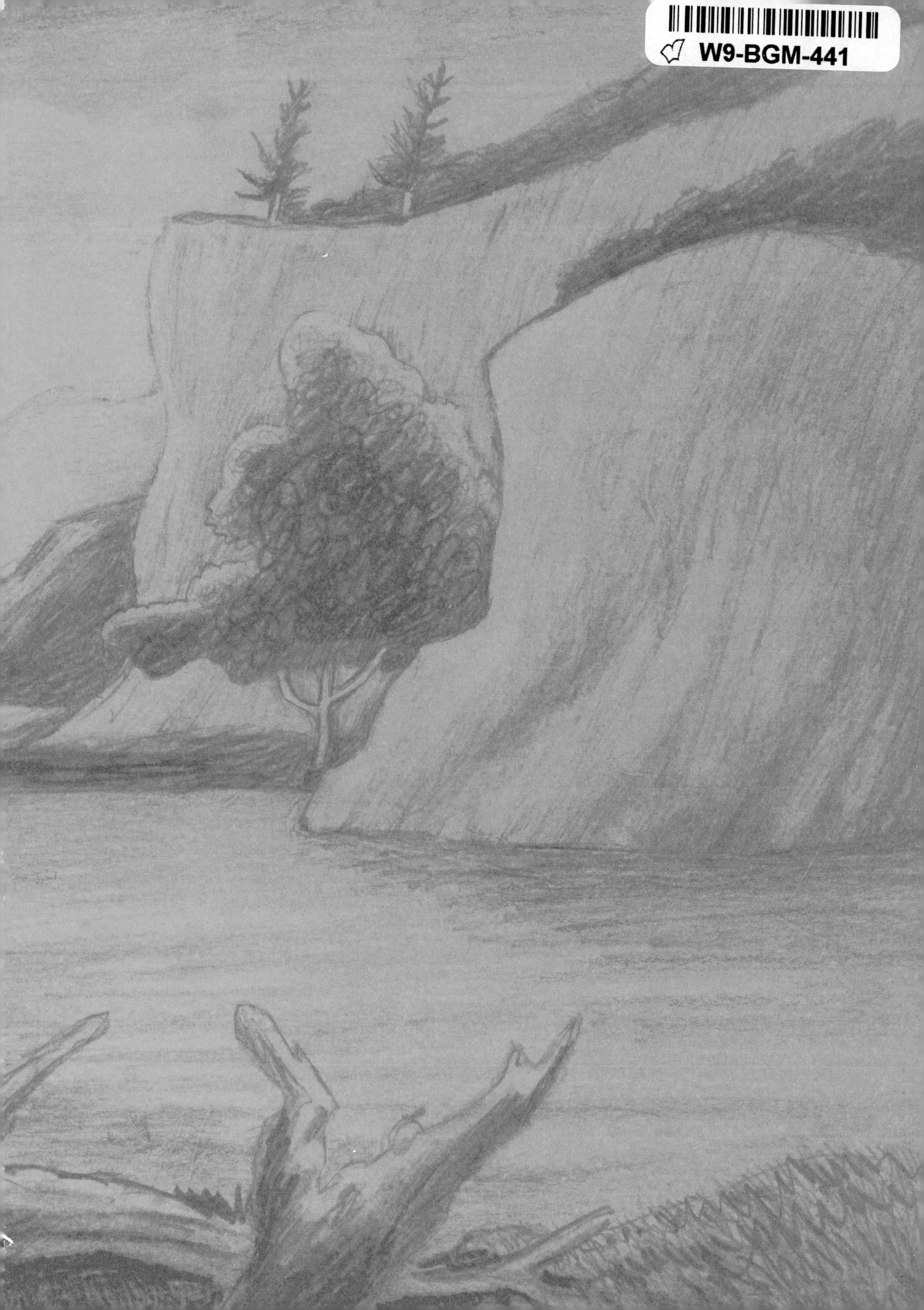

# JAMES STURM'S

# AMERICA

## God, Gold, and Golems

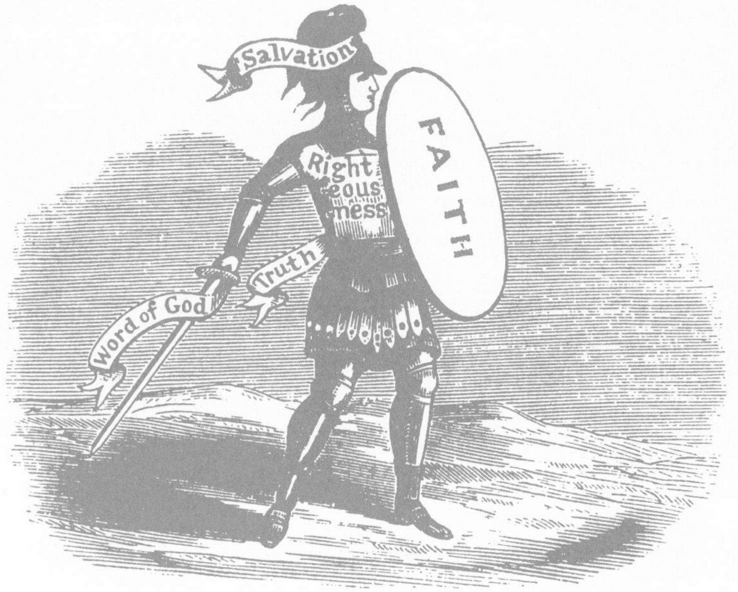
Salvation
Right eous ness
FAITH
Truth
Word of God

MONTREAL
DRAWN & QUARTERLY, PUBLISHERS

Frontier voices were strident and loud enough to be visible.

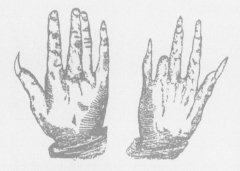

Scarred weapons of the western fighter (useful for gouging).

A Crockett character downed potent drinks with composure.

Cover watercolors by Rachel Gross and James Sturm.

Drawn & Quarterly
Post Office Box 48056
Montreal, Quebec
Canada H2V 4S8
www.drawnandquarterly.com

First hardcover edition: May 2007.
10 9 8 7 6 5 4 3 2 1
Printed in Singapore.

Library and Archives Canada Cataloguing in Publication

Sturm, James, 1965-
    James Sturm's America : God, gold and golems.

Originally publ. under title: The golem's mighty swing.
ISBN 978-1-897299-05-0

    1. United States--History--Comic books, strips, etc.
I. Sturm, James, 1965- Golem's mighty swing. II. Title.
III. Title: God, gold and golems.

PN6727.S88J35 2007      741.5973      C2006-906545-4

Distributed in the USA by:
Farrar, Straus and Giroux
19 Union Square West
New York, NY 10003
Orders: 888-330-8477

Distributed in Canada by:
Raincoast Books
9050 Shaughnessy Street
Vancouver, BC V6P 6E5
Orders: 800-663-5714

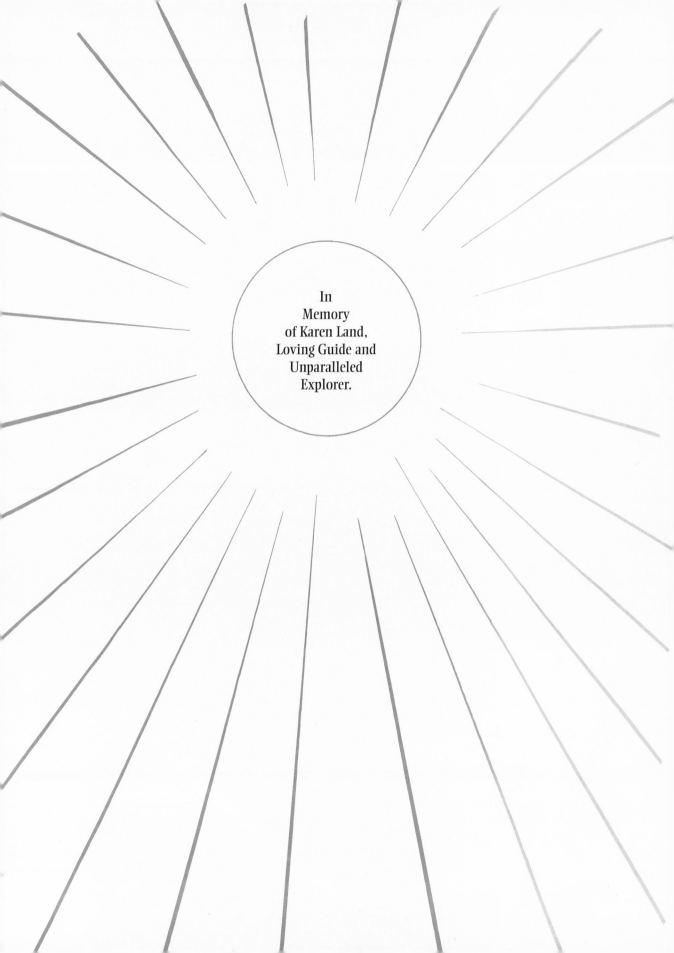

In
Memory
of Karen Land,
Loving Guide and
Unparalleled
Explorer.

WILLIAMS LAND

Arctic Circle

Eskimaux

Wager Str.

NEW

C. Noble

Chesterfield Inlet

NORTH

Rankin Inlet

Hope R.

WALES

Buttons B.

Churchill R.

York Ft.

Nelson R.

NEW

N. Severn R.

C. Henrietta Maria

SOUTH WALES

Albany R.

PARTS

Superior

C. Southampton

HUDSONS

C. Churchill

C. Tatnam

BAY

JAMES

Bay

Rupert R.

Hudsons Str.

LABRADOR
OR
NEW BRITAIN

ESKIMAUX

CANADA

Quebec

NEW
SCOTLAND

C. Sable

land seen by the
Spaniards. 1775

Nootka or
K. George's Sd.

C. Blanco

UNKNOWN

St. Mary

Gr. Fall R.

Huron

Montreal

NEW

C. Blanco

NEW

ALBION

Carmel R.

CALIFORNIA

California

Missouri R.

Panis

Erie

Ontario

Mexic Philadelphia

NEW JERSEY
MARYLAND

VIRGINIA

C. Hatteras

C. Lookout

NEW
Manillo

Great
Teguayo

MEXICO

Cath.
Grande

NEW

NAVAR

St. Fee

Apaches

LOUISI-
ANA

Osavos

Ulf.

Choktaw

CAROLINA

GEORGIA

FLORIDA

Cherokees

C. Fear

Charles Town

Port Royal

St. Augustin

BAHAM.

Mount de
Pinada

St. Christopher
de l'Madelaine

St. Thomas

St. Lucar

Compostella

C. Corientes

Colima

Zacatula

Acapulco

NEW
BISCAY

NEW

MEXICO

Panuco

Vera Cruz

Mexico

St. Bernards B.

GULF OF
MEXICO

B. of Florida

Providence

Cuba

Havana

JAMAICA

Kingston

HISPANIO

C. Honduras

NORTH SE

EAN OR

UTH SEA

Socunusco

I. de la Passion

C. Blanco

SPAIN

Cartagena

Porto
Bello

# CONTENTS

## I. The Revival   *p. 7*

CANE RIDGE, KENTUCKY, 1801; THOUSANDS OF PILGRIMS
LOOK TOWARDS HEAVEN TO FIND SALVATION.


## II. Hundreds of Feet Below Daylight   *p. 33*

SOLOMON'S GULCH, IDAHO, 1886; THE LAST RESIDENTS
OF A MINING TOWN CONTINUE
THEIR DESCENT.


## III. The Golem's Mighty Swing   *p. 83*

SMALL TOWN AMERICA, THE EARLY 1920S;
A BARNSTORMING JEWISH BASEBALL TEAM
CREATE A GOLEM TO DELIVER THEM
FROM THEIR TRIALS.

# THE REVIVAL

## (1801)

THIS BEING *the* FIRST SUMMER *of the* NEW CENTURY
WE INVITE YOU *to* CANE RIDGE, KENTUCKY, *to* BE PART
*of a* CAMP MEETING. THROUGH *the* AGENCY *of* MEN *and* WOMEN
LIKE YOURSELF, THIS REVIVAL WILL LAY *the* GROUNDWORK *for*
GOD'S EMPIRE HERE *on* EARTH. GIVING *a* THOROUGH INSPECTION
*into the* POWER *of* FAITH. INCLUDING *an* ACCURATE HISTORICAL
ACCOUNT *of* RELIGIOUS LIFE *in* EARLY AMERICA.

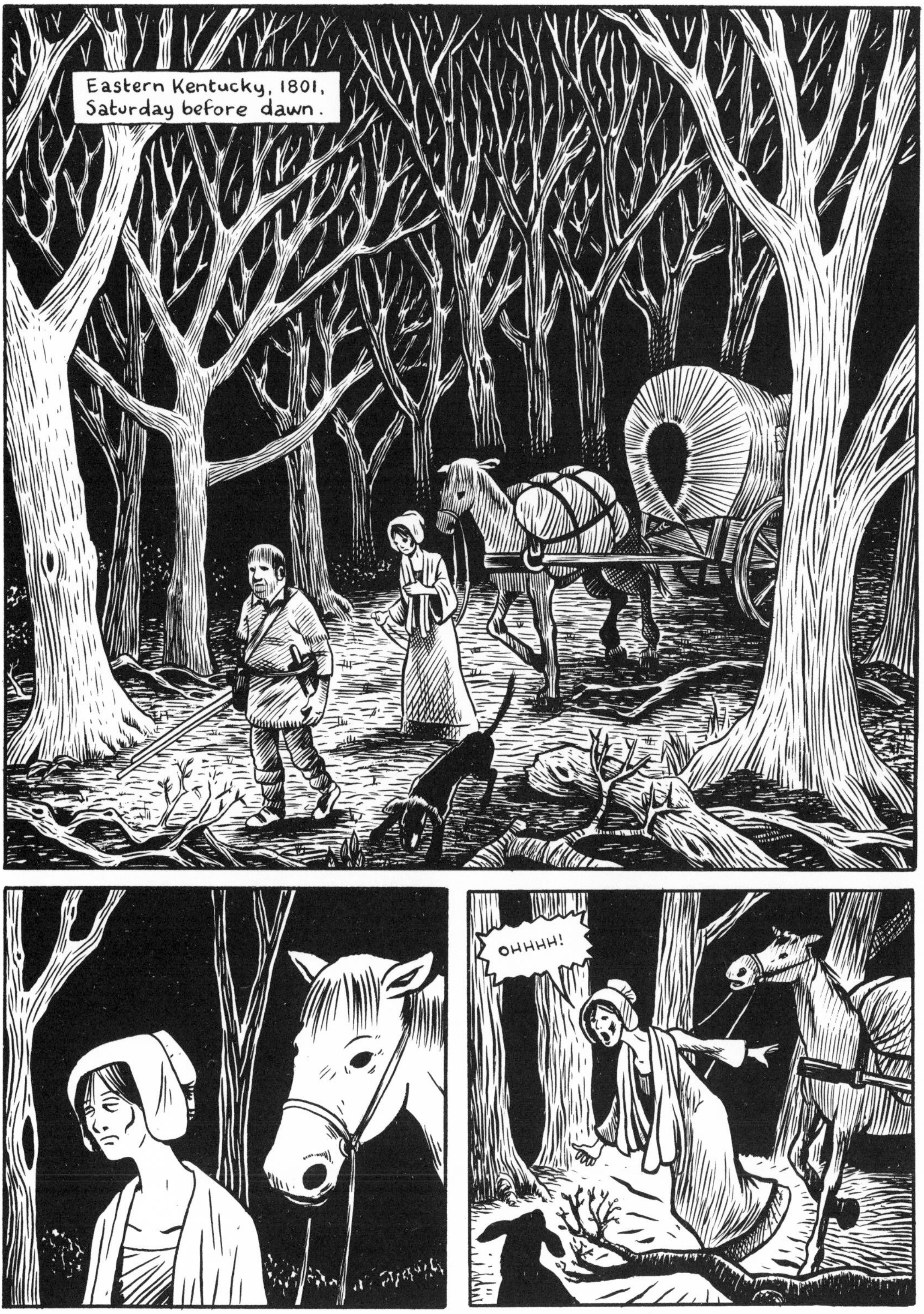
Eastern Kentucky, 1801,
Saturday before dawn.
OHHHH!

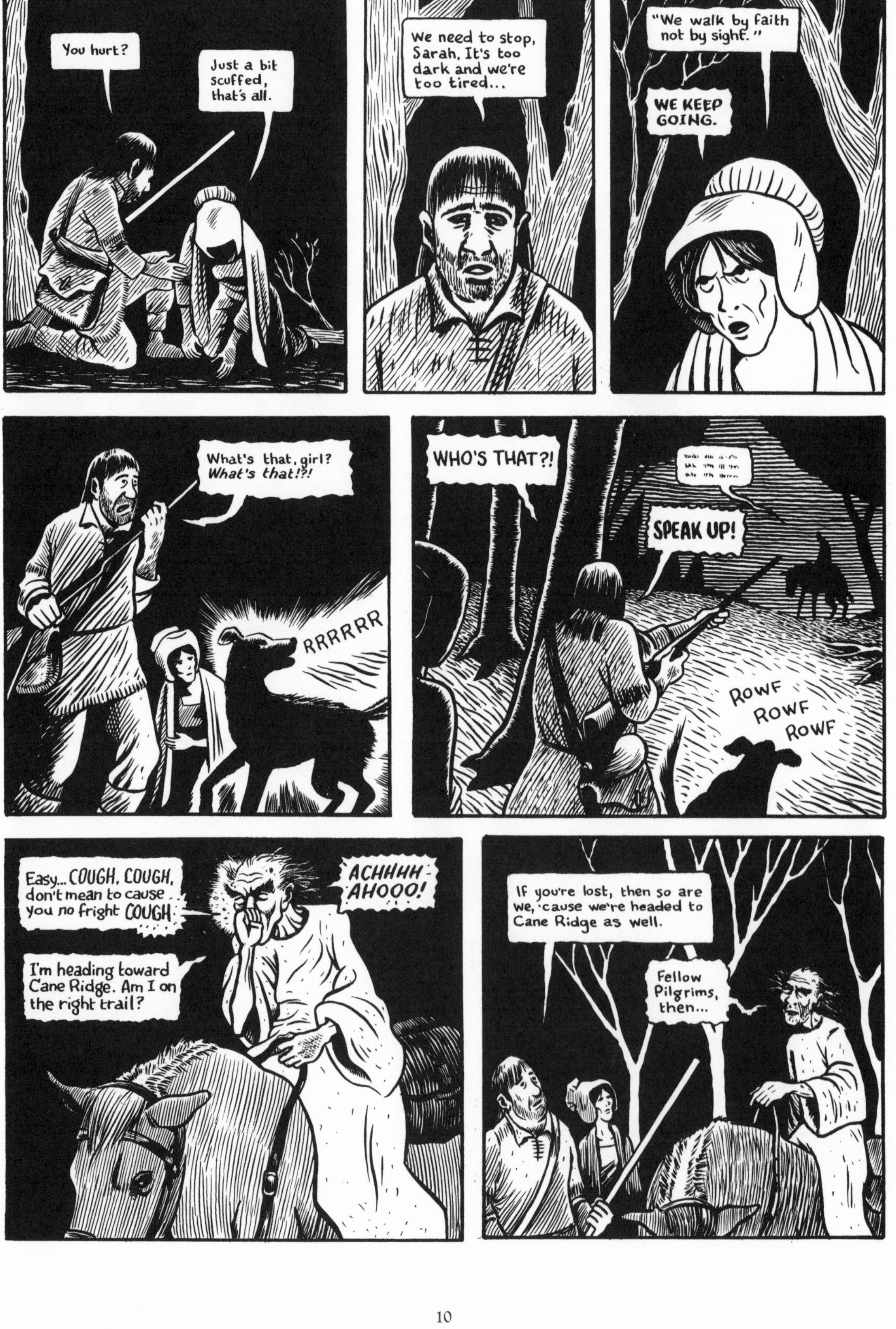
You hurt?
Just a bit scuffed, that's all.
We need to stop, Sarah. It's too dark and we're too tired...
"We walk by faith not by sight."
WE KEEP GOING.
What's that, girl? *What's that!?!*
RRRRRR
WHO'S THAT?!
SPEAK UP!
ROWF ROWF ROWF
Easy... COUGH, COUGH, don't mean to cause you no fright COUGH
ACHHHH-AHOOO!
I'm heading toward Cane Ridge. Am I on the right trail?
If you're lost, then so are we, 'cause we're headed to Cane Ridge as well.
Fellow Pilgrims, then...

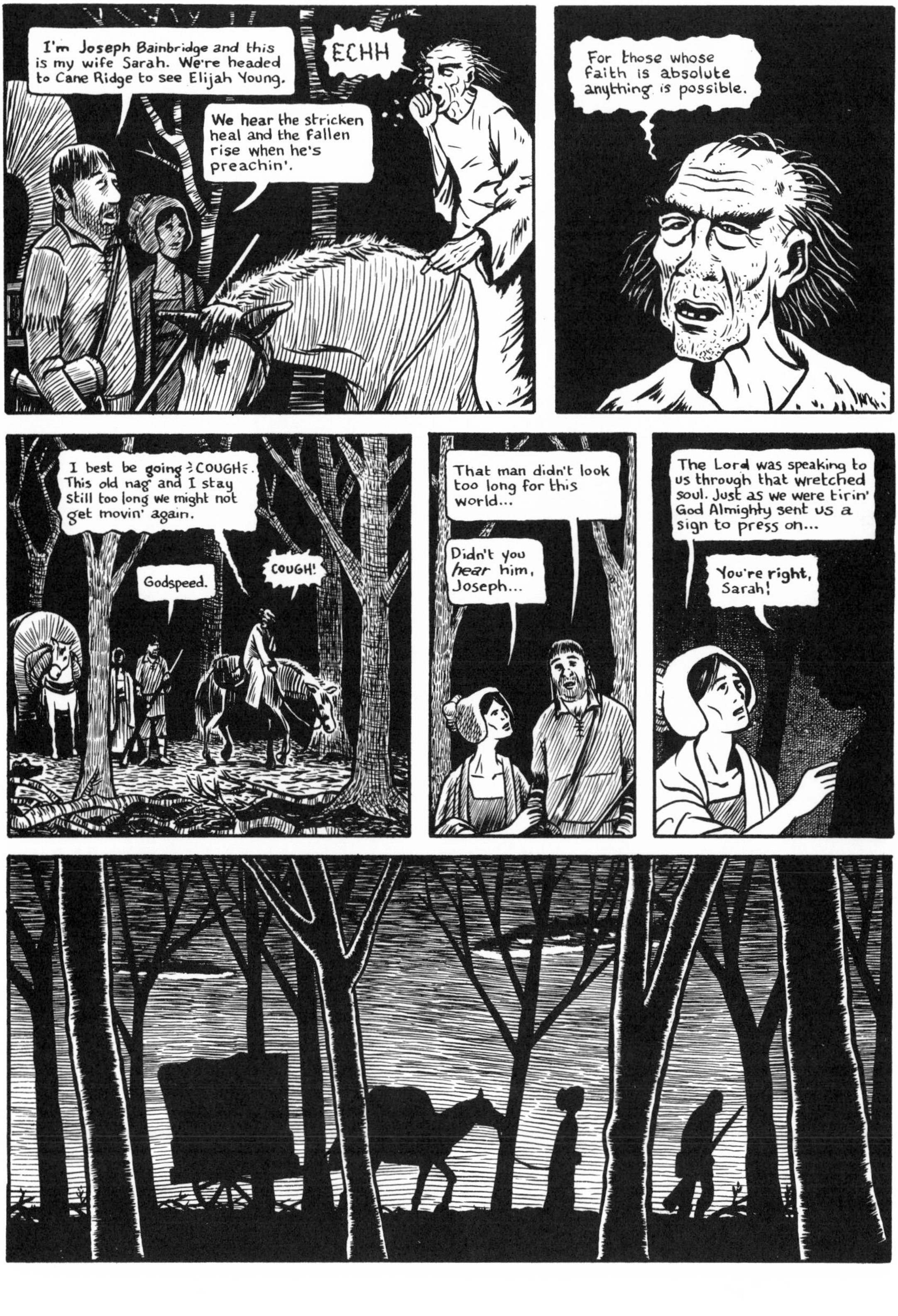
I'm Joseph Bainbridge and this is my wife Sarah. We're headed to Cane Ridge to see Elijah Young.
ECHH
We hear the stricken heal and the fallen rise when he's preachin'.
For those whose faith is absolute anything is possible.
I best be going ≥COUGH≤. This old nag and I stay still too long we might not get movin' again.
Godspeed.
COUGH!
That man didn't look too long for this world...
Didn't you *hear* him, Joseph...
The Lord was speaking to us through that wretched soul. Just as we were tirin' God Almighty sent us a sign to press on...
You're right, Sarah!

Saturday Afternoon, Cane Ridge.

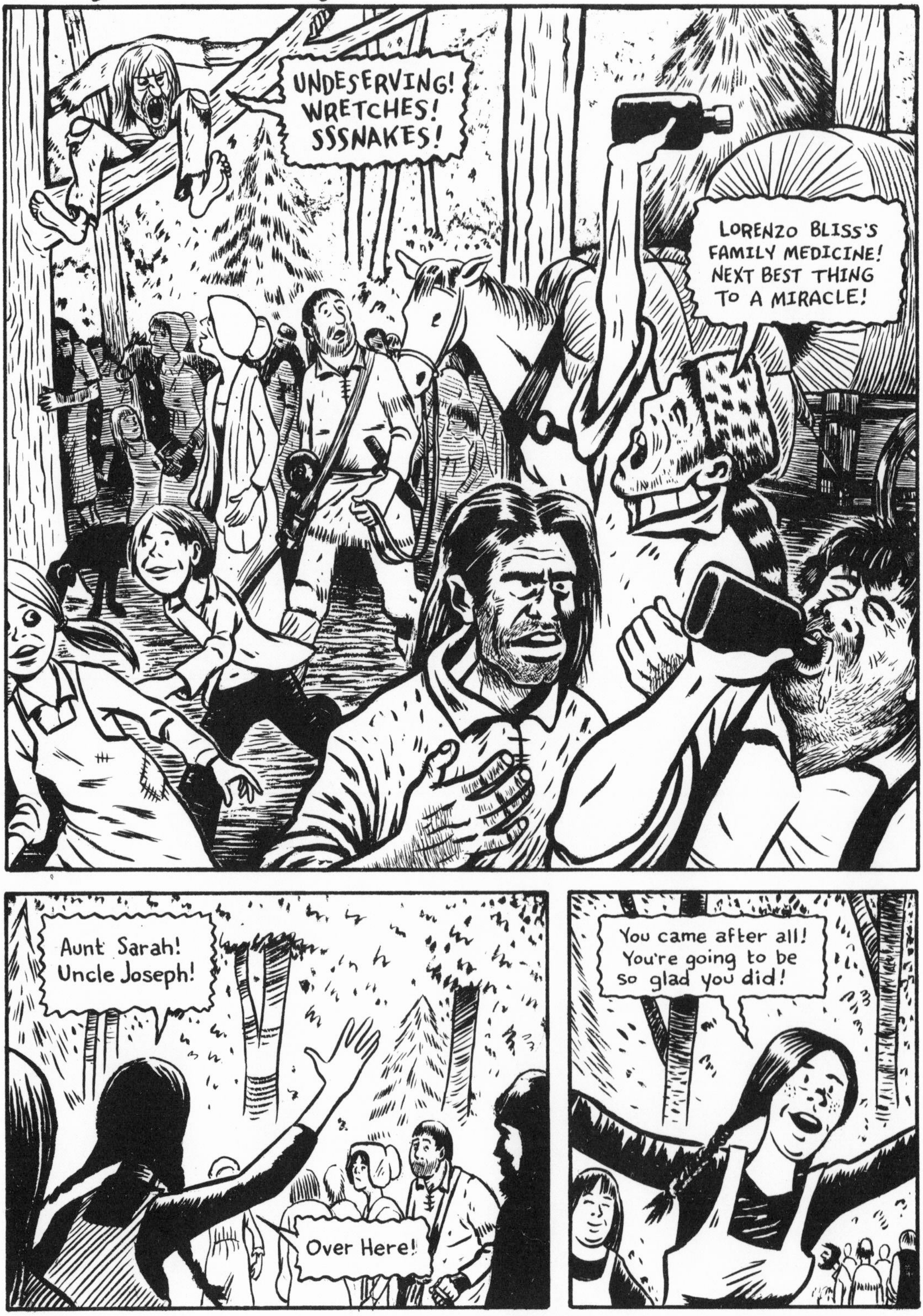
UNDESERVING! WRETCHES! SSSNAKES!
LORENZO BLISS'S FAMILY MEDICINE! NEXT BEST THING TO A MIRACLE!
Aunt Sarah! Uncle Joseph!
Over Here!
You came after all! You're going to be so glad you did!

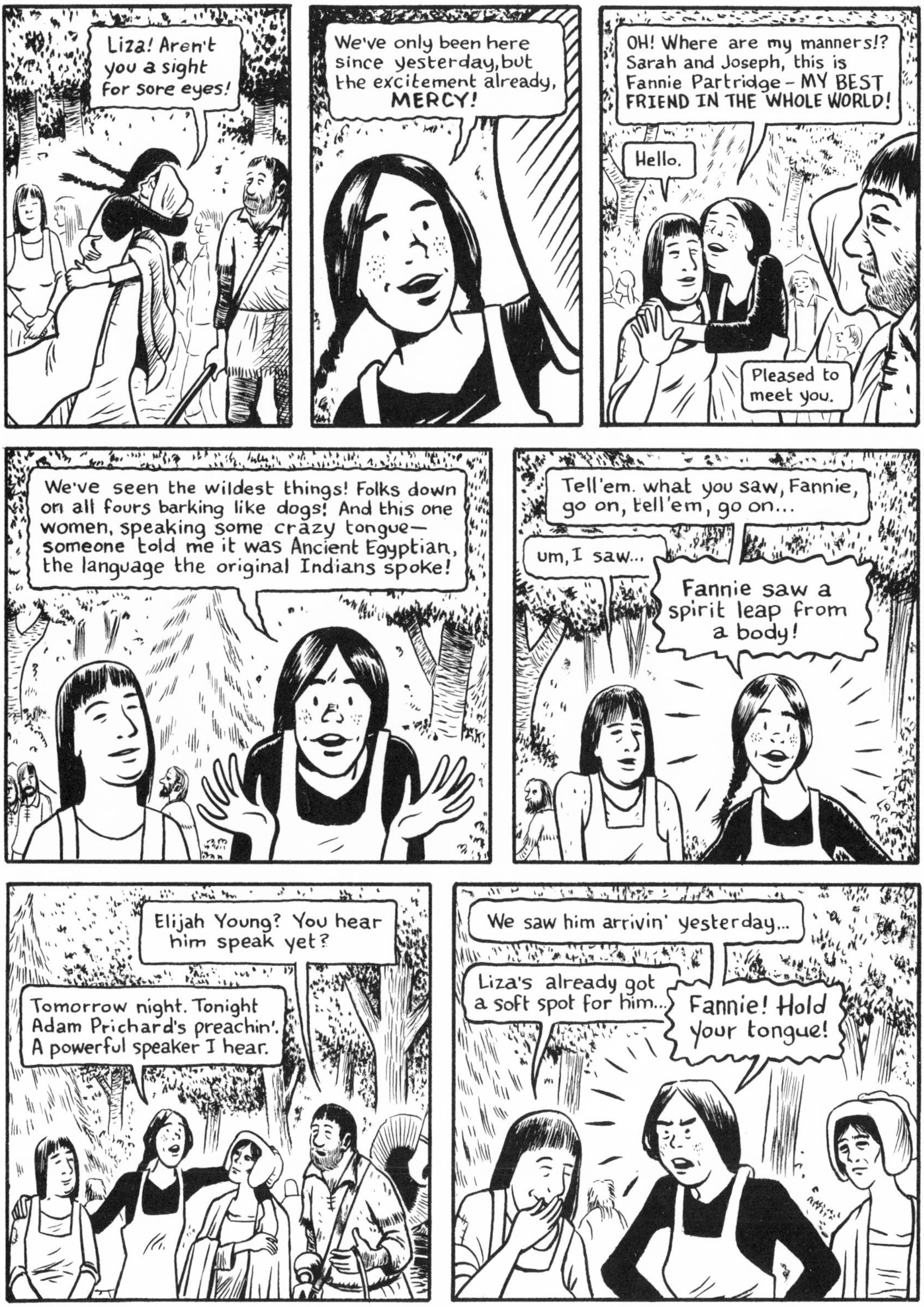
Liza! Aren't you a sight for sore eyes!
We've only been here since yesterday, but the excitement already, MERCY!
OH! Where are my manners!? Sarah and Joseph, this is Fannie Partridge - MY BEST FRIEND IN THE WHOLE WORLD!
Hello.
Pleased to meet you.
We've seen the wildest things! Folks down on all fours barking like dogs! And this one women, speaking some crazy tongue— someone told me it was Ancient Egyptian, the language the original Indians spoke!
Tell'em. what you saw, Fannie, go on, tell'em, go on...
um, I saw...
Fannie saw a spirit leap from a body!
Elijah Young? You hear him speak yet?
Tomorrow night. Tonight Adam Prichard's preachin'. A powerful speaker I hear.
We saw him arrivin' yesterday...
Liza's already got a soft spot for him...
Fannie! Hold your tongue!

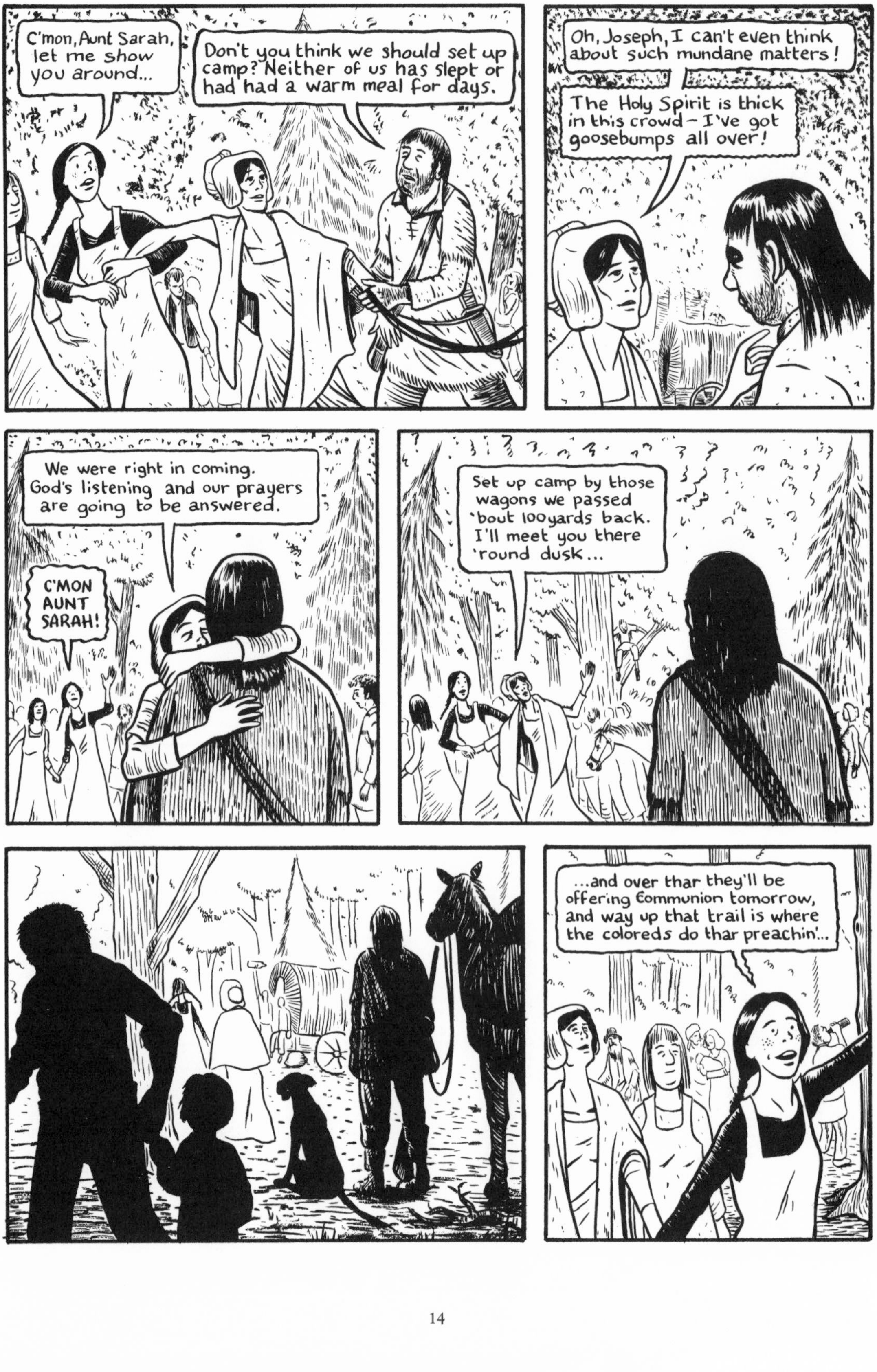
C'mon, Aunt Sarah, let me show you around...
Don't you think we should set up camp? Neither of us has slept or had had a warm meal for days.
Oh, Joseph, I can't even think about such mundane matters!
The Holy Spirit is thick in this crowd – I've got goosebumps all over!
We were right in coming. God's listening and our prayers are going to be answered.
C'MON AUNT SARAH!
Set up camp by those wagons we passed 'bout 100yards back. I'll meet you there 'round dusk...
...and over thar they'll be offering Communion tomorrow, and way up that trail is where the coloreds do thar preachin'...

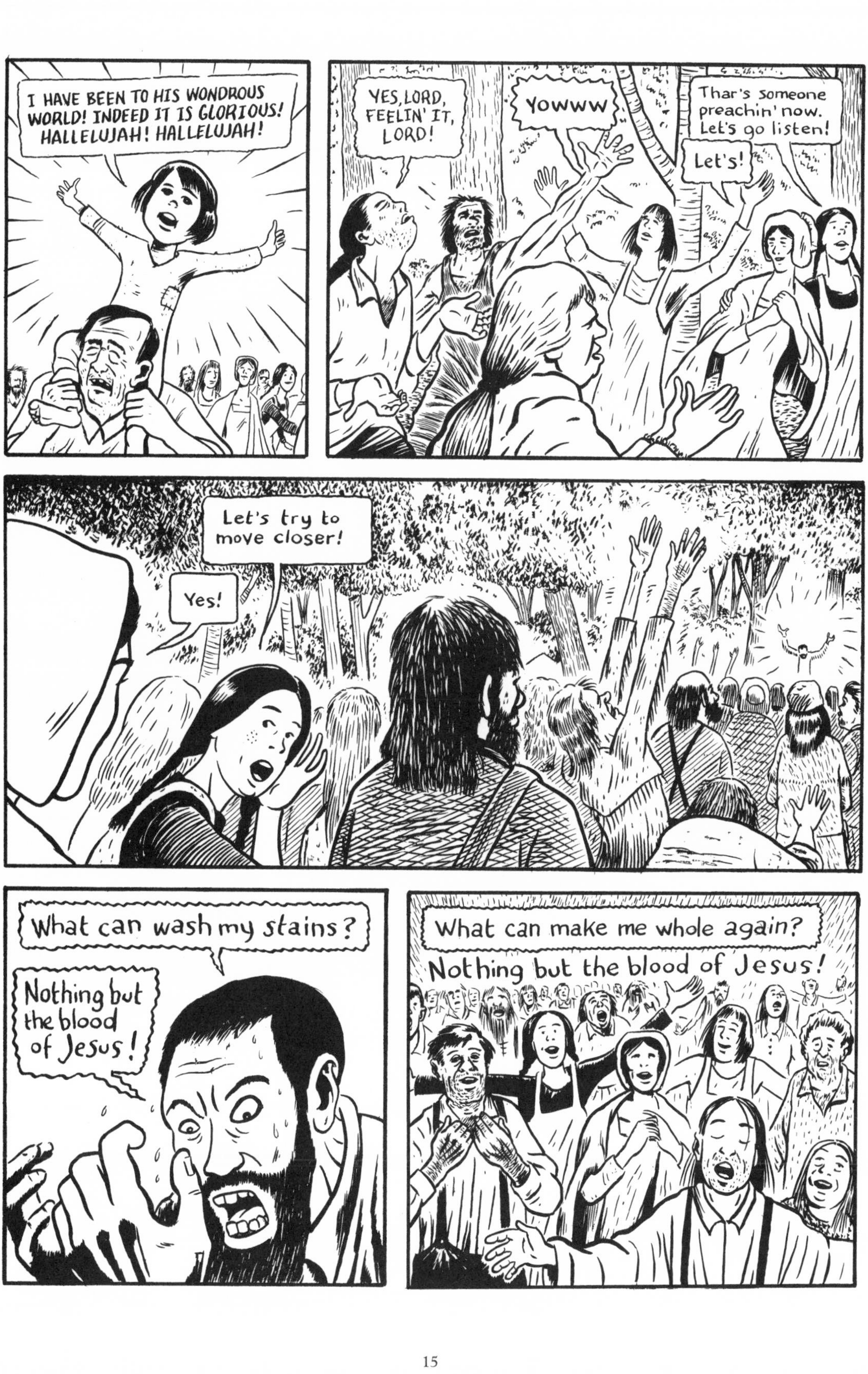
I HAVE BEEN TO HIS WONDROUS WORLD! INDEED IT IS GLORIOUS! HALLELUJAH! HALLELUJAH!
YES, LORD, FEELIN' IT, LORD!
YOWWW
Thar's someone preachin' now. Let's go listen!
Let's!
Let's try to move closer!
Yes!
What can wash my stains?
Nothing but the blood of Jesus!
What can make me whole again?
Nothing but the blood of Jesus!

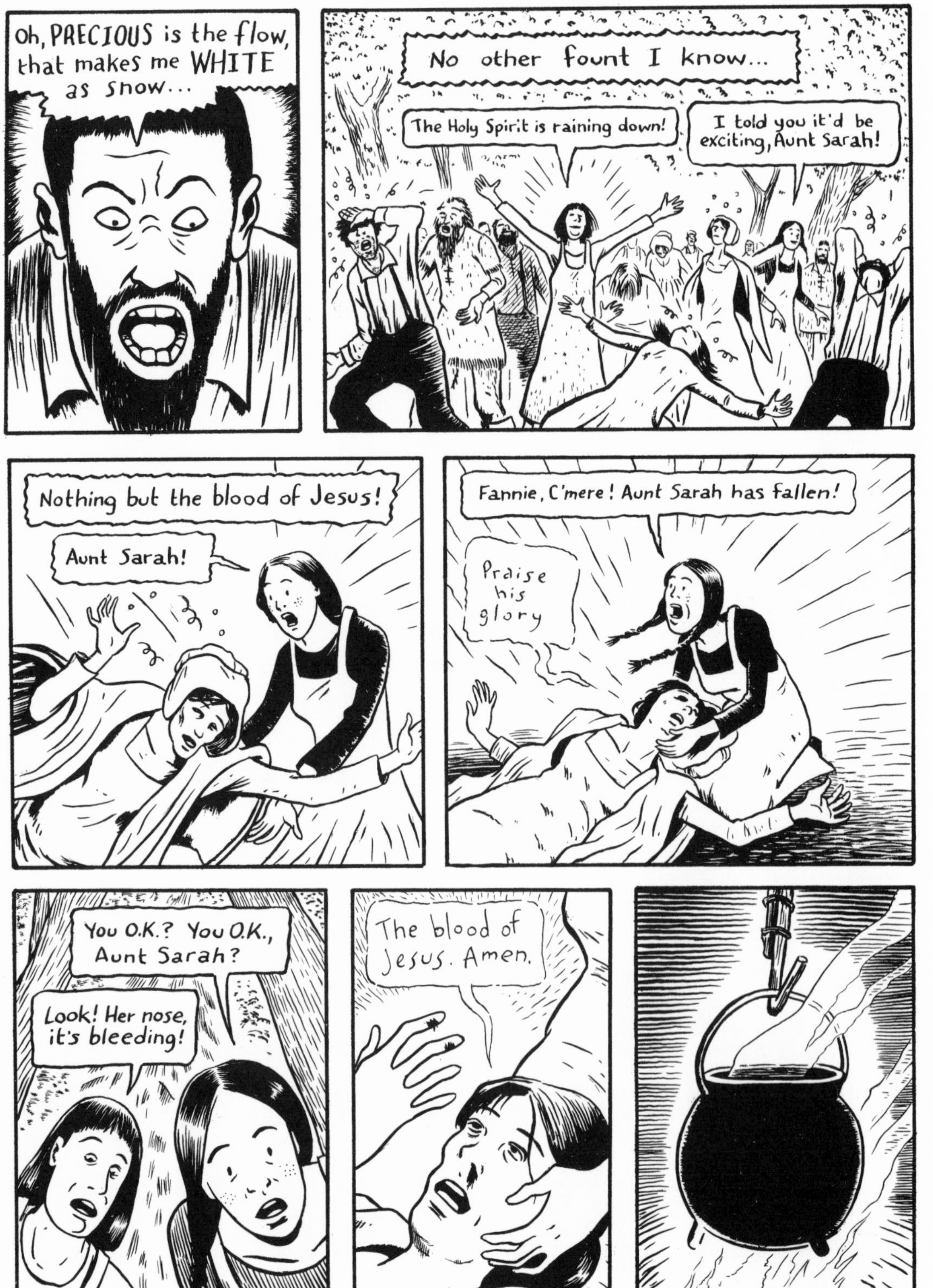
Oh, PRECIOUS is the flow, that makes me WHITE as snow...
No other fount I know...
The Holy Spirit is raining down!
I told you it'd be exciting, Aunt Sarah!
Nothing but the blood of Jesus!
Aunt Sarah!
Fannie, C'mere! Aunt Sarah has fallen!
Praise his glory
You O.K.? You O.K., Aunt Sarah?
Look! Her nose, it's bleeding!
The blood of Jesus. Amen.

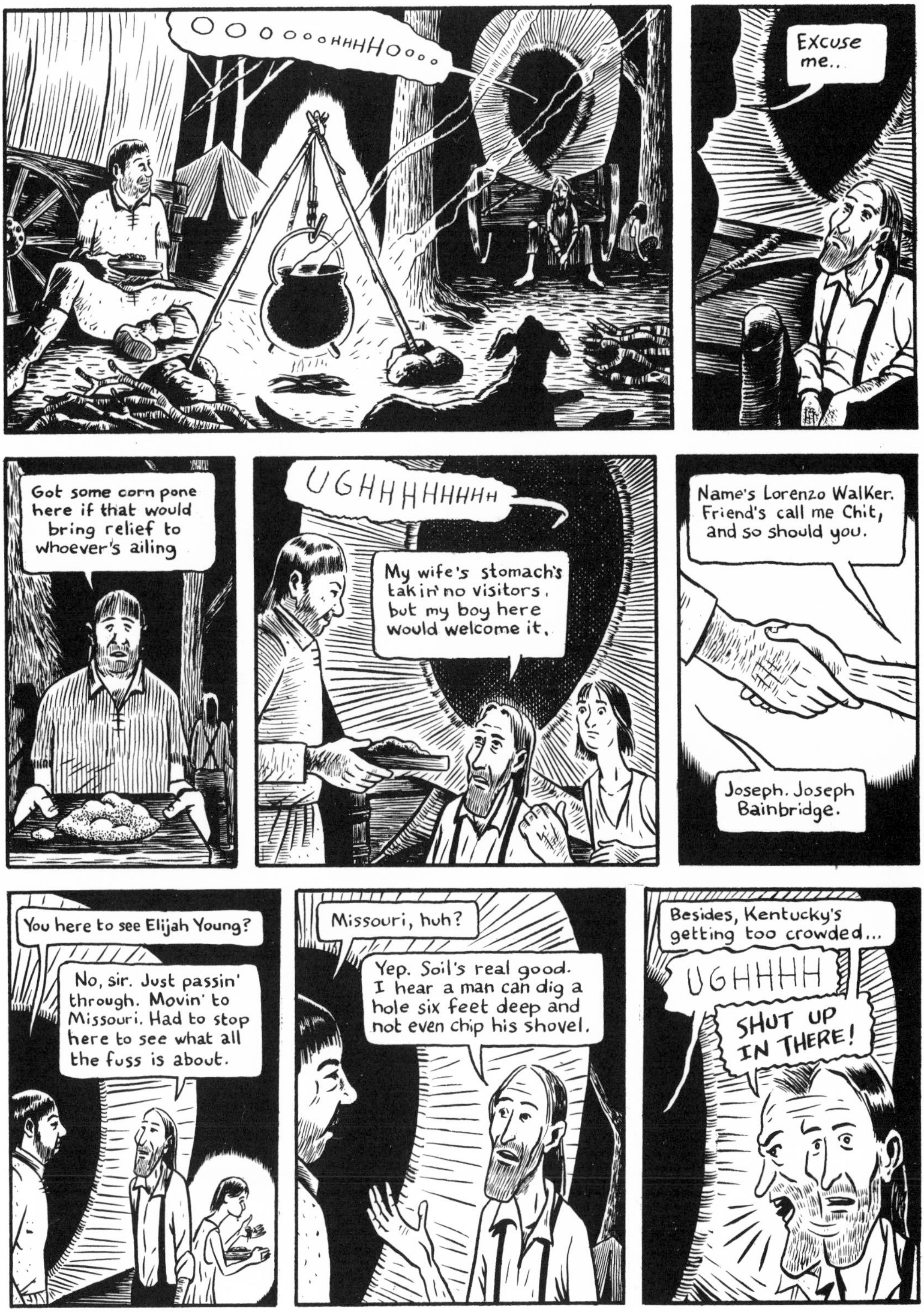
OOOoooHHHHOooo
Excuse me..
Got some corn pone here if that would bring relief to whoever's ailing
UGHHHHHHHH
My wife's stomach's takin' no visitors, but my boy here would welcome it.
Name's Lorenzo Walker. Friend's call me Chit, and so should you.
Joseph. Joseph Bainbridge.
You here to see Elijah Young?
No, sir. Just passin' through. Movin' to Missouri. Had to stop here to see what all the fuss is about.
Missouri, huh?
Yep. Soil's real good. I hear a man can dig a hole six feet deep and not even chip his shovel.
Besides, Kentucky's getting too crowded...
UGHHHH
SHUT UP IN THERE!

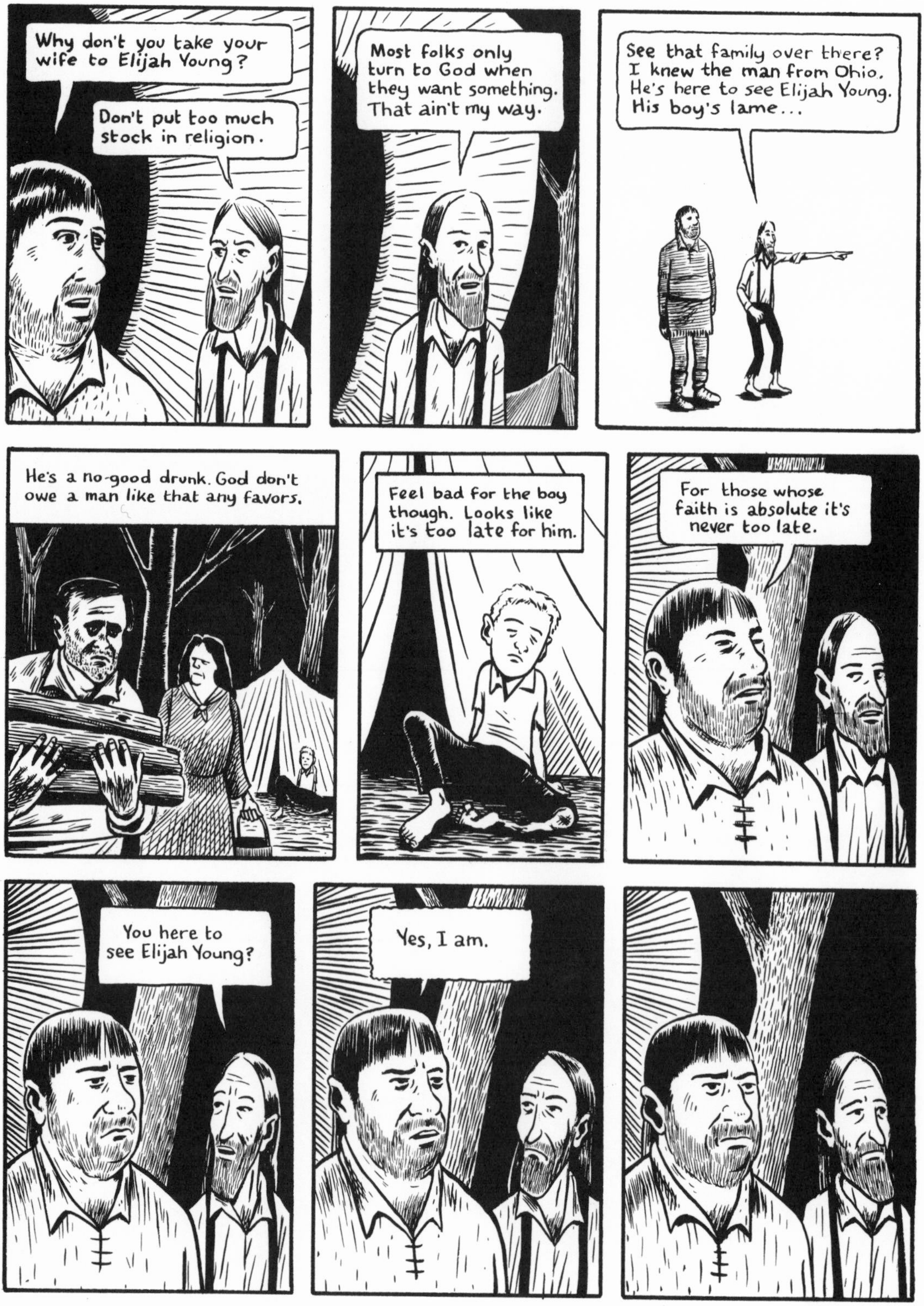
Why don't you take your wife to Elijah Young?
Don't put too much stock in religion.
Most folks only turn to God when they want something. That ain't my way.
See that family over there? I knew the man from Ohio. He's here to see Elijah Young. His boy's lame...
He's a no-good drunk. God don't owe a man like that any favors.
Feel bad for the boy though. Looks like it's too late for him.
For those whose faith is absolute it's never too late.
You here to see Elijah Young?
Yes, I am.

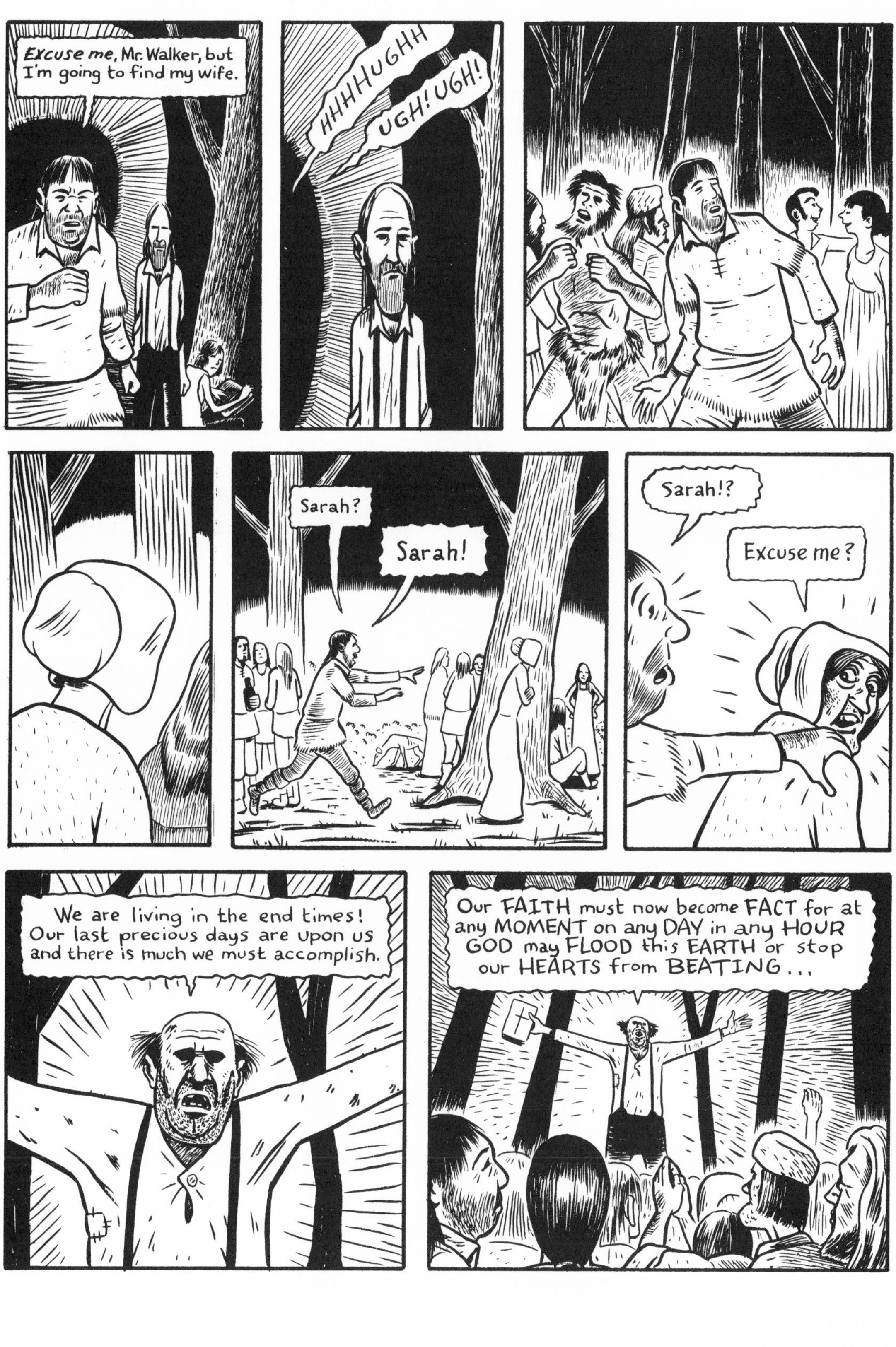
Excuse me, Mr. Walker, but I'm going to find my wife.
HHHHUGHH
UGH! UGH!
Sarah?
Sarah!
Sarah!?
Excuse me?
We are living in the end times! Our last precious days are upon us and there is much we must accomplish.
Our FAITH must now become FACT for at any MOMENT on any DAY in any HOUR GOD may FLOOD this EARTH or stop our HEARTS from BEATING...

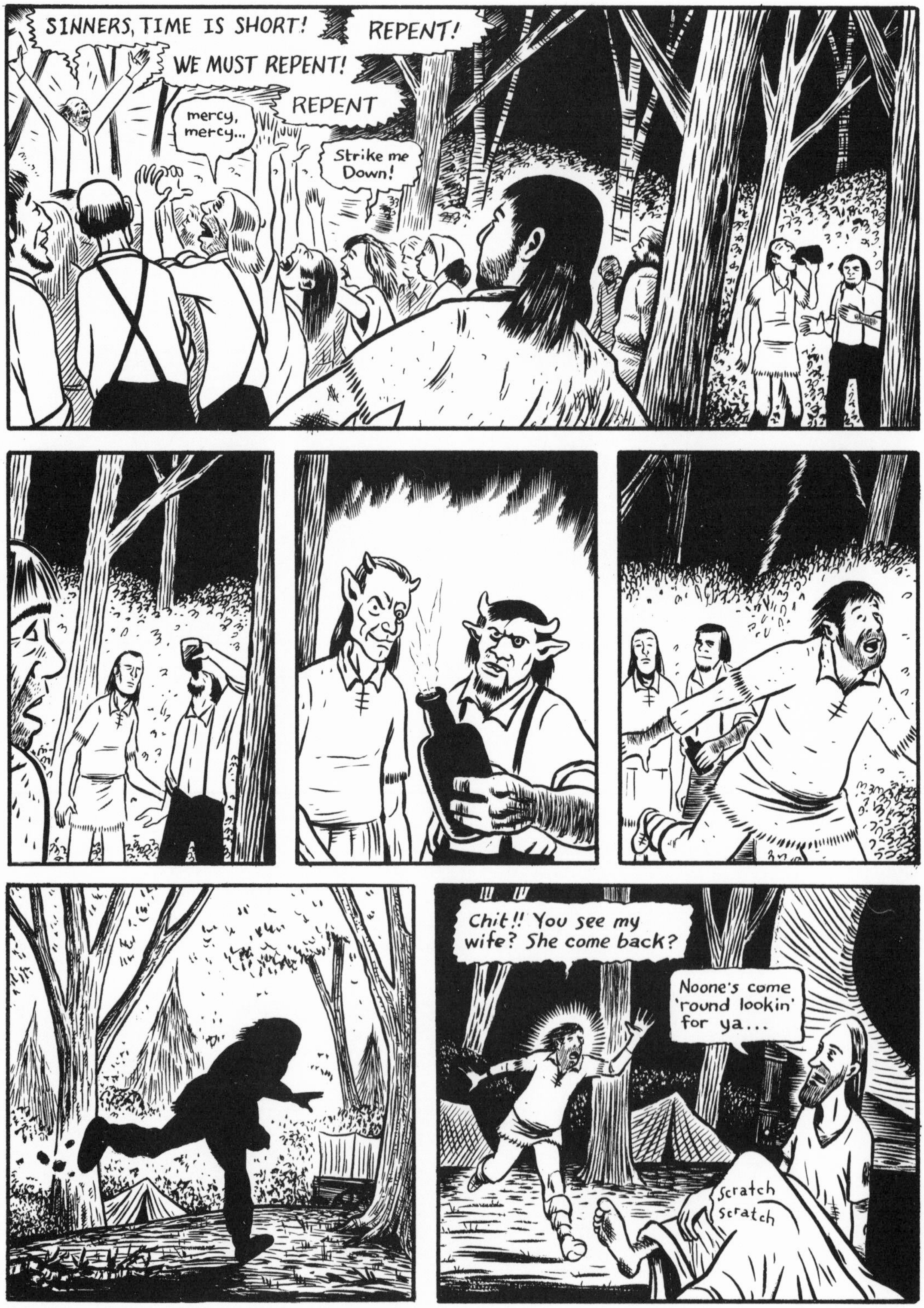
SINNERS, TIME IS SHORT!
REPENT!
WE MUST REPENT!
REPENT
mercy, mercy...
Strike me Down!
Chit!! You see my wife? She come back?
Noone's come 'round lookin' for ya...
scratch scratch

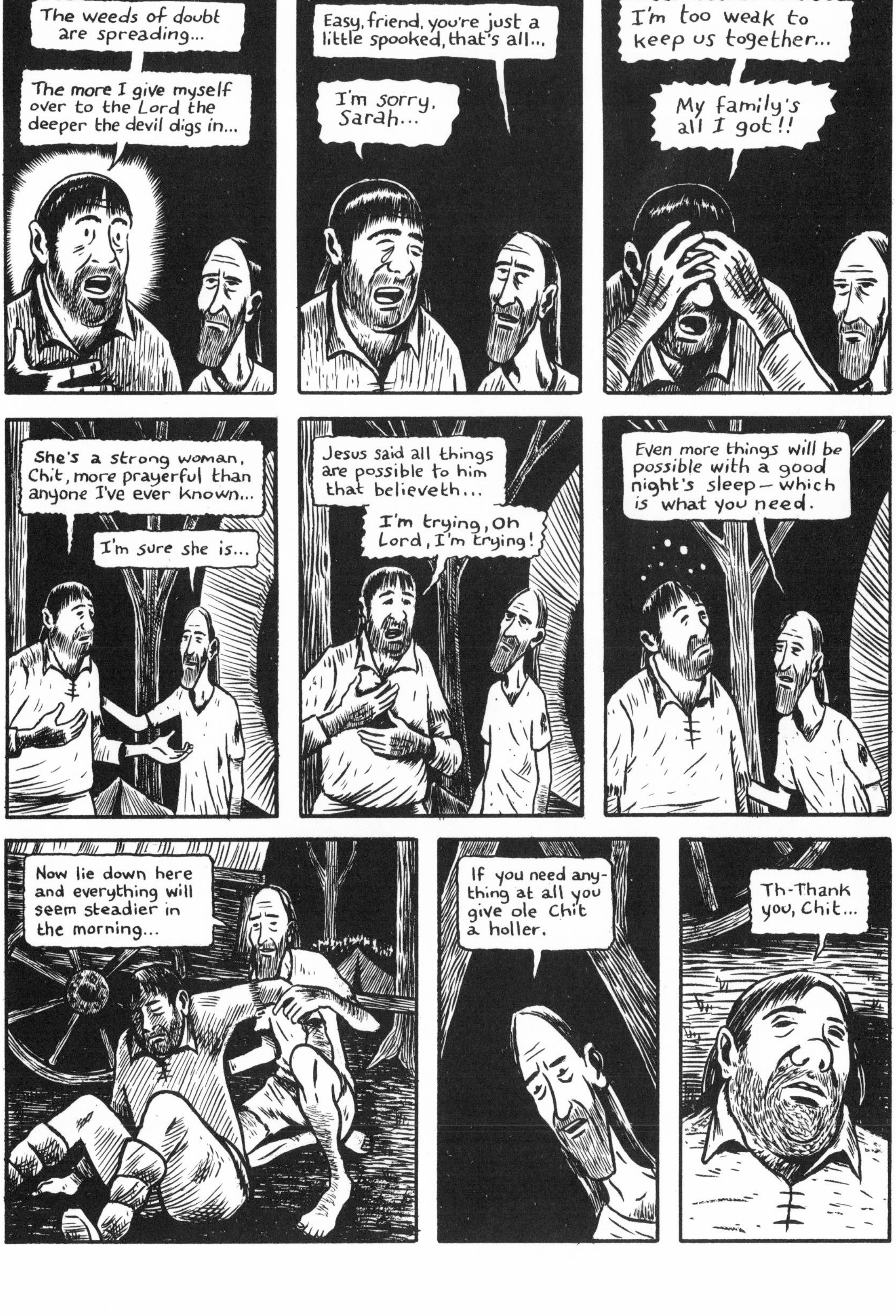
The weeds of doubt are spreading...
The more I give myself over to the Lord the deeper the devil digs in...
Easy, friend, you're just a little spooked, that's all...
I'm sorry, Sarah...
I'm too weak to keep us together...
My family's all I got!!
She's a strong woman, Chit, more prayerful than anyone I've ever known...
I'm sure she is...
Jesus said all things are possible to him that believeth...
I'm trying, Oh Lord, I'm trying!
Even more things will be possible with a good night's sleep—which is what you need.
Now lie down here and everything will seem steadier in the morning...
If you need anything at all you give ole Chit a holler.
Th-Thank you, Chit...

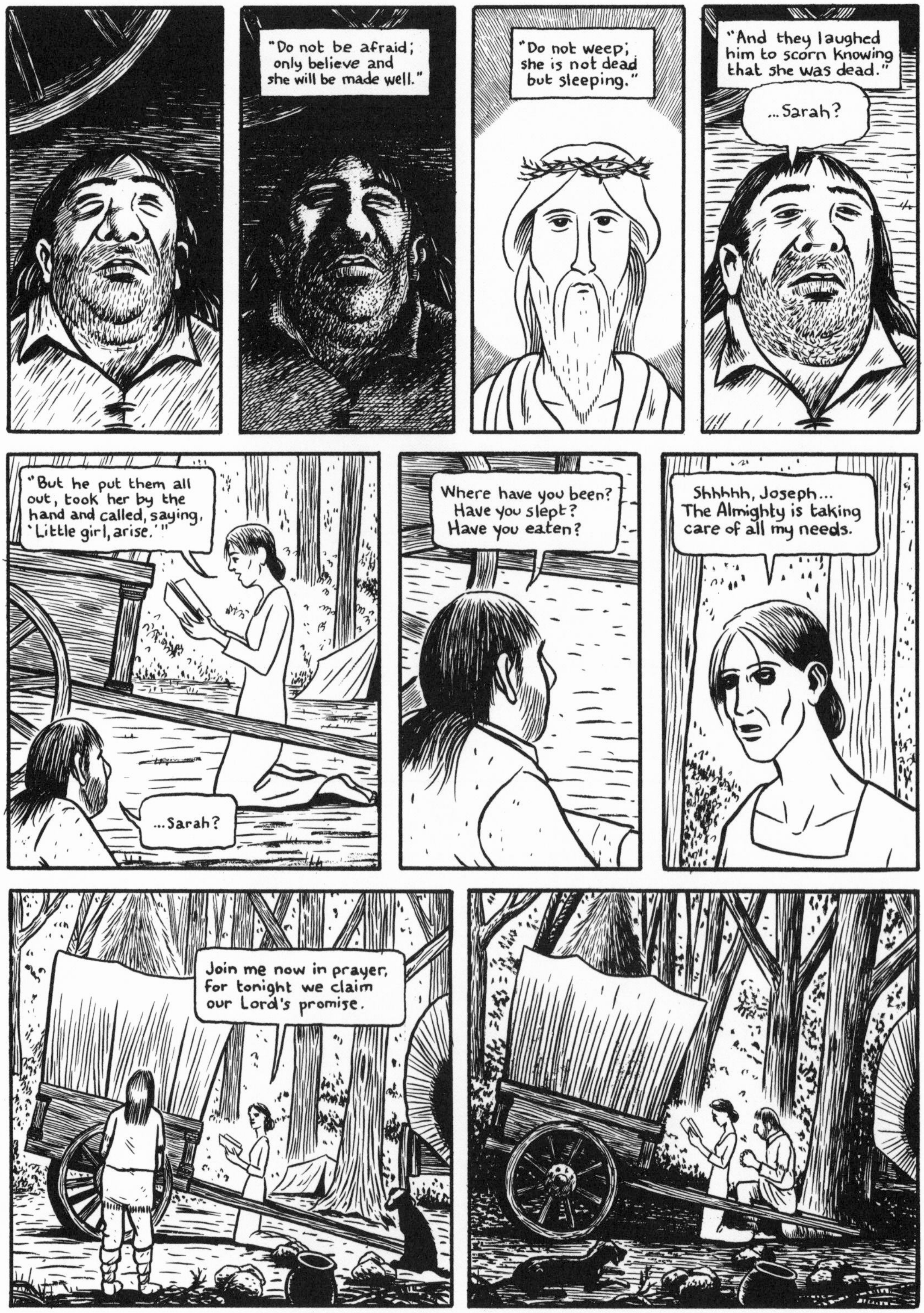
"Do not be afraid; only believe and she will be made well."
"Do not weep; she is not dead but sleeping."
"And they laughed him to scorn knowing that she was dead."
...Sarah?
"But he put them all out, took her by the hand and called, saying, 'Little girl, arise.'"
...Sarah?
Where have you been? Have you slept? Have you eaten?
Shhhhh, Joseph... The Almighty is taking care of all my needs.
Join me now in prayer, for tonight we claim our Lord's promise.

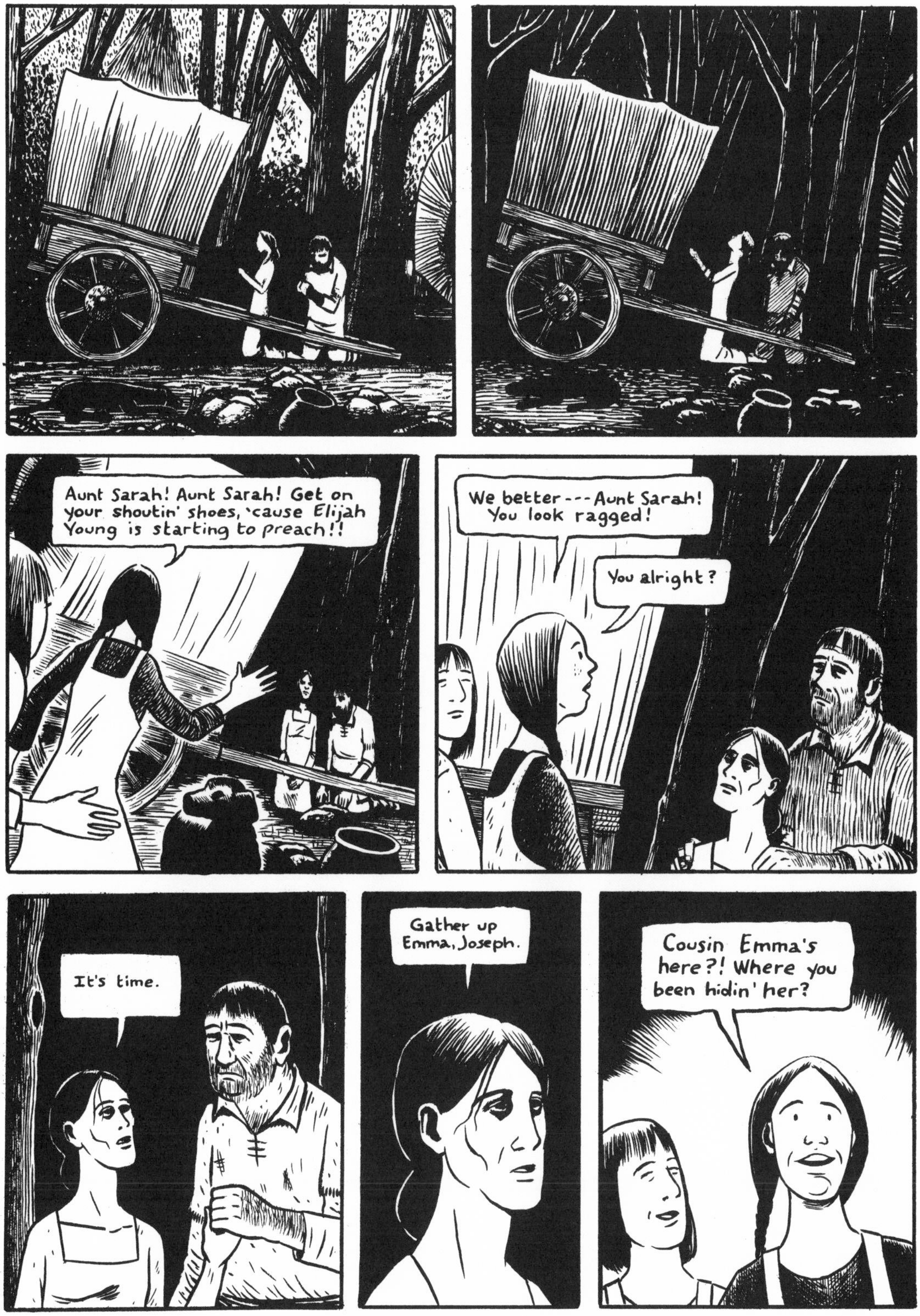
Aunt Sarah! Aunt Sarah! Get on your shoutin' shoes, 'cause Elijah Young is starting to preach!!
We better --- Aunt Sarah! You look ragged!
You alright?
It's time.
Gather up Emma, Joseph.
Cousin Emma's here?! Where you been hidin' her?

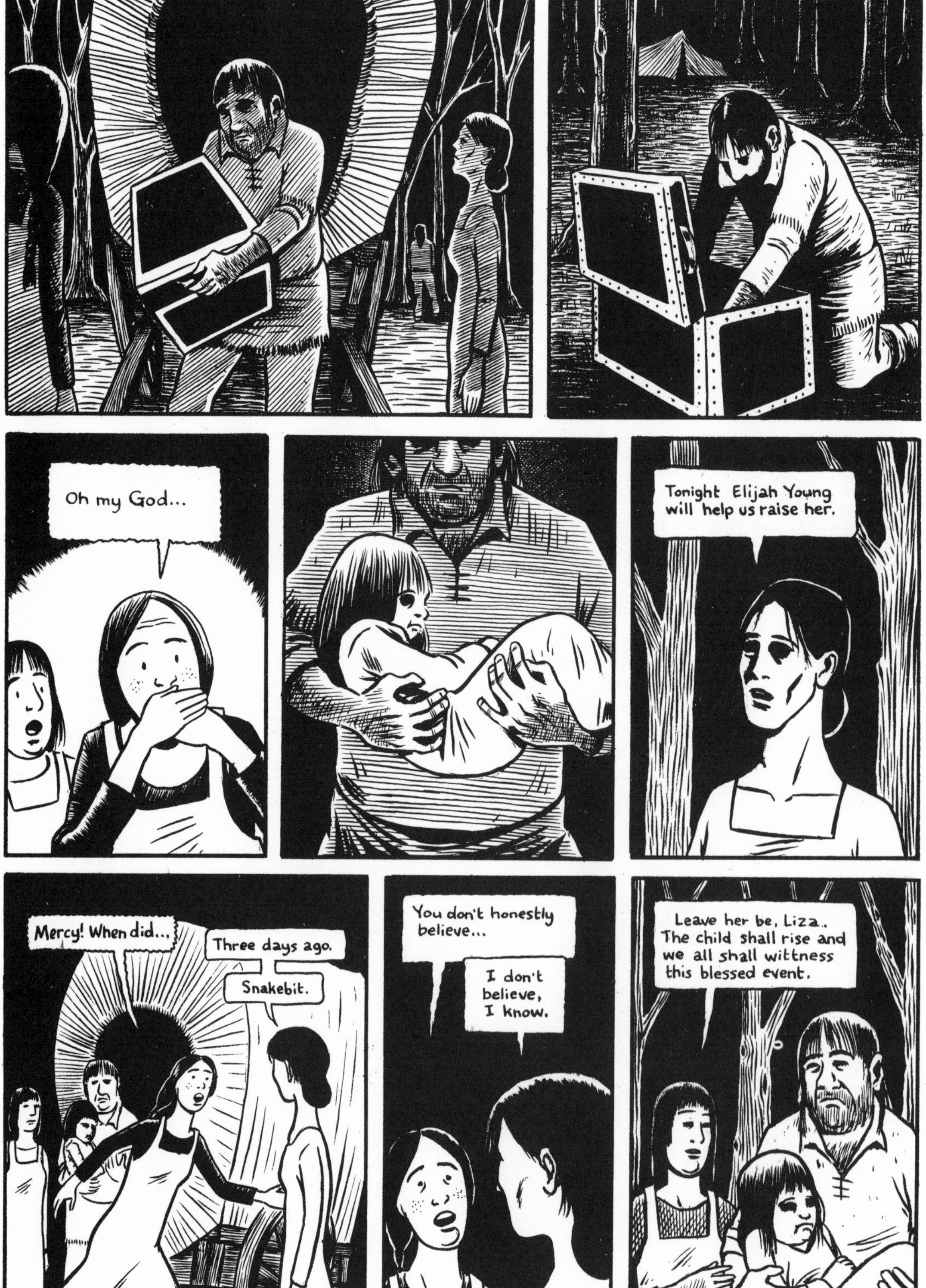
Oh my God...
Tonight Elijah Young will help us raise her.
Mercy! When did...
Three days ago.
Snakebit.
You don't honestly believe...
I don't believe, I know.
Leave her be, Liza.. The child shall rise and we all shall wittness this blessed event.

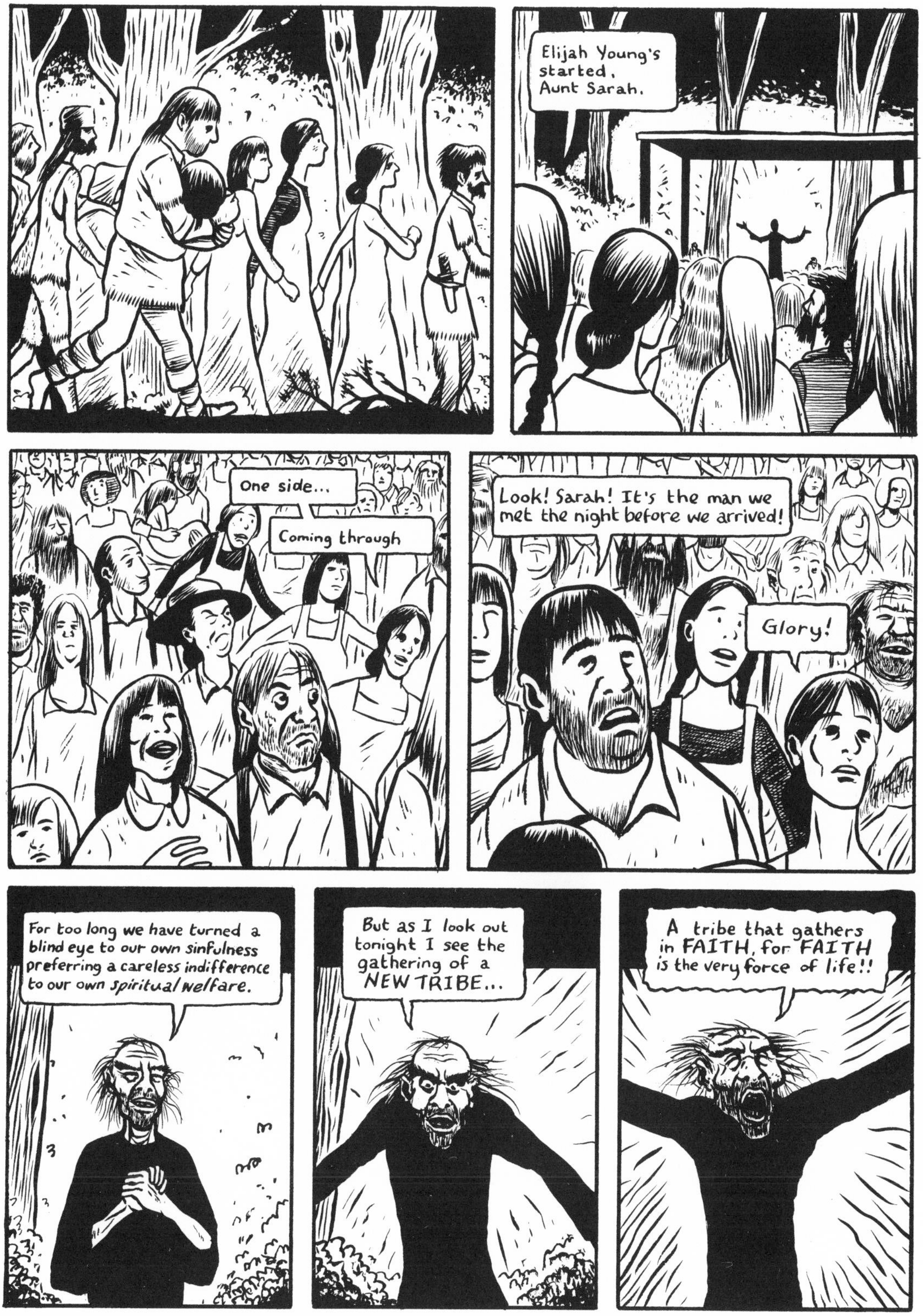
Elijah Young's started, Aunt Sarah.
One side...
Coming through
Look! Sarah! It's the man we met the night before we arrived!
Glory!
For too long we have turned a blind eye to our own sinfulness preferring a careless indifference to our own spiritual welfare.
But as I look out tonight I see the gathering of a NEW TRIBE...
A tribe that gathers in FAITH, for FAITH is the very force of life!!

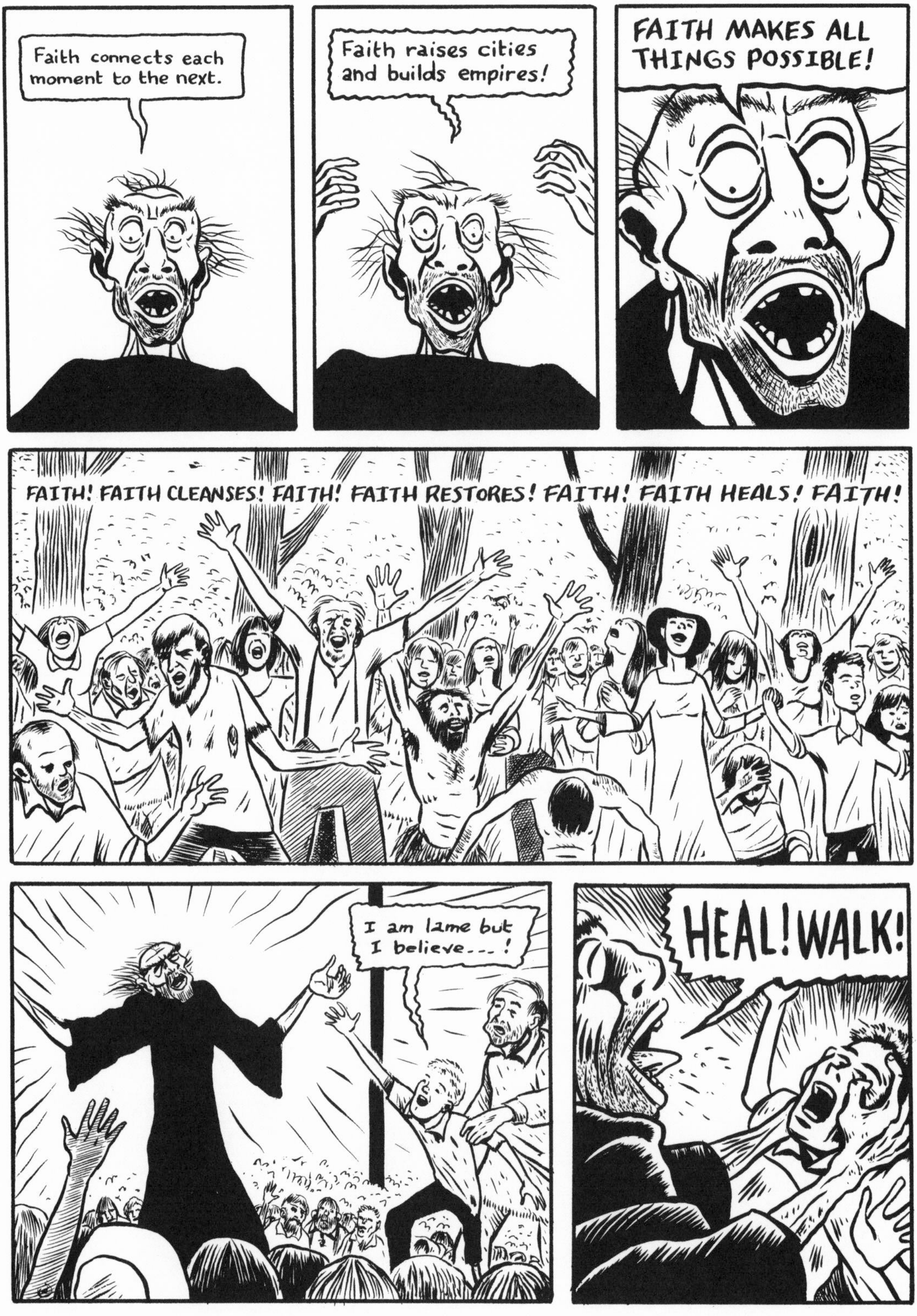
Faith connects each moment to the next.
Faith raises cities and builds empires!
FAITH MAKES ALL THINGS POSSIBLE!
FAITH! FAITH CLEANSES! FAITH! FAITH RESTORES! FAITH! FAITH HEALS! FAITH!
I am lame but I believe...!
HEAL! WALK!

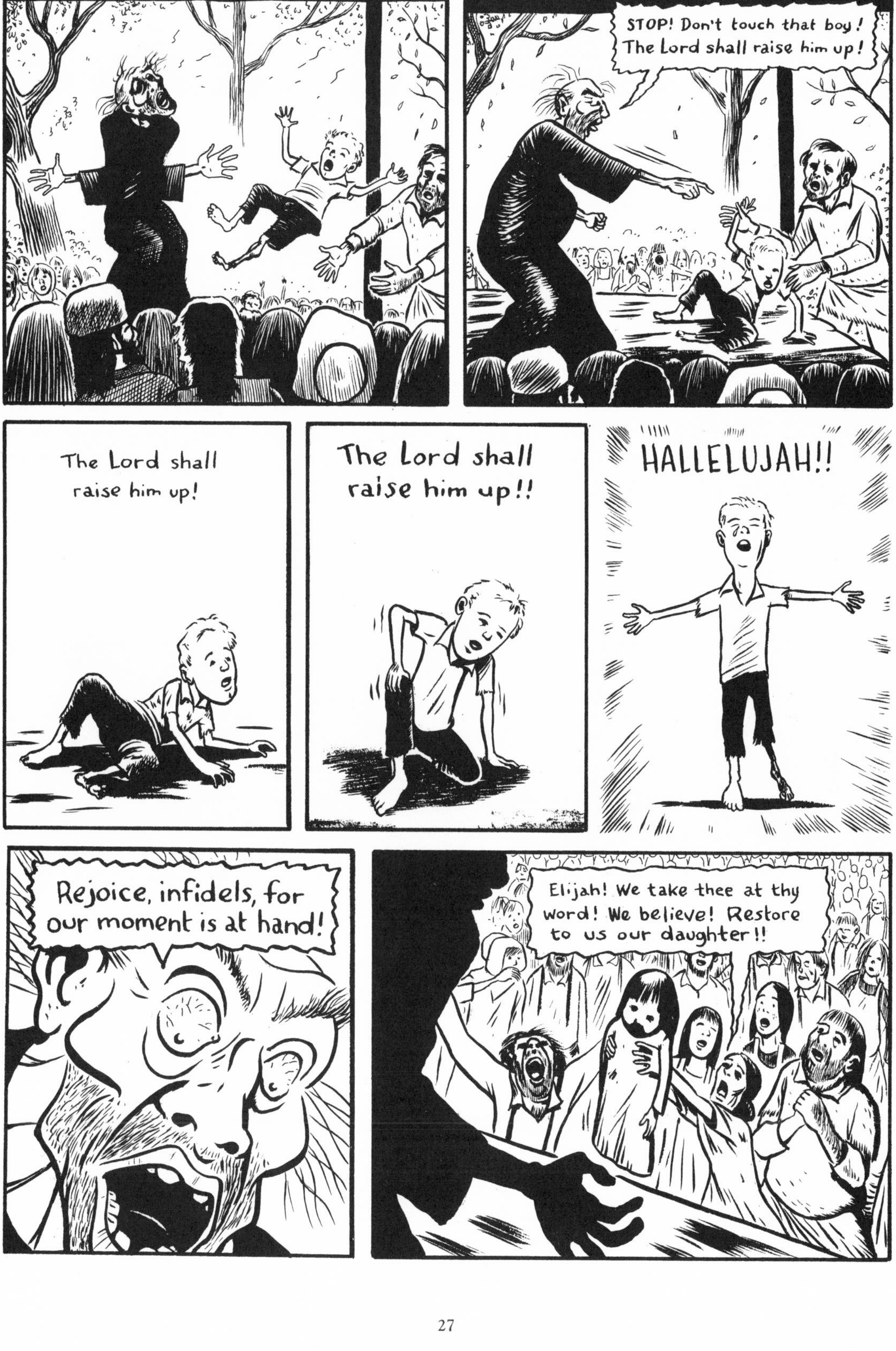
STOP! Don't touch that boy! The Lord shall raise him up!
The Lord shall raise him up!
The Lord shall raise him up!!
HALLELUJAH!!
Rejoice, infidels, for our moment is at hand!
Elijah! We take thee at thy word! We believe! Restore to us our daughter!!

What's this? The roar of the faithful is so quickly muted?!

For those who are Christ's, He will bring them back with him...

Christ's Return! Judgement Day! Who is prepared for Judgement Day!?

WHO is PREPARED to stand NAKED before JESUS and be JUDGED by our all-knowing MASTER?!

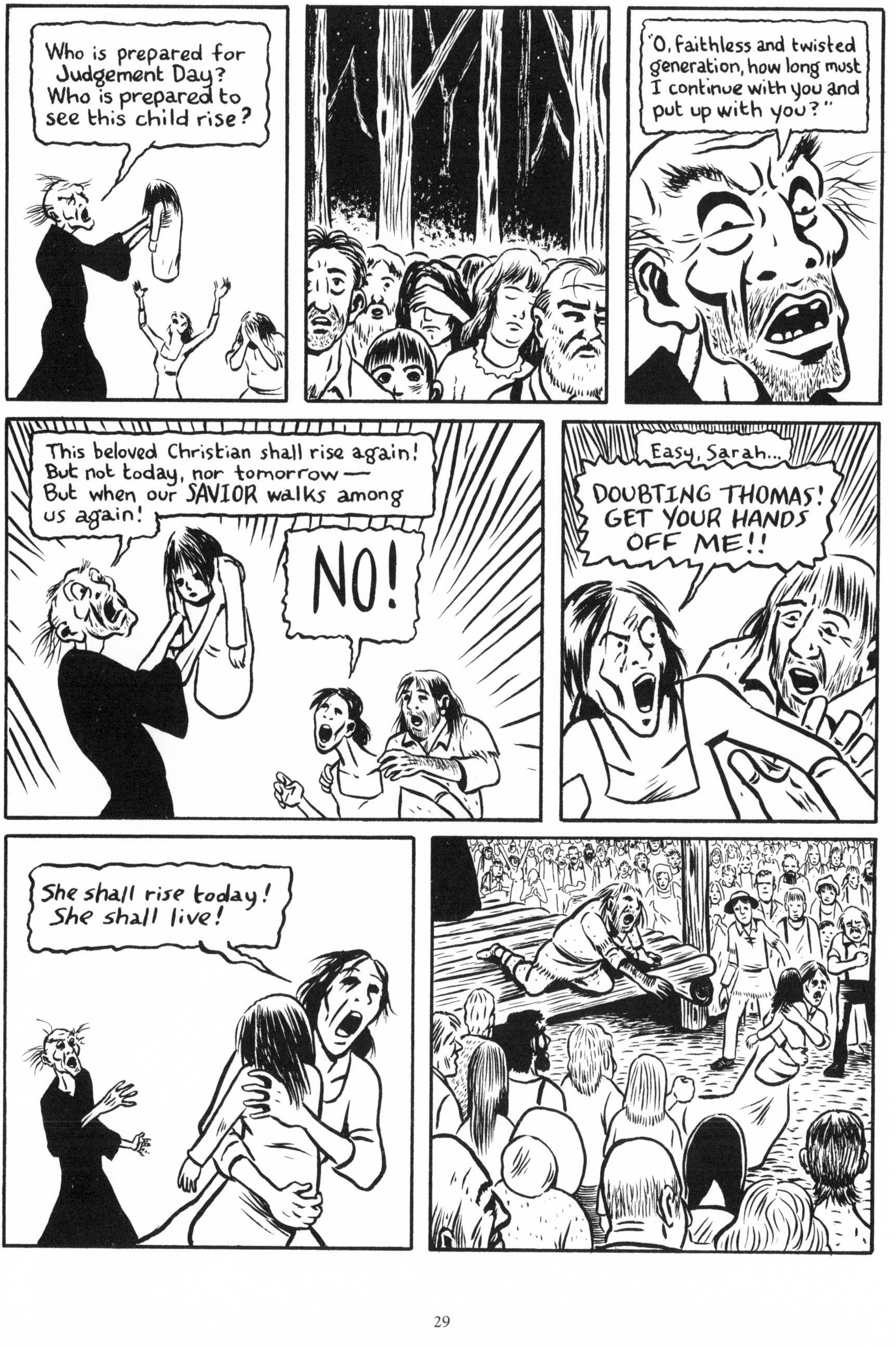

Who is prepared for Judgement Day? Who is prepared to see this child rise?
"O, faithless and twisted generation, how long must I continue with you and put up with you?"
This beloved Christian shall rise again! But not today, nor tomorrow— But when our SAVIOR walks among us again!
NO!
Easy, Sarah...
DOUBTING THOMAS! GET YOUR HANDS OFF ME!!
She shall rise today! She shall live!

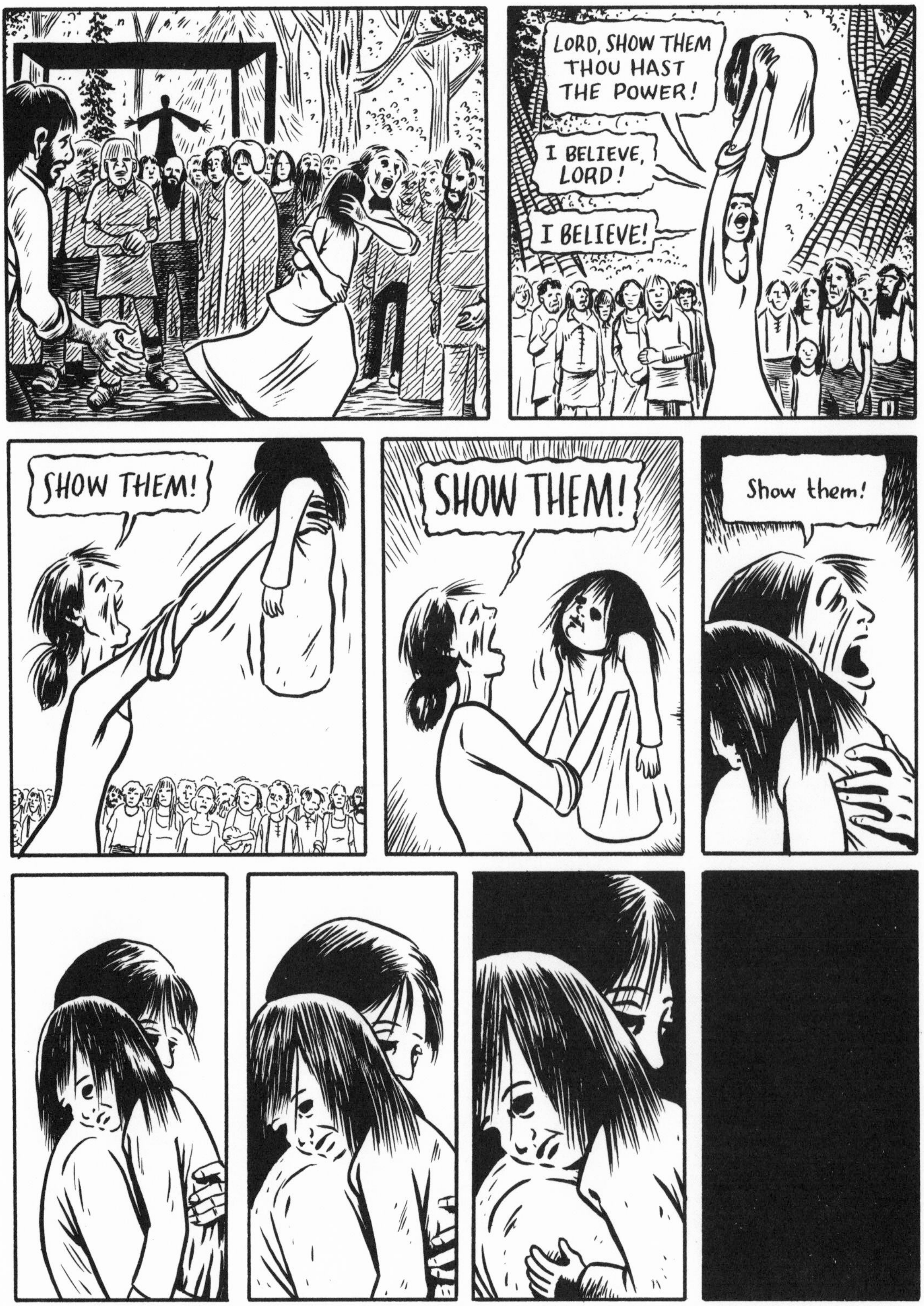
LORD, SHOW THEM THOU HAST THE POWER!
I BELIEVE, LORD!
I BELIEVE!
SHOW THEM!
SHOW THEM!
Show them!

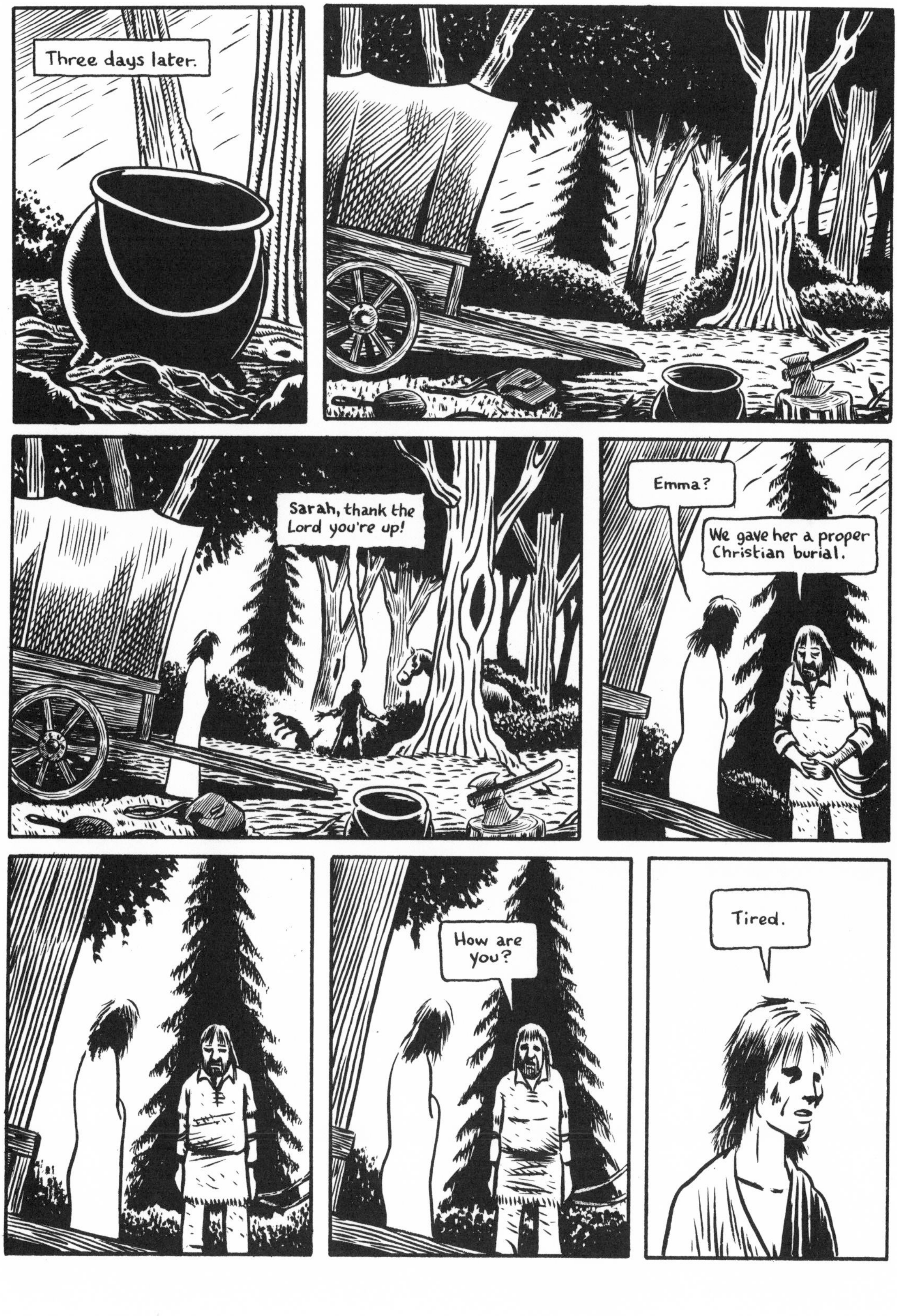
Three days later.
Sarah, thank the Lord you're up!
Emma?
We gave her a proper Christian burial.
How are you?
Tired.

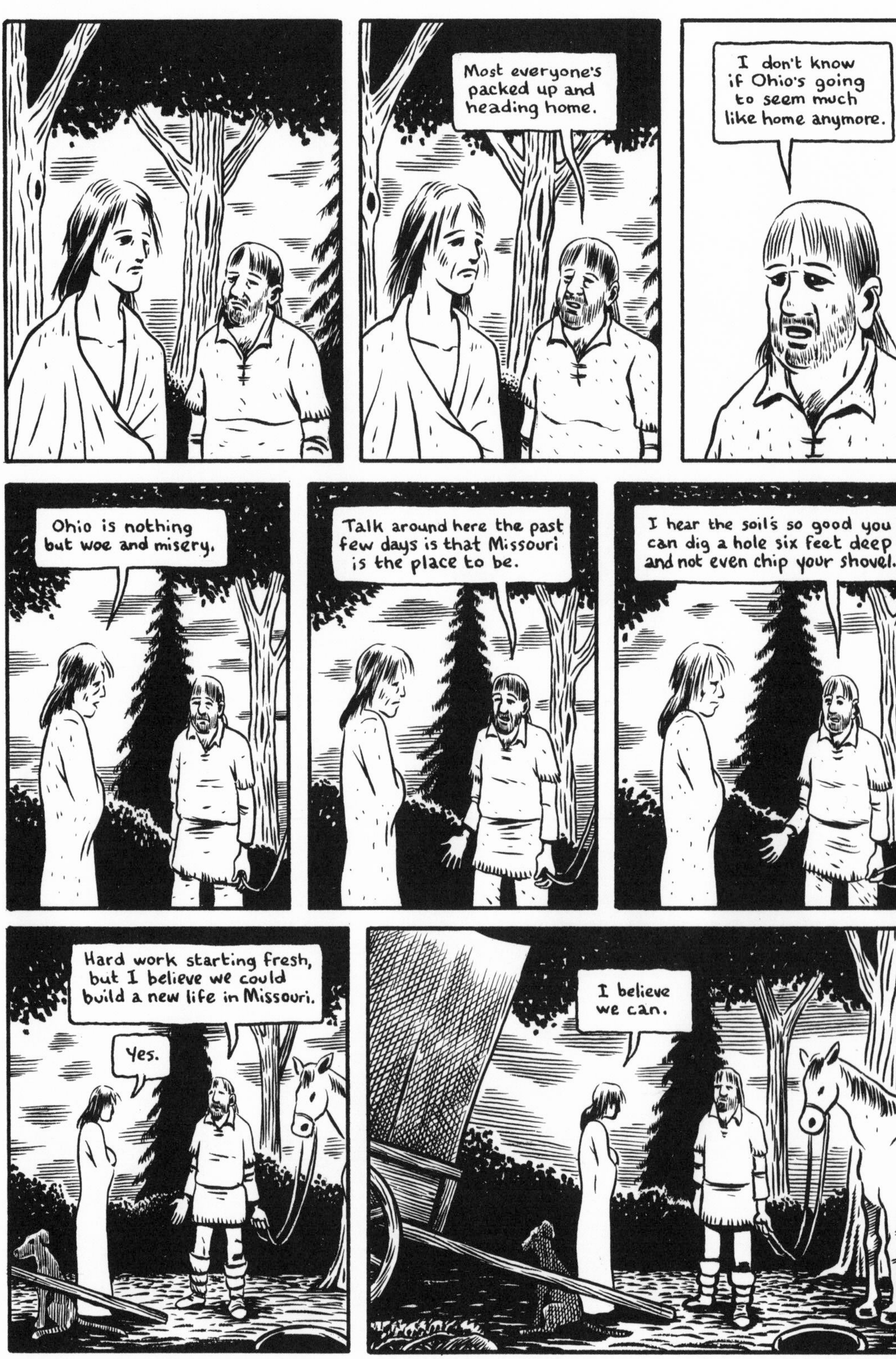
Most everyone's packed up and heading home.
I don't know if Ohio's going to seem much like home anymore.
Ohio is nothing but woe and misery.
Talk around here the past few days is that Missouri is the place to be.
I hear the soil's so good you can dig a hole six feet deep and not even chip your shovel.
Hard work starting fresh, but I believe we could build a new life in Missouri.
Yes.
I believe we can.

# HUNDREDS OF FEET
# BELOW DAYLIGHT

## (1886)

THE LIFE *and* DEATH *of the*
MINING TOWN *of* SOLOMON'S GULCH, IDAHO

# PART ONE

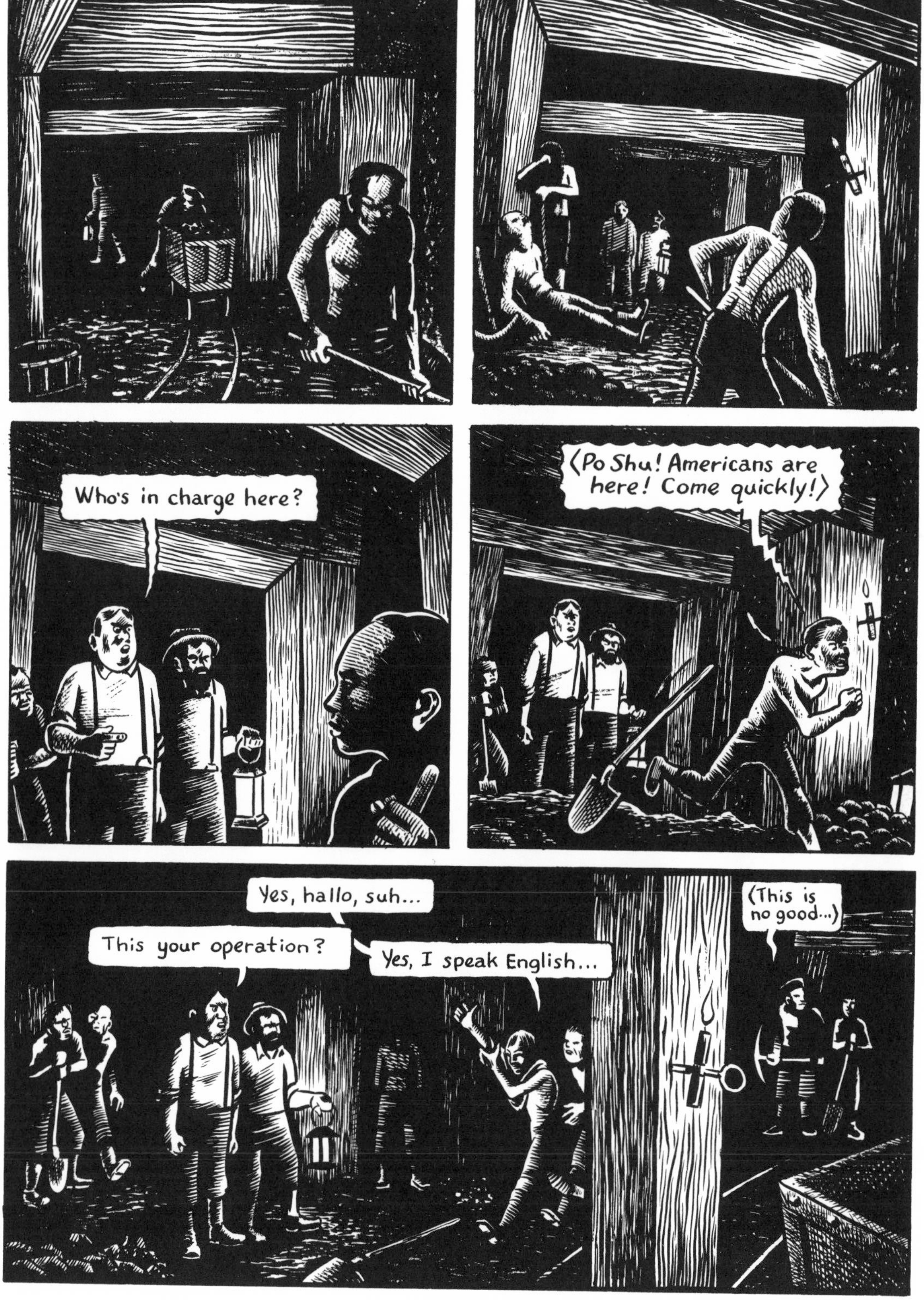
Who's in charge here?
⟨Po Shu! Americans are here! Come quickly!⟩
This your operation?
Yes, hallo, suh...
Yes, I speak English...
⟨This is no good...⟩

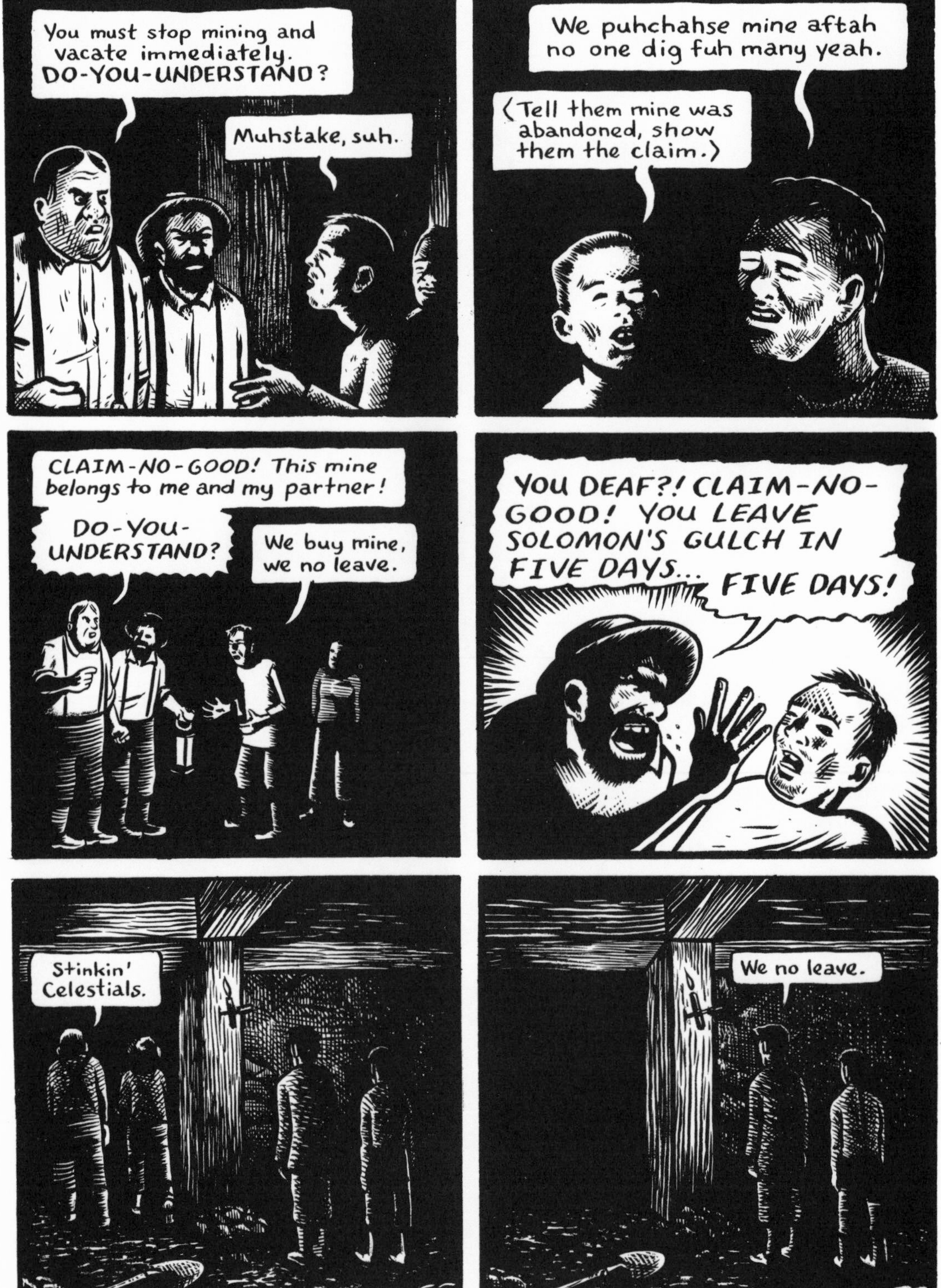

You must stop mining and vacate immediately. DO-YOU-UNDERSTAND?
Muhstake, suh.
We puhchahse mine aftah no one dig fuh many yeah.
⟨Tell them mine was abandoned, show them the claim.⟩
CLAIM-NO-GOOD! This mine belongs to me and my partner!
DO-YOU-UNDERSTAND?
We buy mine, we no leave.
YOU DEAF?! CLAIM-NO-GOOD! YOU LEAVE SOLOMON'S GULCH IN FIVE DAYS... FIVE DAYS!
Stinkin' Celestials.
We no leave.

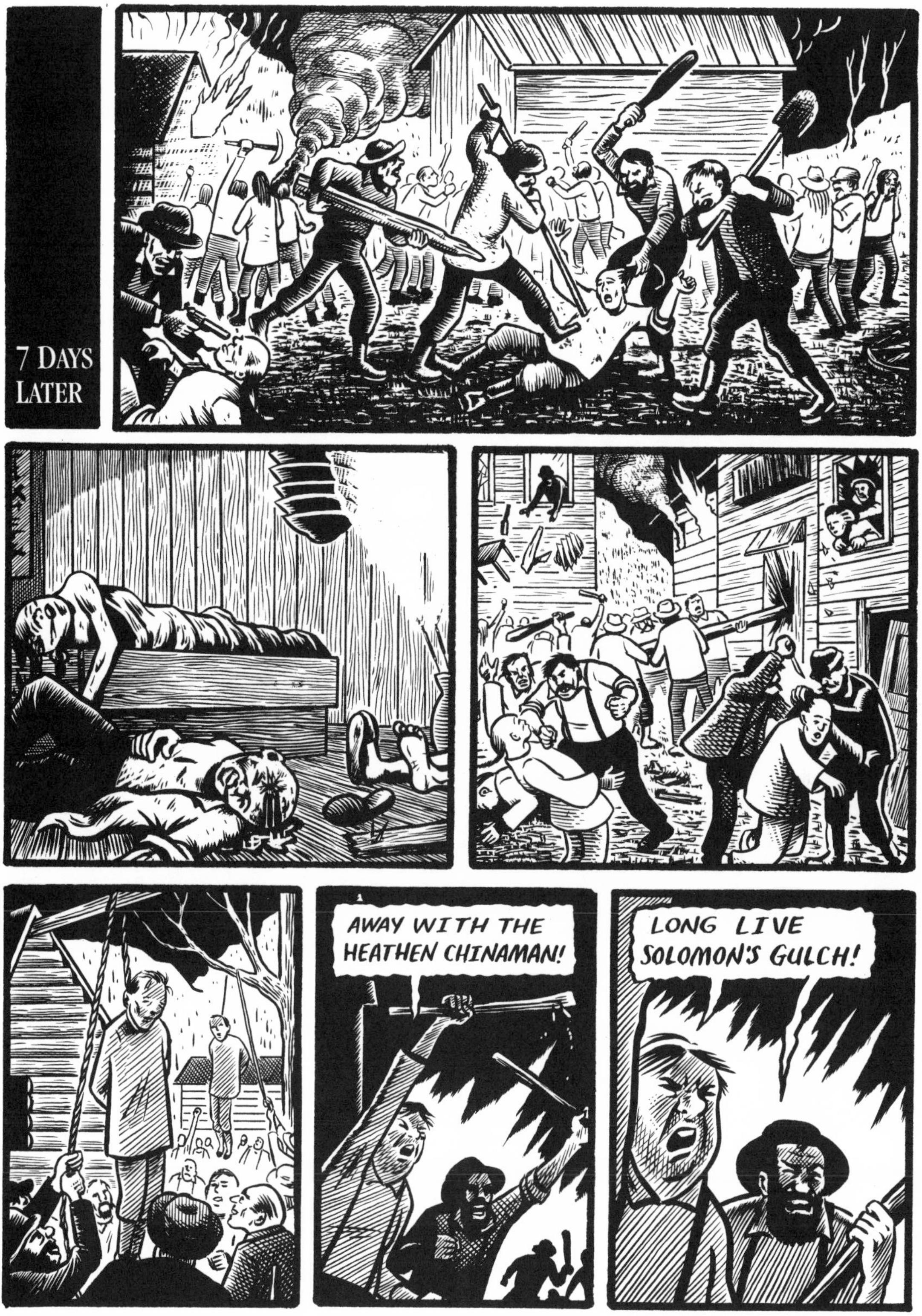
7 DAYS LATER
AWAY WITH THE HEATHEN CHINAMAN!
LONG LIVE SOLOMON'S GULCH!

TEN MONTHS LATER

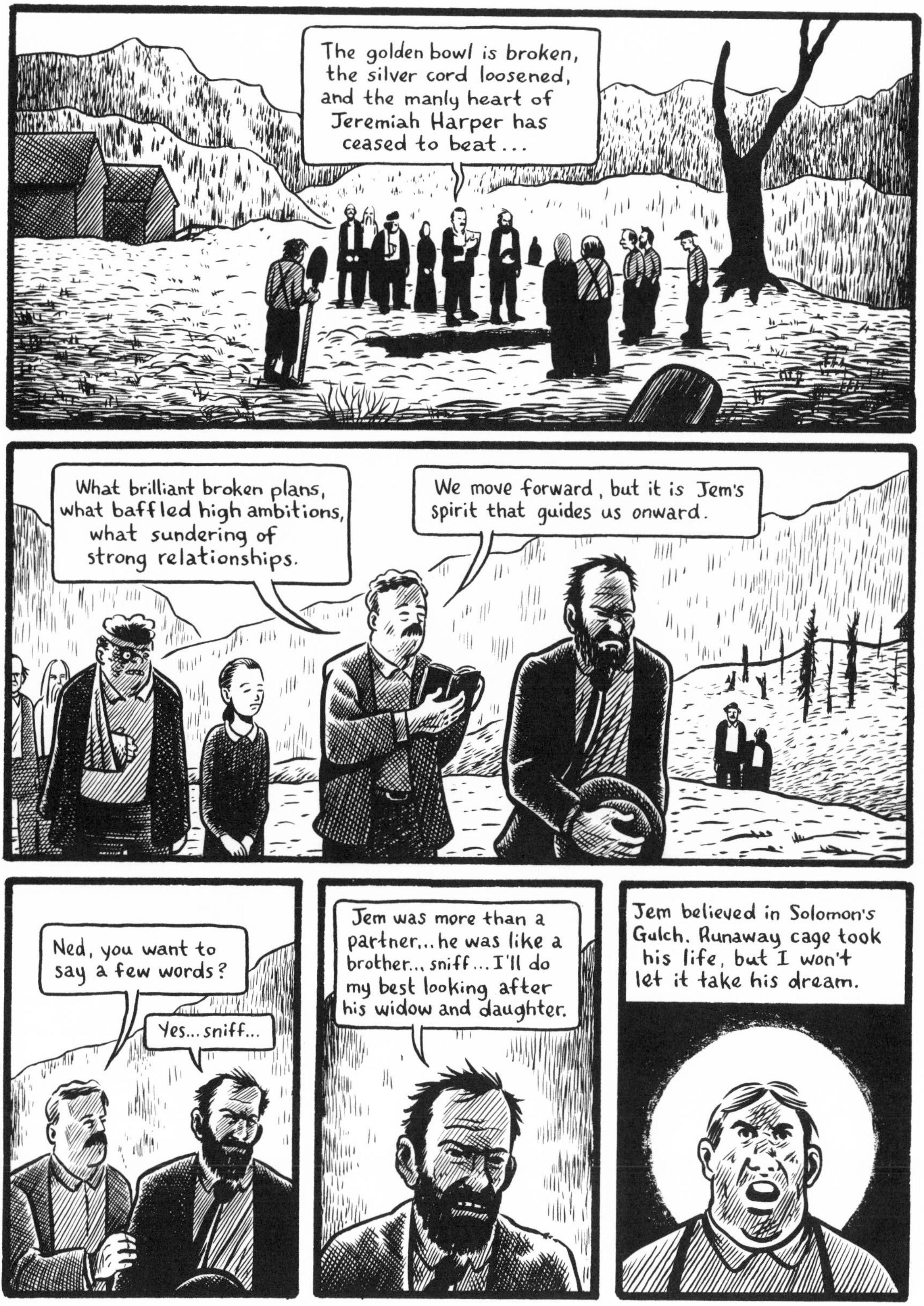

The golden bowl is broken, the silver cord loosened, and the manly heart of Jeremiah Harper has ceased to beat...
What brilliant broken plans, what baffled high ambitions, what sundering of strong relationships.
We move forward, but it is Jem's spirit that guides us onward.
Ned, you want to say a few words?
Yes... sniff...
Jem was more than a partner... he was like a brother... sniff... I'll do my best looking after his widow and daughter.
Jem believed in Solomon's Gulch. Runaway cage took his life, but I won't let it take his dream.

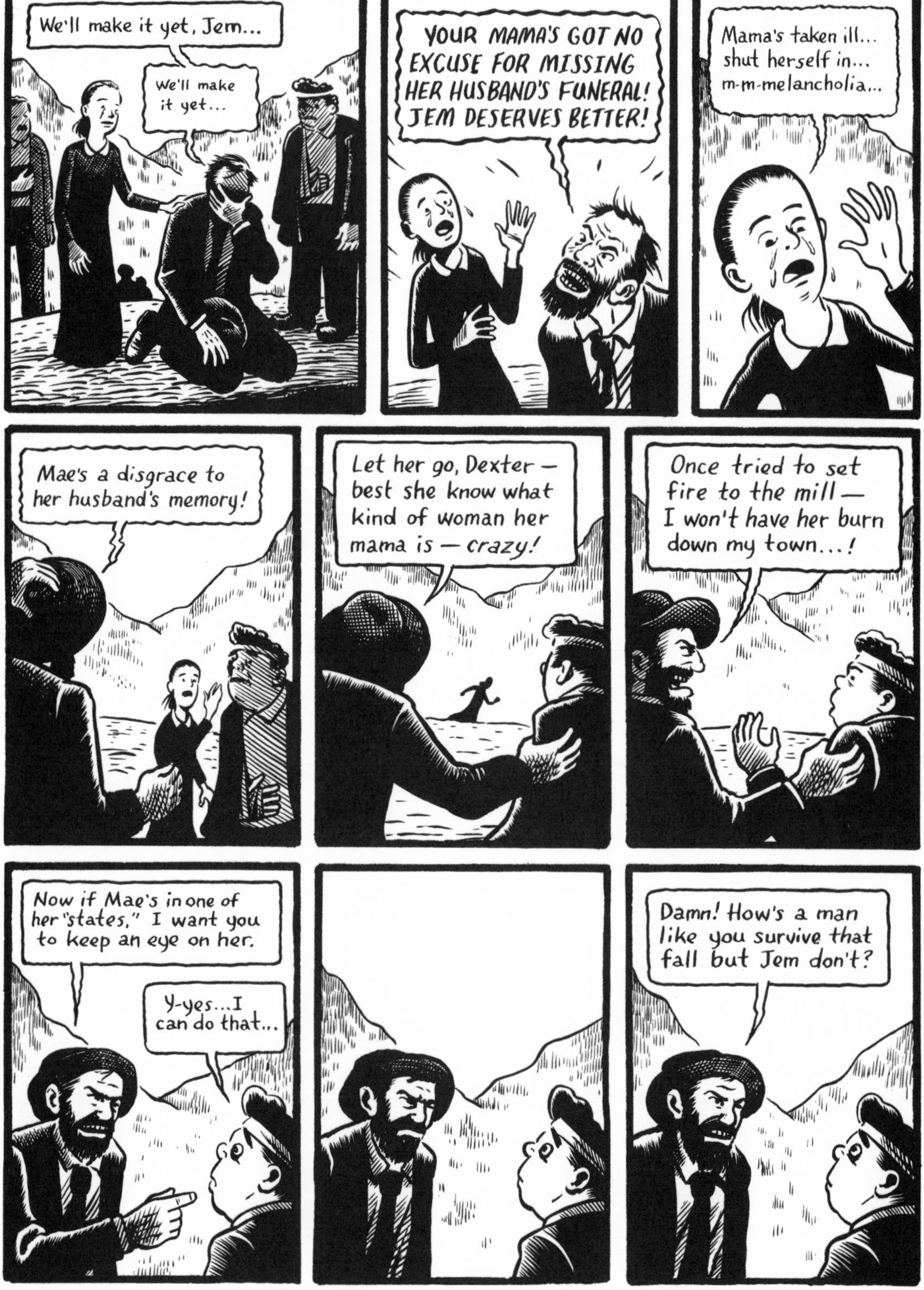
We'll make it yet, Jem...
We'll make it yet...
YOUR MAMA'S GOT NO EXCUSE FOR MISSING HER HUSBAND'S FUNERAL! JEM DESERVES BETTER!
Mama's taken ill... shut herself in... m-m-melancholia...
Mae's a disgrace to her husband's memory!
Let her go, Dexter — best she know what kind of woman her mama is — crazy!
Once tried to set fire to the mill — I won't have her burn down my town...!
Now if Mae's in one of her "states," I want you to keep an eye on her.
Y-yes...I can do that...
Damn! How's a man like you survive that fall but Jem don't?

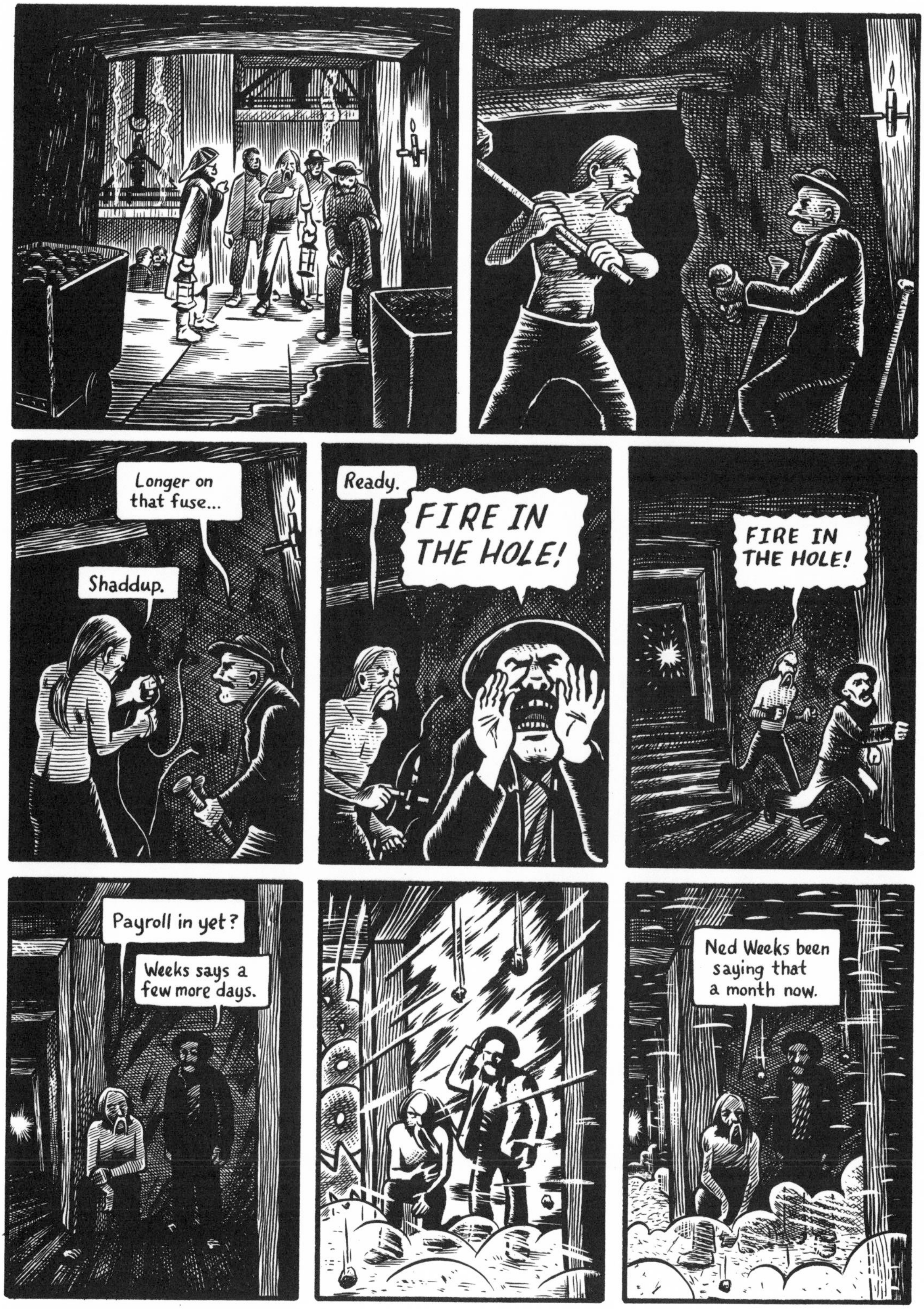
Longer on that fuse...
Shaddup.
Ready.
FIRE IN THE HOLE!
FIRE IN THE HOLE!
Payroll in yet?
Weeks says a few more days.
Ned Weeks been saying that a month now.

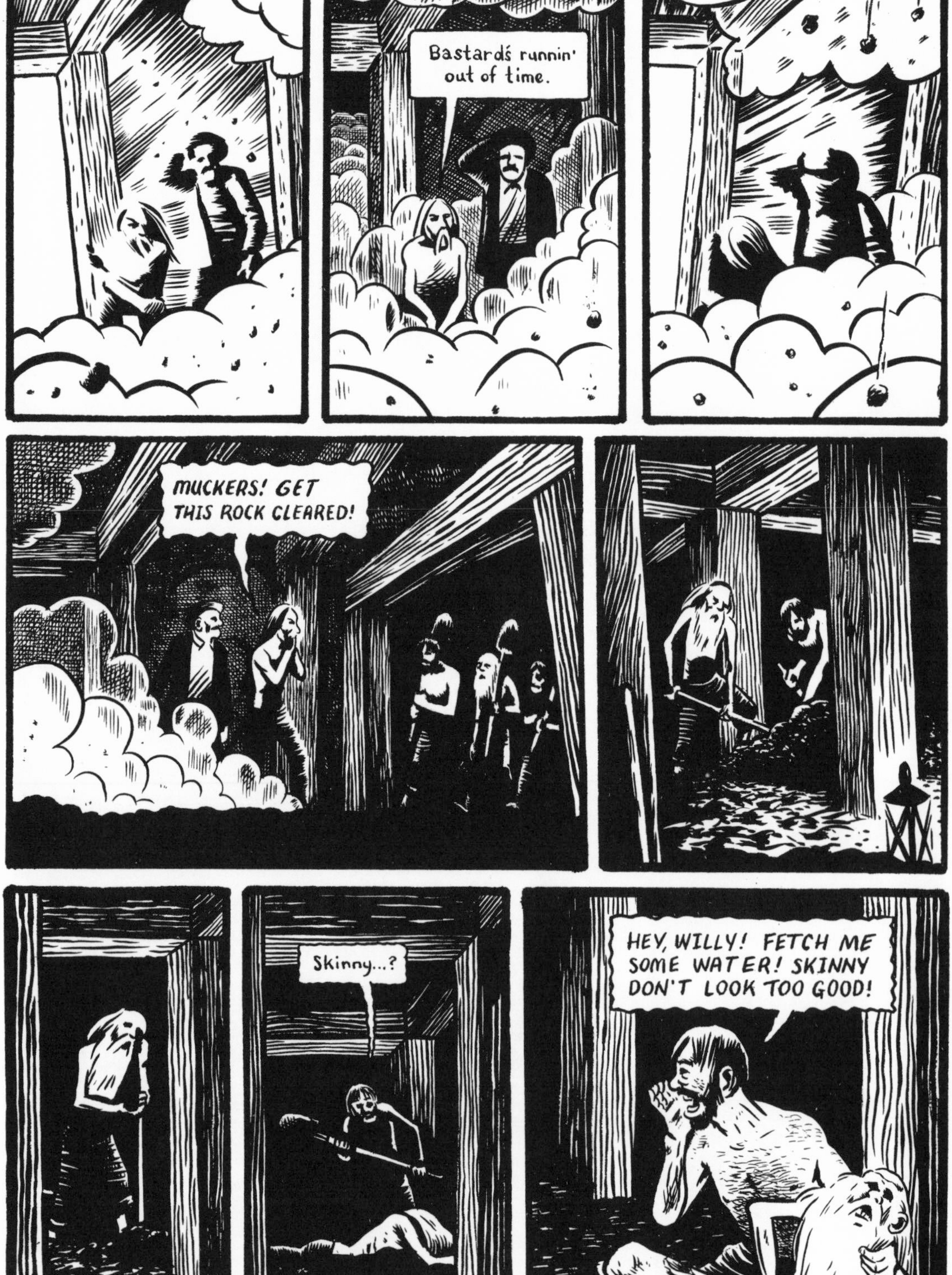
Bastard's runnin' out of time.
MUCKERS! GET THIS ROCK CLEARED!
Skinny...?
HEY, WILLY! FETCH ME SOME WATER! SKINNY DON'T LOOK TOO GOOD!

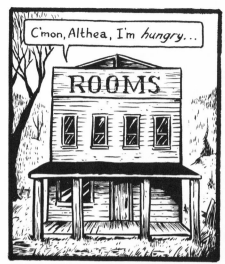

C'mon, Althea, I'm *hungry...*

ROOMS

You wait and eat with the rest of the men.

How 'bout one of those biscuits?

NO!

These are for Mama. She needs to eat.

Give me those— I'll take 'em to Mae!

I'm *in charge* of keeping an eye on her.

OPEN UP, MAE! Got a plateful of biscuits.

Mae? You there? You alright?

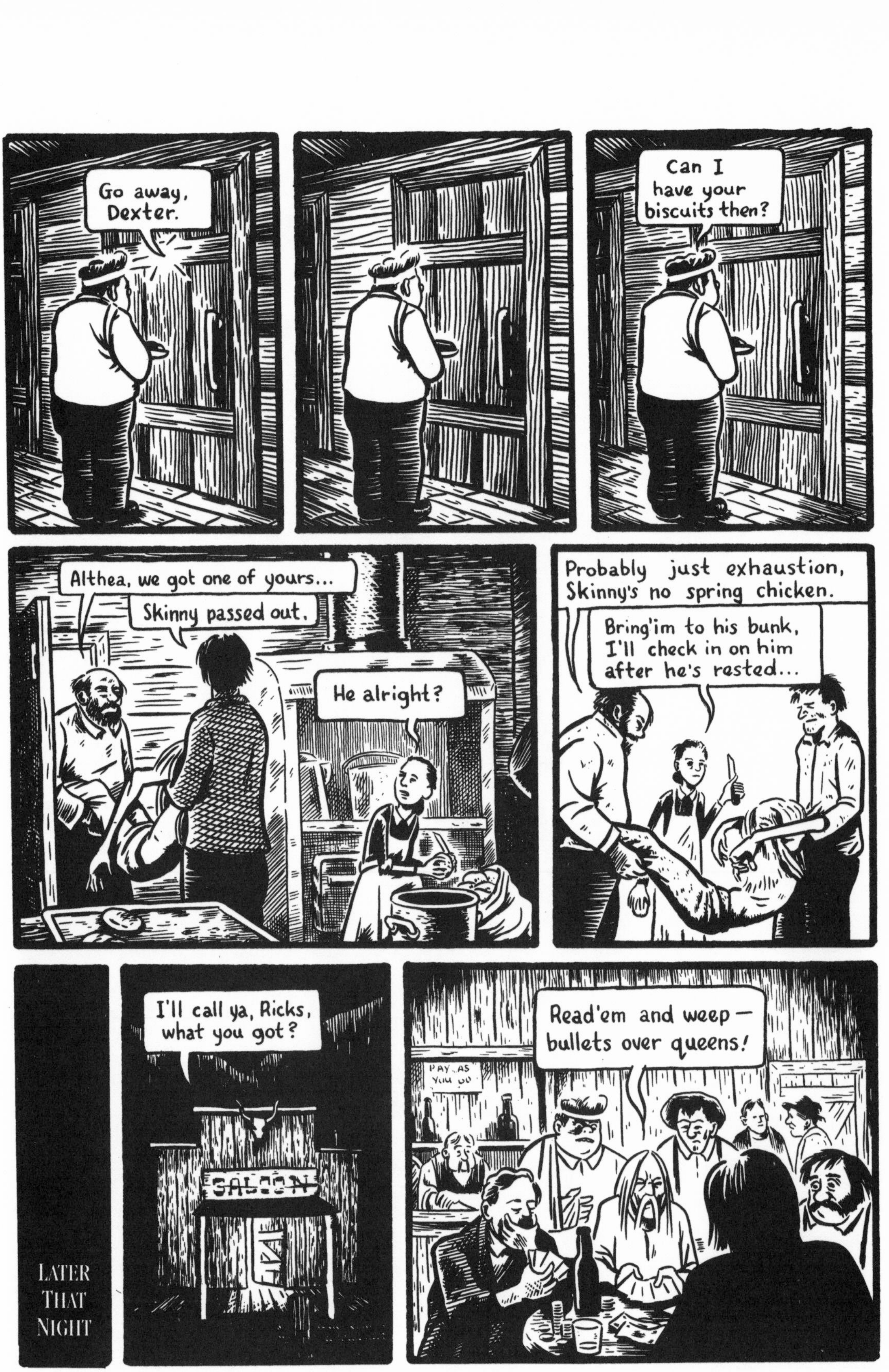
Go away, Dexter.
Can I have your biscuits then?
Althea, we got one of yours...
Skinny passed out.
He alright?
Probably just exhaustion, Skinny's no spring chicken.
Bring'im to his bunk, I'll check in on him after he's rested...
LATER THAT NIGHT
I'll call ya, Ricks, what you got?
SALOON
PAY AS YOU GO
Read'em and weep— bullets over queens!

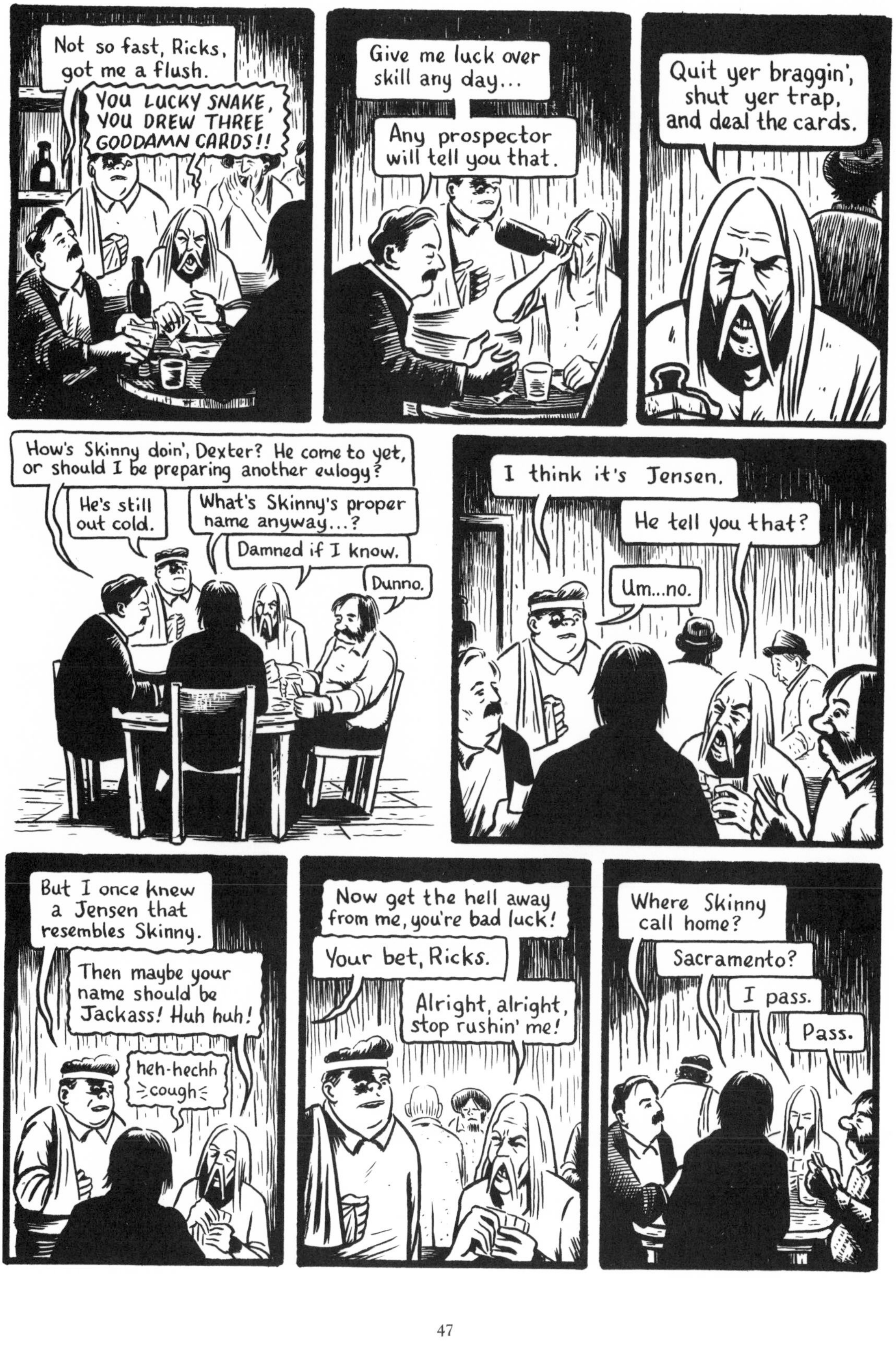
Not so fast, Ricks, got me a flush.
YOU LUCKY SNAKE, YOU DREW THREE GODDAMN CARDS!!
Give me luck over skill any day...
Any prospector will tell you that.
Quit yer braggin', shut yer trap, and deal the cards.
How's Skinny doin', Dexter? He come to yet, or should I be preparing another eulogy?
He's still out cold.
What's Skinny's proper name anyway...?
Damned if I know.
Dunno.
I think it's Jensen.
He tell you that?
Um...no.
But I once knew a Jensen that resembles Skinny.
Then maybe your name should be Jackass! Huh huh!
heh-hechh
cough
Now get the hell away from me, you're bad luck!
Your bet, Ricks.
Alright, alright, stop rushin' me!
Where Skinny call home?
Sacramento?
I pass.
Pass.

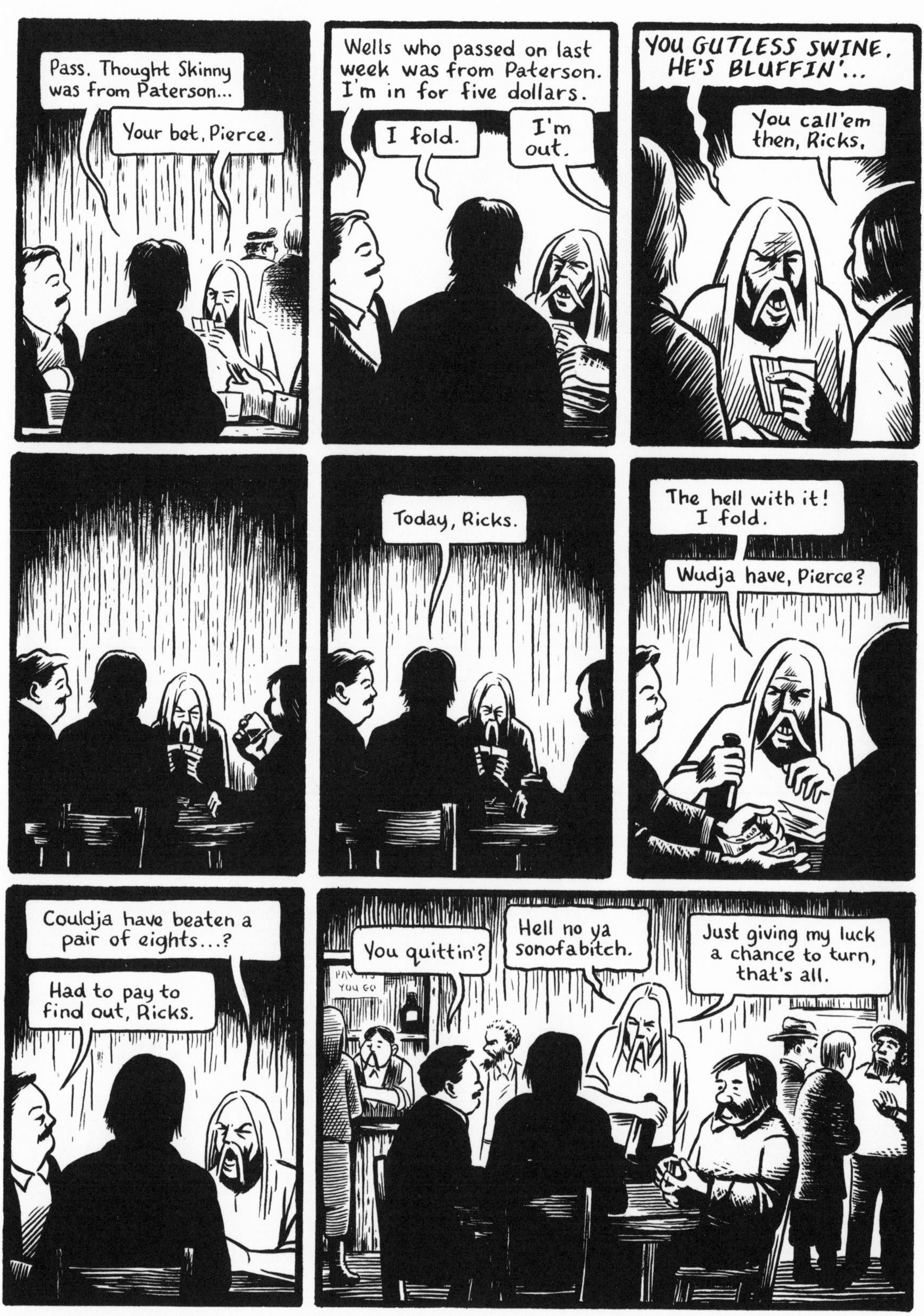

Pass. Thought Skinny was from Paterson...
Your bet, Pierce.
Wells who passed on last week was from Paterson. I'm in for five dollars.
I fold.
I'm out.
YOU GUTLESS SWINE. HE'S BLUFFIN'...
You call'em then, Ricks.
Today, Ricks.
The hell with it! I fold.
Wudja have, Pierce?
Couldja have beaten a pair of eights...?
Had to pay to find out, Ricks.
You quittin'?
Hell no ya sonofabitch.
Just giving my luck a chance to turn, that's all.

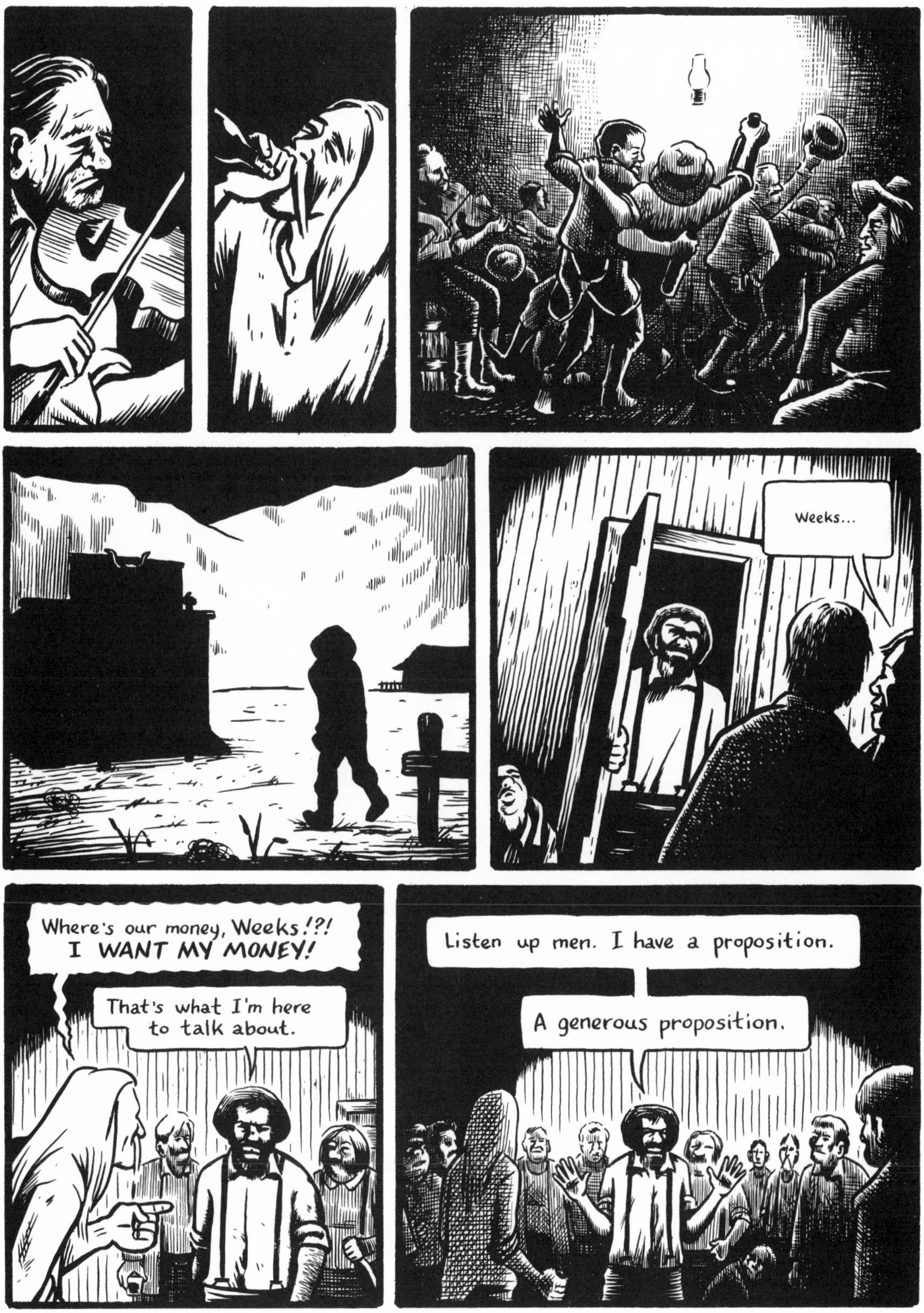
Weeks...
Where's our money, Weeks!?!
I WANT MY MONEY!
That's what I'm here to talk about.
Listen up men. I have a proposition.
A generous proposition.

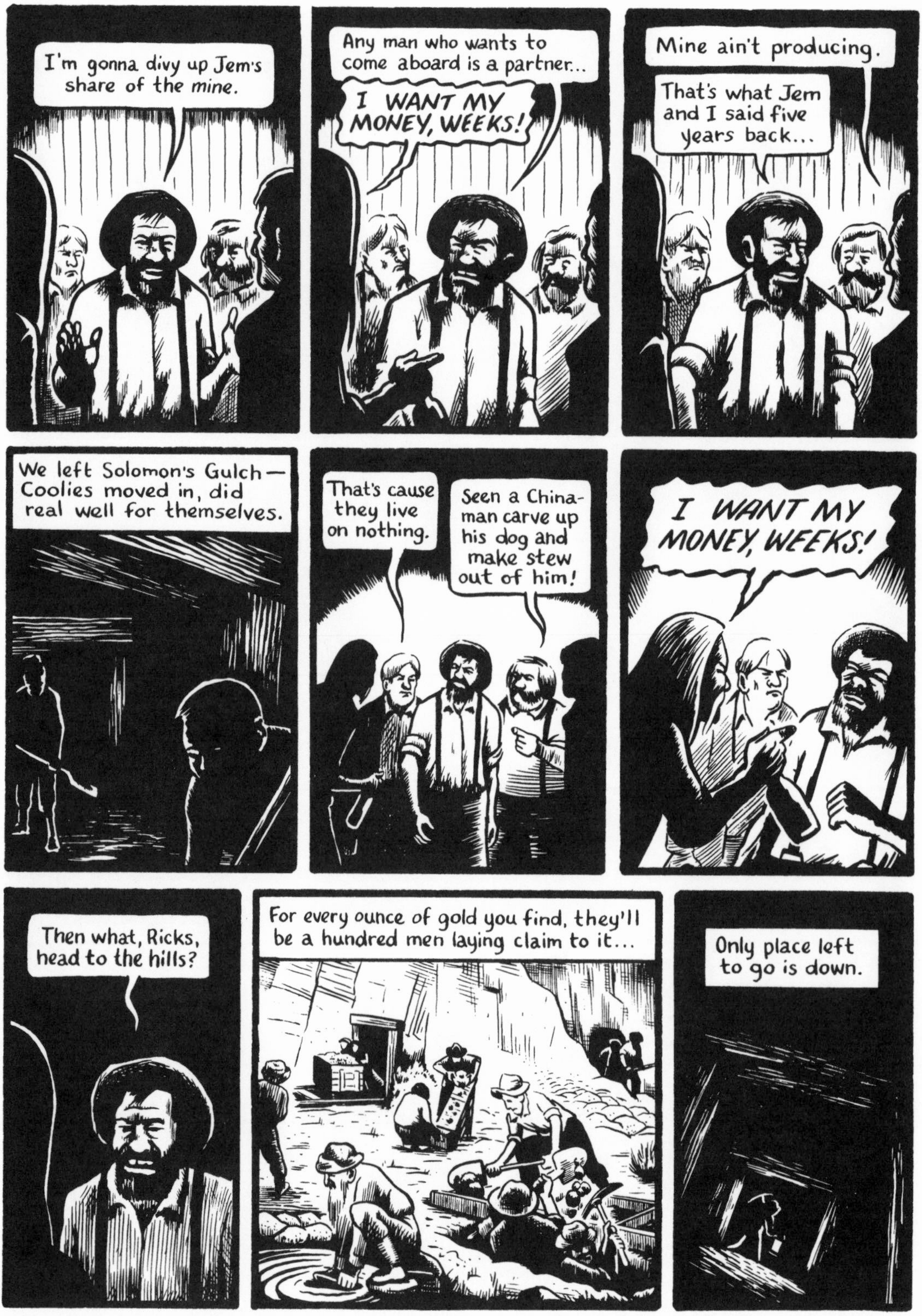
I'm gonna divy up Jem's share of the mine.
Any man who wants to come aboard is a partner...
I WANT MY MONEY, WEEKS!
Mine ain't producing.
That's what Jem and I said five years back...
We left Solomon's Gulch— Coolies moved in, did real well for themselves.
That's cause they live on nothing.
Seen a China-man carve up his dog and make stew out of him!
I WANT MY MONEY, WEEKS!
Then what, Ricks, head to the hills?
For every ounce of gold you find, they'll be a hundred men laying claim to it...
Only place left to go is down.

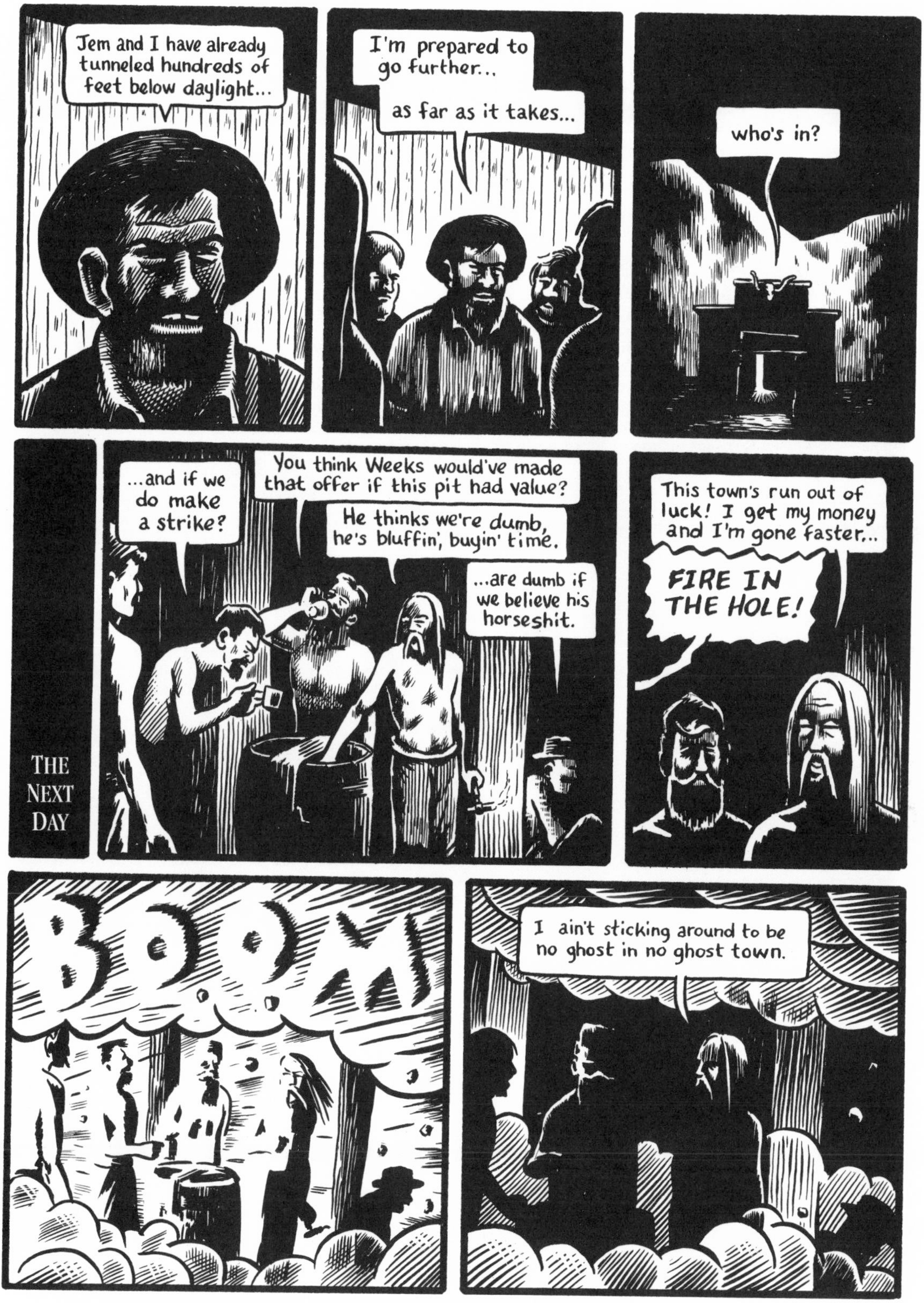

Jem and I have already tunneled hundreds of feet below daylight...
I'm prepared to go further...
as far as it takes...
who's in?
THE NEXT DAY
...and if we do make a strike?
You think Weeks would've made that offer if this pit had value?
He thinks we're dumb, he's bluffin', buyin' time.
...are dumb if we believe his horseshit.
This town's run out of luck! I get my money and I'm gone faster...
FIRE IN THE HOLE!
BOOM!
I ain't sticking around to be no ghost in no ghost town.

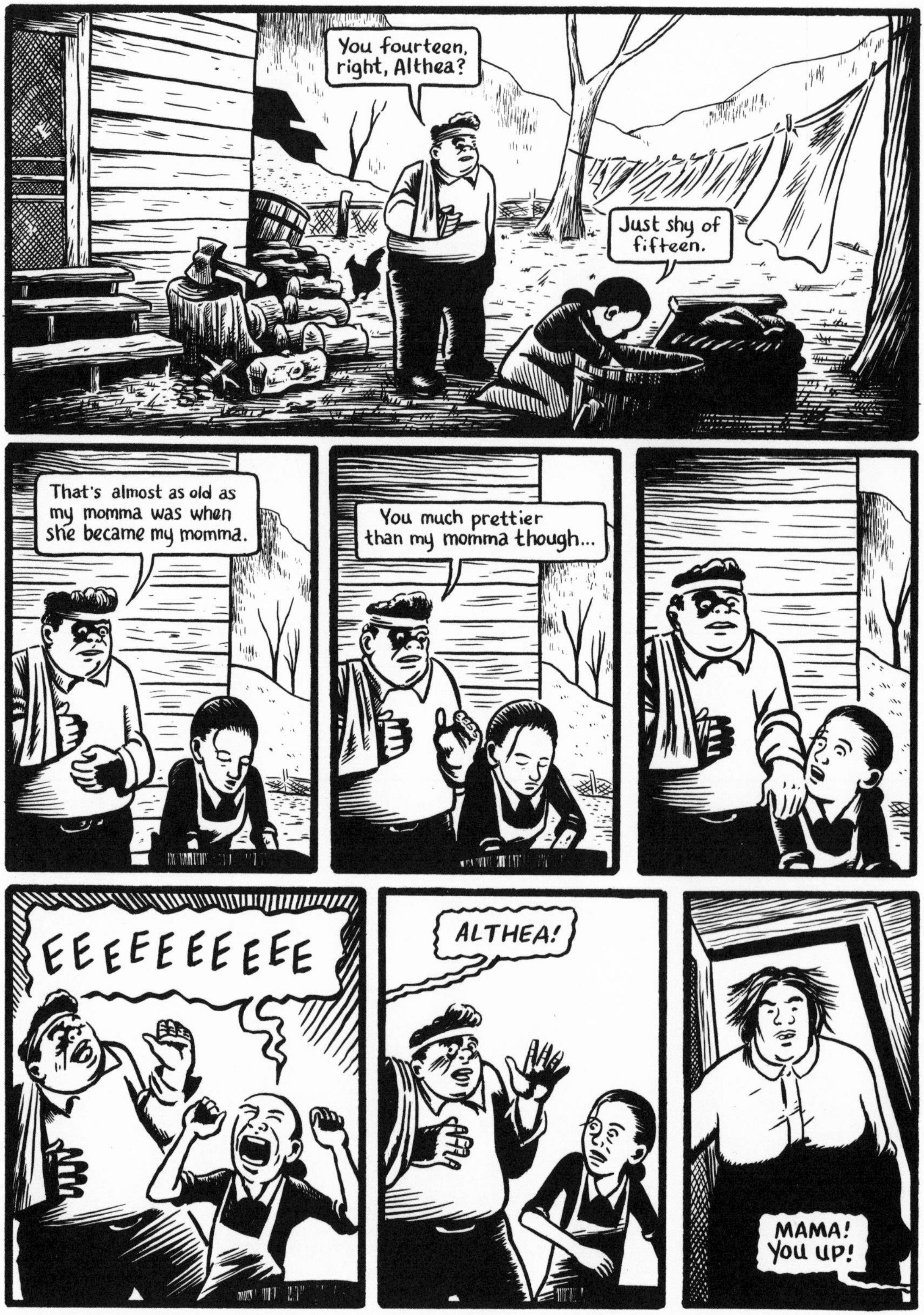
You fourteen, right, Althea?
Just shy of fifteen.
That's almost as old as my momma was when she became my momma.
You much prettier than my momma though...
EEEEEEEEEE
ALTHEA!
MAMA! You up!

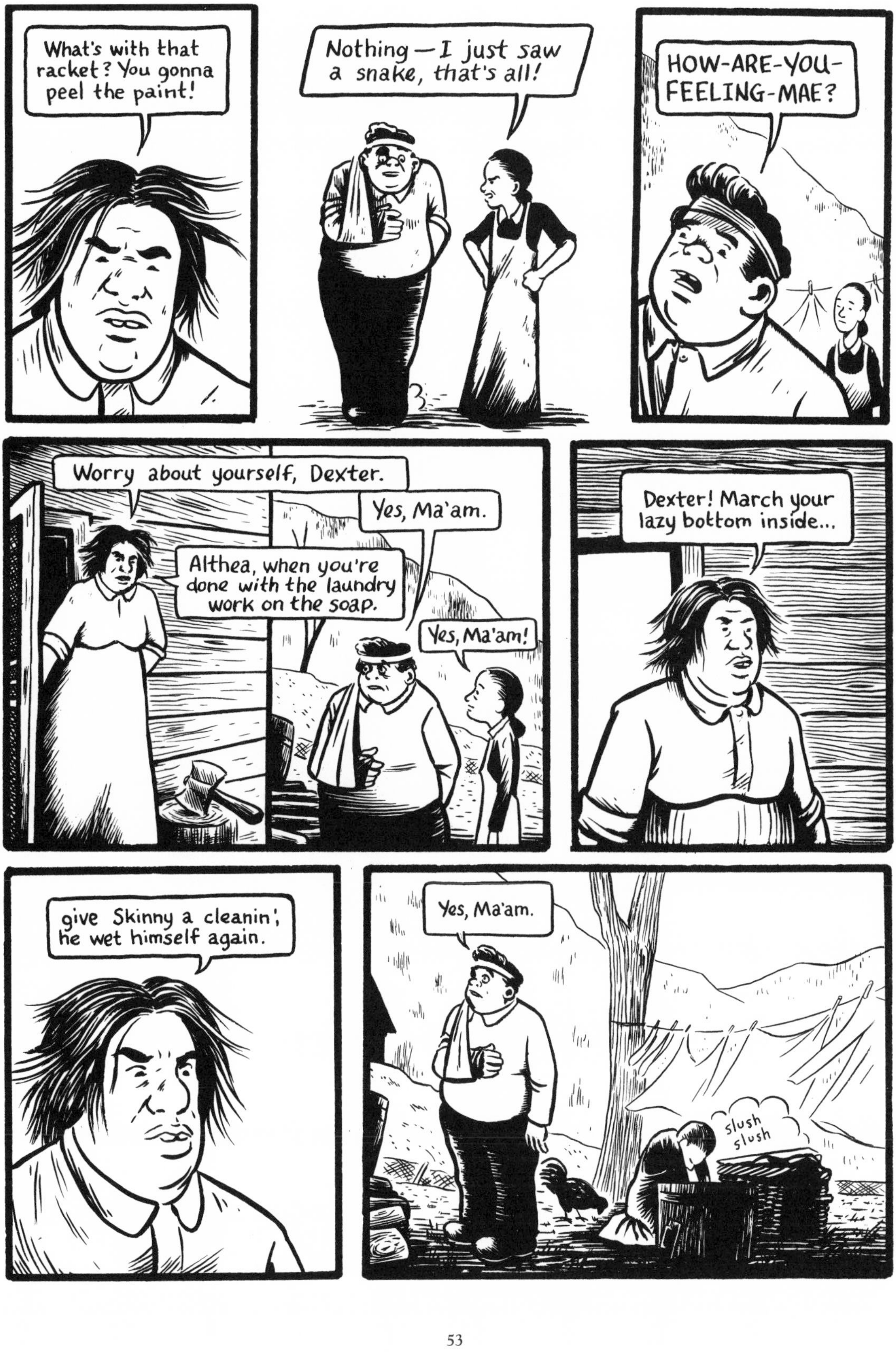
What's with that racket? You gonna peel the paint!
Nothing — I just saw a snake, that's all!
HOW-ARE-YOU-FEELING-MAE?
Worry about yourself, Dexter.
Althea, when you're done with the laundry work on the soap.
Yes, Ma'am.
Yes, Ma'am!
Dexter! March your lazy bottom inside...
give Skinny a cleanin', he wet himself again.
Yes, Ma'am.
slush slush

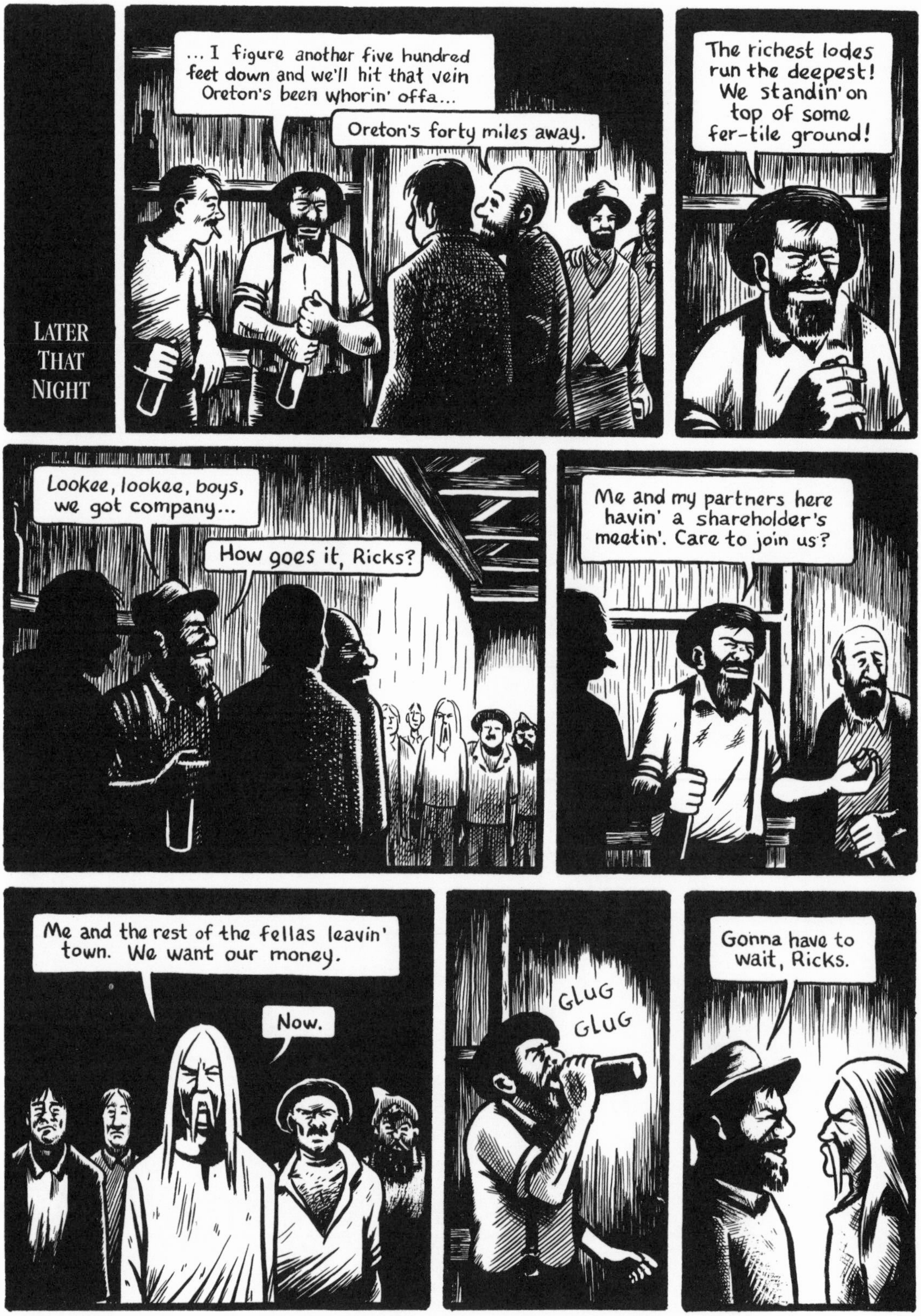
LATER THAT NIGHT
... I figure another five hundred feet down and we'll hit that vein Oreton's been whorin' offa...
Oreton's forty miles away.
The richest lodes run the deepest! We standin' on top of some fer-tile ground!
Lookee, lookee, boys, we got company...
How goes it, Ricks?
Me and my partners here havin' a shareholder's meetin'. Care to join us?
Me and the rest of the fellas leavin' town. We want our money.
Now.
GLUG GLUG
Gonna have to wait, Ricks.

Things alittle mixed up since Jem died. Gotta get the books in order.

You got till the end of the week, Weeks. Come Saturday, no excuses.

You'll always be a poor man, Ricks— ain't got the guts to make it big.

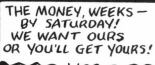

THE MONEY, WEEKS — BY SATURDAY! WE WANT OURS OR YOU'LL GET YOURS!

LEAVE YOU COWARDS! I'LL BE DRINKING CHAMPAGNE ON YOUR GRAVES!

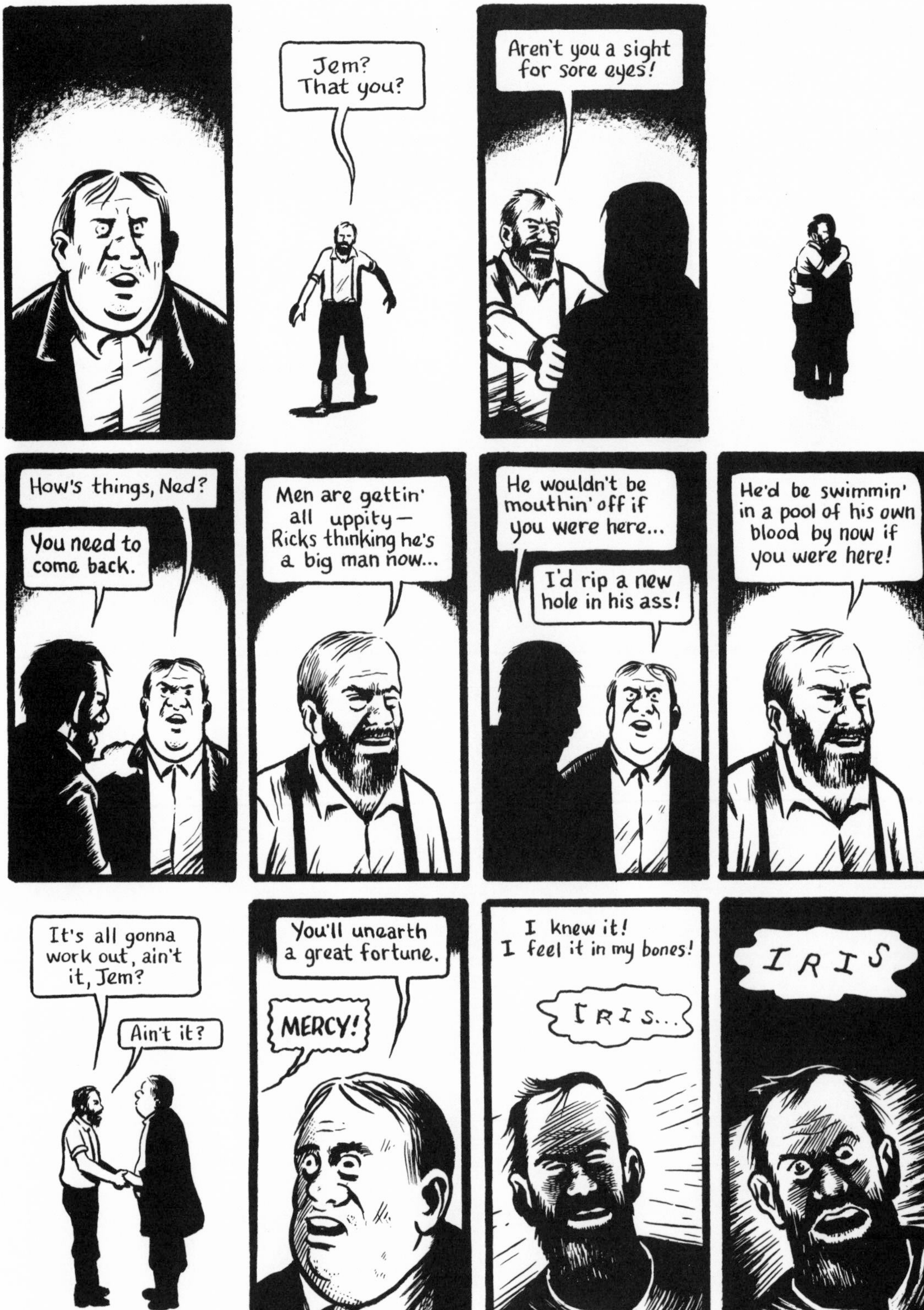

Jem? That you?
Aren't you a sight for sore eyes!
How's things, Ned?
You need to come back.
Men are gettin' all uppity— Ricks thinking he's a big man now...
He wouldn't be mouthin' off if you were here...
I'd rip a new hole in his ass!
He'd be swimmin' in a pool of his own blood by now if you were here!
It's all gonna work out, ain't it, Jem?
Ain't it?
You'll unearth a great fortune.
MERCY!
I knew it! I feel it in my bones!
IRIS...
IRIS

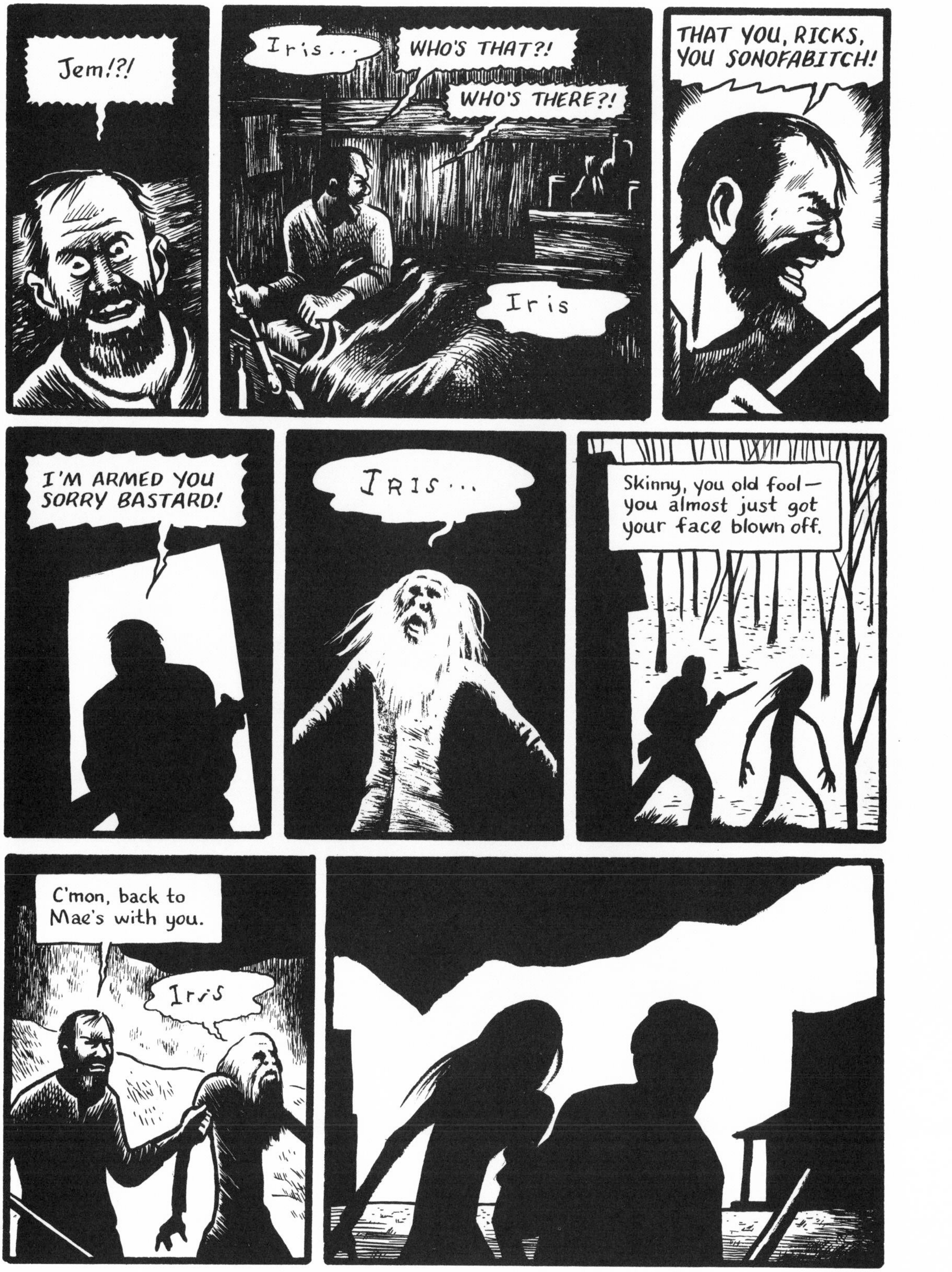
Jem!?!
Iris...
WHO'S THAT?!
WHO'S THERE?!
Iris
THAT YOU, RICKS, YOU SONOFABITCH!
I'M ARMED YOU SORRY BASTARD!
IRIS...
Skinny, you old fool—you almost just got your face blown off.
C'mon, back to Mae's with you.
Iris

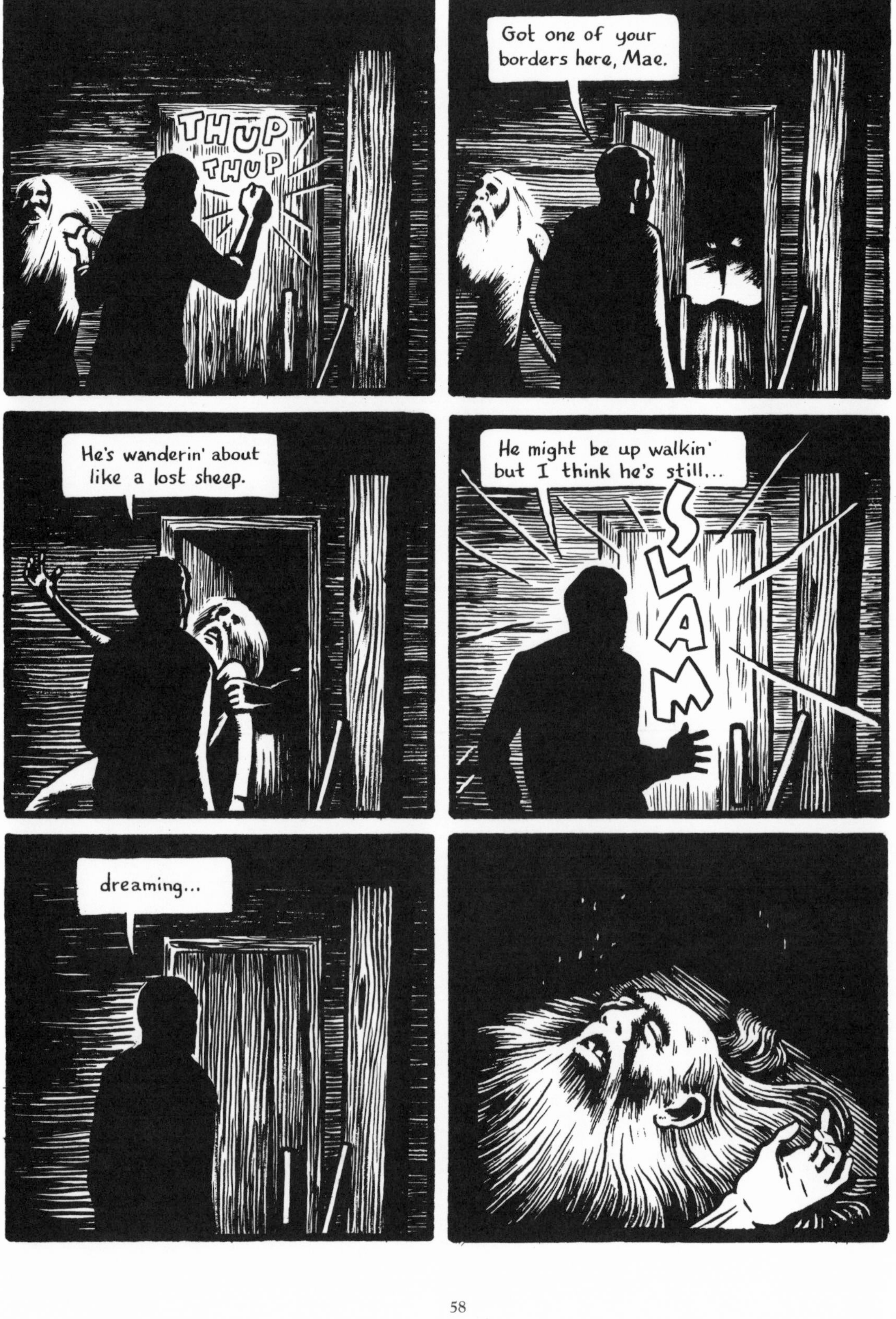
THUP
THUP
Got one of your borders here, Mae.
He's wanderin' about like a lost sheep.
He might be up walkin' but I think he's still...
SLAM
dreaming...

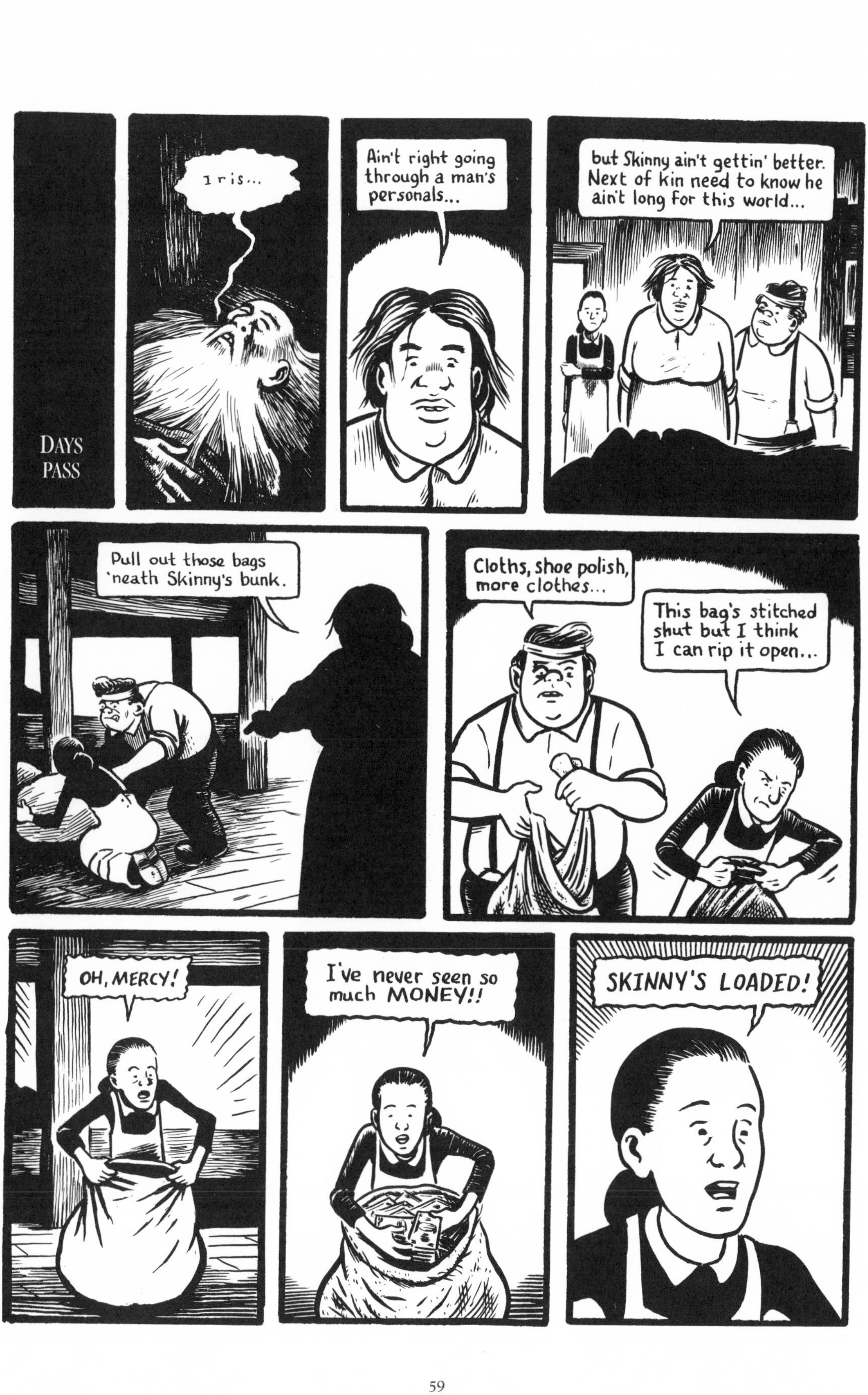
DAYS PASS
Iris...
Ain't right going through a man's personals...
but Skinny ain't gettin' better. Next of kin need to know he ain't long for this world...
Pull out those bags 'neath Skinny's bunk.
Cloths, shoe polish, more clothes...
This bag's stitched shut but I think I can rip it open...
OH, MERCY!
I've never seen so much MONEY!!
SKINNY'S LOADED!

PART TWO

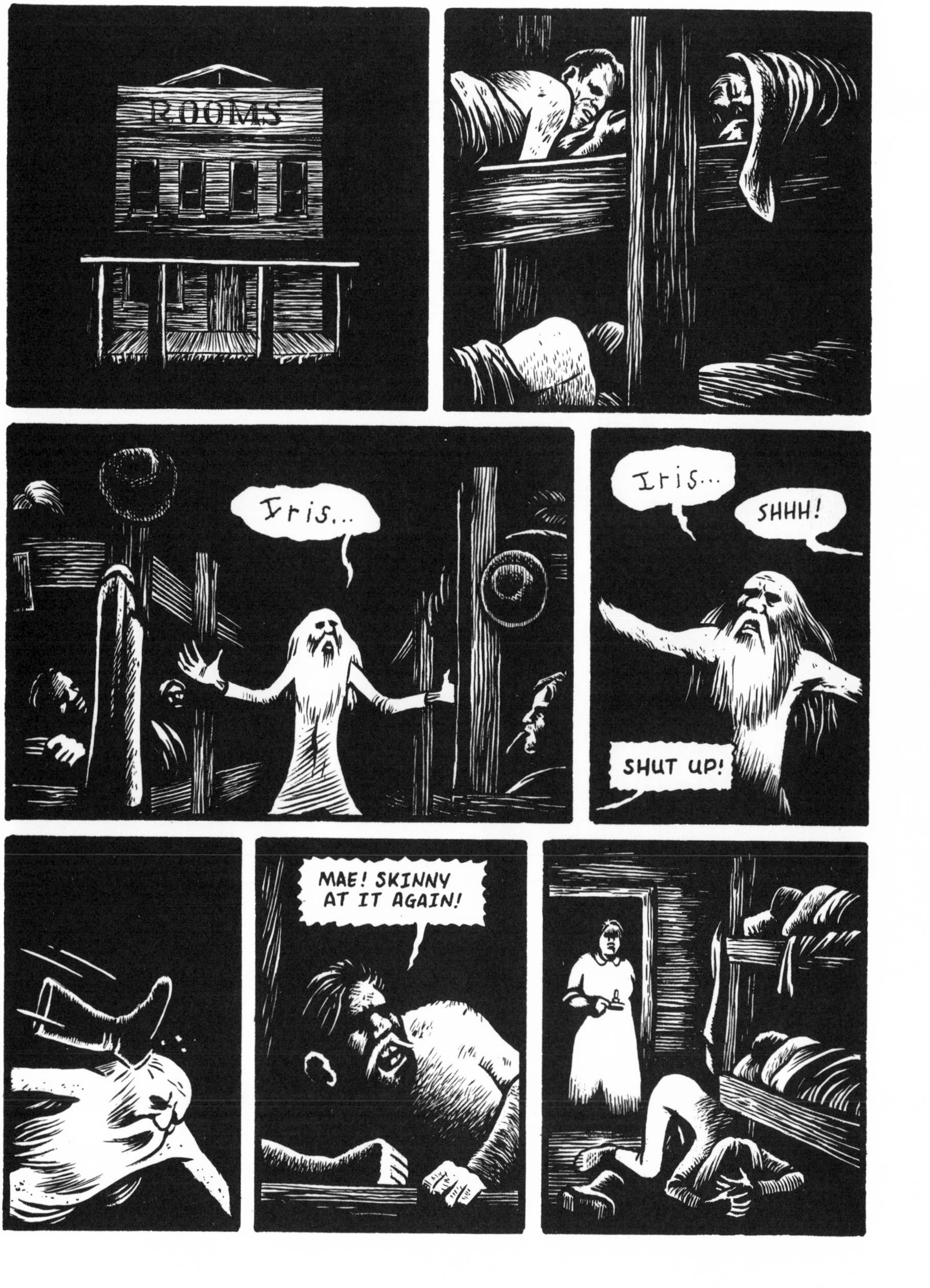
ROOMS
Iris...
Iris...
SHHH!
SHUT UP!
MAE! SKINNY AT IT AGAIN!

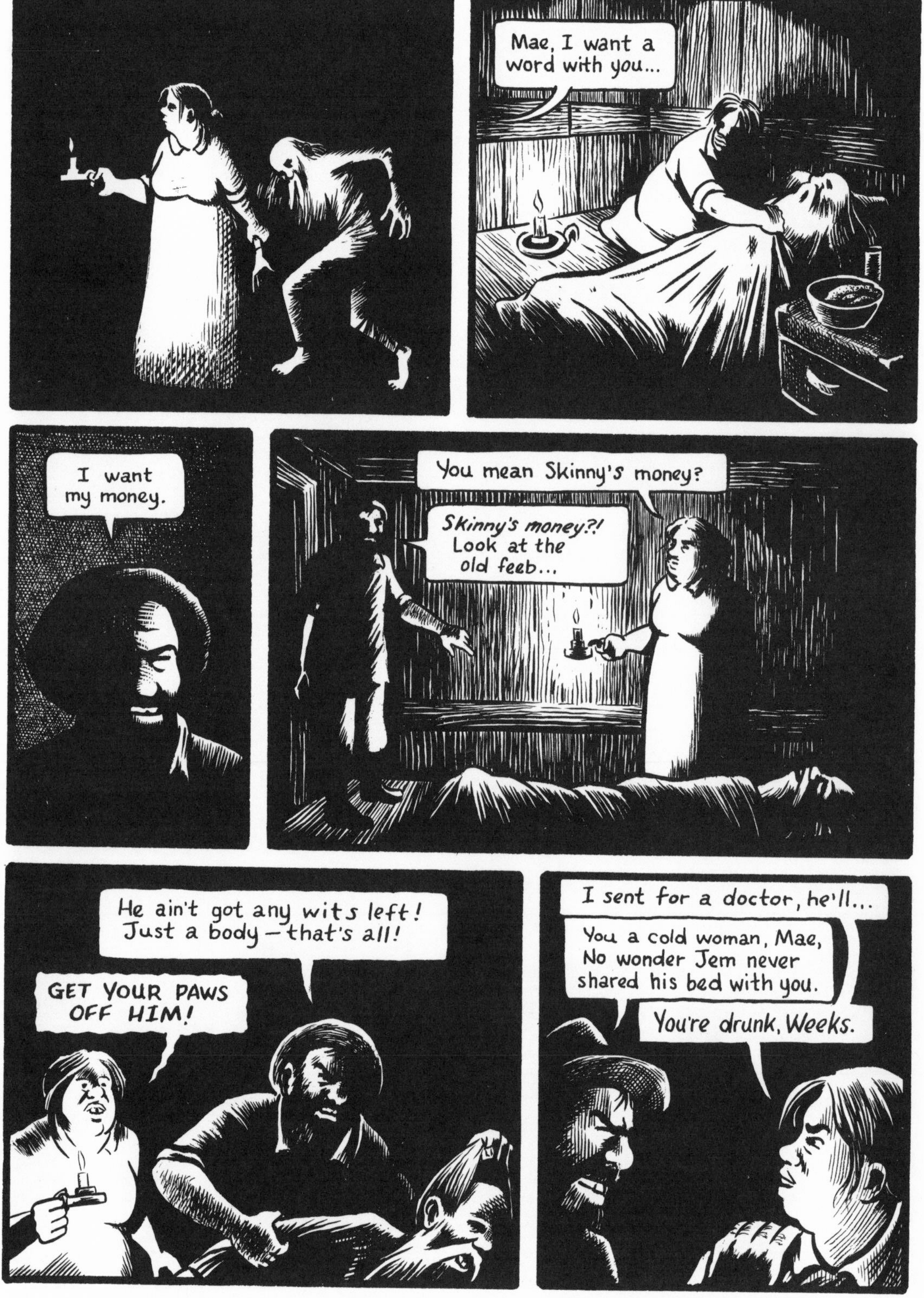
Mae, I want a word with you...
I want my money.
You mean Skinny's money?
Skinny's money?! Look at the old feeb...
He ain't got any wits left! Just a body — that's all!
GET YOUR PAWS OFF HIM!
I sent for a doctor, he'll...
You a cold woman, Mae, No wonder Jem never shared his bed with you.
You're drunk, Weeks.

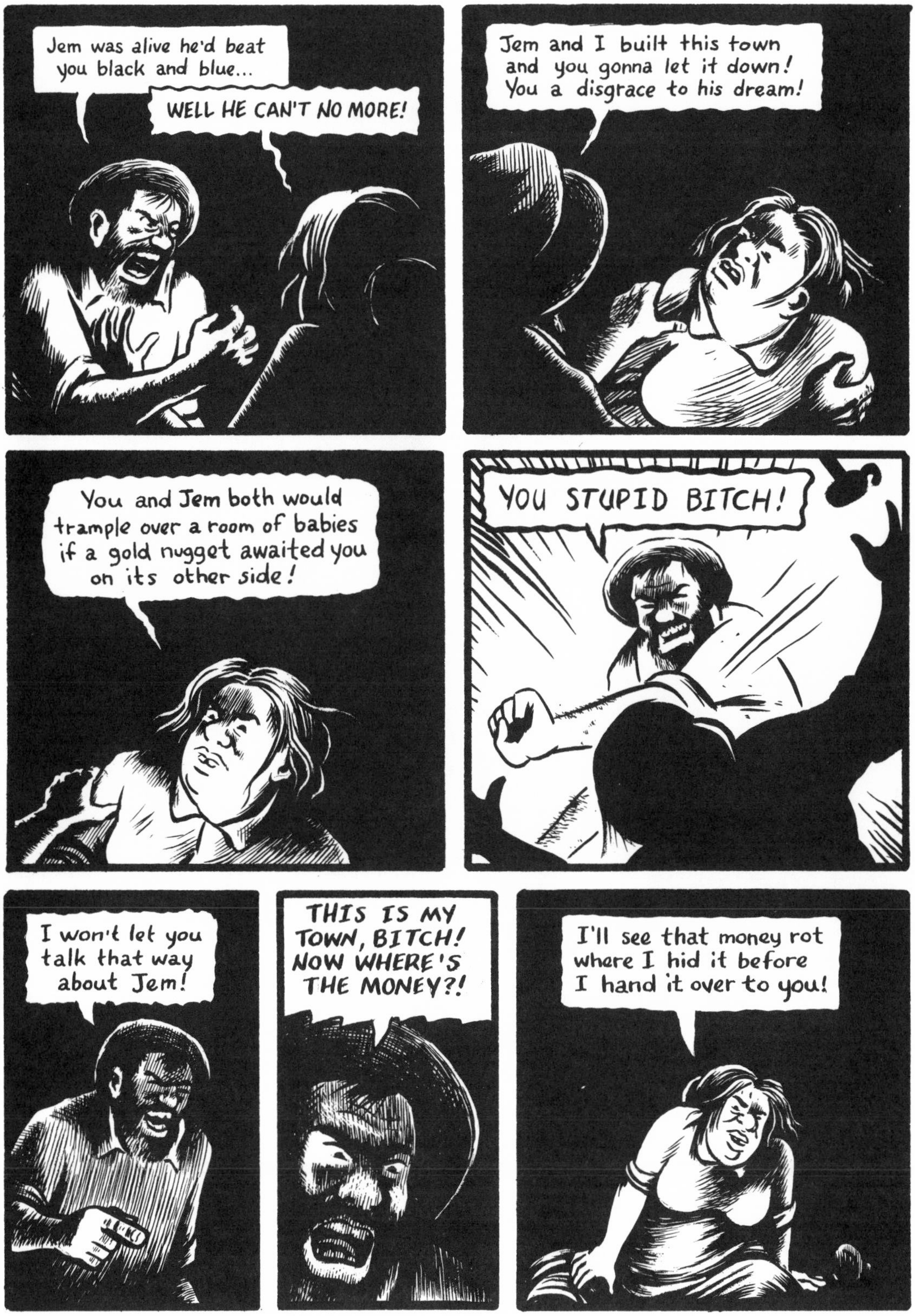
Jem was alive he'd beat you black and blue...
WELL HE CAN'T NO MORE!
Jem and I built this town and you gonna let it down! You a disgrace to his dream!
You and Jem both would trample over a room of babies if a gold nugget awaited you on its other side!
YOU STUPID BITCH!
I won't let you talk that way about Jem!
THIS IS MY TOWN, BITCH! NOW WHERE'S THE MONEY?!
I'll see that money rot where I hid it before I hand it over to you!

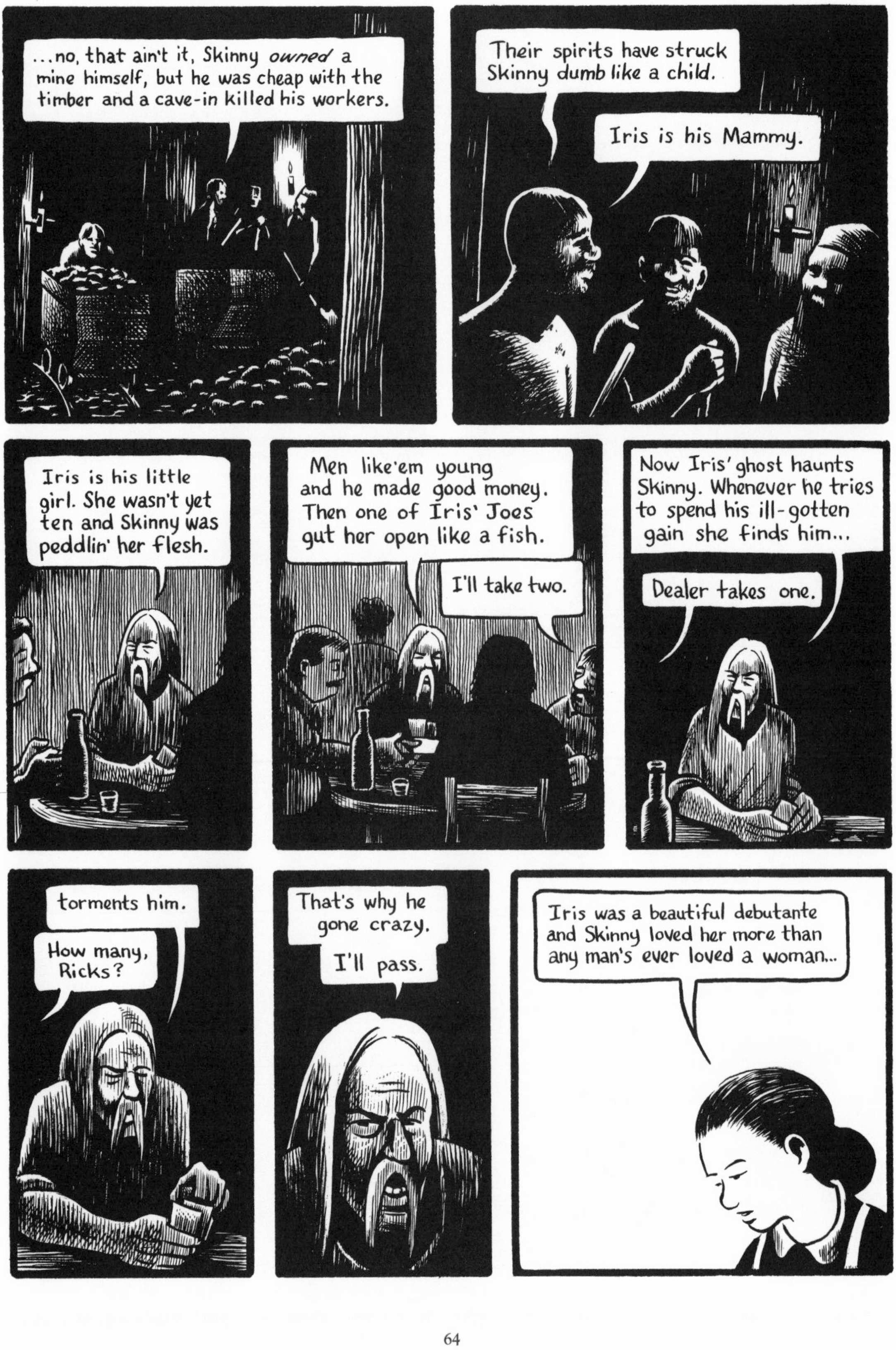
...no, that ain't it, Skinny *owned* a mine himself, but he was cheap with the timber and a cave-in killed his workers.
Their spirits have struck Skinny dumb like a child.
Iris is his Mammy.
Iris is his little girl. She wasn't yet ten and Skinny was peddlin' her flesh.
Men like'em young and he made good money. Then one of Iris' Joes gut her open like a fish.
I'll take two.
Now Iris' ghost haunts Skinny. Whenever he tries to spend his ill-gotten gain she finds him...
Dealer takes one.
torments him.
How many, Ricks?
That's why he gone crazy.
I'll pass.
Iris was a beautiful debutante and Skinny loved her more than any man's ever loved a woman...

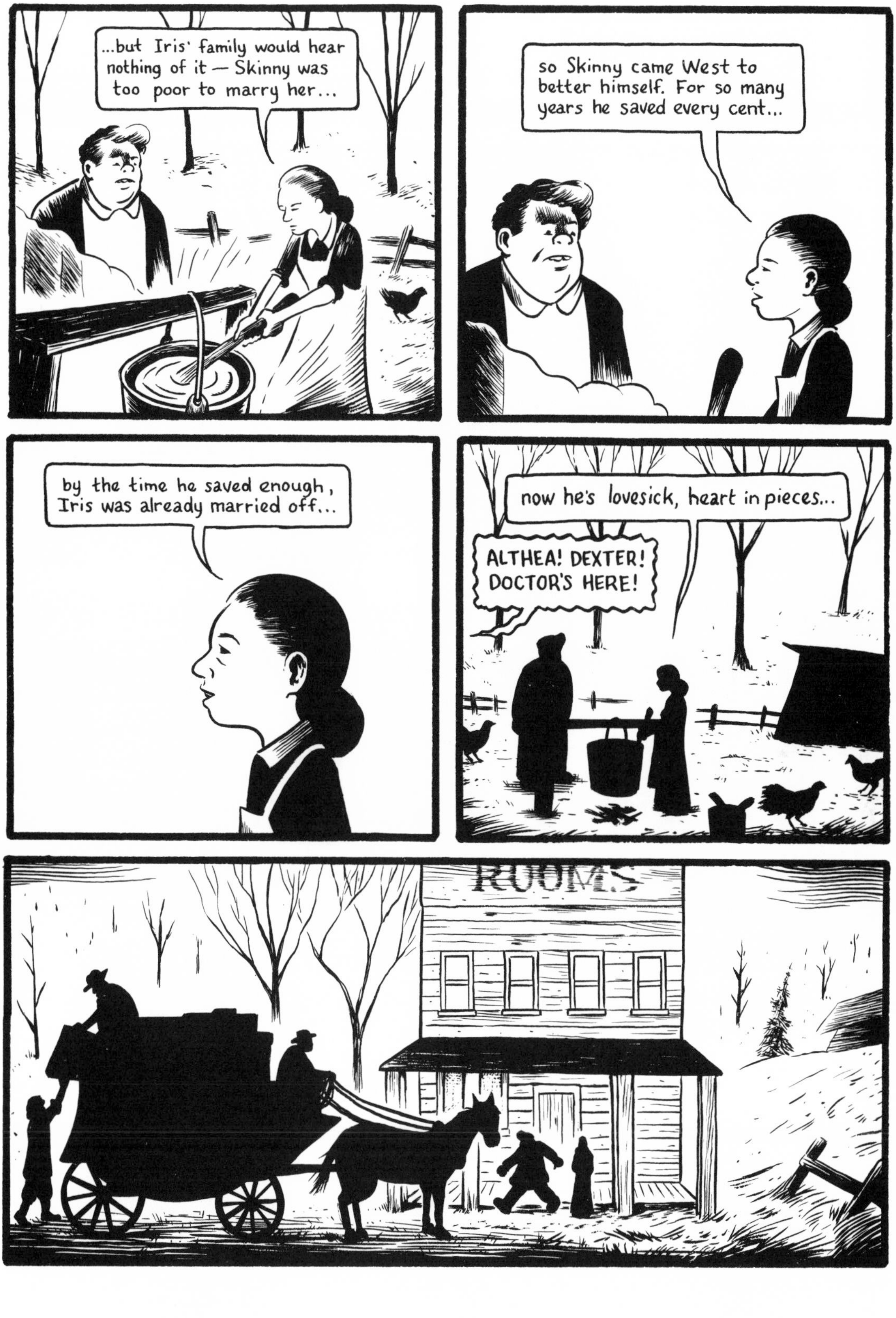
...but Iris' family would hear nothing of it — Skinny was too poor to marry her...
so Skinny came West to better himself. For so many years he saved every cent...
by the time he saved enough, Iris was already married off...
now he's lovesick, heart in pieces...
ALTHEA! DEXTER! DOCTOR'S HERE!
ROOMS

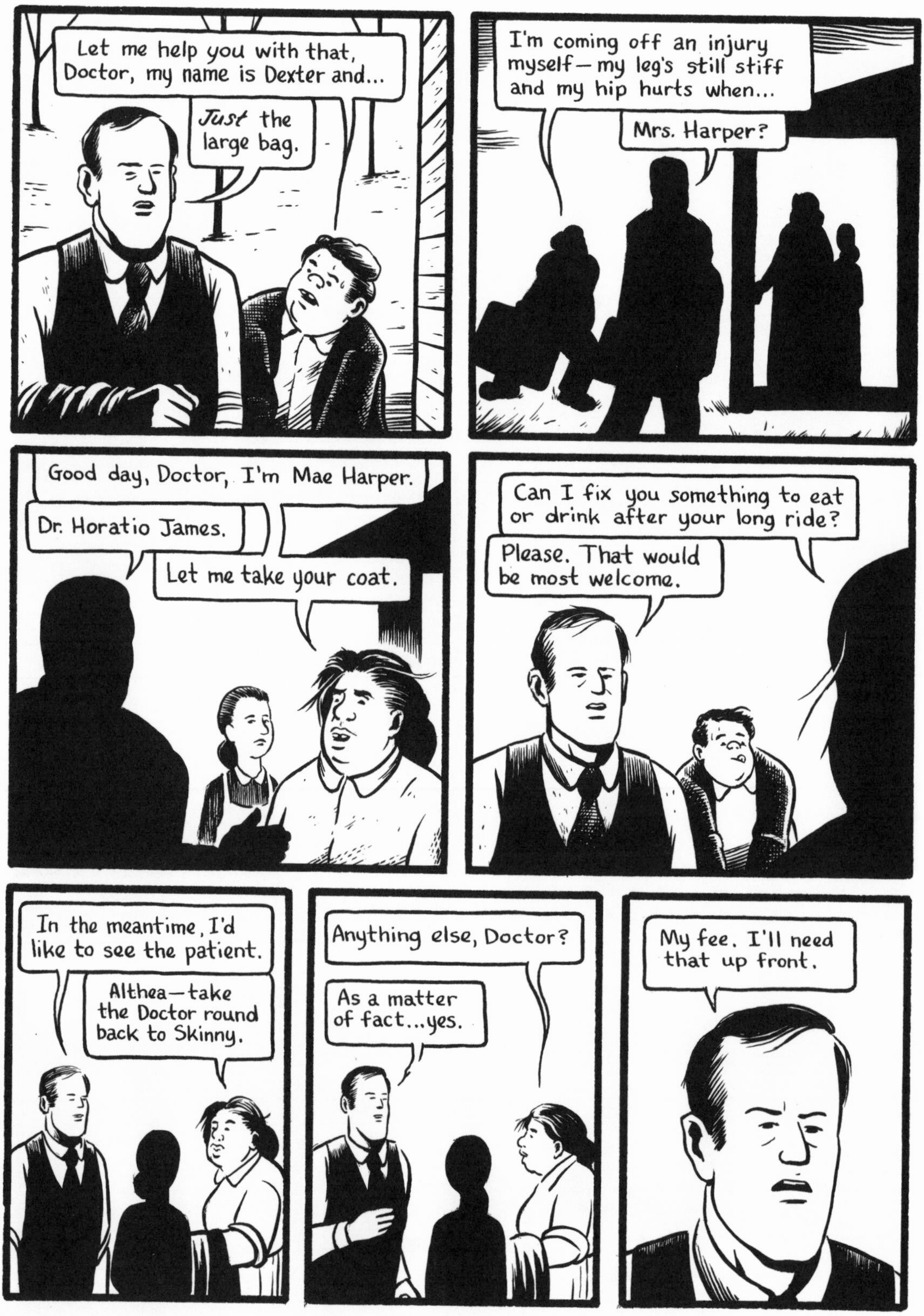

Let me help you with that, Doctor, my name is Dexter and...
*Just* the large bag.
I'm coming off an injury myself—my leg's still stiff and my hip hurts when...
Mrs. Harper?
Good day, Doctor, I'm Mae Harper.
Dr. Horatio James.
Let me take your coat.
Can I fix you something to eat or drink after your long ride?
Please. That would be most welcome.
In the meantime, I'd like to see the patient.
Althea—take the Doctor round back to Skinny.
Anything else, Doctor?
As a matter of fact...yes.
My fee. I'll need that up front.

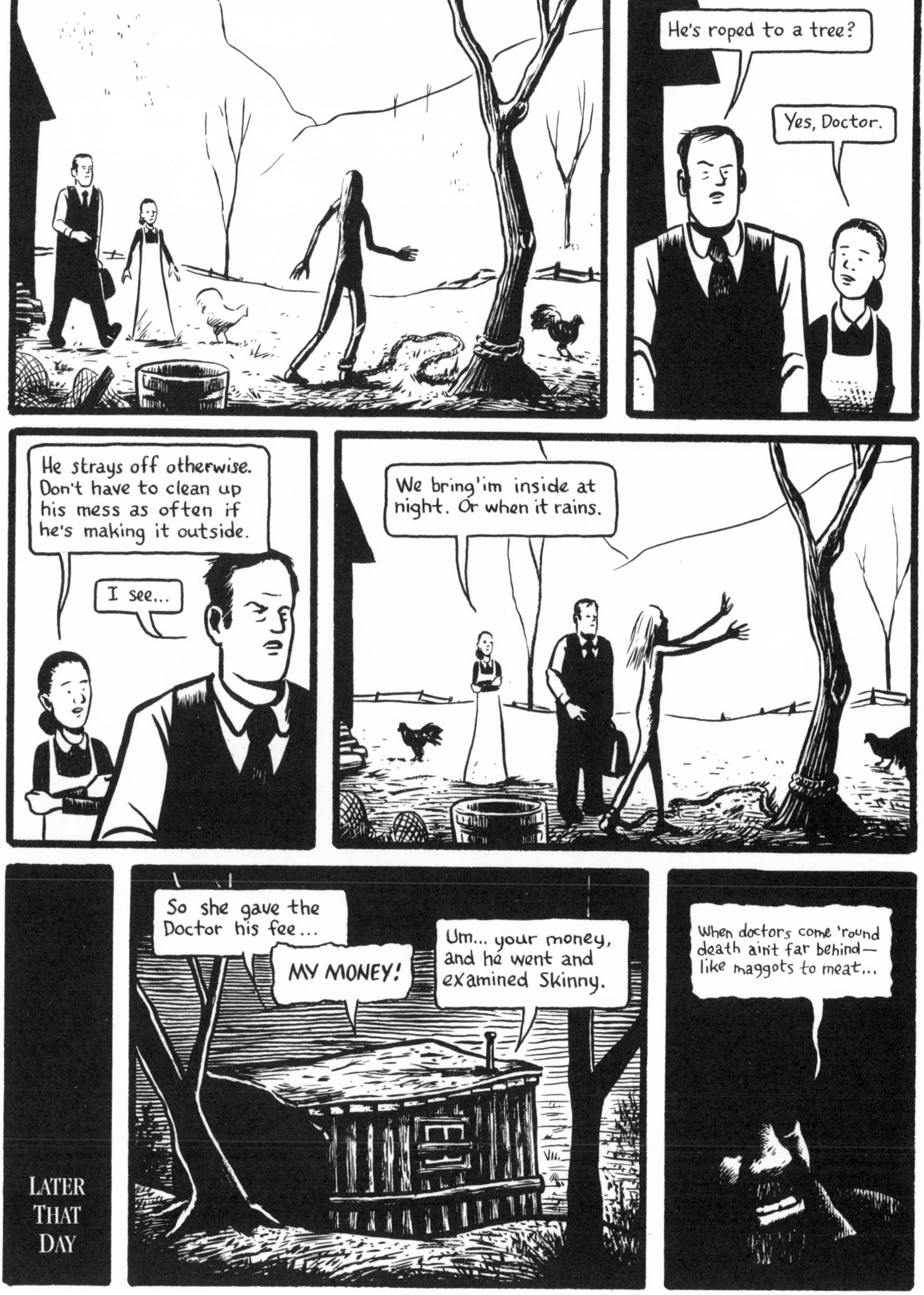

He's roped to a tree?
Yes, Doctor.
He strays off otherwise. Don't have to clean up his mess as often if he's making it outside.
I see...
We bring'im inside at night. Or when it rains.
LATER THAT DAY
So she gave the Doctor his fee...
MY MONEY!
Um... your money, and he went and examined Skinny.
When doctors come 'round death ain't far behind— like maggots to meat...

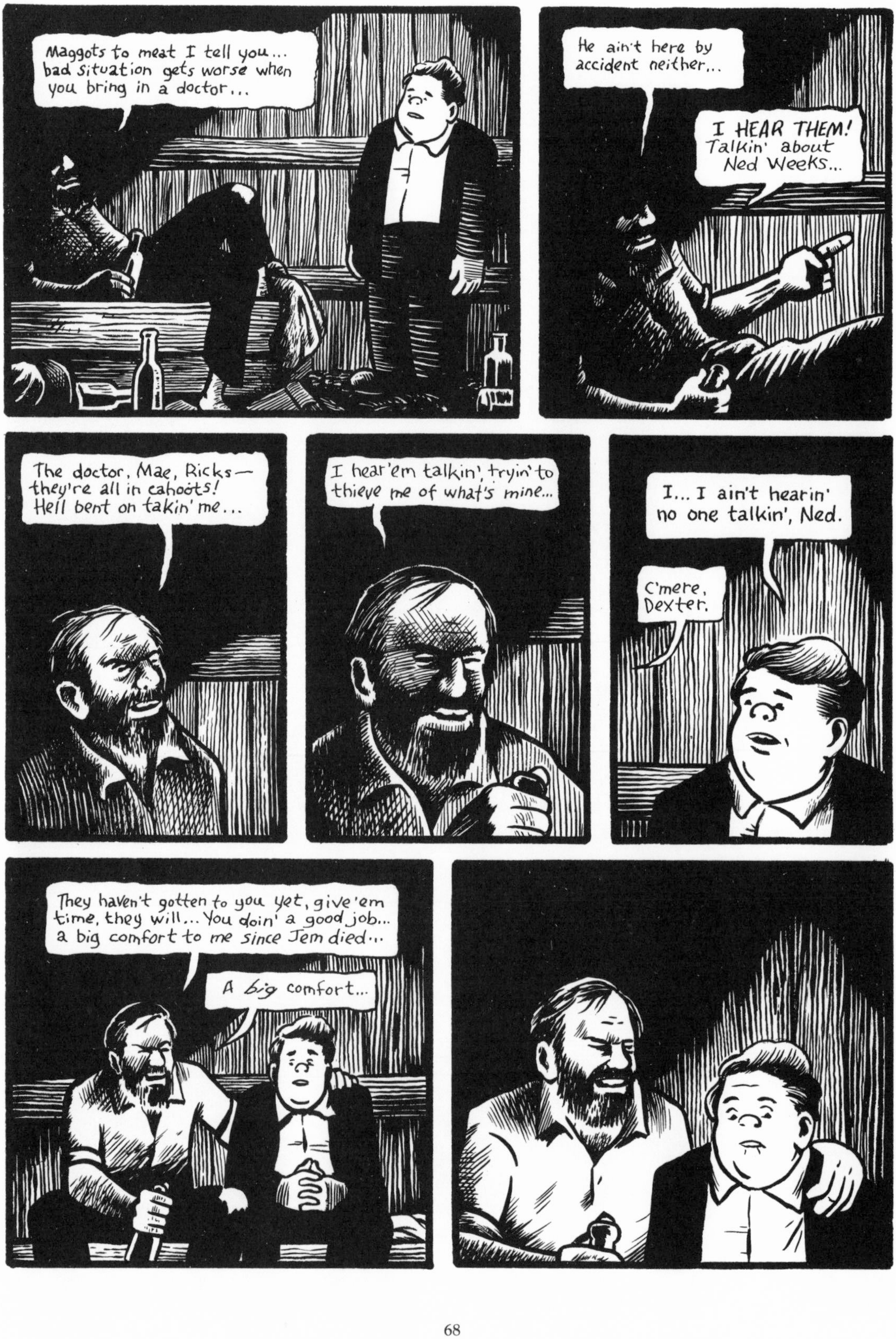
Maggots to meat I tell you... bad situation gets worse when you bring in a doctor...
He ain't here by accident neither...
I HEAR THEM! Talkin' about Ned Weeks...
The doctor, Mae, Ricks— they're all in cahoots! Hell bent on takin' me...
I hear'em talkin', tryin' to thieve me of what's mine...
I... I ain't hearin' no one talkin', Ned.
C'mere, Dexter.
They haven't gotten to you yet, give'em time, they will... You doin' a good job... a big comfort to me since Jem died...
A *big* comfort...

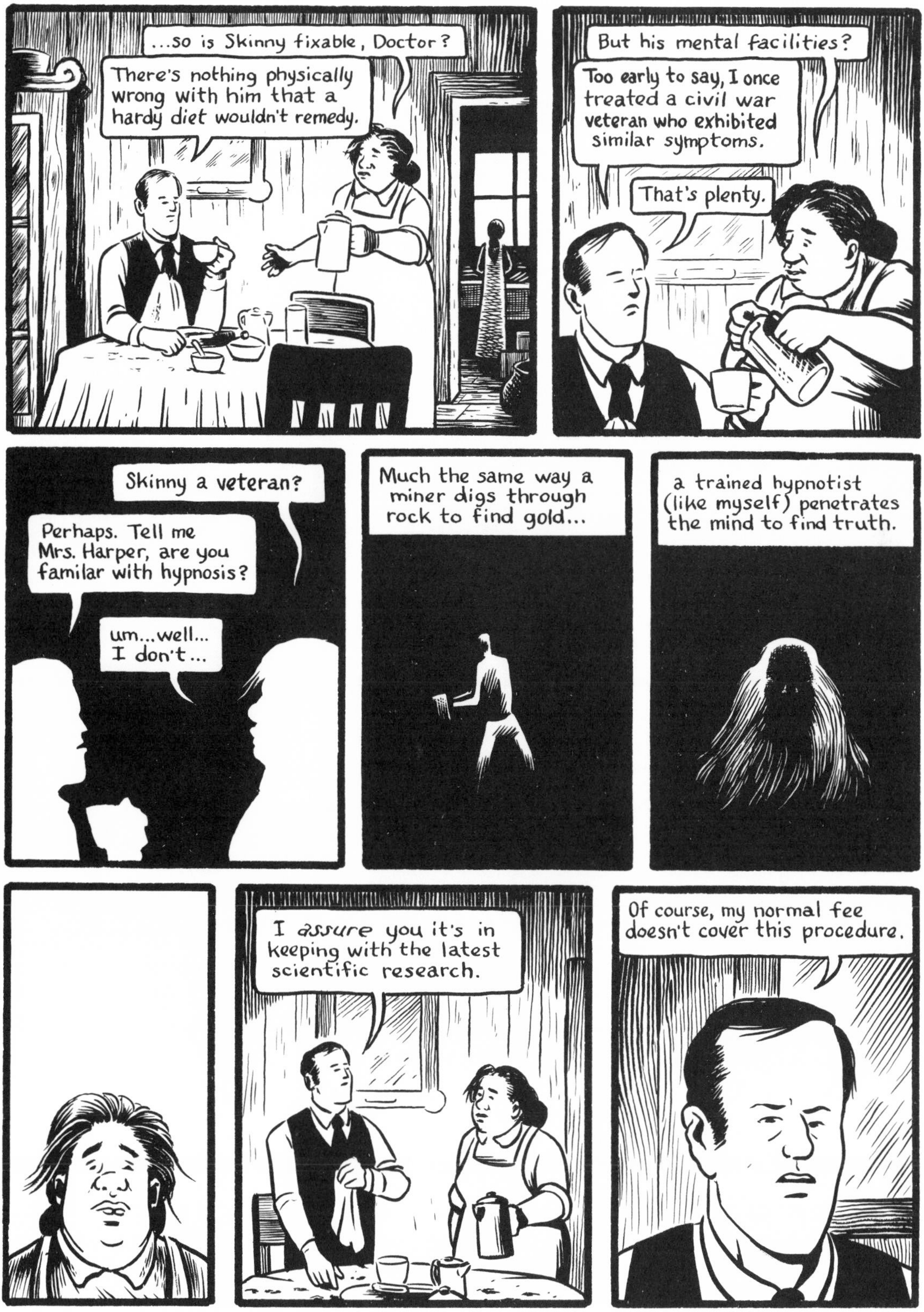
...so is Skinny fixable, Doctor?
There's nothing physically wrong with him that a hardy diet wouldn't remedy.
But his mental facilities?
Too early to say, I once treated a civil war veteran who exhibited similar symptoms.
That's plenty.
Skinny a veteran?
Perhaps. Tell me Mrs. Harper, are you familar with hypnosis?
um...well... I don't...
Much the same way a miner digs through rock to find gold...
a trained hypnotist (like myself) penetrates the mind to find truth.
I *assure* you it's in keeping with the latest scientific research.
Of course, my normal fee doesn't cover this procedure.

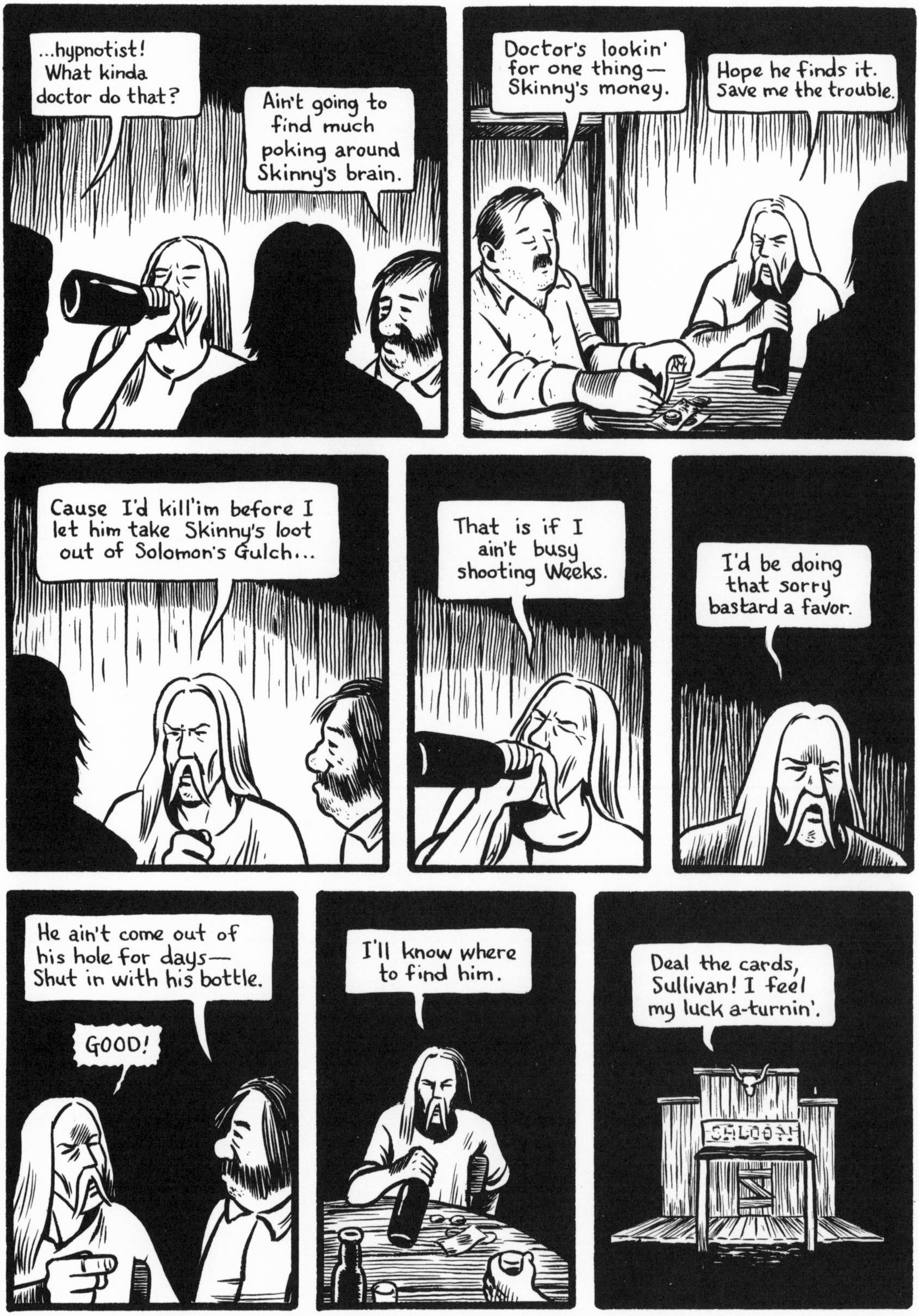
...hypnotist! What kinda doctor do that?
Ain't going to find much poking around Skinny's brain.
Doctor's lookin' for one thing— Skinny's money.
Hope he finds it. Save me the trouble.
Cause I'd kill'im before I let him take Skinny's loot out of Solomon's Gulch...
That is if I ain't busy shooting Weeks.
I'd be doing that sorry bastard a favor.
He ain't come out of his hole for days— Shut in with his bottle.
GOOD!
I'll know where to find him.
Deal the cards, Sullivan! I feel my luck a-turnin'.
SALOON

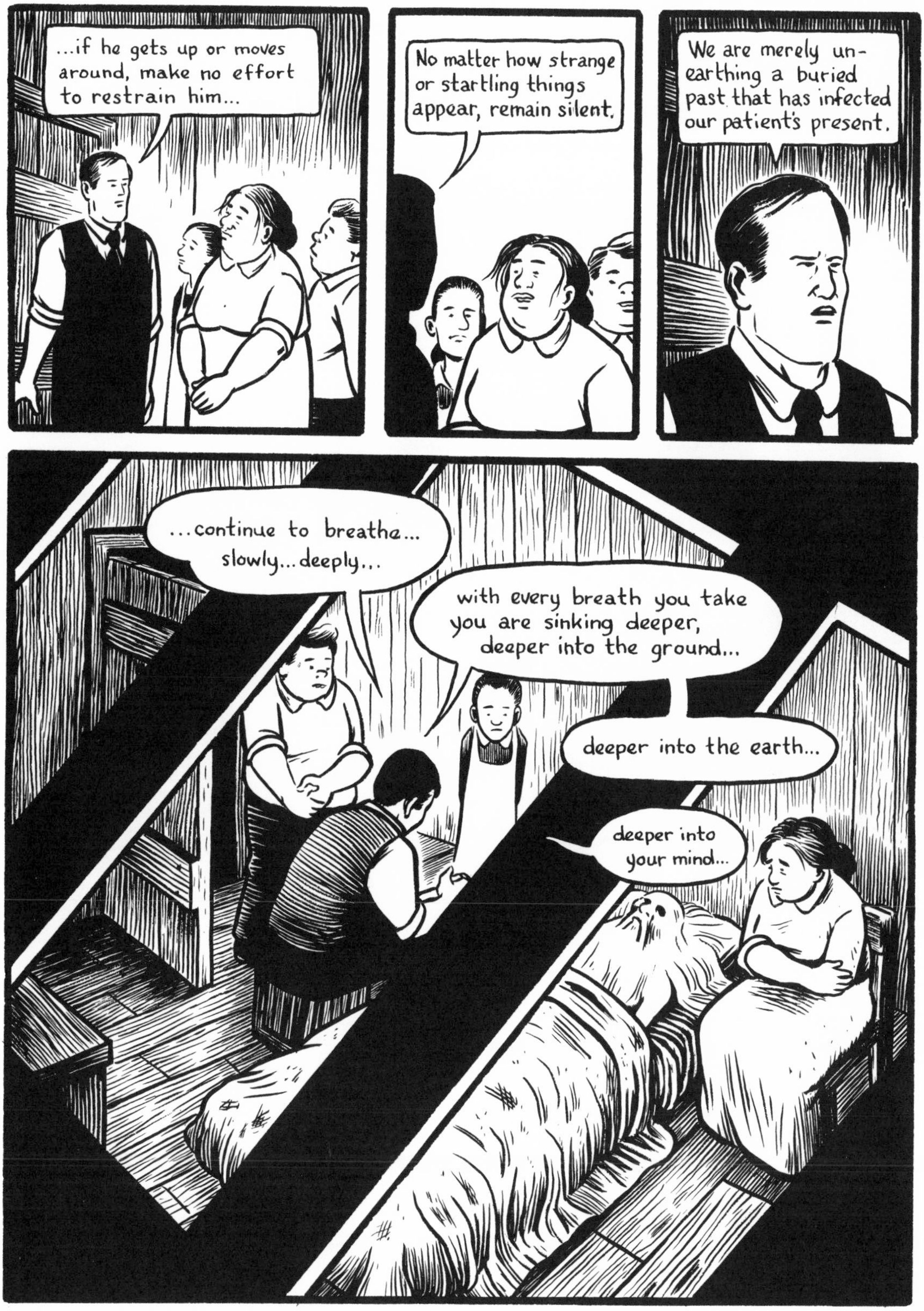
...if he gets up or moves around, make no effort to restrain him...
No matter how strange or startling things appear, remain silent.
We are merely unearthing a buried past that has infected our patient's present.
...continue to breathe... slowly...deeply...
with every breath you take you are sinking deeper, deeper into the ground...
deeper into the earth...
deeper into your mind...

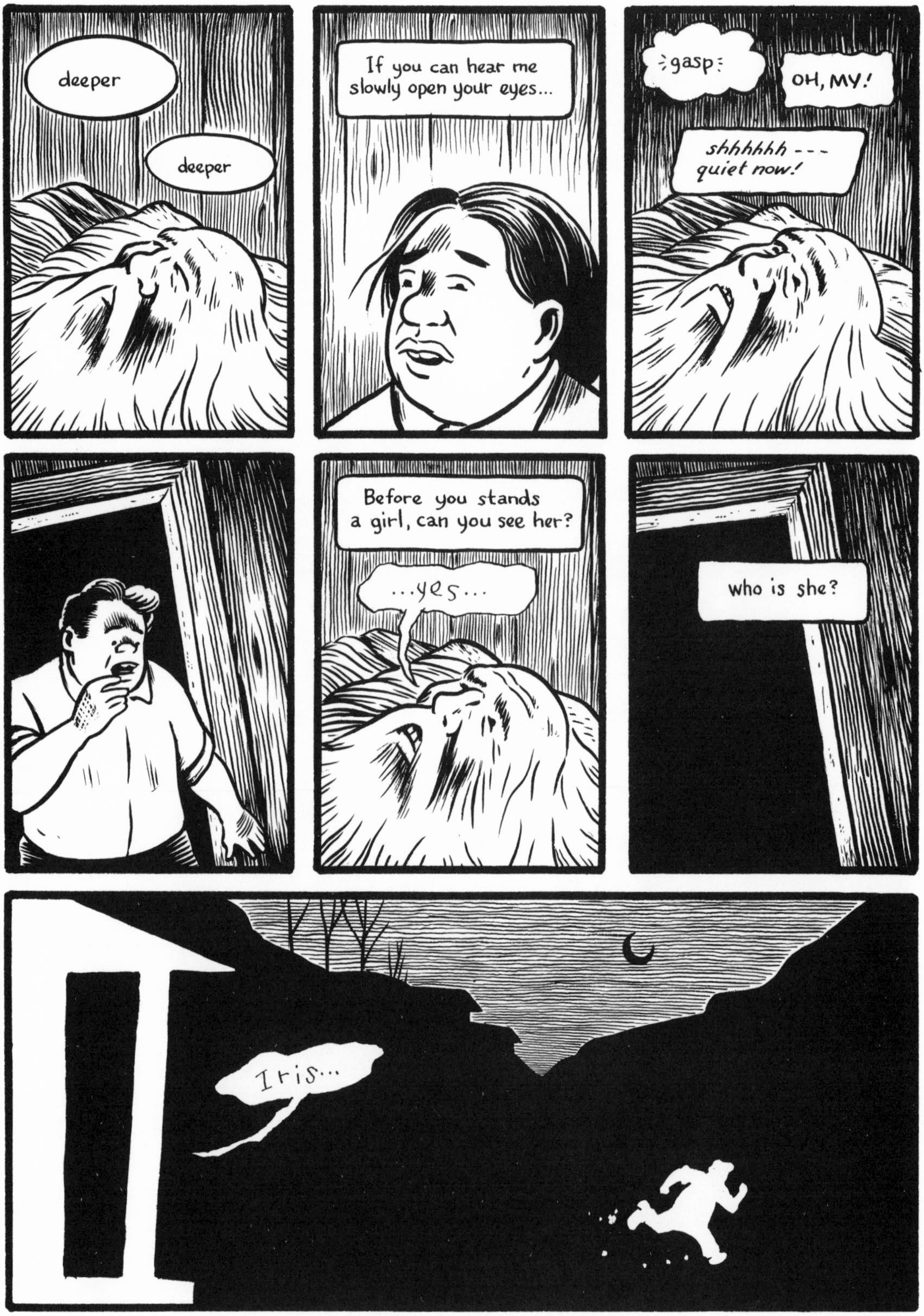
deeper
deeper
If you can hear me slowly open your eyes...
gasp
OH, MY!
shhhhhh --- quiet now!
Before you stands a girl, can you see her?
...yes...
who is she?
Iris...

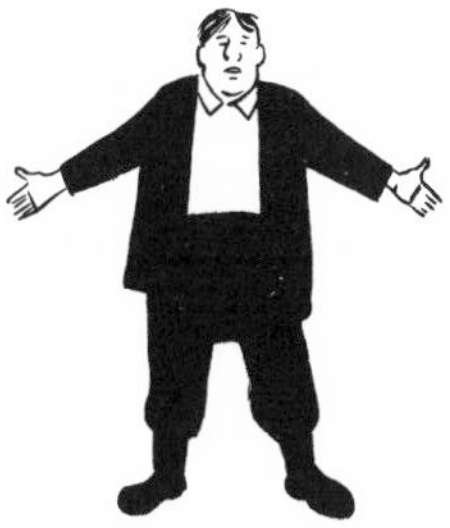

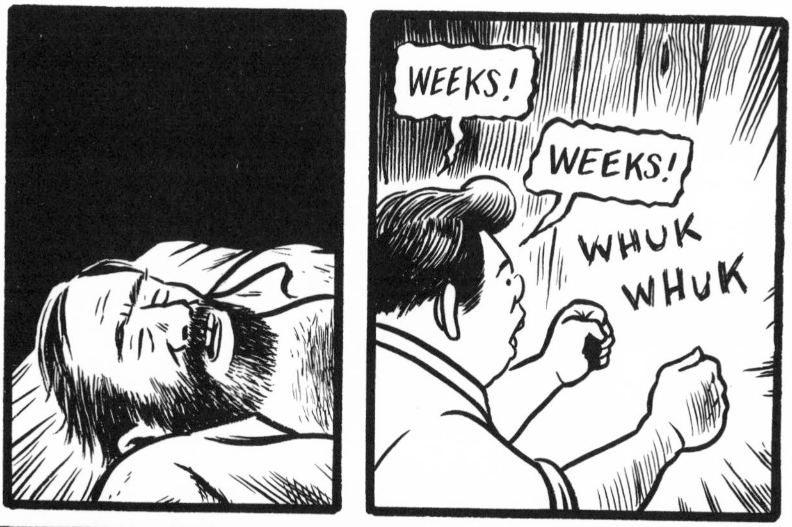
WEEKS!
WEEKS!
WHUK WHUK

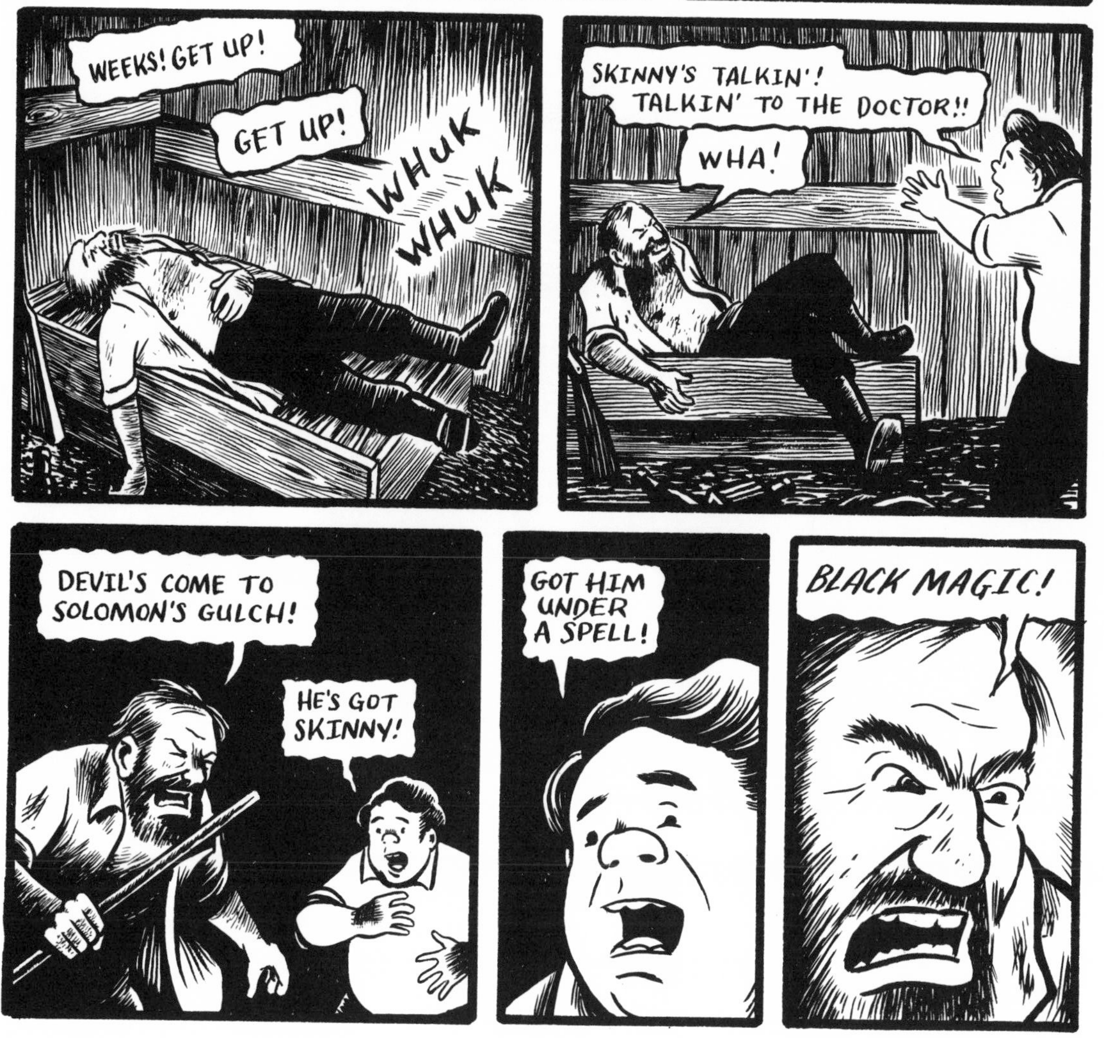
WEEKS! GET UP!
GET UP!
WHUK WHUK
SKINNY'S TALKIN'! TALKIN' TO THE DOCTOR!!
WHA!
DEVIL'S COME TO SOLOMON'S GULCH!
HE'S GOT SKINNY!
GOT HIM UNDER A SPELL!
BLACK MAGIC!

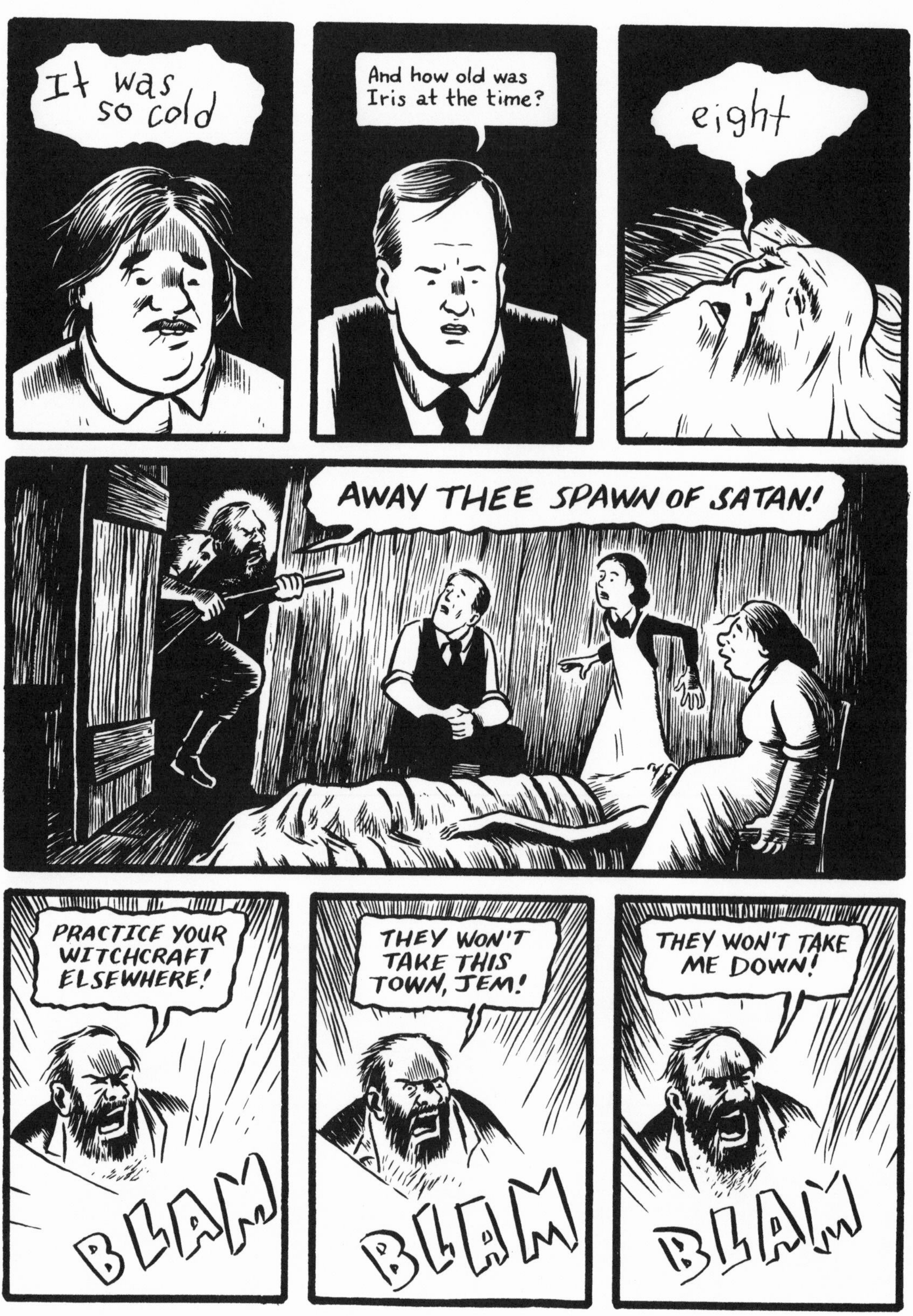
It was so cold
And how old was Iris at the time?
eight
AWAY THEE SPAWN OF SATAN!
PRACTICE YOUR WITCHCRAFT ELSEWHERE!
BLAM
THEY WON'T TAKE THIS TOWN, JEM!
BLAM
THEY WON'T TAKE ME DOWN!
BLAM

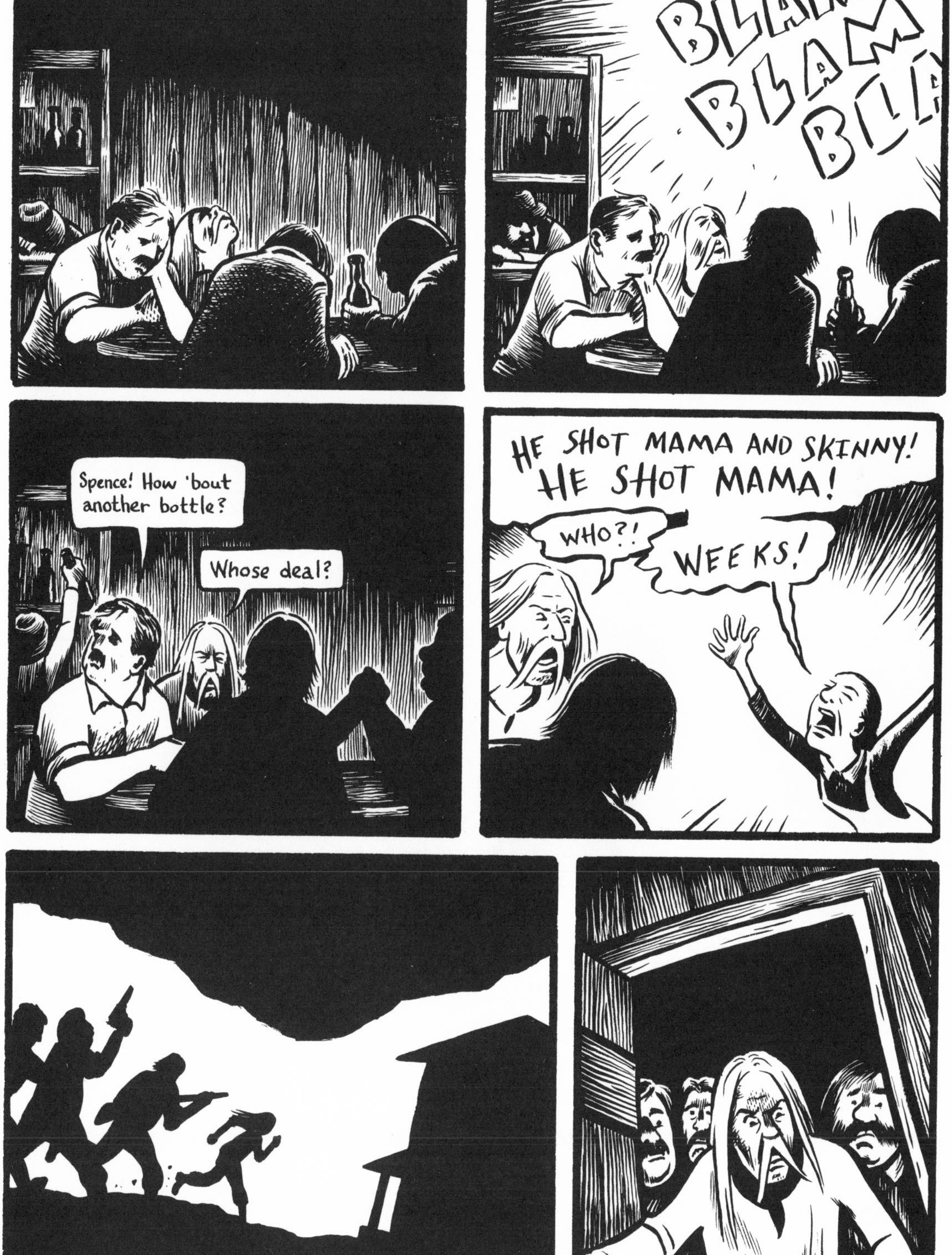
BLAM
BLAM
BLA
Spence! How 'bout another bottle?
Whose deal?
HE SHOT MAMA AND SKINNY!
HE SHOT MAMA!
WHO?!
WEEKS!

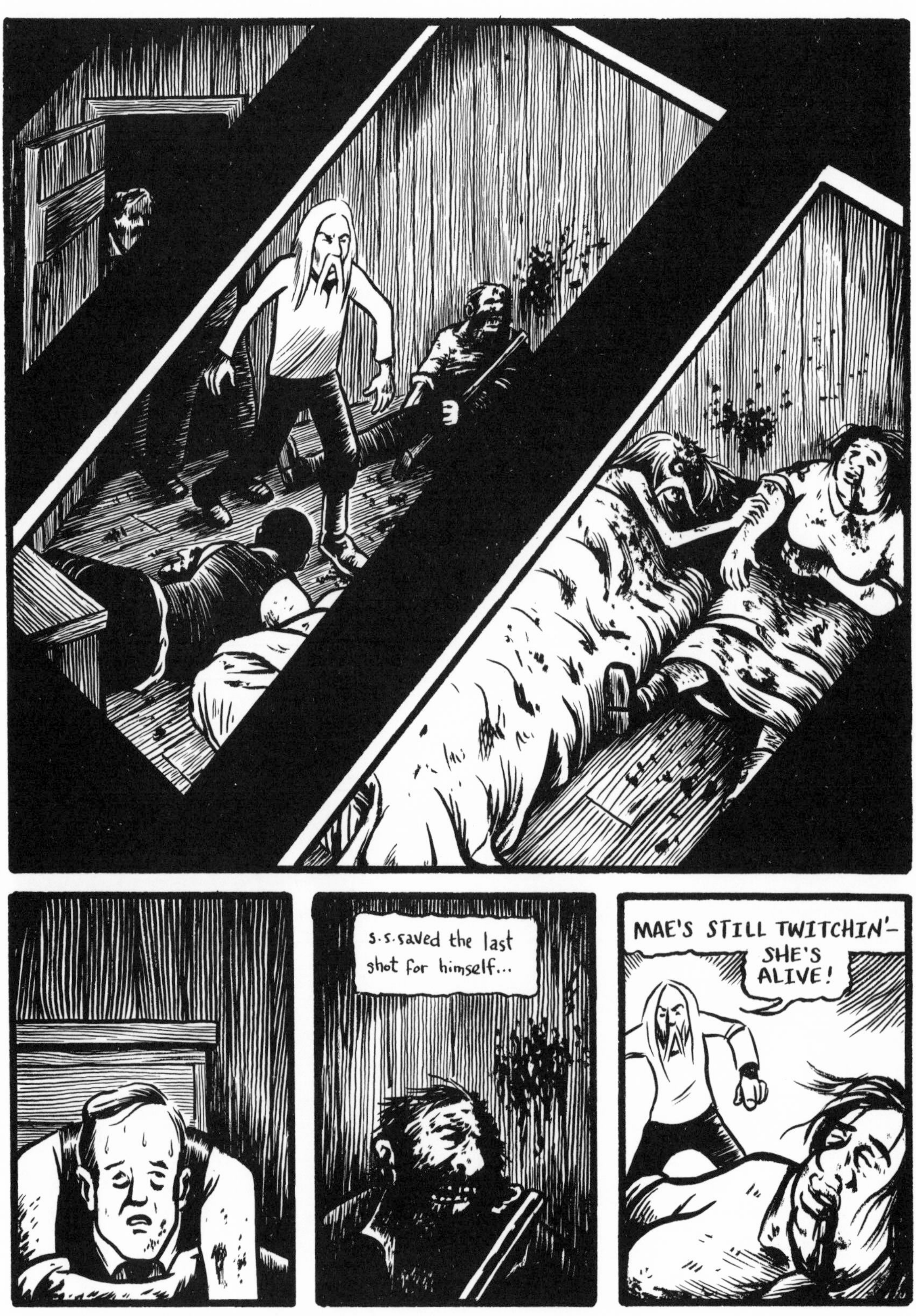
s.s. saved the last shot for himself...
MAE'S STILL TWITCHIN'-
SHE'S ALIVE!

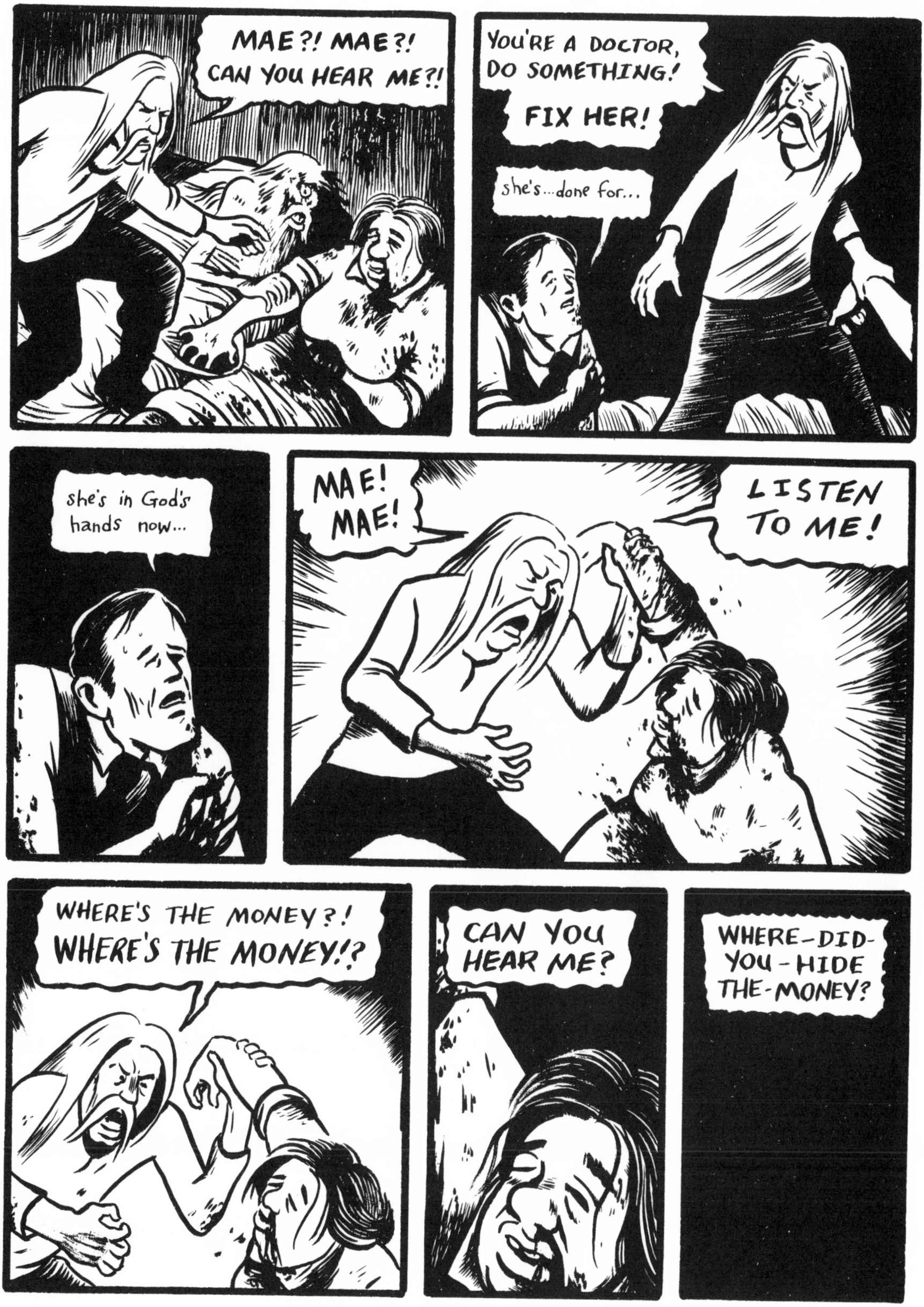
MAE?! MAE?! CAN YOU HEAR ME?!
YOU'RE A DOCTOR, DO SOMETHING!
FIX HER!
she's...done for...
she's in God's hands now...
MAE! MAE!
LISTEN TO ME!
WHERE'S THE MONEY?! WHERE'S THE MONEY!?
CAN YOU HEAR ME?
WHERE-DID-YOU-HIDE THE-MONEY?

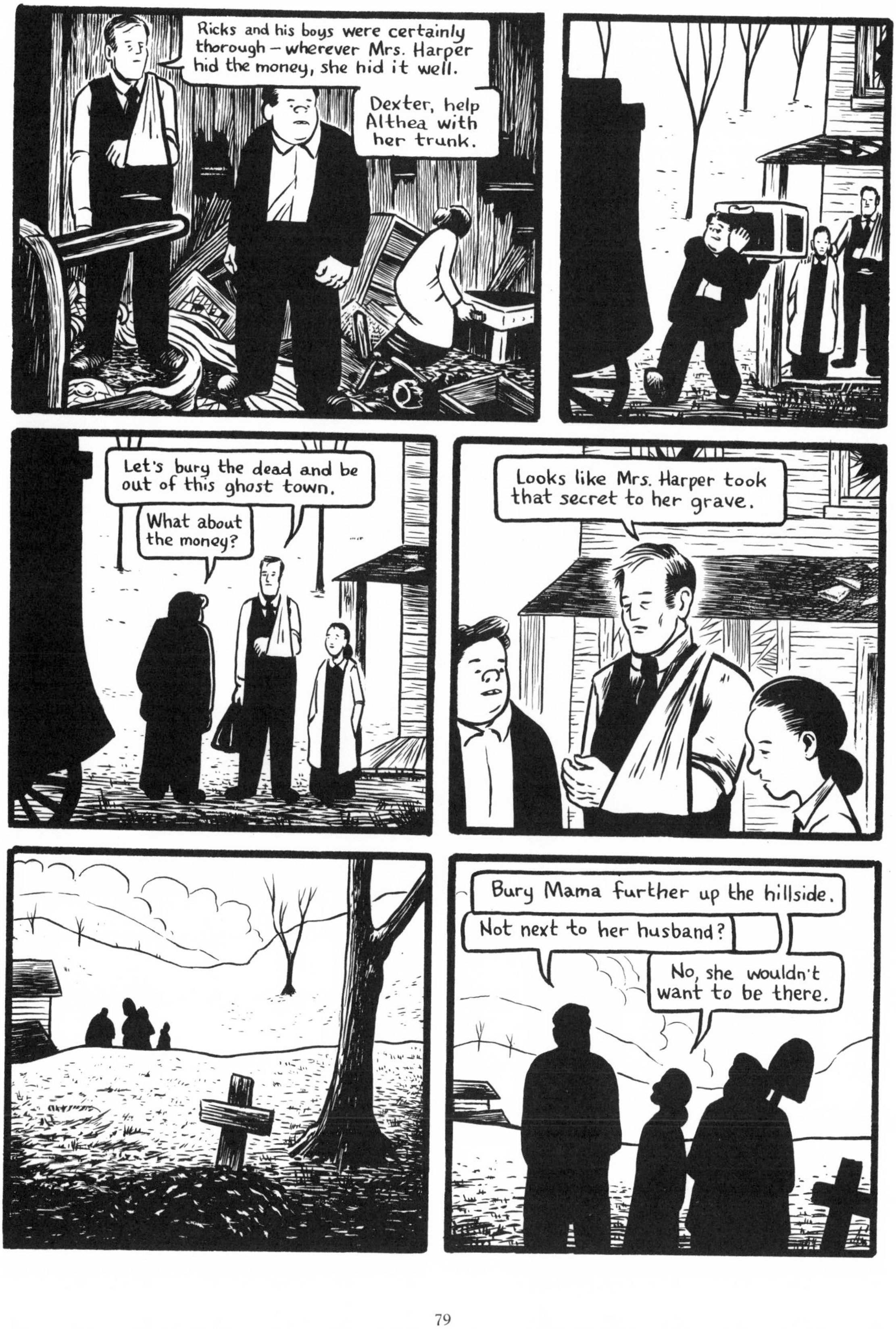

Ricks and his boys were certainly thorough – wherever Mrs. Harper hid the money, she hid it well.
Dexter, help Althea with her trunk.
Let's bury the dead and be out of this ghost town.
What about the money?
Looks like Mrs. Harper took that secret to her grave.
Bury Mama further up the hillside.
Not next to her husband?
No, she wouldn't want to be there.

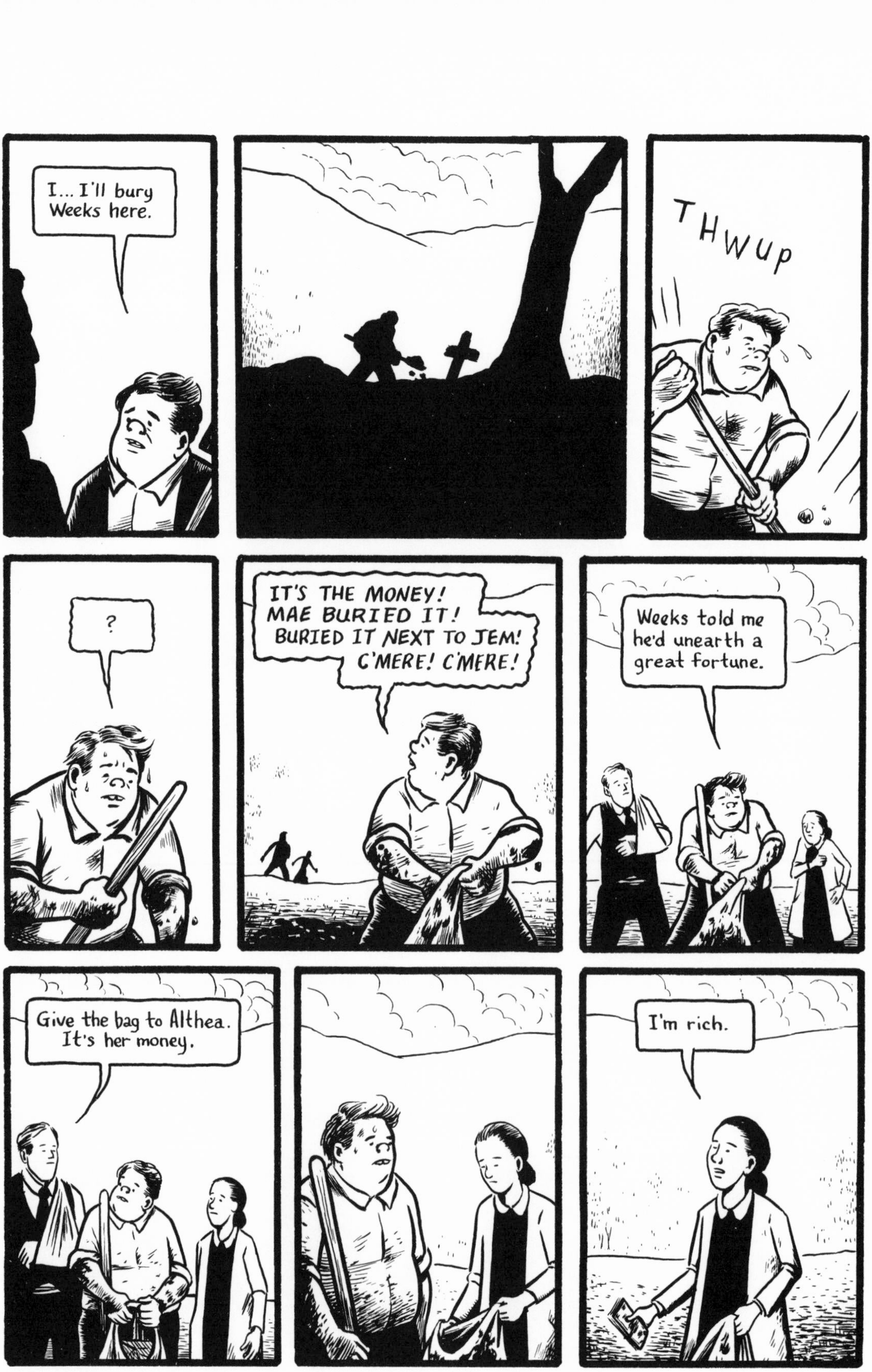

I... I'll bury Weeks here.
THWUP
?
IT'S THE MONEY! MAE BURIED IT! BURIED IT NEXT TO JEM! C'MERE! C'MERE!
Weeks told me he'd unearth a great fortune.
Give the bag to Althea. It's her money.
I'm rich.

# THE GOLEM'S MIGHTY SWING

## (Early 1920s)

"THE PUBLIC *is* EAGER *for* SPECTACLE,
THEY DON'T SPLIT HAIRS."

# BASEBALL

World's Champion Traveling Baseball Team!

## STARS ✡ OF ✡ DAVID

### THE BEARDED WANDERING WONDERS

### VS

## FOREST GROVE SPARTANS

# FRIDAY, AUGUST 16

## ADMISSION 50¢          3:00 P.M.

THREE YEAR RECORD
1919 Won 110, Tied 3 of 162 Games
1920 Won 92, Tied 4 of 143 Games
1921 Won 136, Tied 1 of 160 Games
Average 20,000 Miles by Autobus Each Year

## A REAL
## PARK PACKING
## ATTRACTION

Formerly of the Boston Red Sox
Noah Strauss "The Zion Lion"

## RESERVED SEATING FOR WHITES

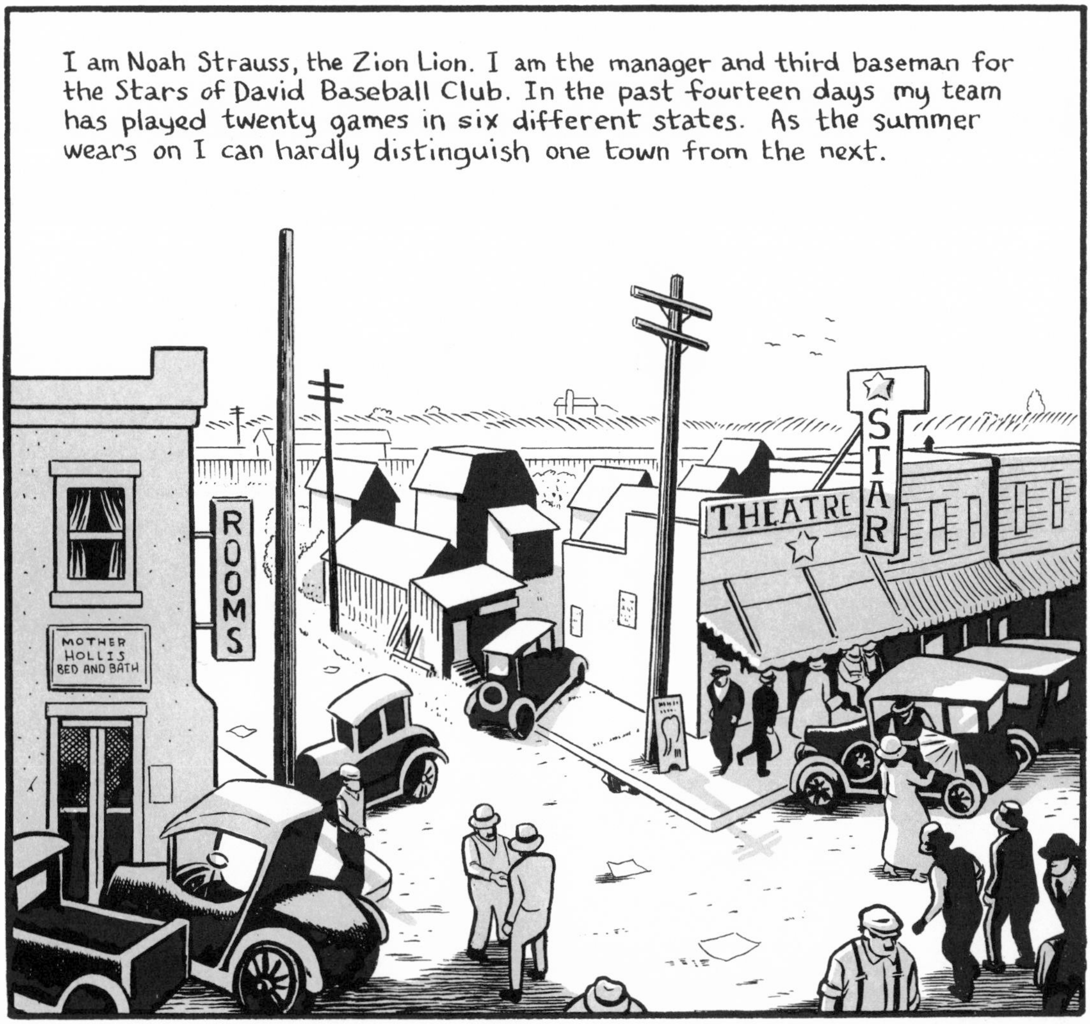
I am Noah Strauss, the Zion Lion. I am the manager and third baseman for the Stars of David Baseball Club. In the past fourteen days my team has played twenty games in six different states. As the summer wears on I can hardly distinguish one town from the next.
ROOMS
MOTHER HOLLIS BED AND BATH
THEATRE
STAR

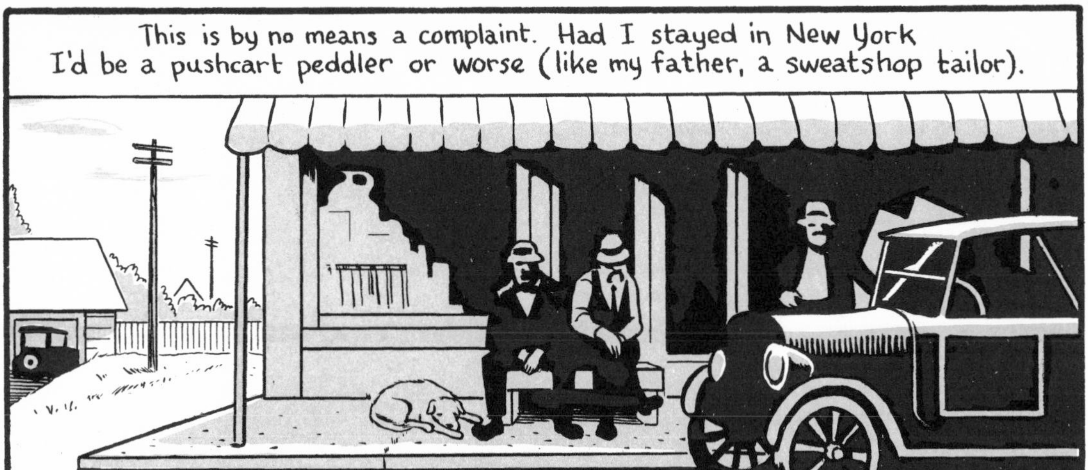
This is by no means a complaint. Had I stayed in New York I'd be a pushcart peddler or worse (like my father, a sweatshop tailor).

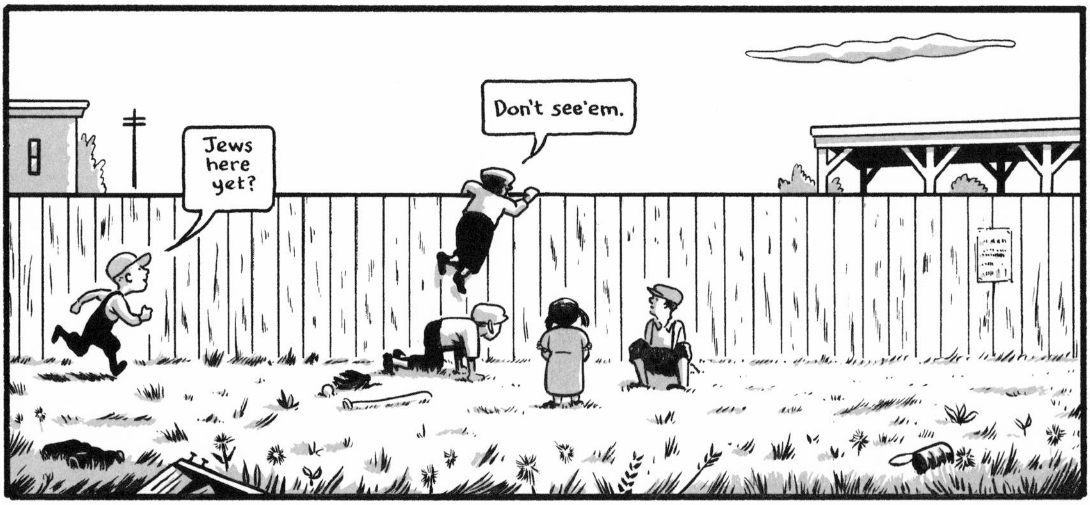
Jews here yet?
Don't see'em.

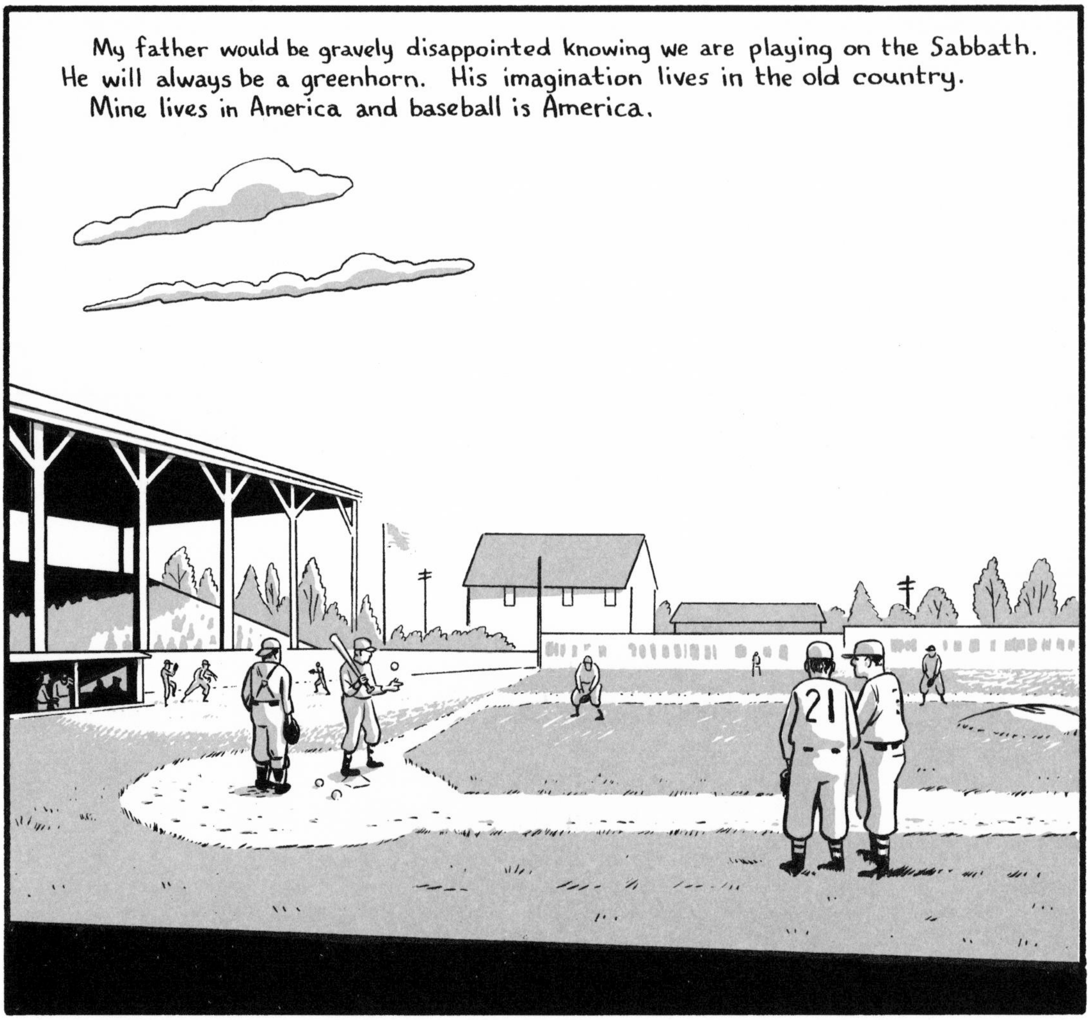
My father would be gravely disappointed knowing we are playing on the Sabbath. He will always be a greenhorn. His imagination lives in the old country. Mine lives in America and baseball is America.
21

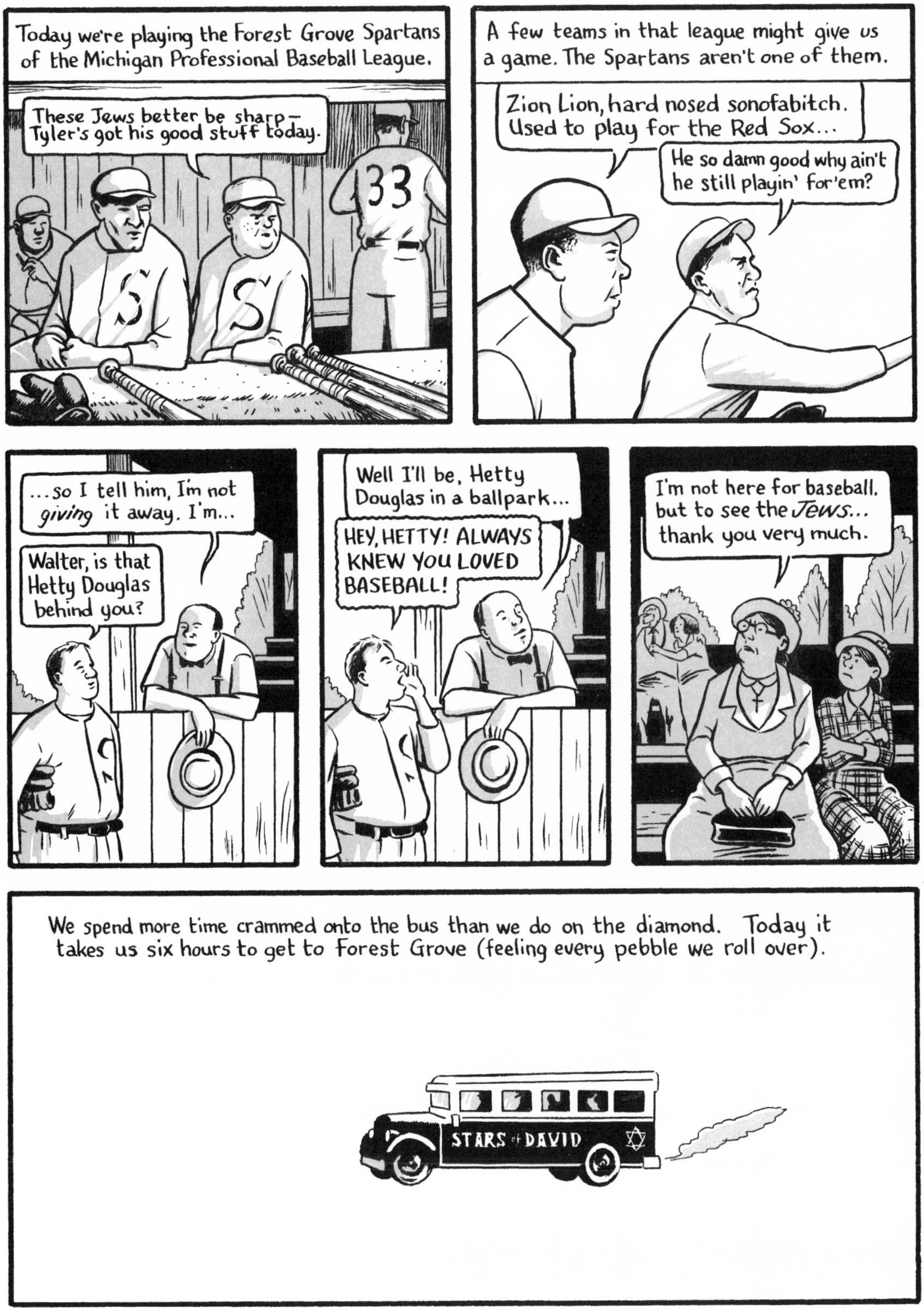
Today we're playing the Forest Grove Spartans of the Michigan Professional Baseball League.
These Jews better be sharp— Tyler's got his good stuff today.
33
A few teams in that league might give us a game. The Spartans aren't one of them.
Zion Lion, hard nosed sonofabitch. Used to play for the Red Sox...
He so damn good why ain't he still playin' for 'em?
...so I tell him, I'm not *giving* it away. I'm...
Walter, is that Hetty Douglas behind you?
Well I'll be, Hetty Douglas in a ballpark...
HEY, HETTY! ALWAYS KNEW YOU LOVED BASEBALL!
I'm not here for baseball, but to see the *JEWS*... thank you very much.
We spend more time crammed onto the bus than we do on the diamond. Today it takes us six hours to get to Forest Grove (feeling every pebble we roll over).
STARS of DAVID

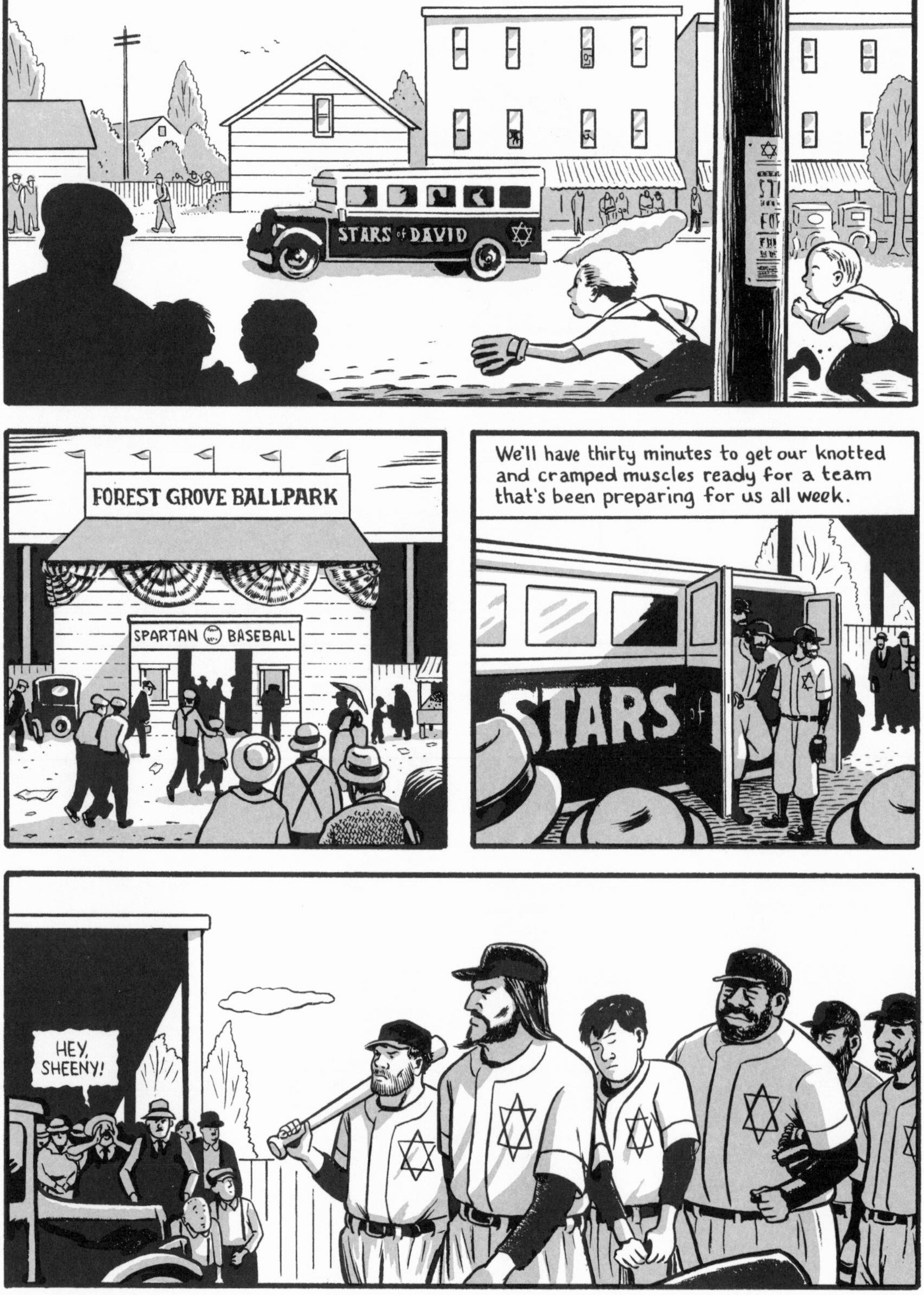
STARS of DAVID
FOREST GROVE BALLPARK
SPARTAN BASEBALL
We'll have thirty minutes to get our knotted and cramped muscles ready for a team that's been preparing for us all week.
STARS
HEY, SHEENY!

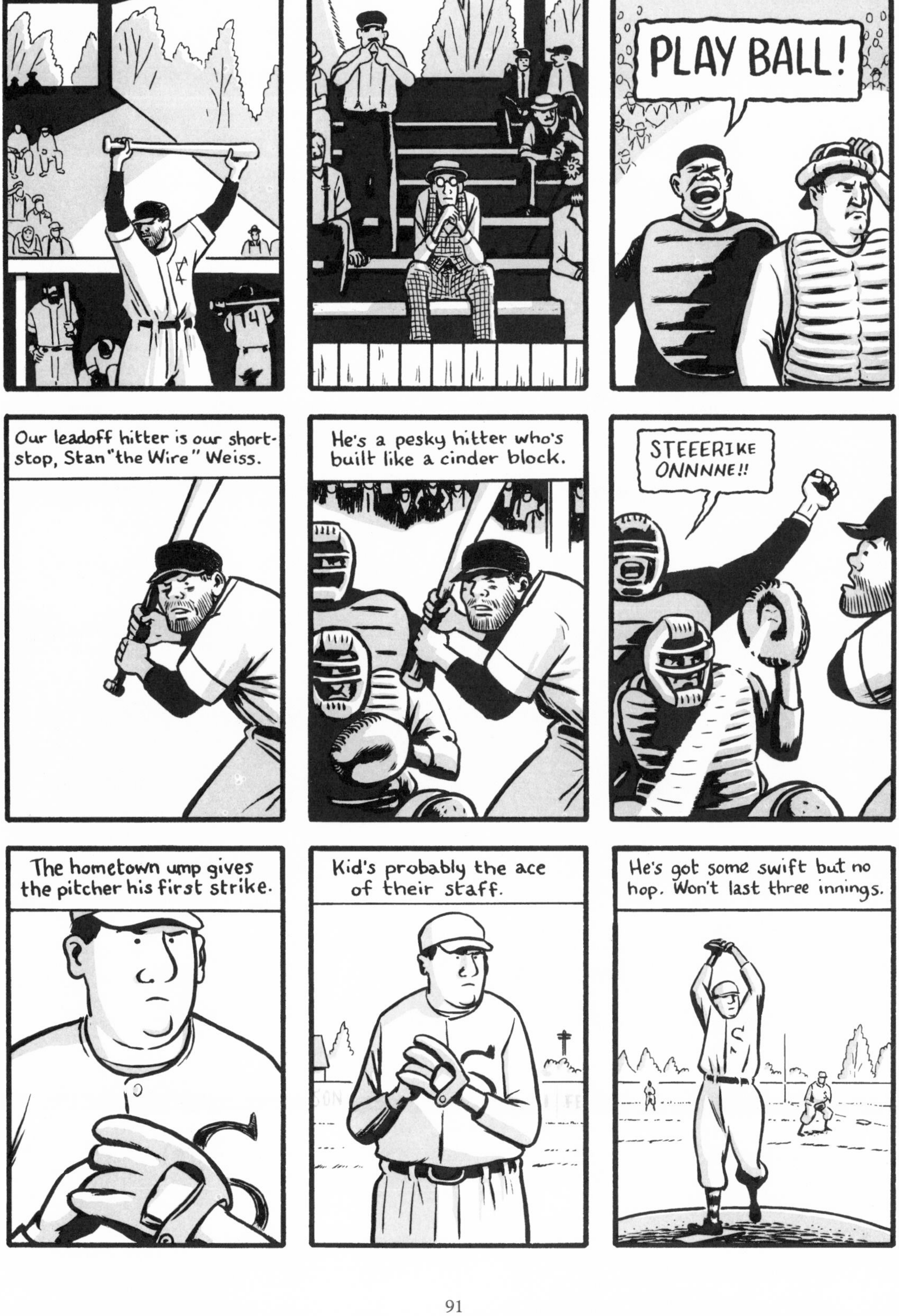
PLAY BALL!
Our leadoff hitter is our short-stop, Stan "the Wire" Weiss.
He's a pesky hitter who's built like a cinder block.
STEEERIKE ONNNNE!!
The hometown ump gives the pitcher his first strike.
Kid's probably the ace of their staff.
He's got some swift but no hop. Won't last three innings.

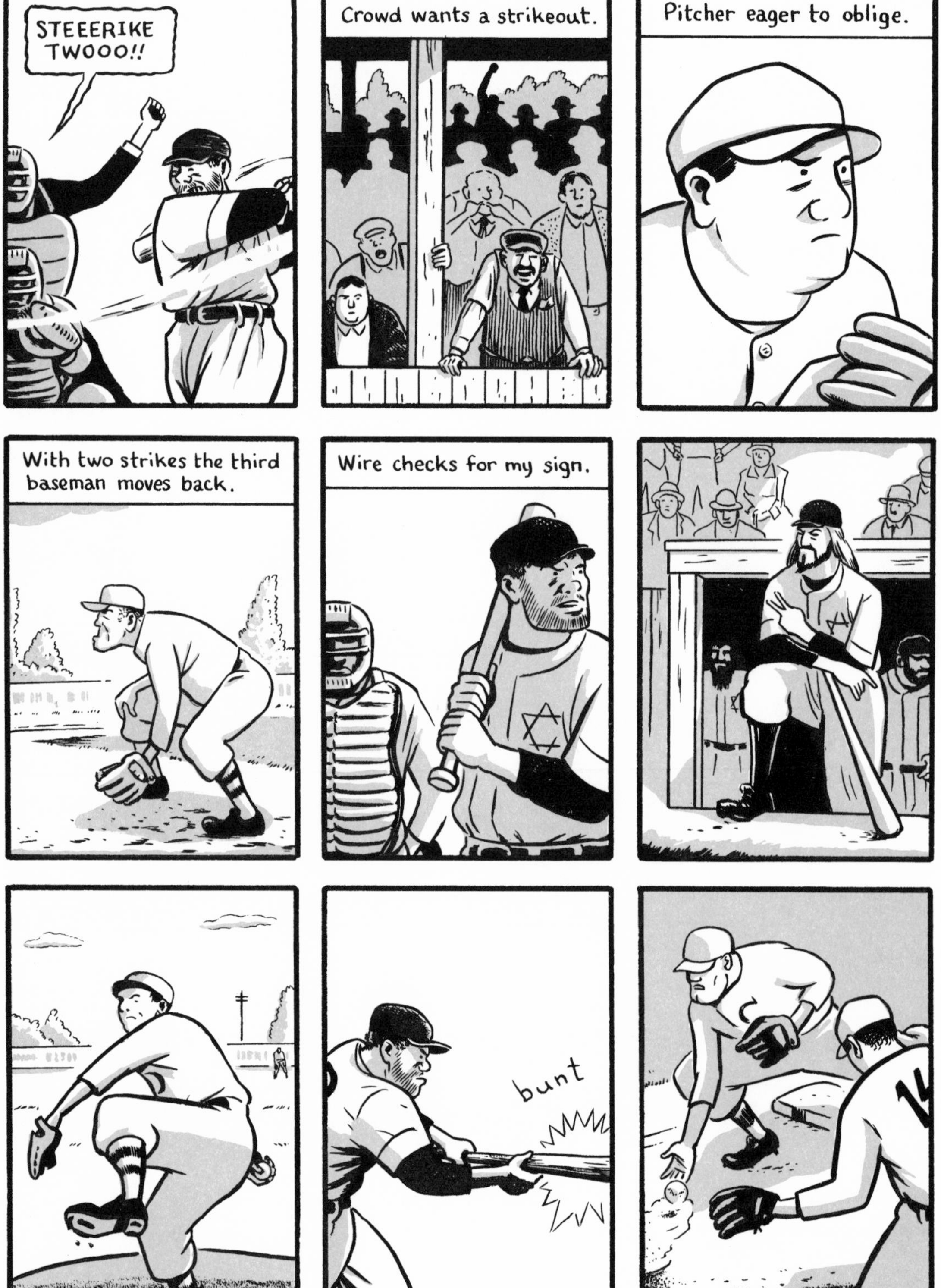
STEEERIKE TWOOO!!
Crowd wants a strikeout.
Pitcher eager to oblige.
With two strikes the third baseman moves back.
Wire checks for my sign.
bunt

Not even a throw.

One on, no out.

Next up is our second baseman, Moishe. Mo is sixteen. He is also my younger brother.

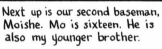

Time out, Fred.

TIME OUT!

The Jew at the plate is just a kid. That's not a beard, it's shoe polish.

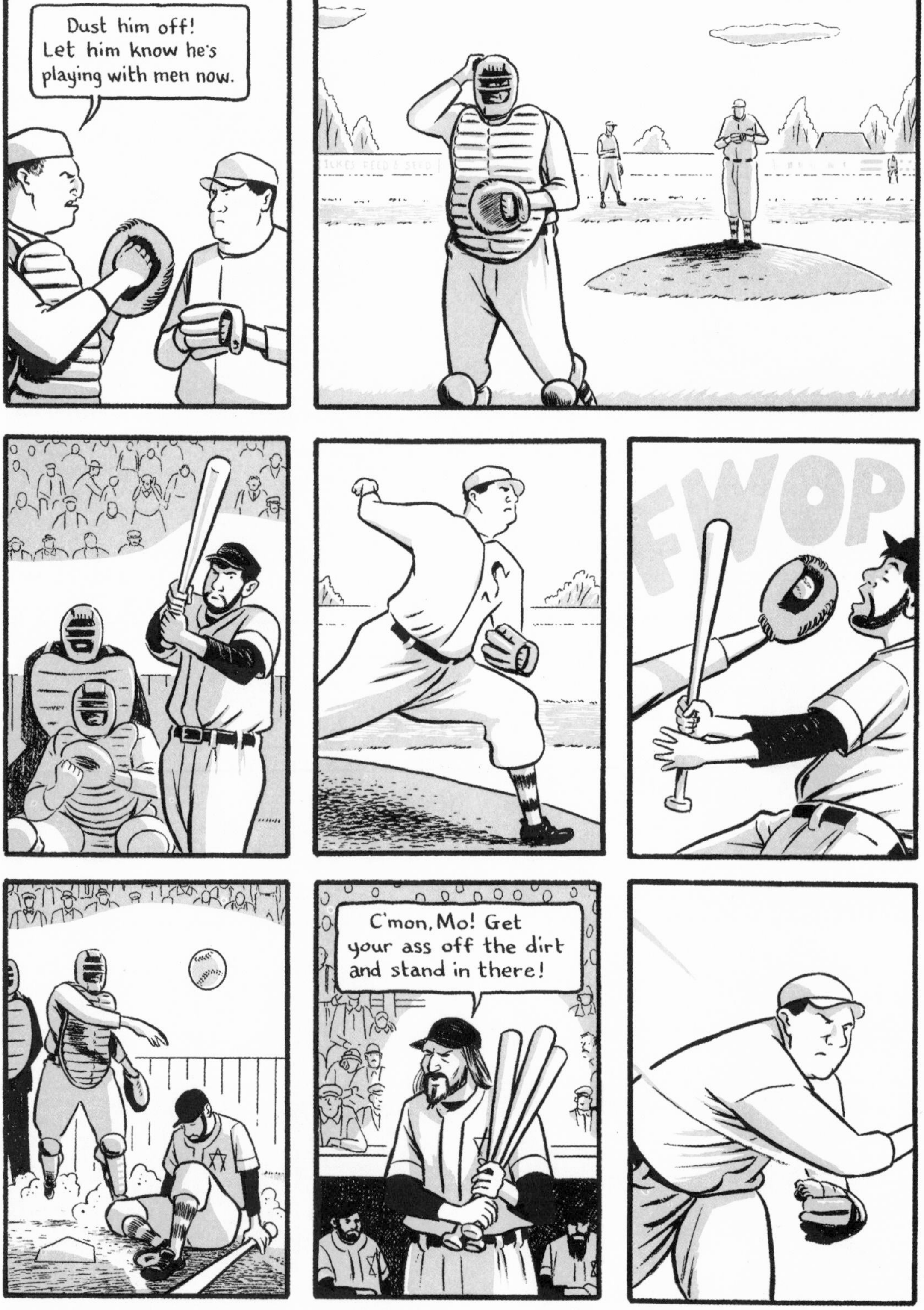
Dust him off! Let him know he's playing with men now.
FWOP
C'mon, Mo! Get your ass off the dirt and stand in there!

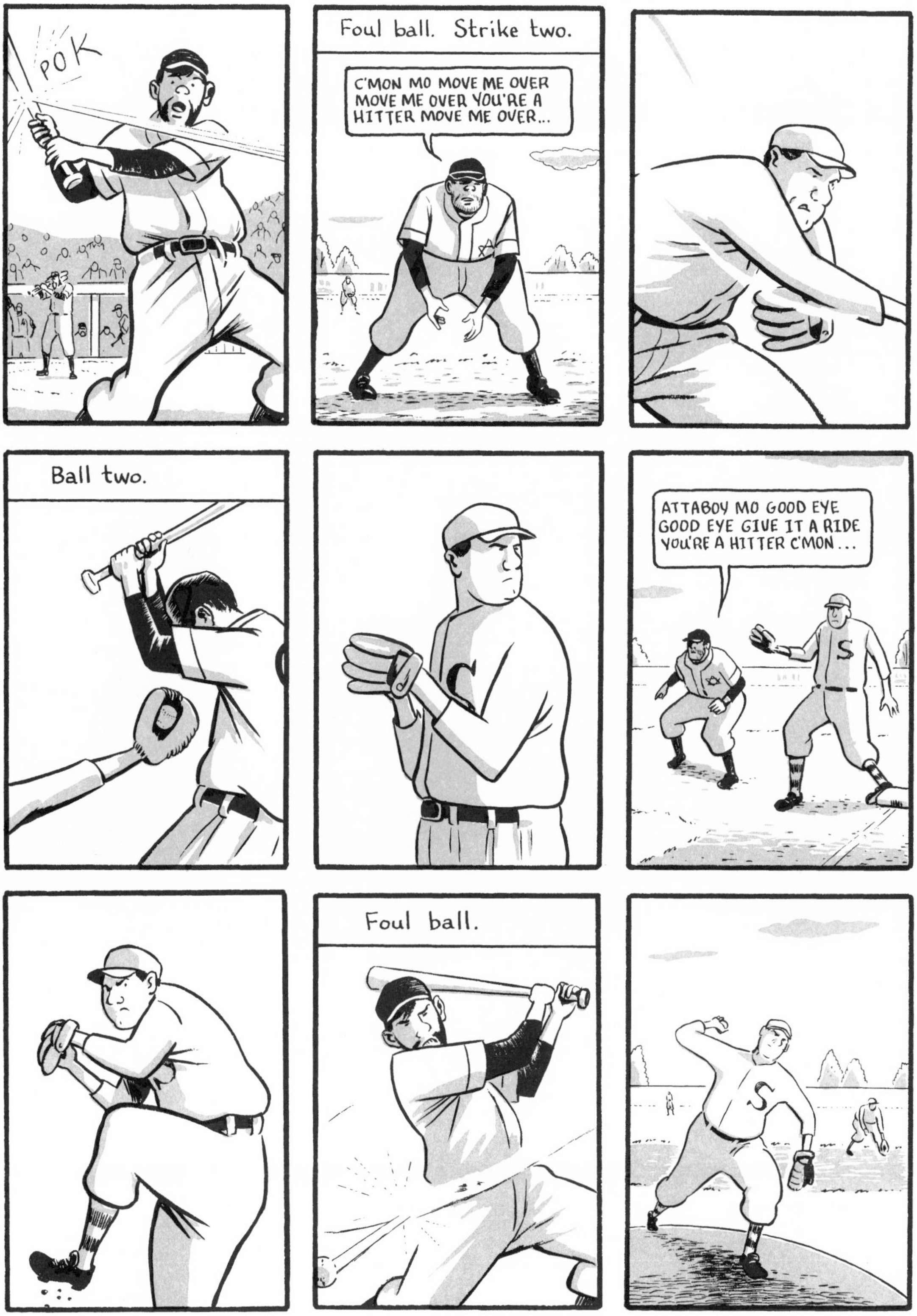
POK
Foul ball. Strike two.
C'MON MO MOVE ME OVER MOVE ME OVER YOU'RE A HITTER MOVE ME OVER...
Ball two.
ATTABOY MO GOOD EYE GOOD EYE GIVE IT A RIDE YOU'RE A HITTER C'MON...
Foul ball.

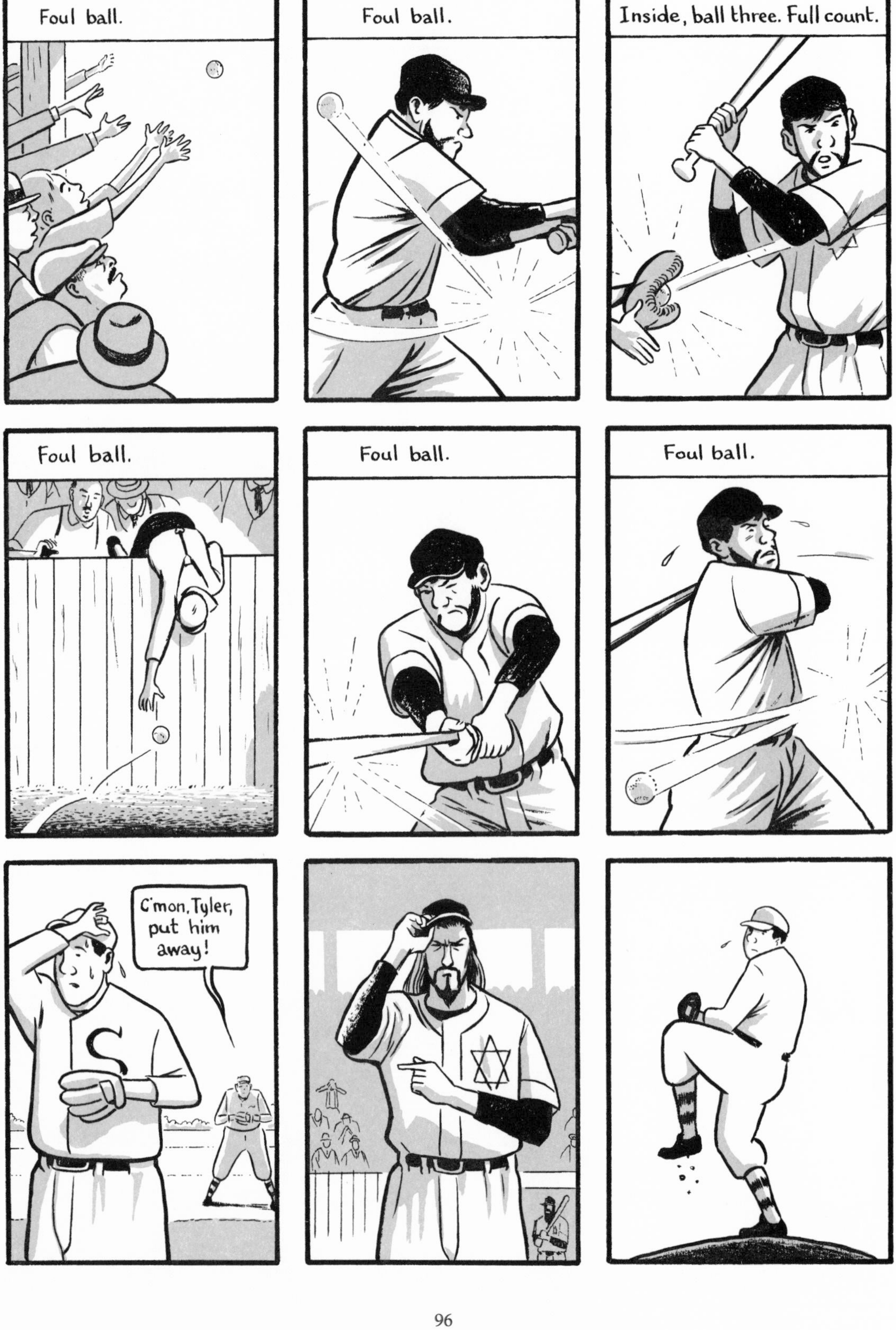
Foul ball.
Foul ball.
Inside, ball three. Full count.
Foul ball.
Foul ball.
Foul ball.
C'mon, Tyler, put him away!

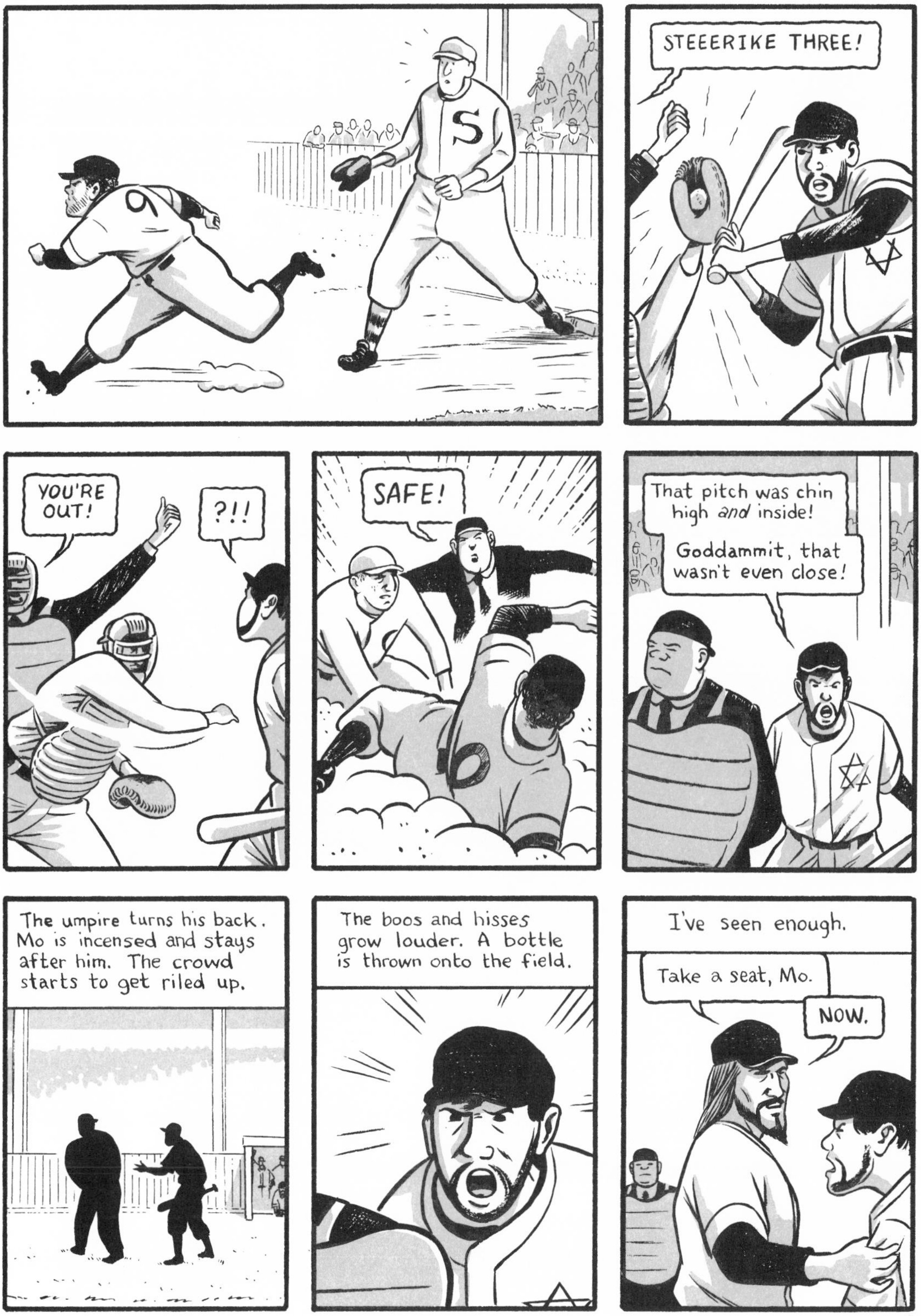
STEEERIKE THREE!
YOU'RE OUT!
?!!
SAFE!
That pitch was chin high *and* inside!
Goddammit, that wasn't even close!
The umpire turns his back. Mo is incensed and stays after him. The crowd starts to get riled up.
The boos and hisses grow louder. A bottle is thrown onto the field.
I've seen enough.
Take a seat, Mo.
NOW.

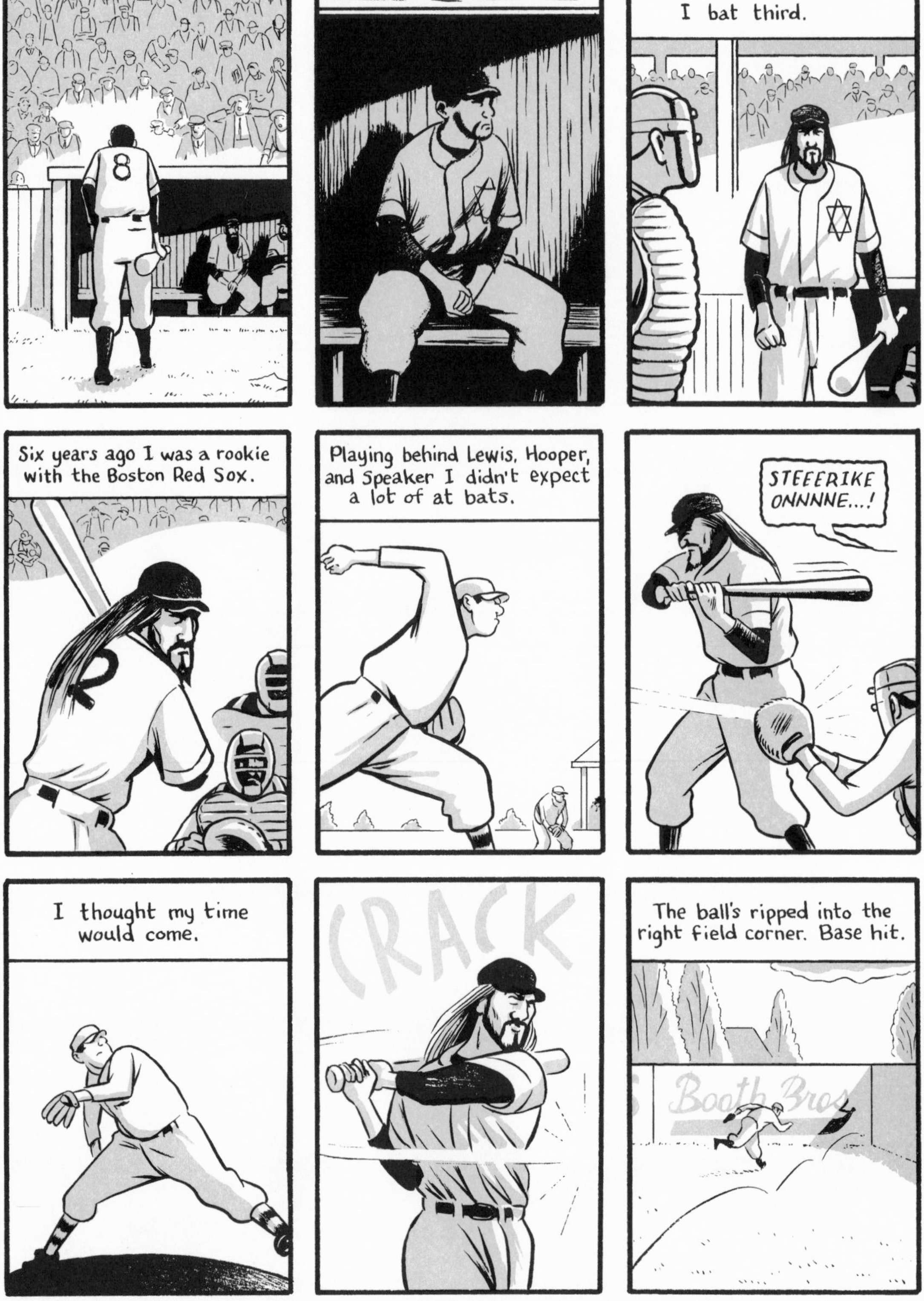
I bat third.
Six years ago I was a rookie with the Boston Red Sox.
Playing behind Lewis, Hooper, and Speaker I didn't expect a lot of at bats.
STEEERIKE ONNNNE...!
I thought my time would come.
CRACK
The ball's ripped into the right field corner. Base hit.
Booth Bros

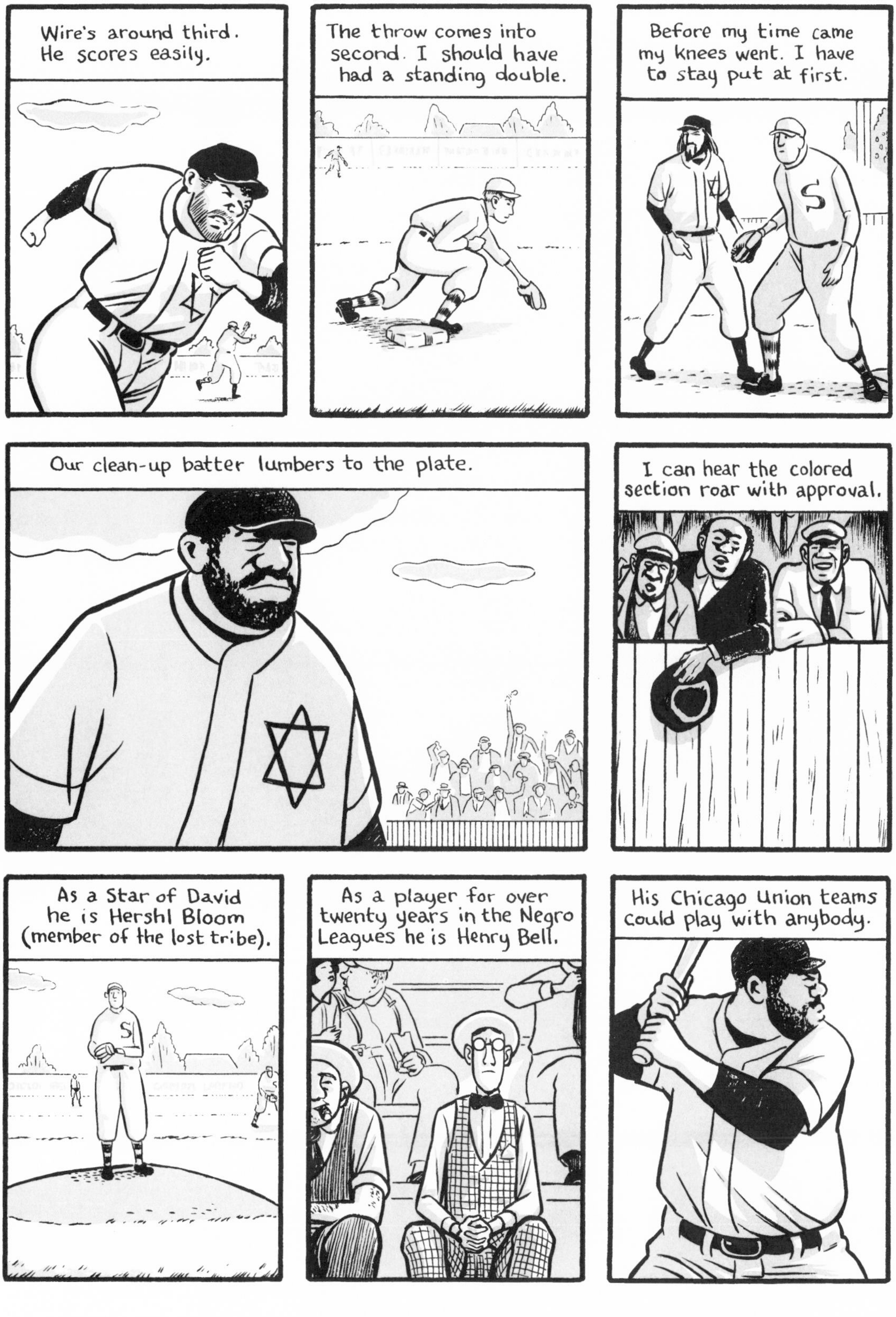
Wire's around third. He scores easily.
The throw comes into second. I should have had a standing double.
Before my time came my knees went. I have to stay put at first.
Our clean-up batter lumbers to the plate.
I can hear the colored section roar with approval.
As a Star of David he is Hershl Bloom (member of the lost tribe).
As a player for over twenty years in the Negro Leagues he is Henry Bell.
His Chicago Union teams could play with anybody.

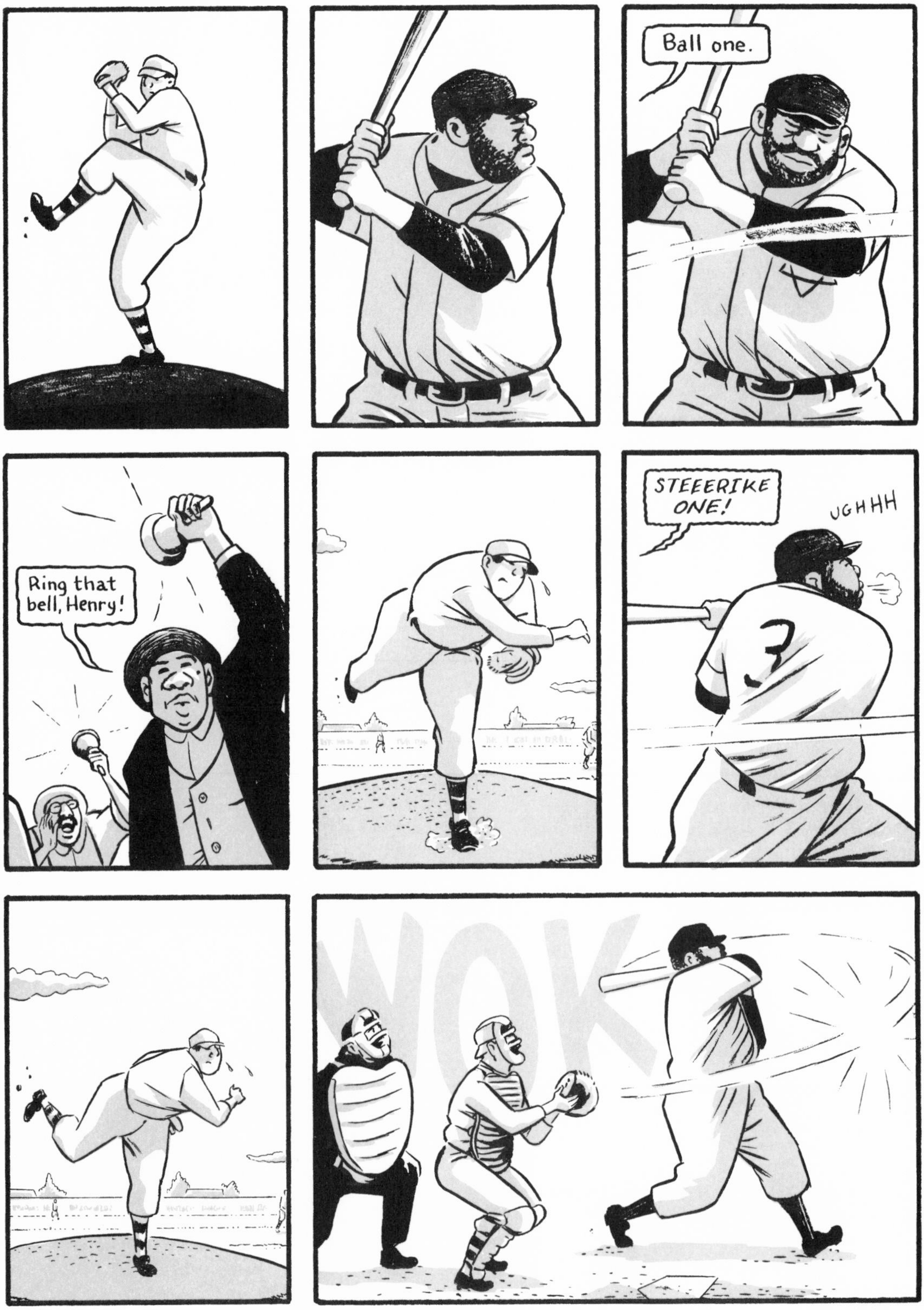
Ball one.
Ring that bell, Henry!
STEEERIKE ONE!
UGHHH
WOK

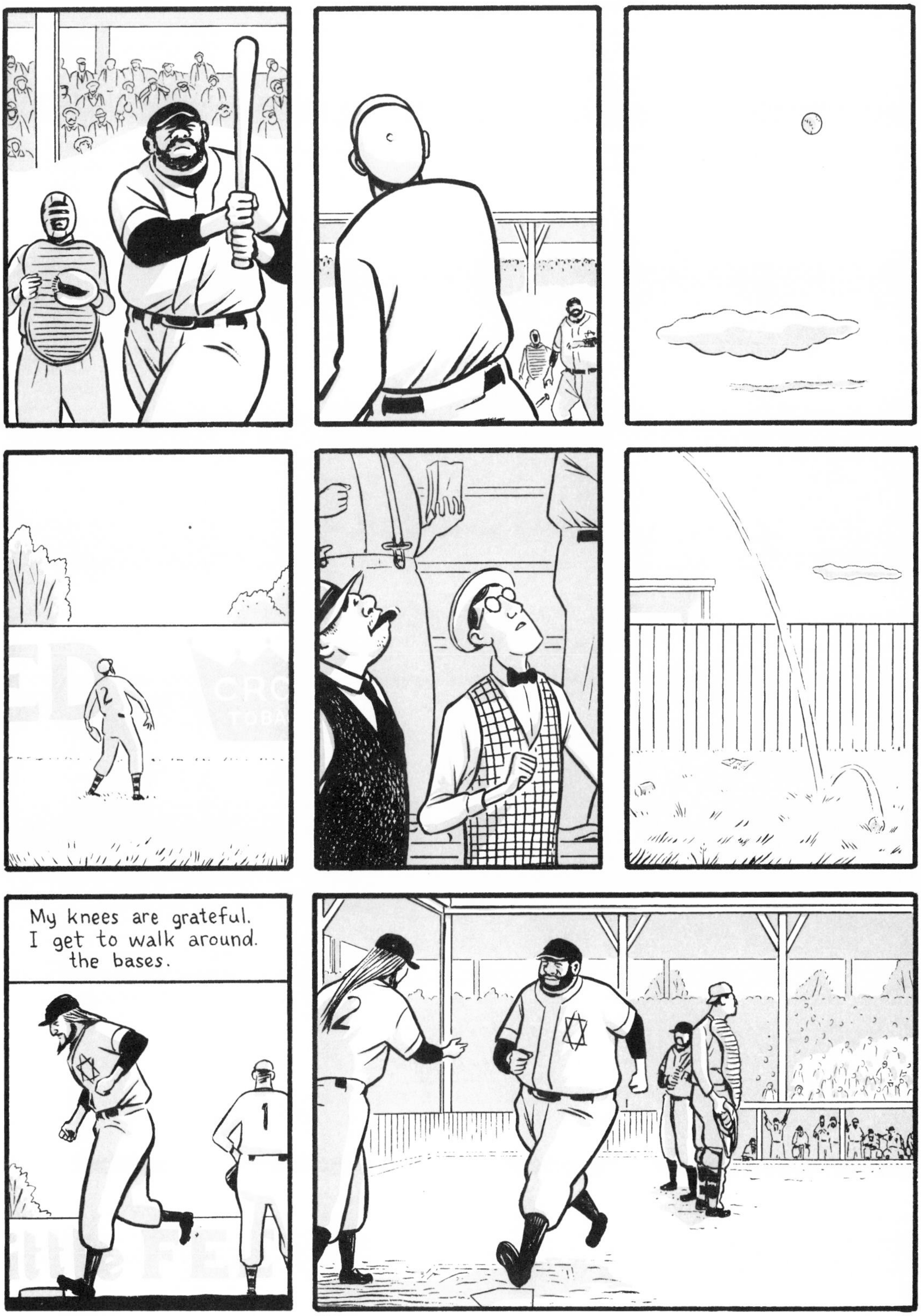
My knees are grateful. I get to walk around the bases.

The rest of the game is sloppy as we play down to the level of our opponent. Mo's error in the fourth costs us two runs.

| VISITORS | 4 | 2 | 1 | 0 | 2 | 0 | 1 | 0 | | 1 | 0 |
| SPARTANS | 0 | 0 | 1 | 3 | 0 | 0 | 1 | 2 | | | 7 |

Bottom of the eighth: Forest Grove continues to put runs on the board. Another single, another run in.

The crowd rises to its feet, rallying their team.

My pitcher, Buttercup Lev, is throwing on only two days rest. He's already thrown 130 pitches.

Buttercup is a slowball pitcher, so even when fresh he's not going to overwhelm anyone.

He hits the corners and changes speed (slow and slower).

You could count the stiches on the ball as it crosses the plate.

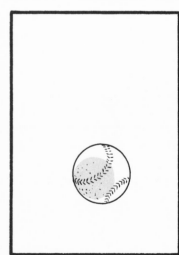

102

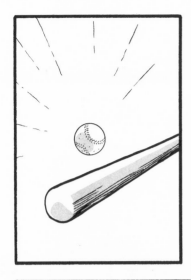

Ball's hit hard, the runner at first **takes off**...

What should have been a double in the gap is plucked out of the air by Mo.

On his way down he fires a bullet to first.

Runner doesn't get back in time, double play.

We're out of the inning. To the ninth.

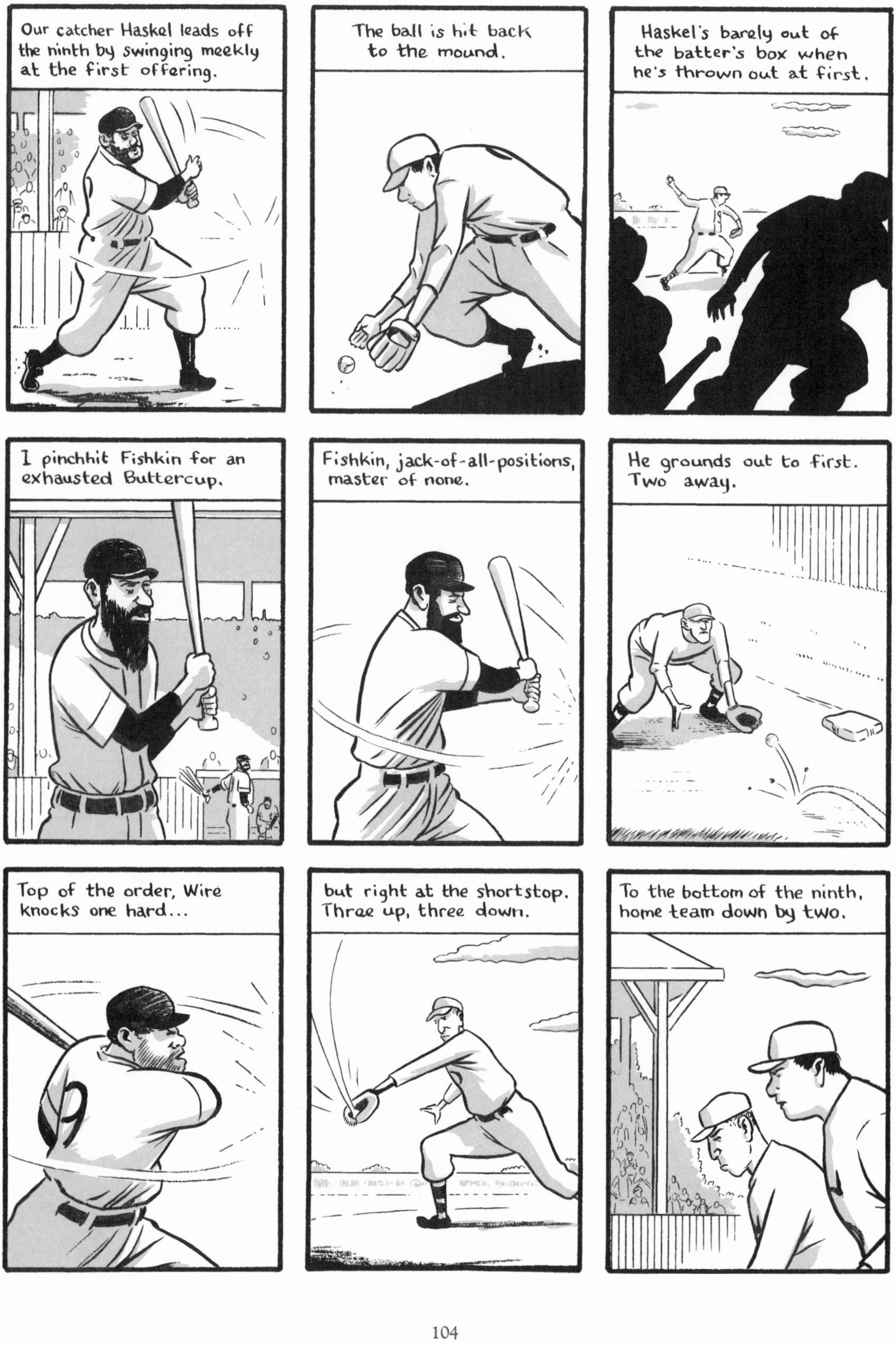
Our catcher Haskel leads off the ninth by swinging meekly at the first offering.
The ball is hit back to the mound.
Haskel's barely out of the batter's box when he's thrown out at first.
I pinchhit Fishkin for an exhausted Buttercup.
Fishkin, jack-of-all-positions, master of none.
He grounds out to first. Two away.
Top of the order, Wire knocks one hard...
but right at the shortstop. Three up, three down.
To the bottom of the ninth, home team down by two.

Fishkin takes over at first from Henry.

Henry relieves Buttercup on the mound. His old arm can still throw smoke for an inning or two.

The first hitter's bat never leaves his shoulders.

STEEERIKE THREEE!

The second batter tries to bunt his way on...

He pops out to the catcher.

The third batter nicks one towards me at third.

Game over. We win.

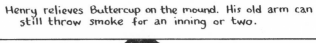

105

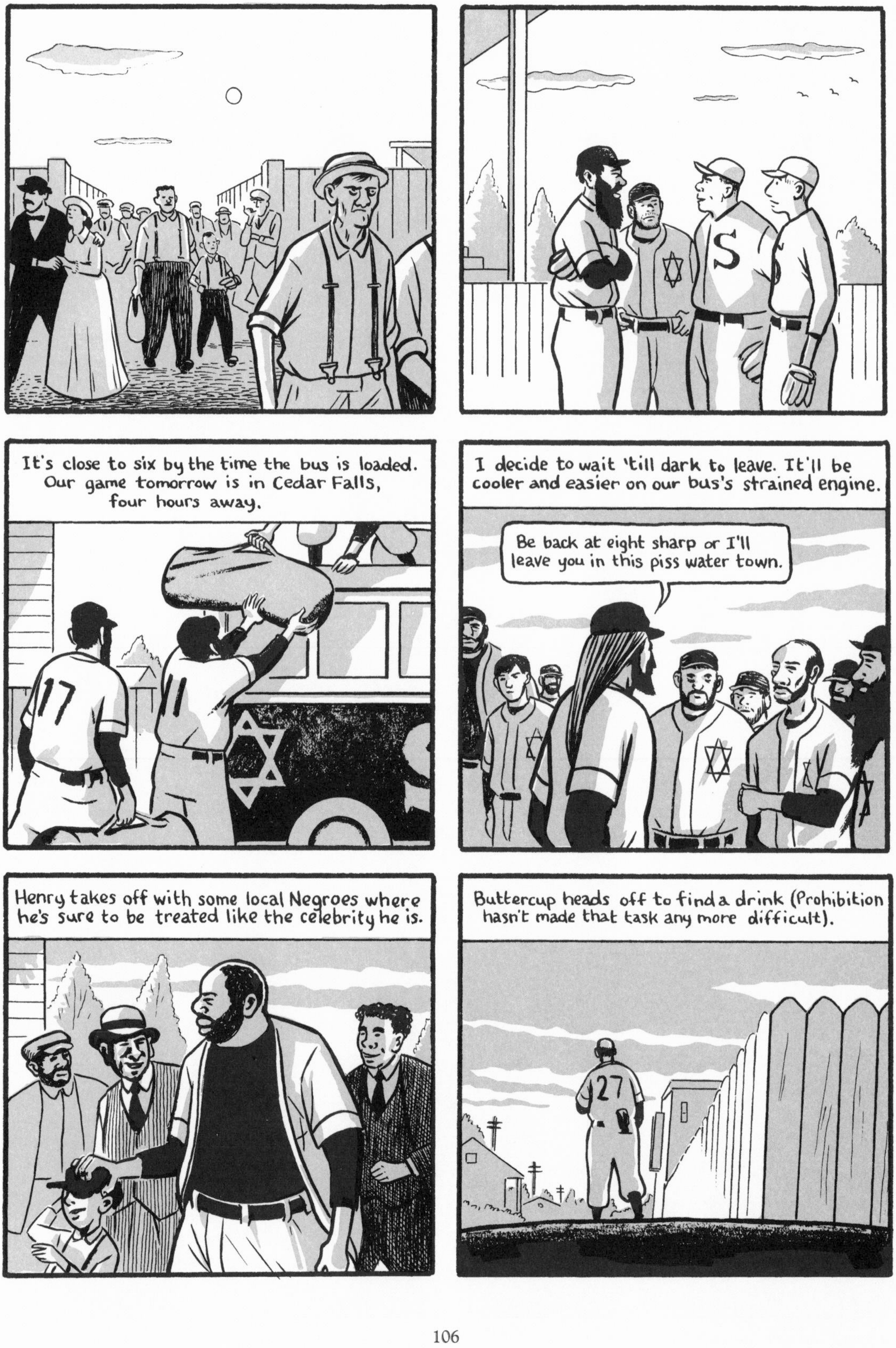
It's close to six by the time the bus is loaded. Our game tomorrow is in Cedar Falls, four hours away.
I decide to wait 'till dark to leave. It'll be cooler and easier on our bus's strained engine.
Be back at eight sharp or I'll leave you in this piss water town.
Henry takes off with some local Negroes where he's sure to be treated like the celebrity he is.
Buttercup heads off to find a drink (Prohibition hasn't made that task any more difficult).

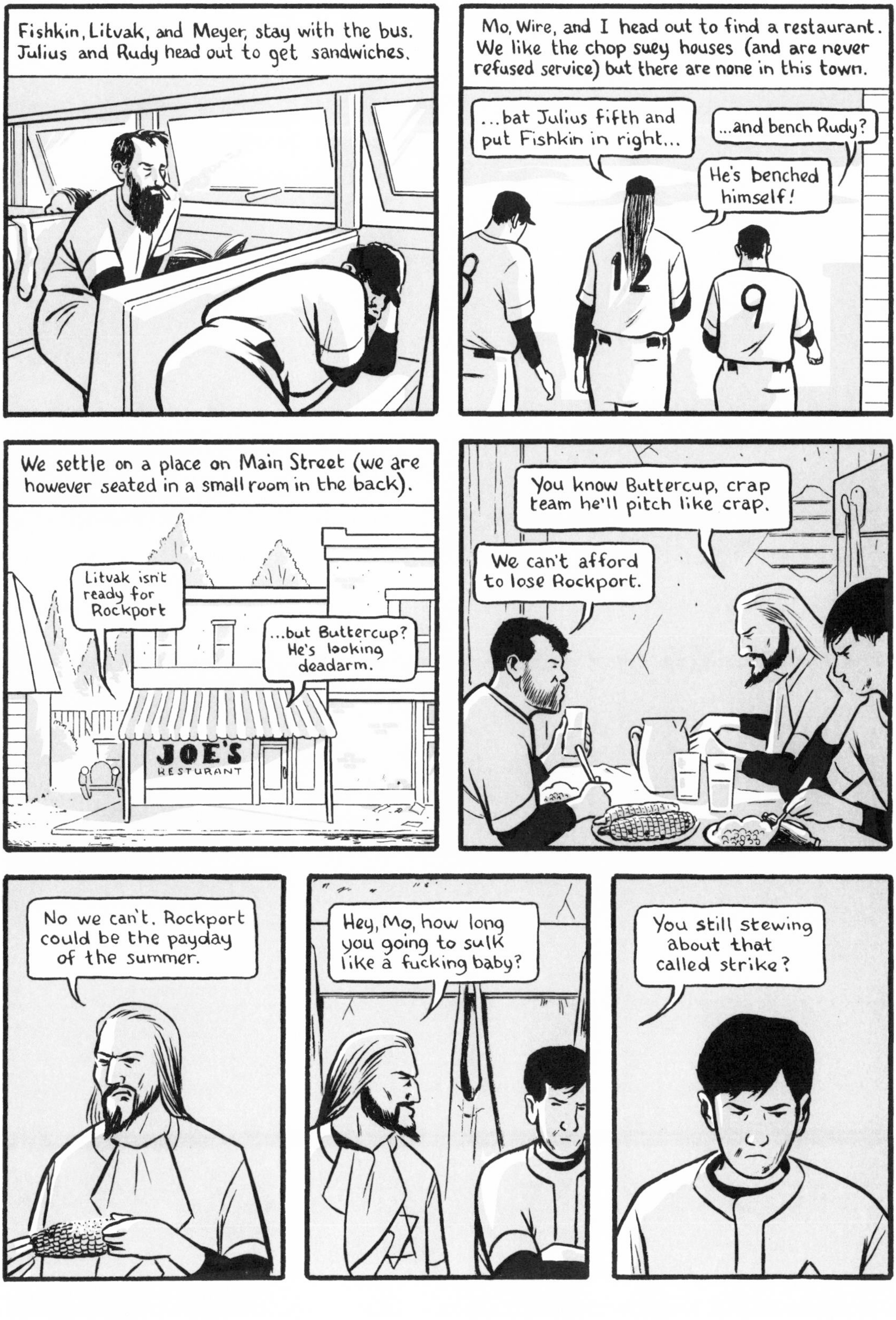

Fishkin, Litvak, and Meyer, stay with the bus. Julius and Rudy head out to get sandwiches.
Mo, Wire, and I head out to find a restaurant. We like the chop suey houses (and are never refused service) but there are none in this town.
...bat Julius fifth and put Fishkin in right...
...and bench Rudy?
He's benched himself!
We settle on a place on Main Street (we are however seated in a small room in the back).
Litvak isn't ready for Rockport
...but Buttercup? He's looking deadarm.
JOE'S
RESTURANT
You know Buttercup, crap team he'll pitch like crap.
We can't afford to lose Rockport.
No we can't. Rockport could be the payday of the summer.
Hey, Mo, how long you going to sulk like a fucking baby?
You still stewing about that called strike?

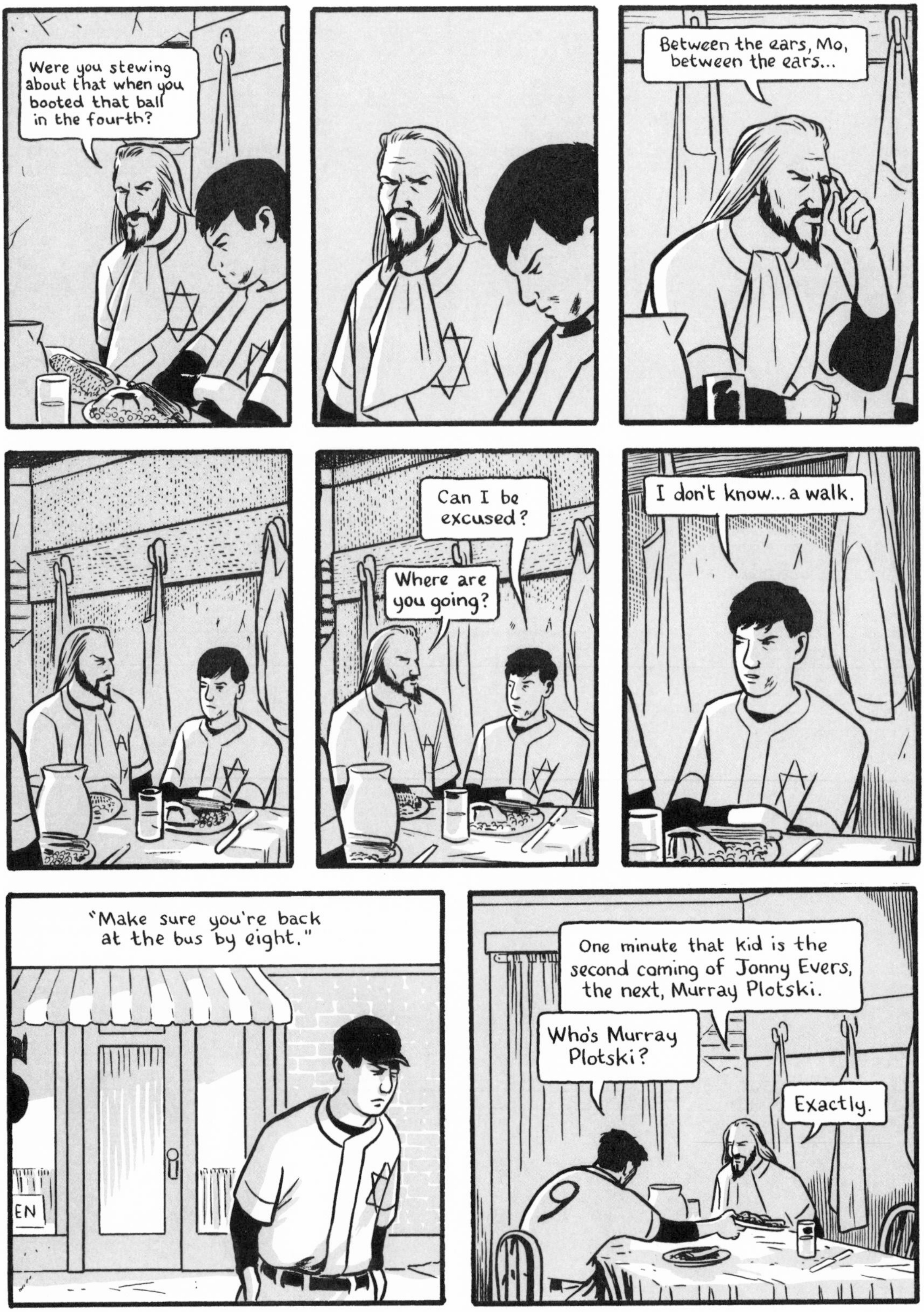
Were you stewing about that when you booted that ball in the fourth?
Between the ears, Mo, between the ears...
Can I be excused?
Where are you going?
I don't know... a walk.
"Make sure you're back at the bus by eight."
EN
One minute that kid is the second coming of Jonny Evers, the next, Murray Plotski.
Who's Murray Plotski?
Exactly.

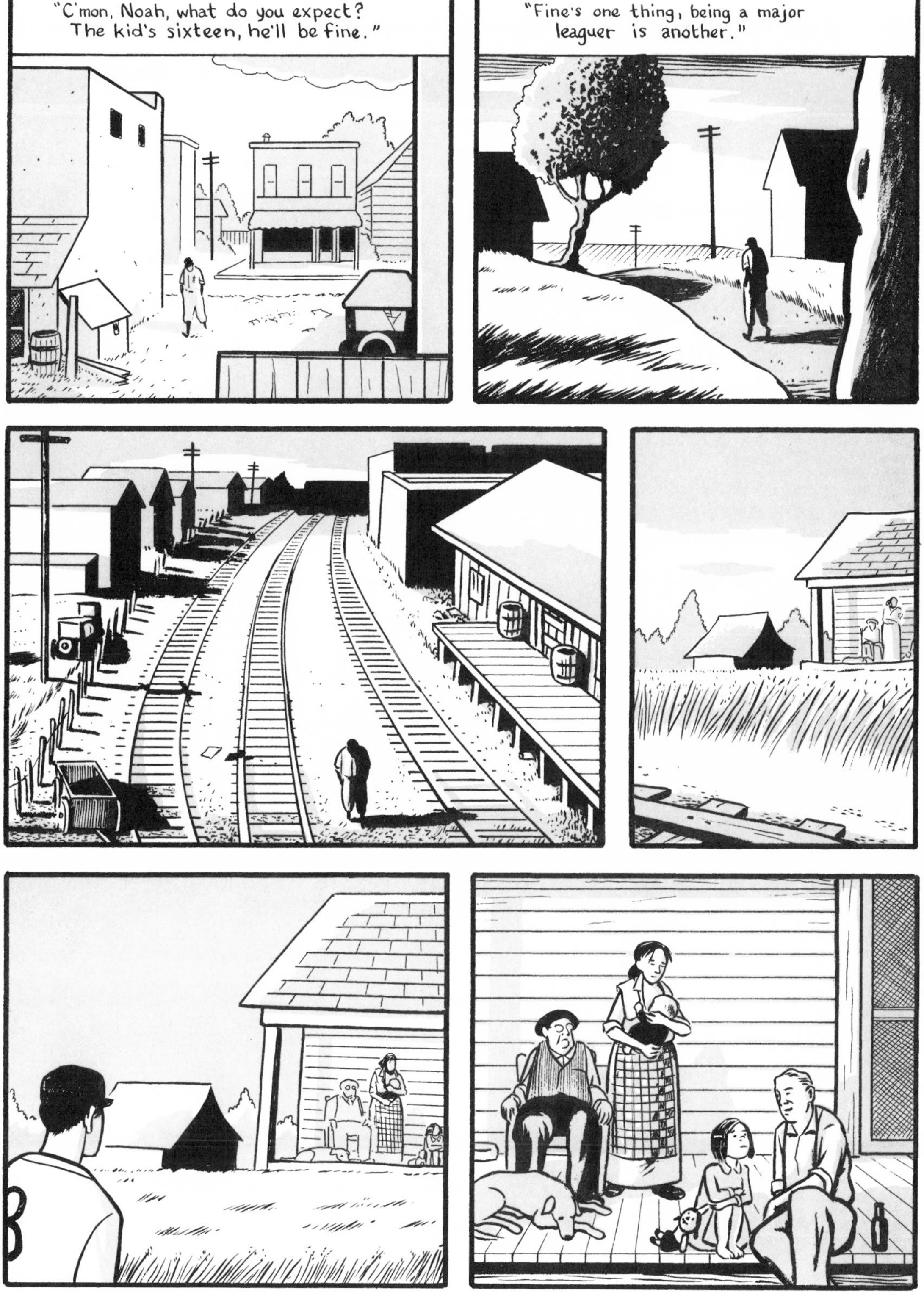
"C'mon, Noah, what do you expect? The kid's sixteen, he'll be fine."
"Fine's one thing, being a major leaguer is another."

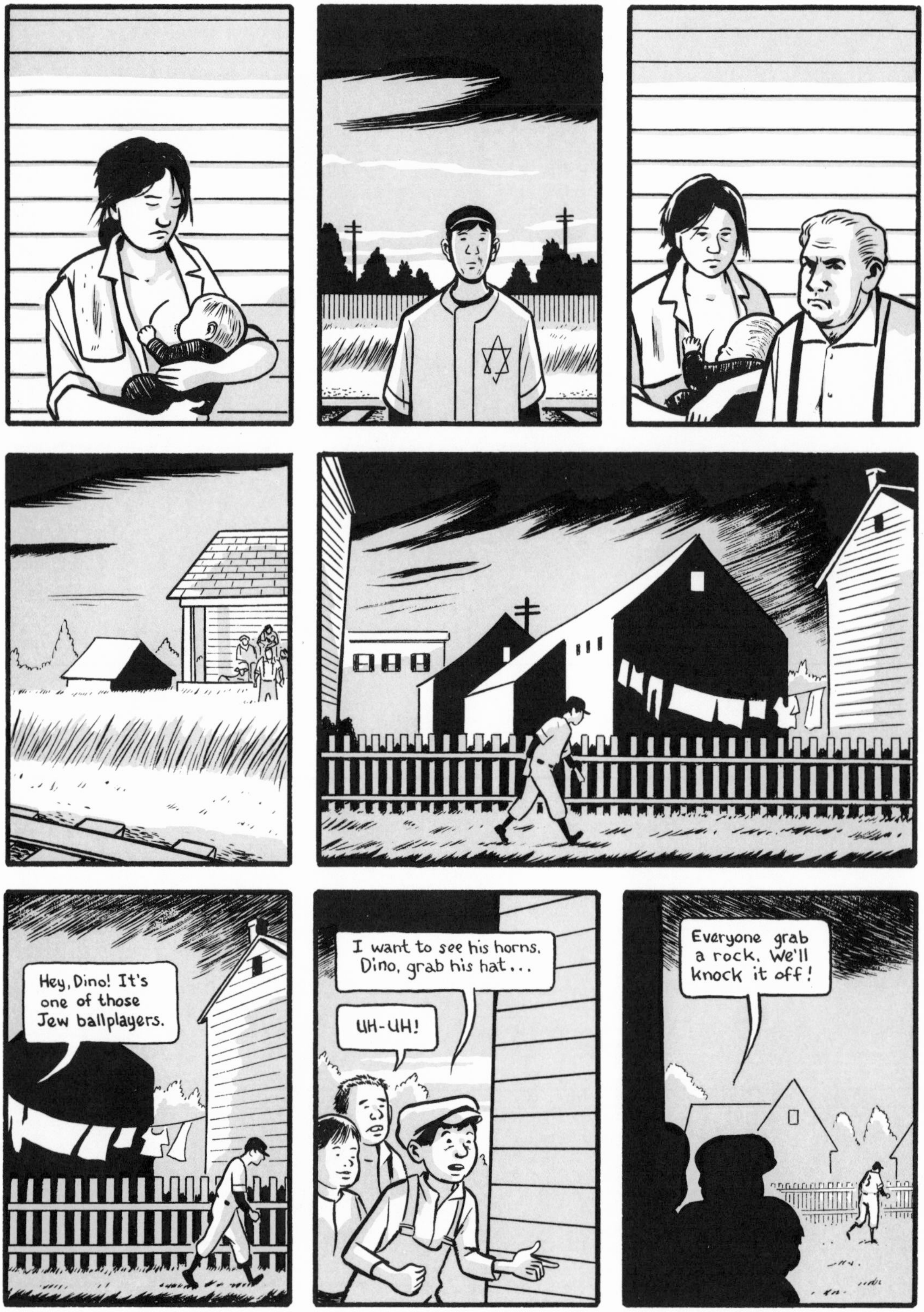
Hey, Dino! It's one of those Jew ballplayers.
I want to see his horns. Dino, grab his hat...
UH-UH!
Everyone grab a rock. We'll knock it off!

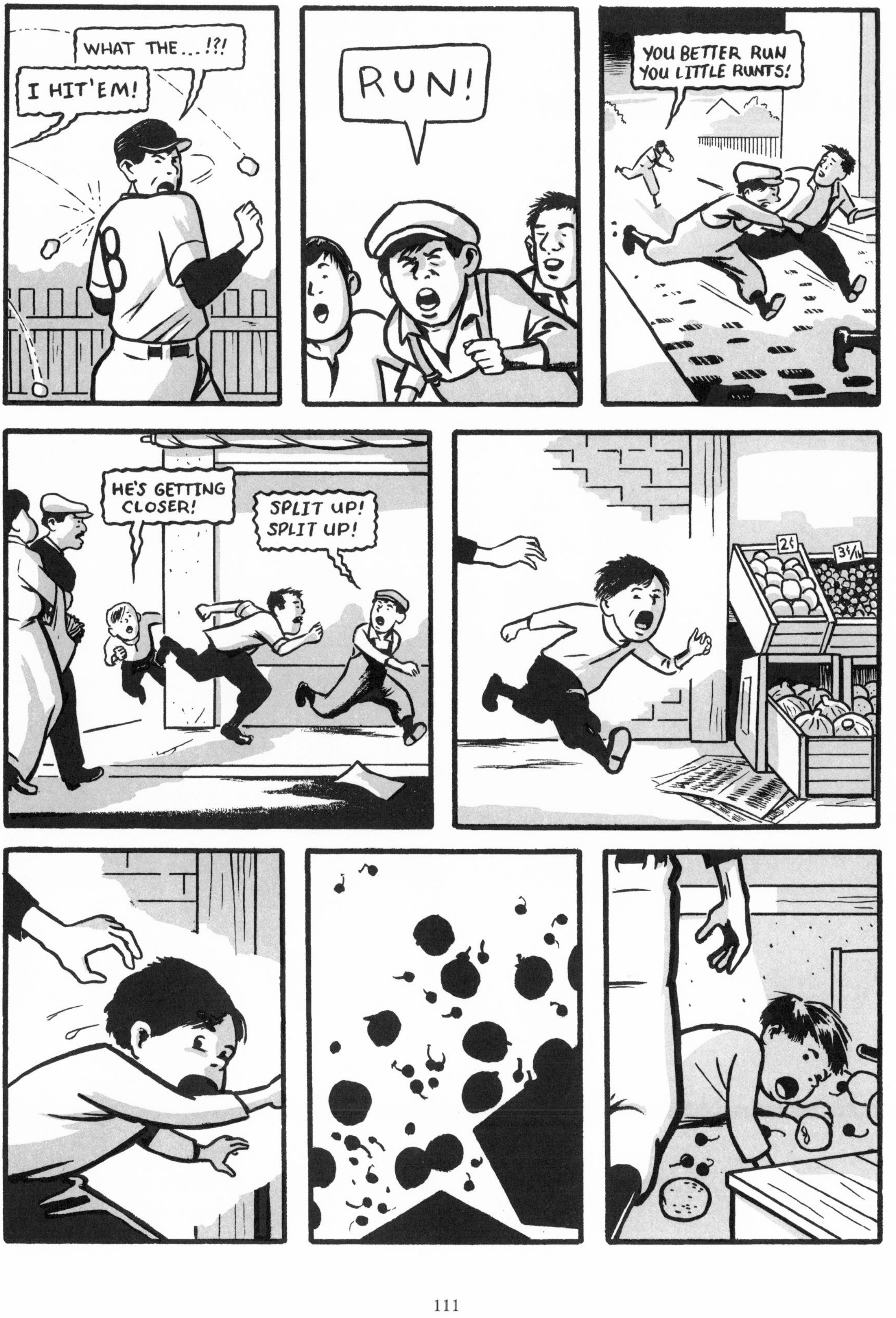
WHAT THE...!?!
I HIT'EM!
RUN!
YOU BETTER RUN YOU LITTLE RUNTS!
HE'S GETTING CLOSER!
SPLIT UP! SPLIT UP!
2¢
3¢/lb

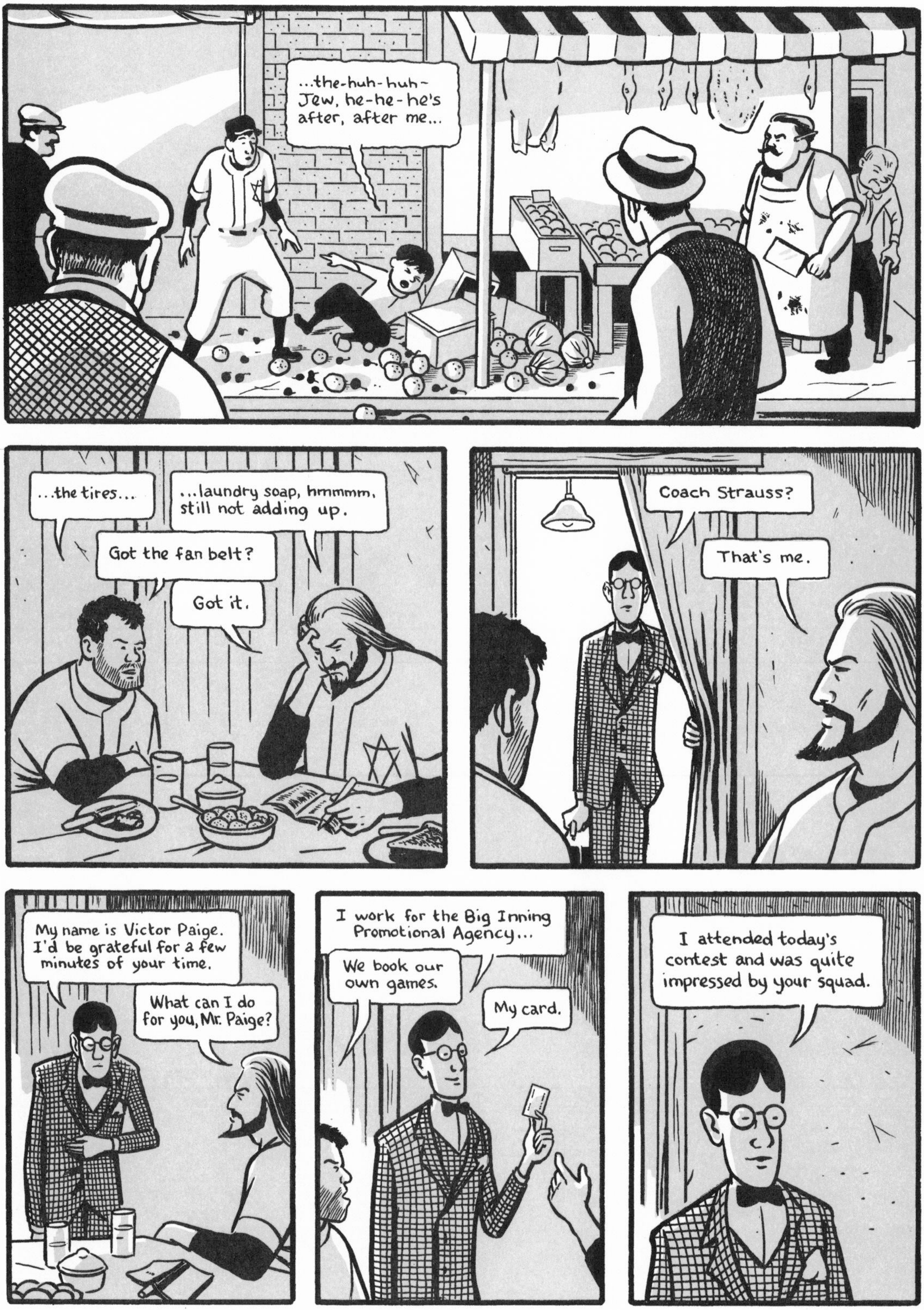
...the-huh-huh-
Jew, he-he-he's
after, after me...
...the tires...
...laundry soap, hmmmm,
still not adding up.
Got the fan belt?
Got it.
Coach Strauss?
That's me.
My name is Victor Paige.
I'd be grateful for a few
minutes of your time.
What can I do
for you, Mr. Paige?
I work for the Big Inning
Promotional Agency...
We book our
own games.
My card.
I attended today's
contest and was quite
impressed by your squad.

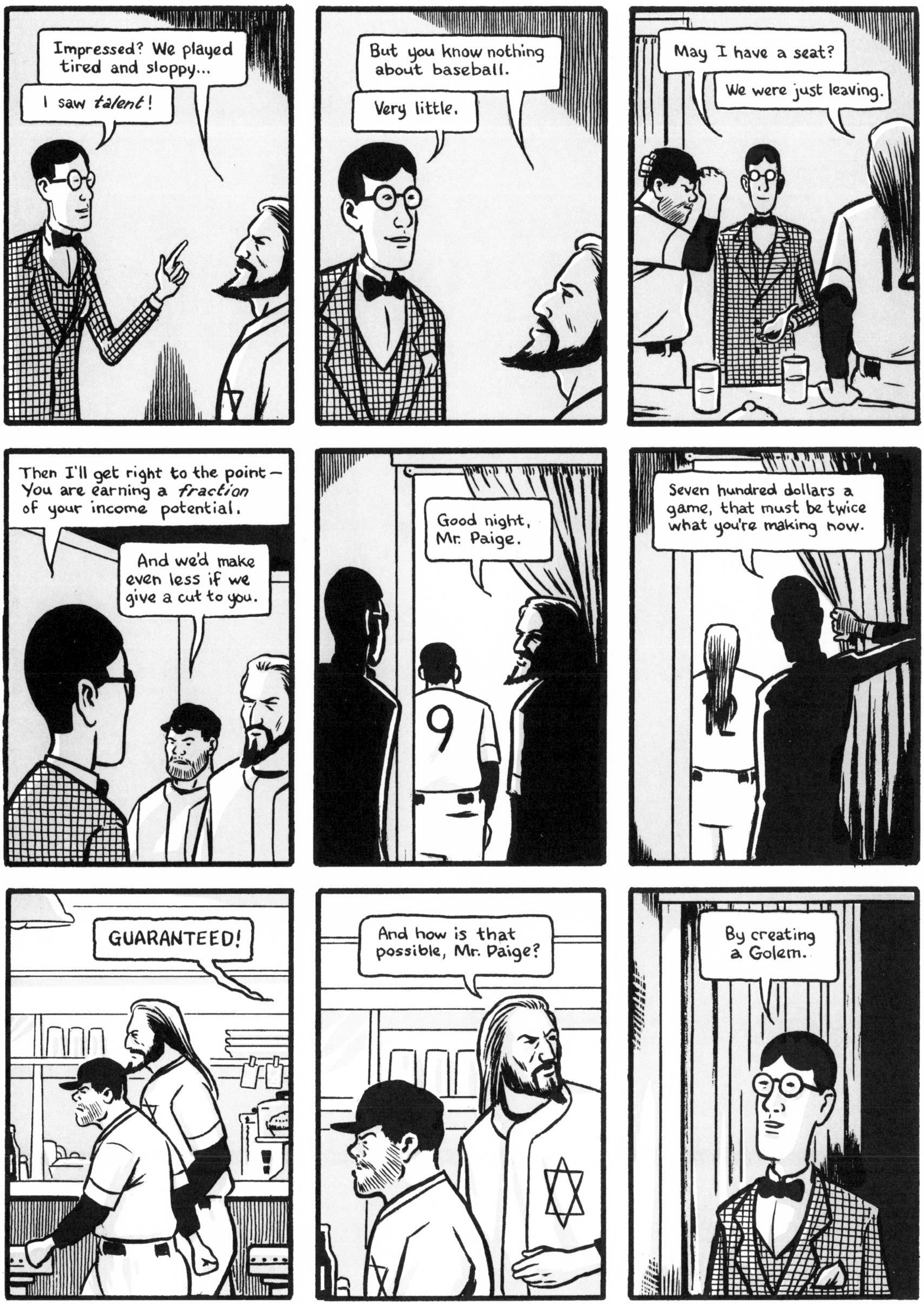
Impressed? We played tired and sloppy...
I saw *talent*!
But you know nothing about baseball.
Very little.
May I have a seat?
We were just leaving.
Then I'll get right to the point — You are earning a *fraction* of your income potential.
And we'd make even less if we give a cut to you.
Good night, Mr. Paige.
Seven hundred dollars a game, that must be twice what you're making now.
GUARANTEED!
And how is that possible, Mr. Paige?
By creating a Golem.

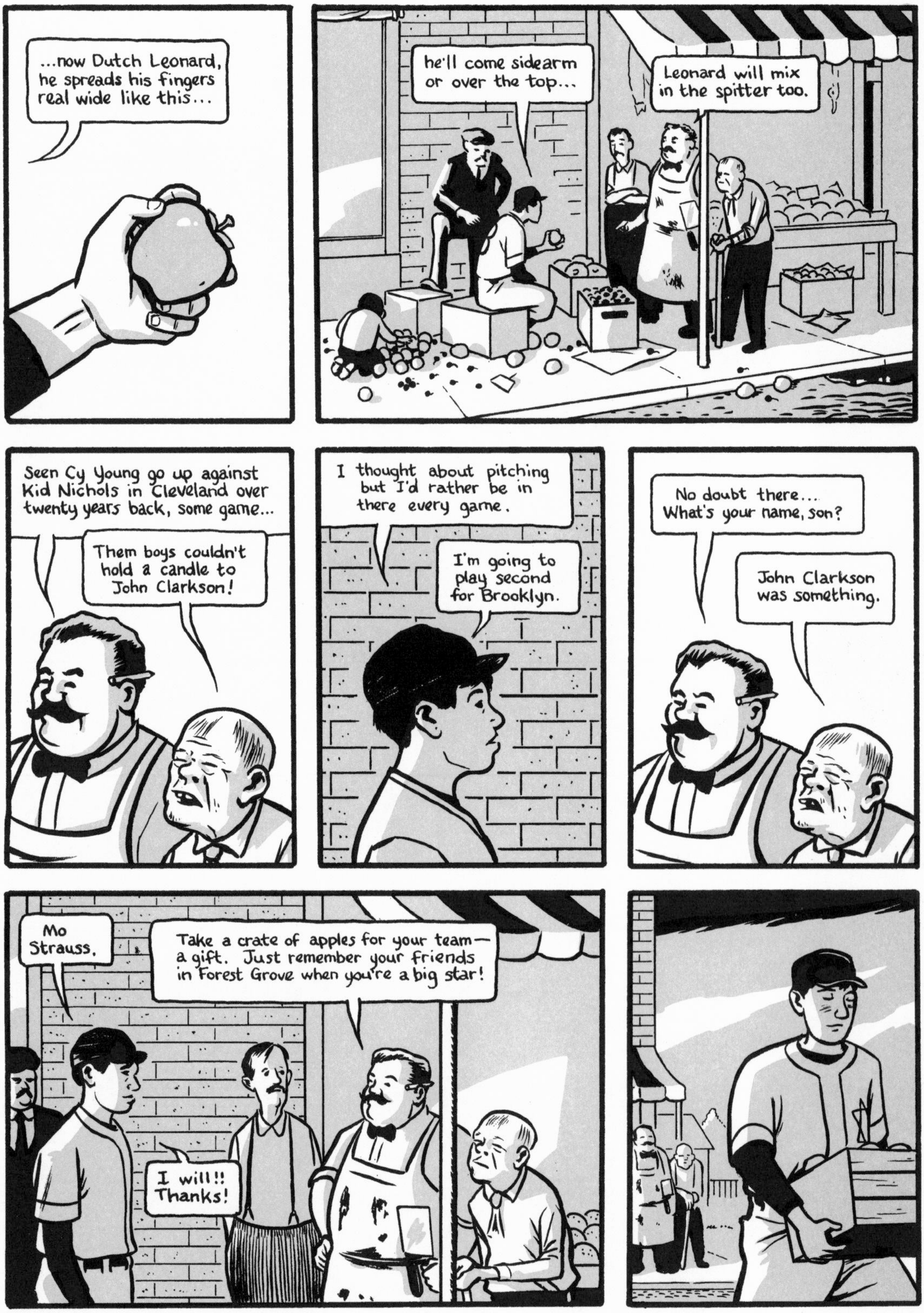
...now Dutch Leonard, he spreads his fingers real wide like this...
he'll come sidearm or over the top...
Leonard will mix in the spitter too.
Seen Cy Young go up against Kid Nichols in Cleveland over twenty years back, some game...
Them boys couldn't hold a candle to John Clarkson!
I thought about pitching but I'd rather be in there every game.
I'm going to play second for Brooklyn.
No doubt there... What's your name, son?
John Clarkson was something.
Mo Strauss.
Take a crate of apples for your team— a gift. Just remember your friends in Forest Grove when you're a big star!
I will!! Thanks!

"Show after show, week after week, month after month, the Criterion Theatre packed! Crowds held in awe by the mythical Jewish legend.

The Golem has captivated New York."

My agency has procured the actual costume worn in the film. All the way from Germany.

Hey, Noah, he wants you to dress up like that big goon.

Well, forget it!

No, no, no, nooooo...! It's not *you* who would play the Golem (you're all wrong for the part). It would be your first baseman, Hershl Bloom.

It's *Henry*, and he's not even Jewish...

But you *pretend* he is for your team...

as you pretend your younger brother can grow a beard...

It's all just a conceit isn't it, Coach Strauss?

"The public is eager for spectacle...

"they don't split hairs."

I'm sure Hershl, excuse me, *Henry* will embrace this new role. Negroes, after all, are born performers.

One game. One game to prove how lucrative a partnership with my agency would be.

Let us step up to the plate and "swat" a "dinger" for you.

I'm sorry, Mr. Paige, but I'll have to decline your offer...

I'm more interested in baseball than sideshows.

click

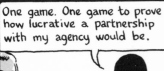

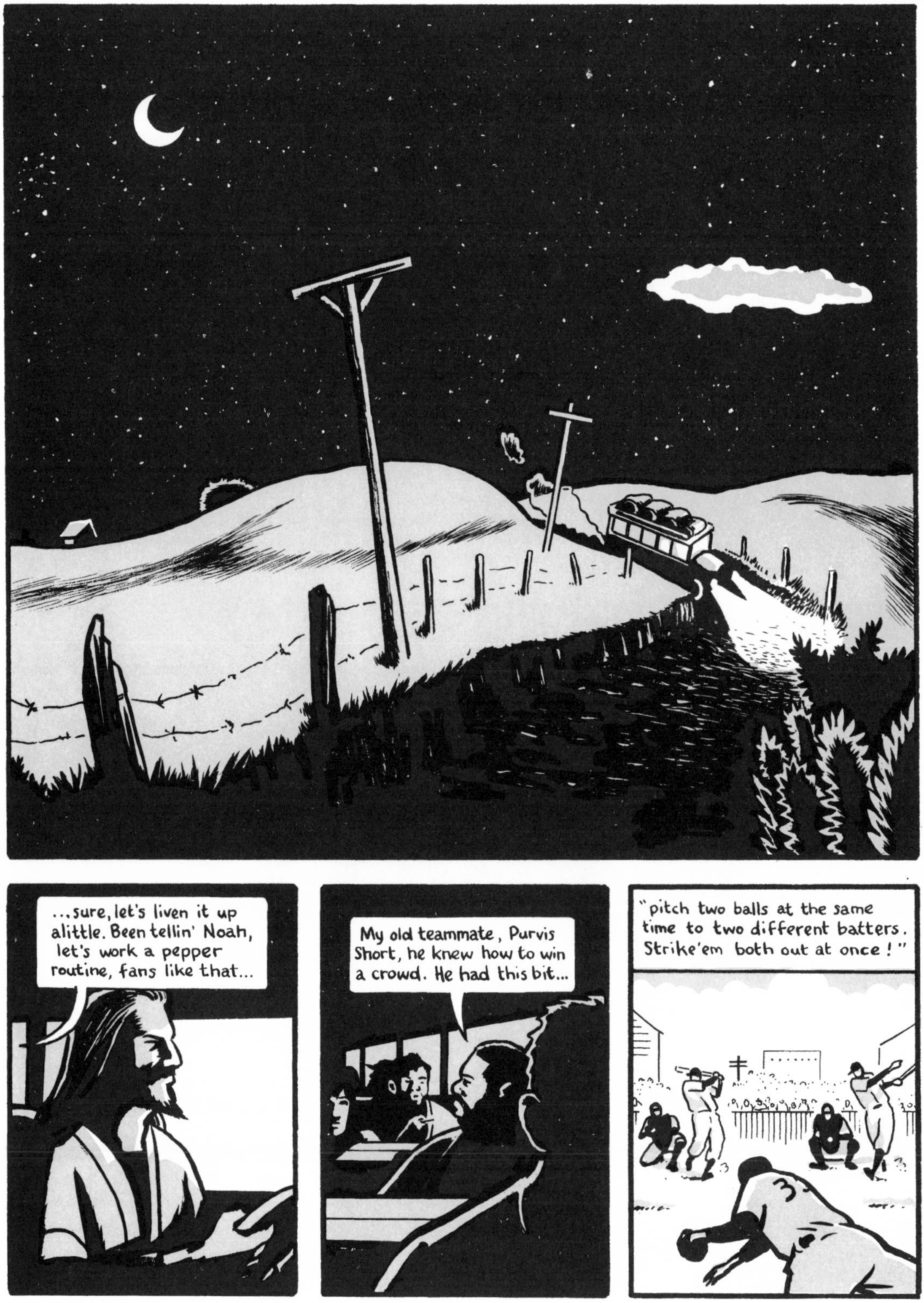
...sure, let's liven it up alittle. Been tellin' Noah, let's work a pepper routine, fans like that...
My old teammate, Purvis Short, he knew how to win a crowd. He had this bit...
"pitch two balls at the same time to two different batters. Strike'em both out at once!"
3

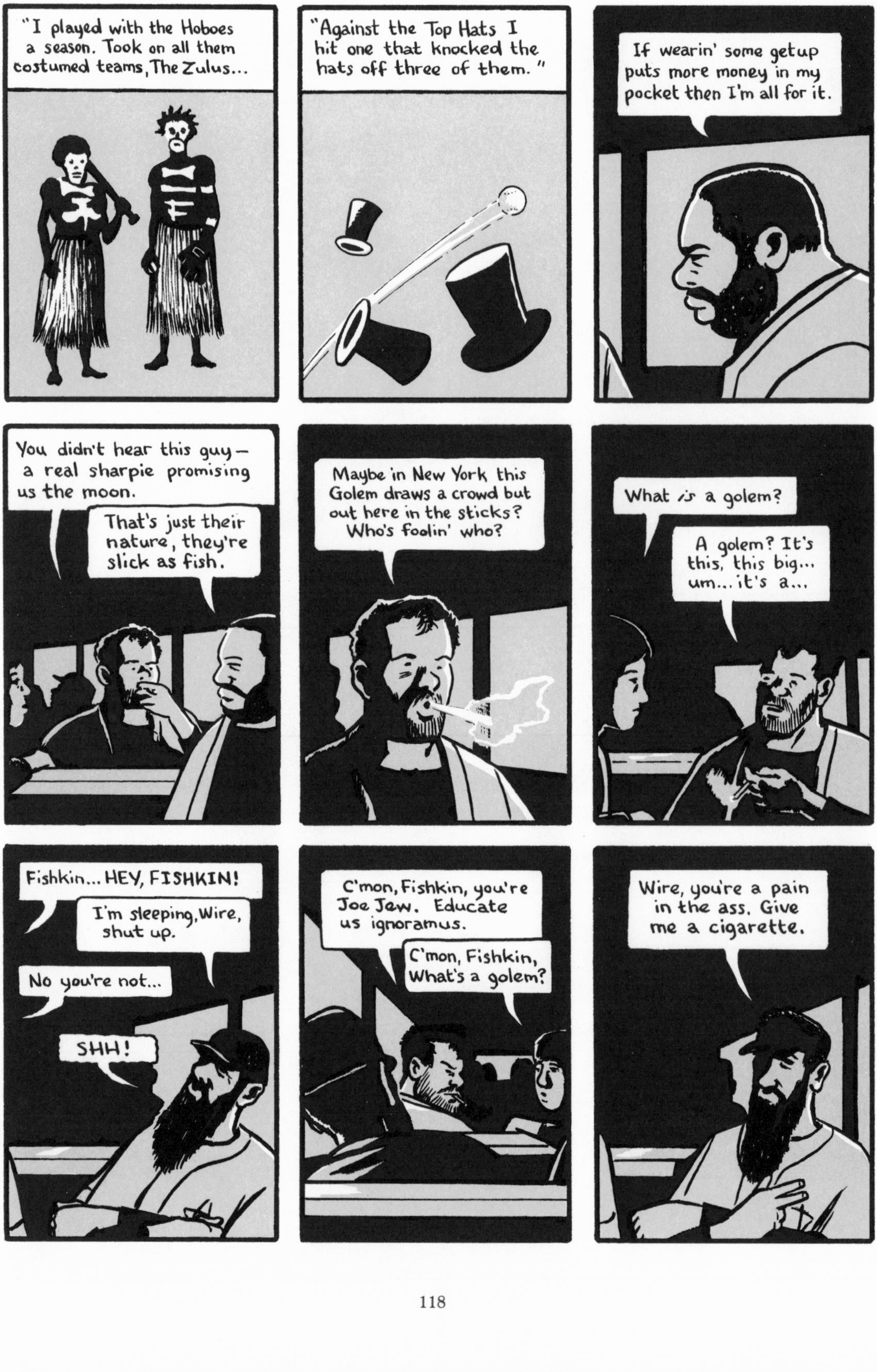
"I played with the Hoboes a season. Took on all them costumed teams, The Zulus...
"Against the Top Hats I hit one that knocked the hats off three of them."
If wearin' some getup puts more money in my pocket then I'm all for it.
You didn't hear this guy— a real sharpie promising us the moon.
That's just their nature, they're slick as fish.
Maybe in New York this Golem draws a crowd but out here in the sticks? Who's foolin' who?
What *is* a golem?
A golem? It's this, this big... um... it's a...
Fishkin... HEY, FISHKIN!
I'm sleeping, Wire, shut up.
No you're not...
SHH!
C'mon, Fishkin, you're Joe Jew. Educate us ignoramus.
C'mon, Fishkin, What's a golem?
Wire, you're a pain in the ass. Give me a cigarette.

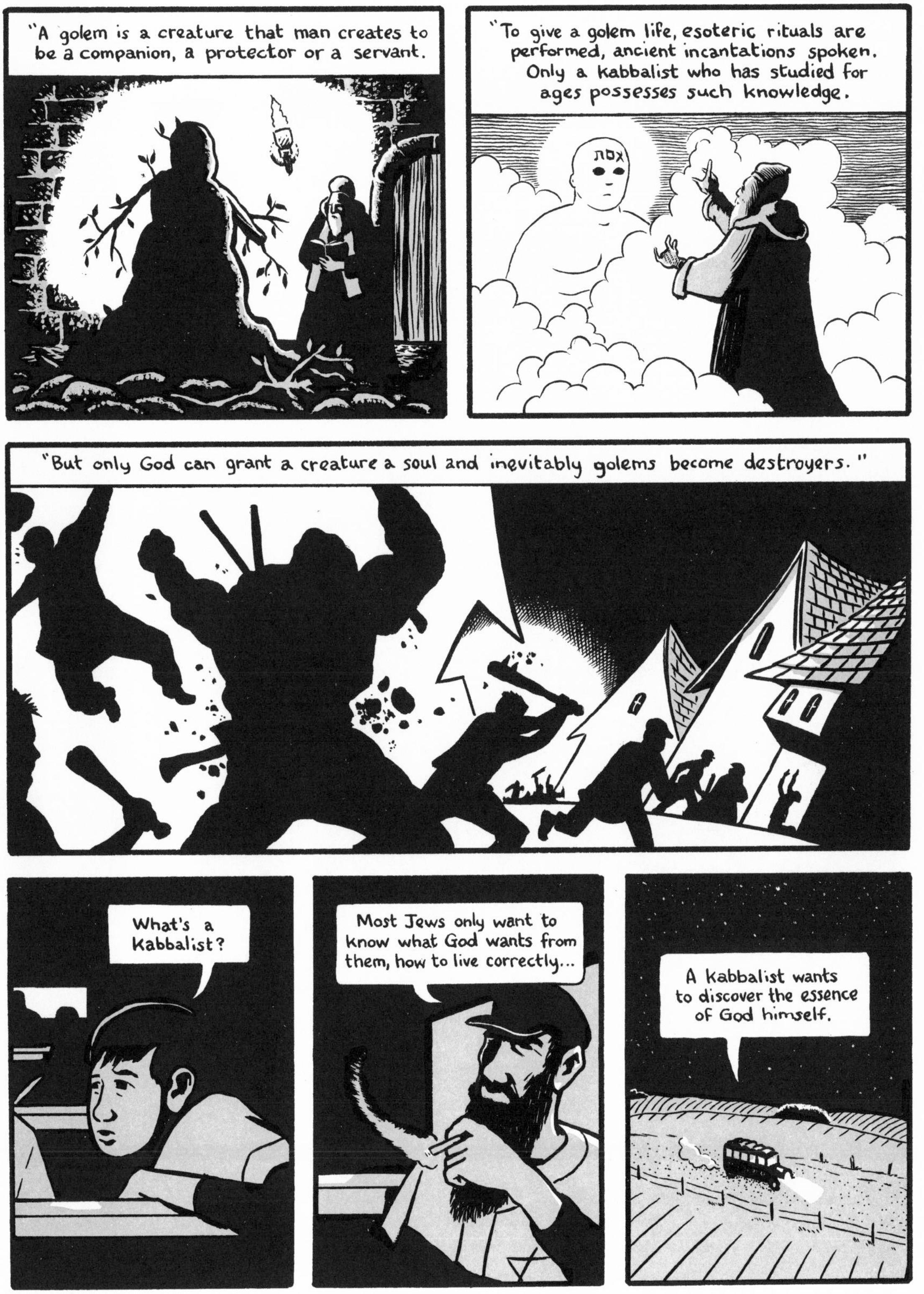
"A golem is a creature that man creates to be a companion, a protector or a servant.
"To give a golem life, esoteric rituals are performed, ancient incantations spoken. Only a kabbalist who has studied for ages possesses such knowledge.
אמת
"But only God can grant a creature a soul and inevitably golems become destroyers."
What's a Kabbalist?
Most Jews only want to know what God wants from them, how to live correctly...
A kabbalist wants to discover the essence of God himself.

Had a humpback mascot. Won fourteen in a row when he joined the team.

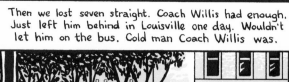

Then we lost seven straight. Coach Willis had enough. Just left him behind in Louisville one day. Wouldn't let him on the bus. Cold man Coach Willis was.

Cedar Falls thirty miles.

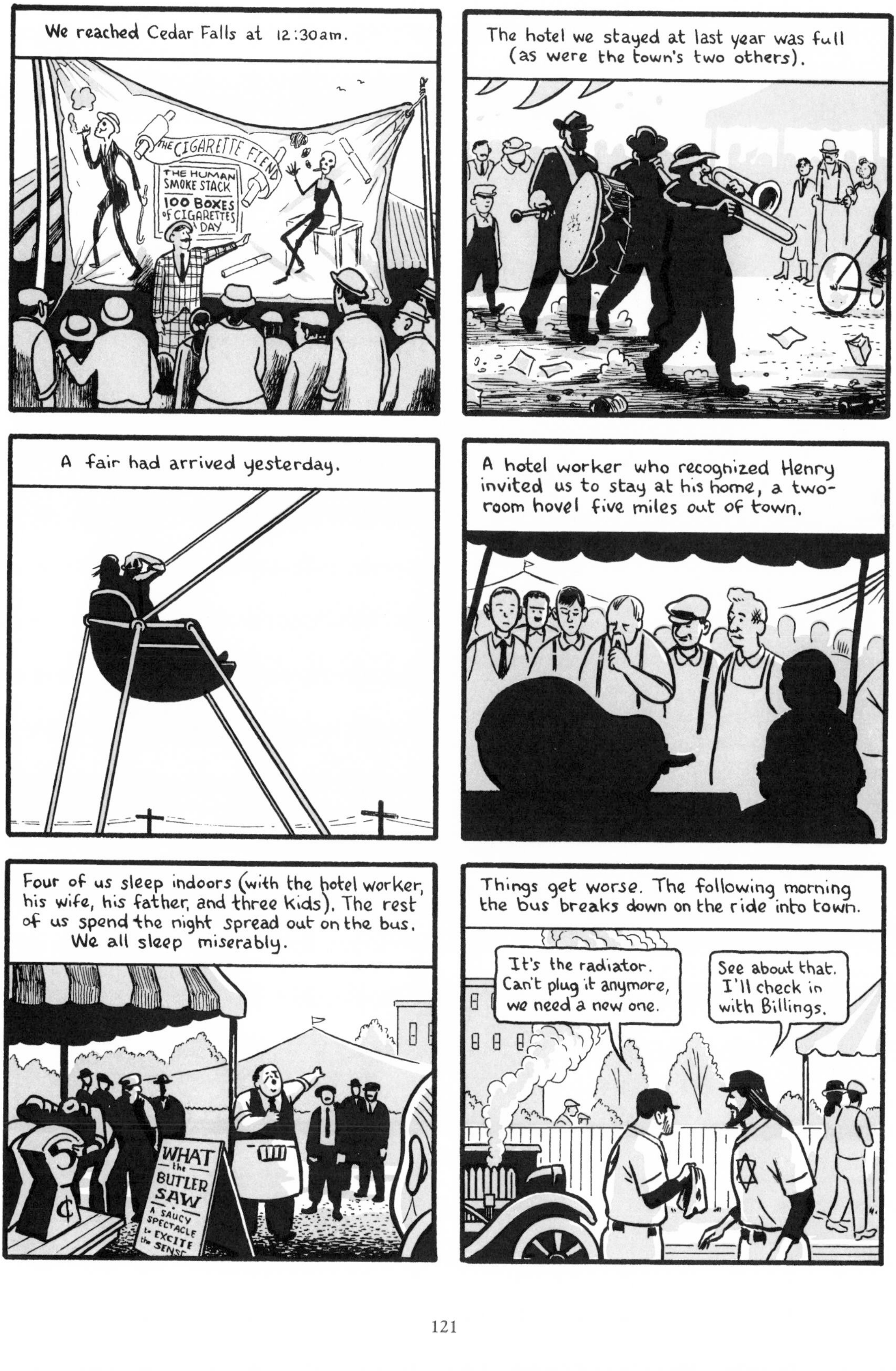
We reached Cedar Falls at 12:30am.
THE CIGARETTE FIEND
THE HUMAN SMOKE STACK
100 BOXES of CIGARETTES a DAY
The hotel we stayed at last year was full (as were the town's two others).
A fair had arrived yesterday.
A hotel worker who recognized Henry invited us to stay at his home, a two-room hovel five miles out of town.
Four of us sleep indoors (with the hotel worker, his wife, his father, and three kids). The rest of us spend the night spread out on the bus. We all sleep miserably.
WHAT the BUTLER SAW
A SAUCY SPECTACLE to EXCITE
Things get worse. The following morning the bus breaks down on the ride into town.
It's the radiator. Can't plug it anymore, we need a new one.
See about that. I'll check in with Billings.

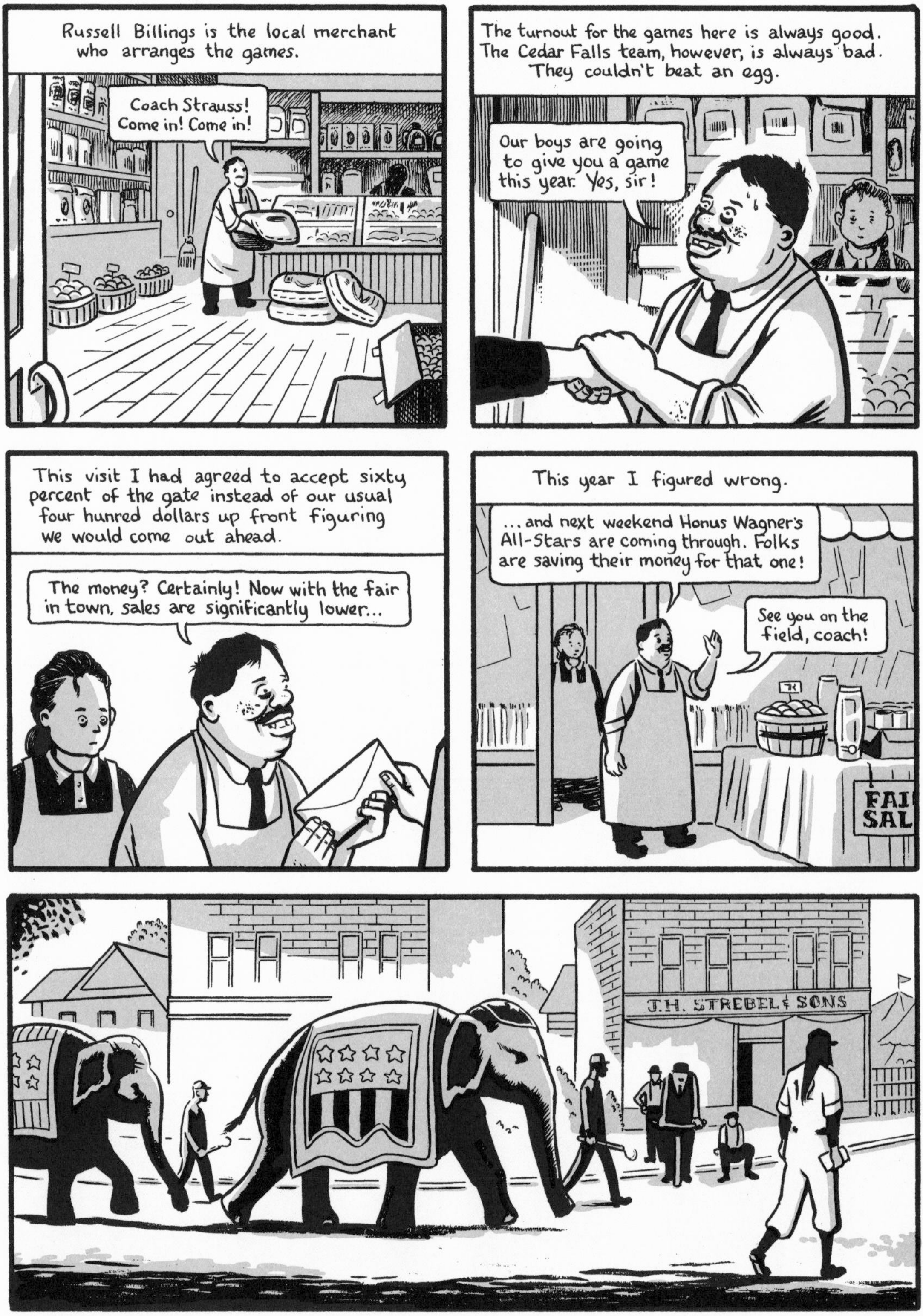
Russell Billings is the local merchant who arranges the games.
Coach Strauss! Come in! Come in!
The turnout for the games here is always good. The Cedar Falls team, however, is always bad. They couldn't beat an egg.
Our boys are going to give you a game this year. Yes, sir!
This visit I had agreed to accept sixty percent of the gate instead of our usual four hunred dollars up front figuring we would come out ahead.
The money? Certainly! Now with the fair in town, sales are significantly lower...
This year I figured wrong.
...and next weekend Honus Wagner's All-Stars are coming through. Folks are saving their money for that one!
See you on the field, coach!
J.H. STREBEL & SONS

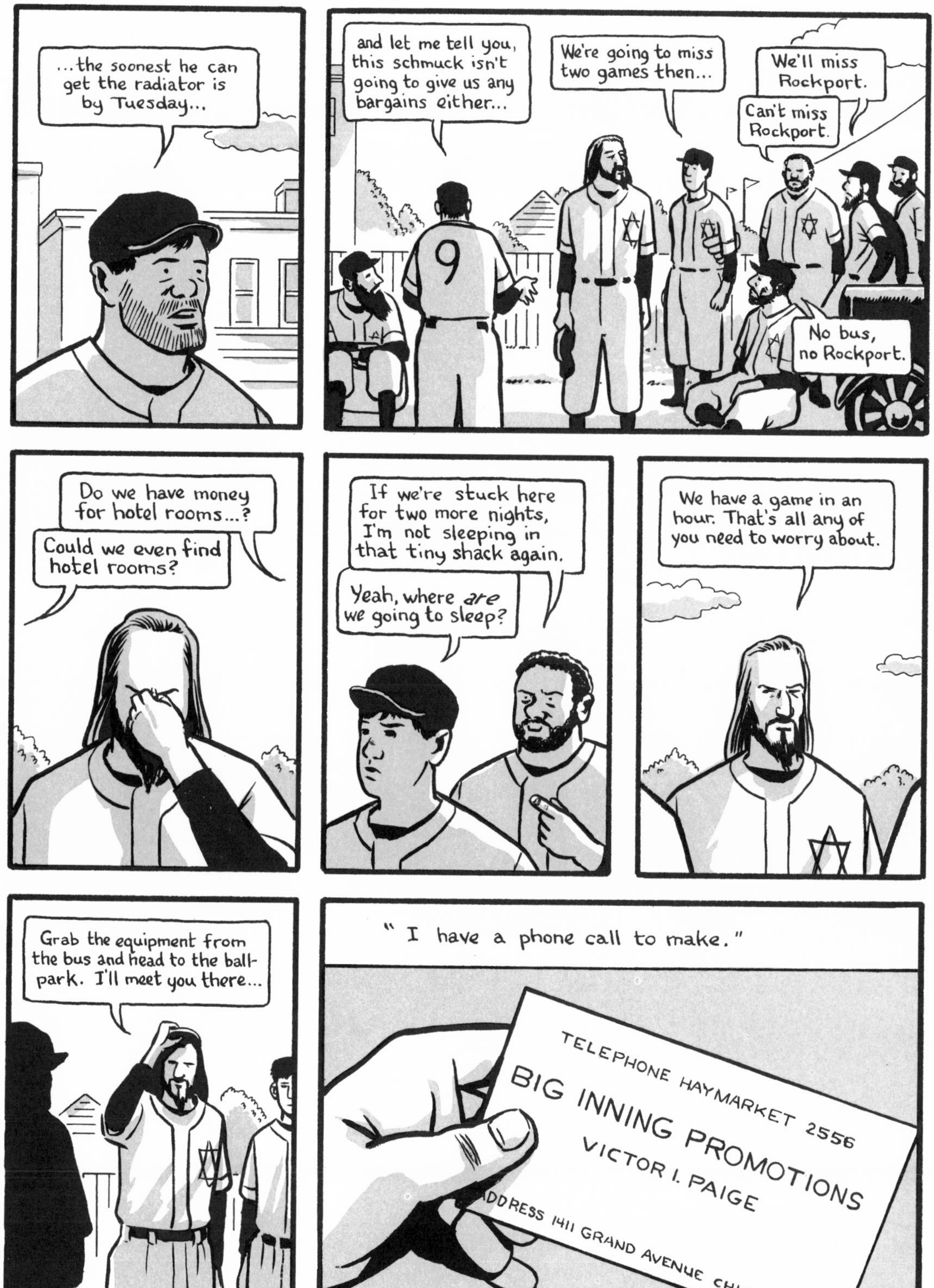
...the soonest he can get the radiator is by Tuesday...
and let me tell you, this schmuck isn't going to give us any bargains either...
We're going to miss two games then...
We'll miss Rockport.
Can't miss Rockport.
No bus, no Rockport.
Do we have money for hotel rooms...?
Could we even find hotel rooms?
If we're stuck here for two more nights, I'm not sleeping in that tiny shack again.
Yeah, where *are* we going to sleep?
We have a game in an hour. That's all any of you need to worry about.
Grab the equipment from the bus and head to the ball-park. I'll meet you there...
"I have a phone call to make."
TELEPHONE HAYMARKET 2556
BIG INNING PROMOTIONS
VICTOR I. PAIGE
ADDRESS 1411 GRAND AVENUE CHICAGO, ILL

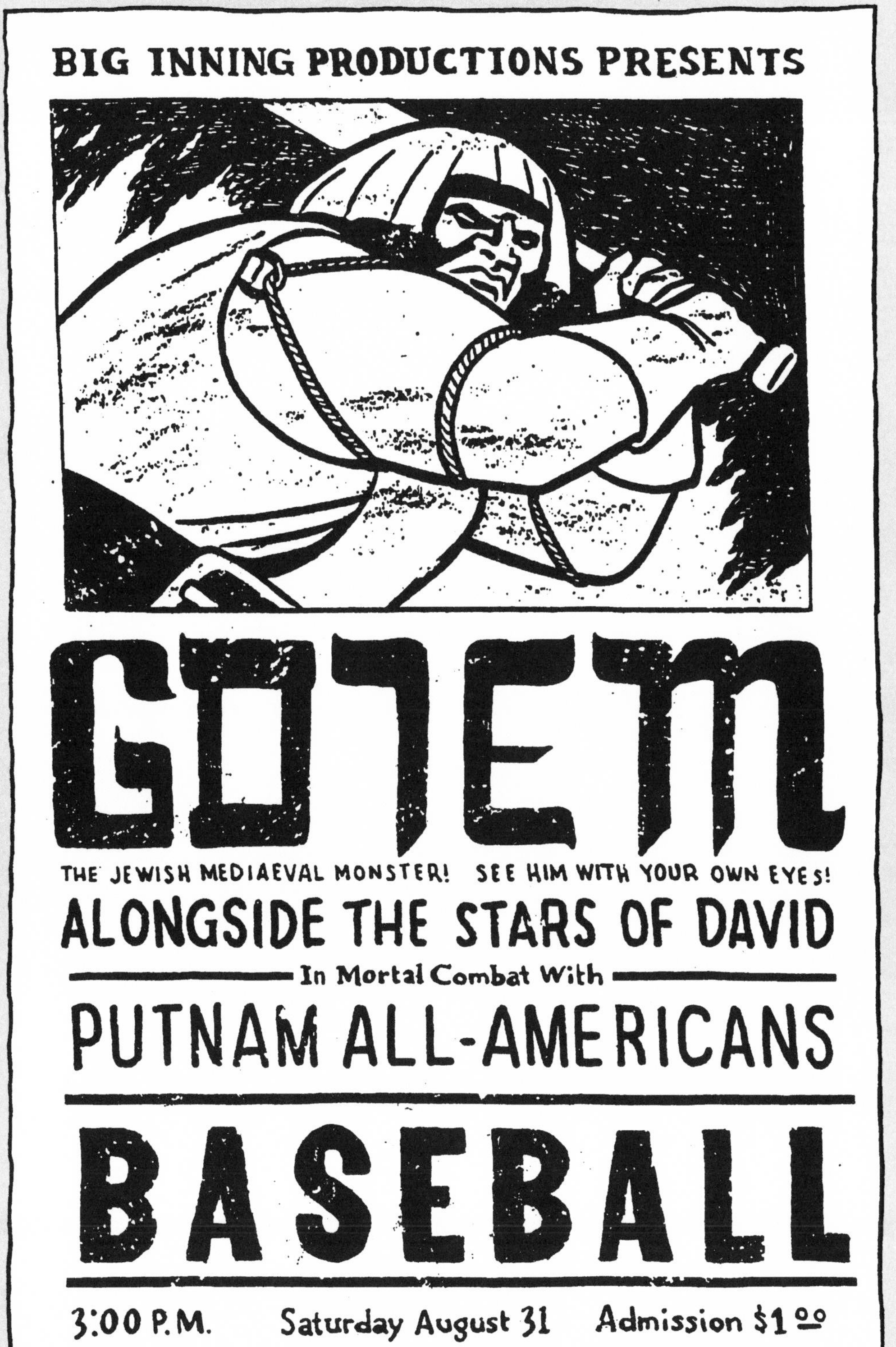
BIG INNING PRODUCTIONS PRESENTS
GOLEM
THE JEWISH MEDIAEVAL MONSTER! SEE HIM WITH YOUR OWN EYES!
ALONGSIDE THE STARS OF DAVID
In Mortal Combat With
PUTNAM ALL-AMERICANS
BASEBALL
3:00 P.M. Saturday August 31 Admission $1.00

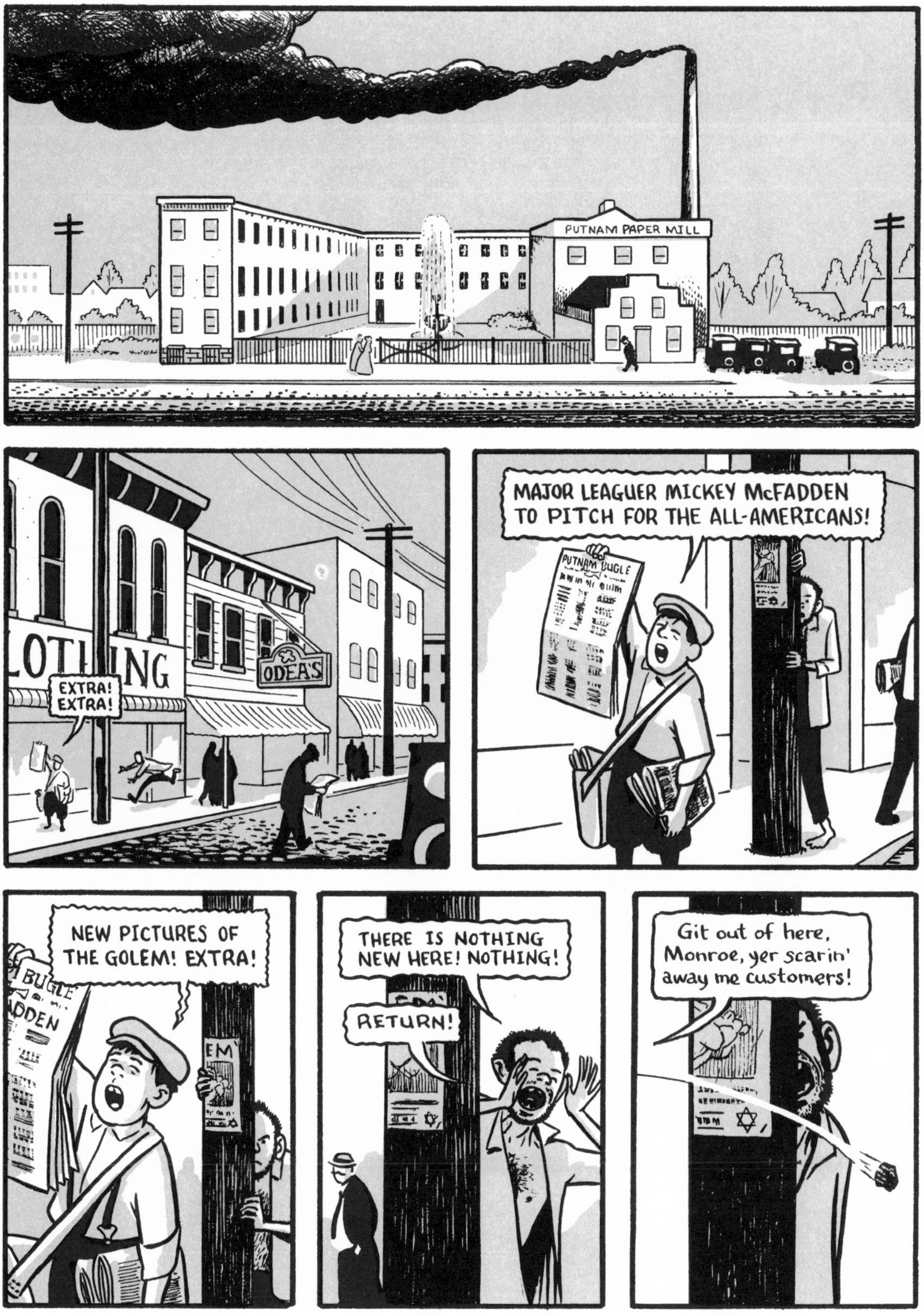
PUTNAM PAPER MILL
LOTHING
ODEA'S
EXTRA! EXTRA!
MAJOR LEAGUER MICKEY McFADDEN TO PITCH FOR THE ALL-AMERICANS!
PUTNAM BUGLE
NEW PICTURES OF THE GOLEM! EXTRA!
THERE IS NOTHING NEW HERE! NOTHING!
RETURN!
Git out of here, Monroe, yer scarin' away me customers!

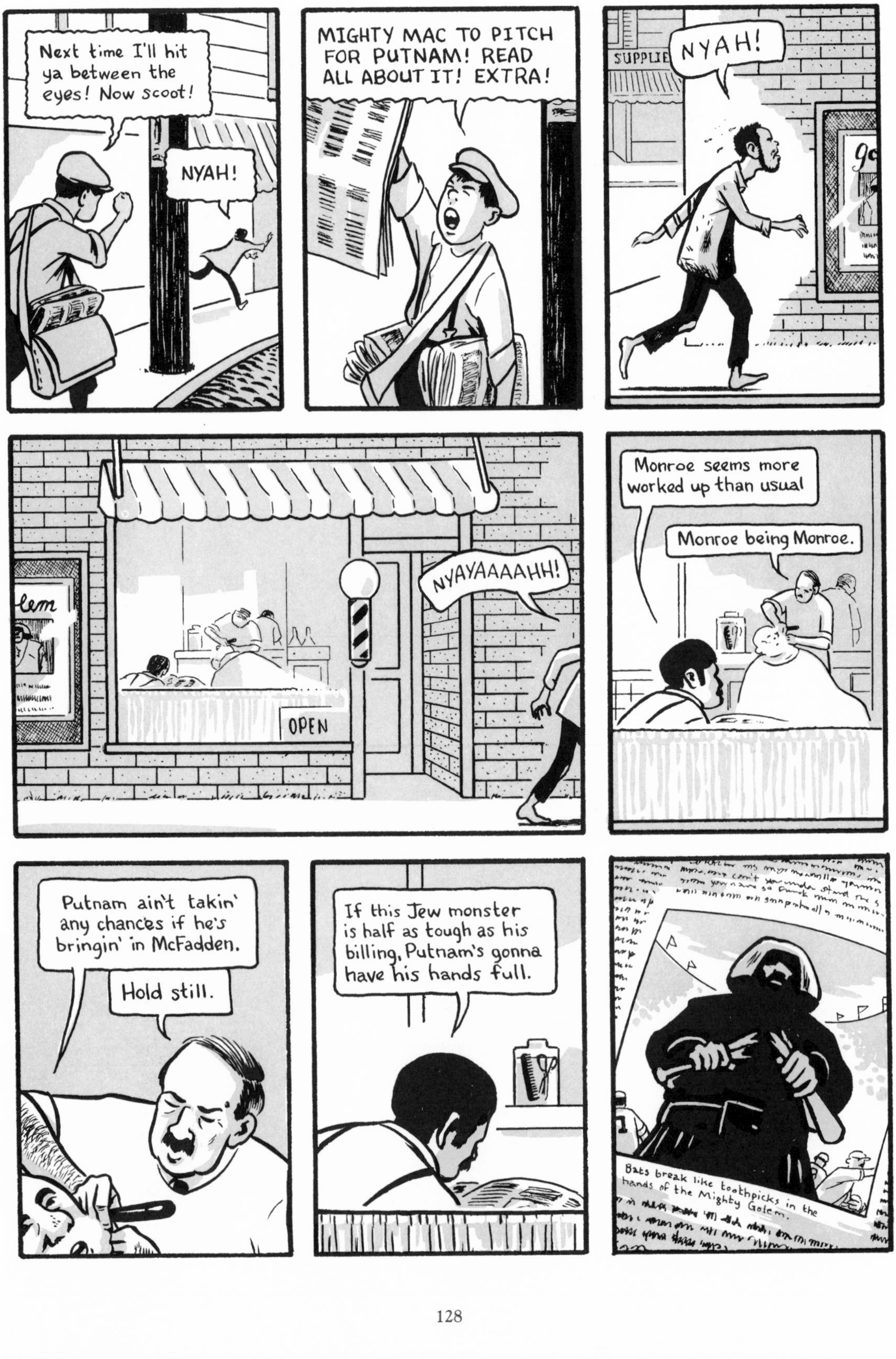
Next time I'll hit ya between the eyes! Now scoot!
NYAH!
MIGHTY MAC TO PITCH FOR PUTNAM! READ ALL ABOUT IT! EXTRA!
SUPPLIE
NYAH!
OPEN
NYAYAAAAHH!
Monroe seems more worked up than usual
Monroe being Monroe.
Putnam ain't takin' any chances if he's bringin' in McFadden.
Hold still.
If this Jew monster is half as tough as his billing, Putnam's gonna have his hands full.
Bats break like toothpicks in the hands of the Mighty Golem.

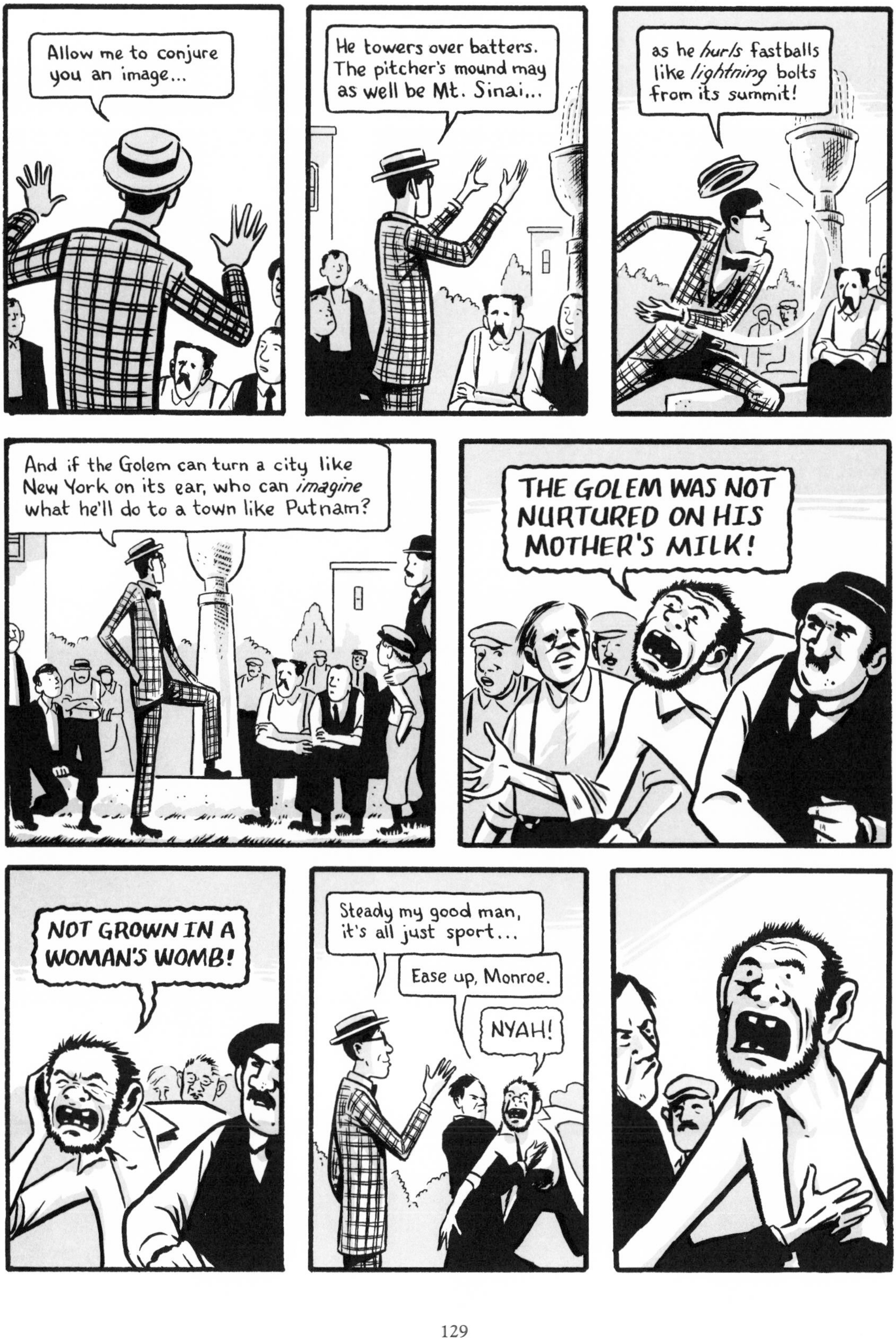
Allow me to conjure you an image...
He towers over batters. The pitcher's mound may as well be Mt. Sinai...
as he *hurls* fastballs like *lightning* bolts from its summit!
And if the Golem can turn a city like New York on its ear, who can *imagine* what he'll do to a town like Putnam?
THE GOLEM WAS NOT NURTURED ON HIS MOTHER'S MILK!
NOT GROWN IN A WOMAN'S WOMB!
Steady my good man, it's all just sport...
Ease up, Monroe.
NYAH!

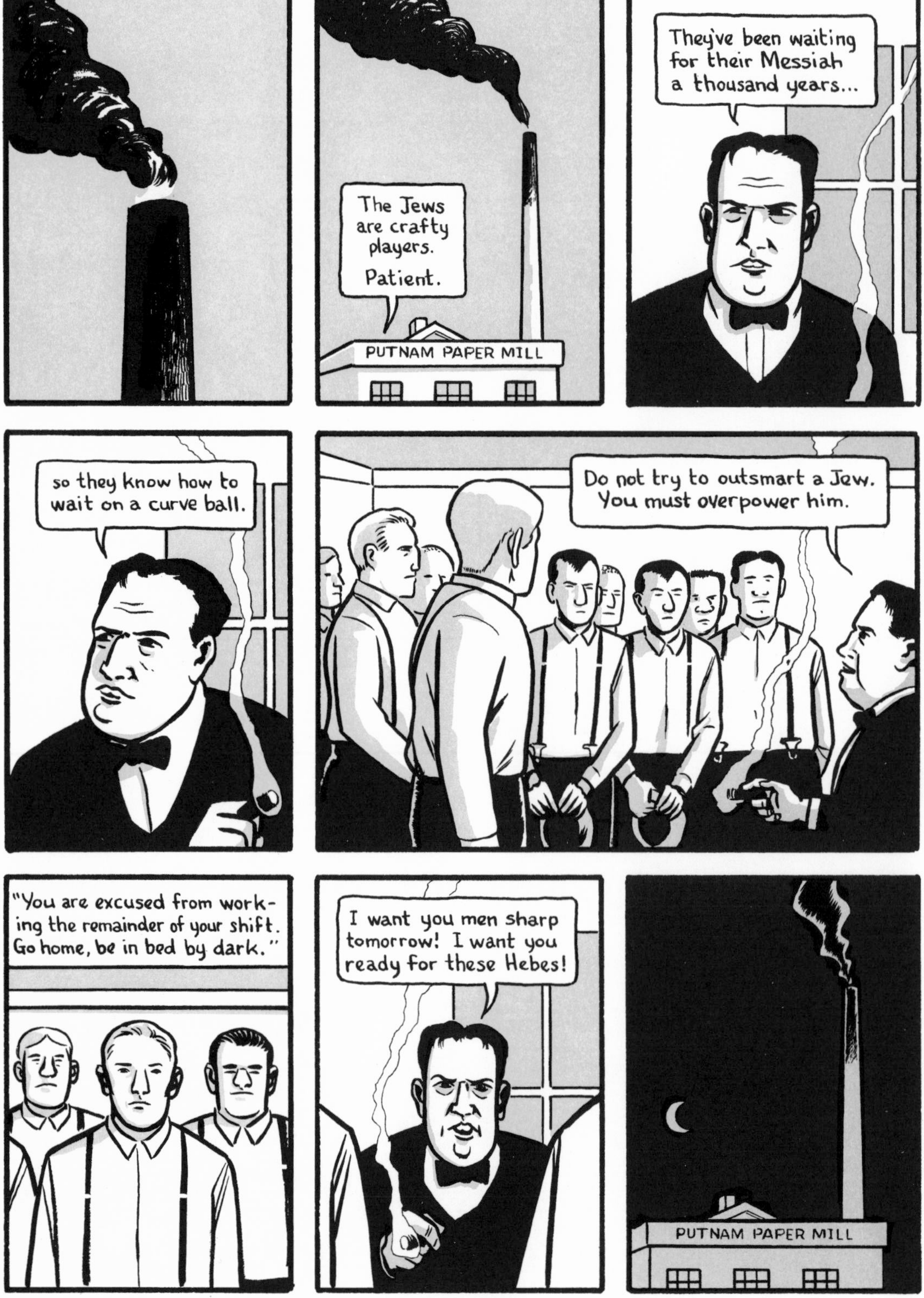
The Jews are crafty players.
Patient.
PUTNAM PAPER MILL
They've been waiting for their Messiah a thousand years...
so they know how to wait on a curve ball.
Do not try to outsmart a Jew. You must overpower him.
"You are excused from working the remainder of your shift. Go home, be in bed by dark."
I want you men sharp tomorrow! I want you ready for these Hebes!
PUTNAM PAPER MILL

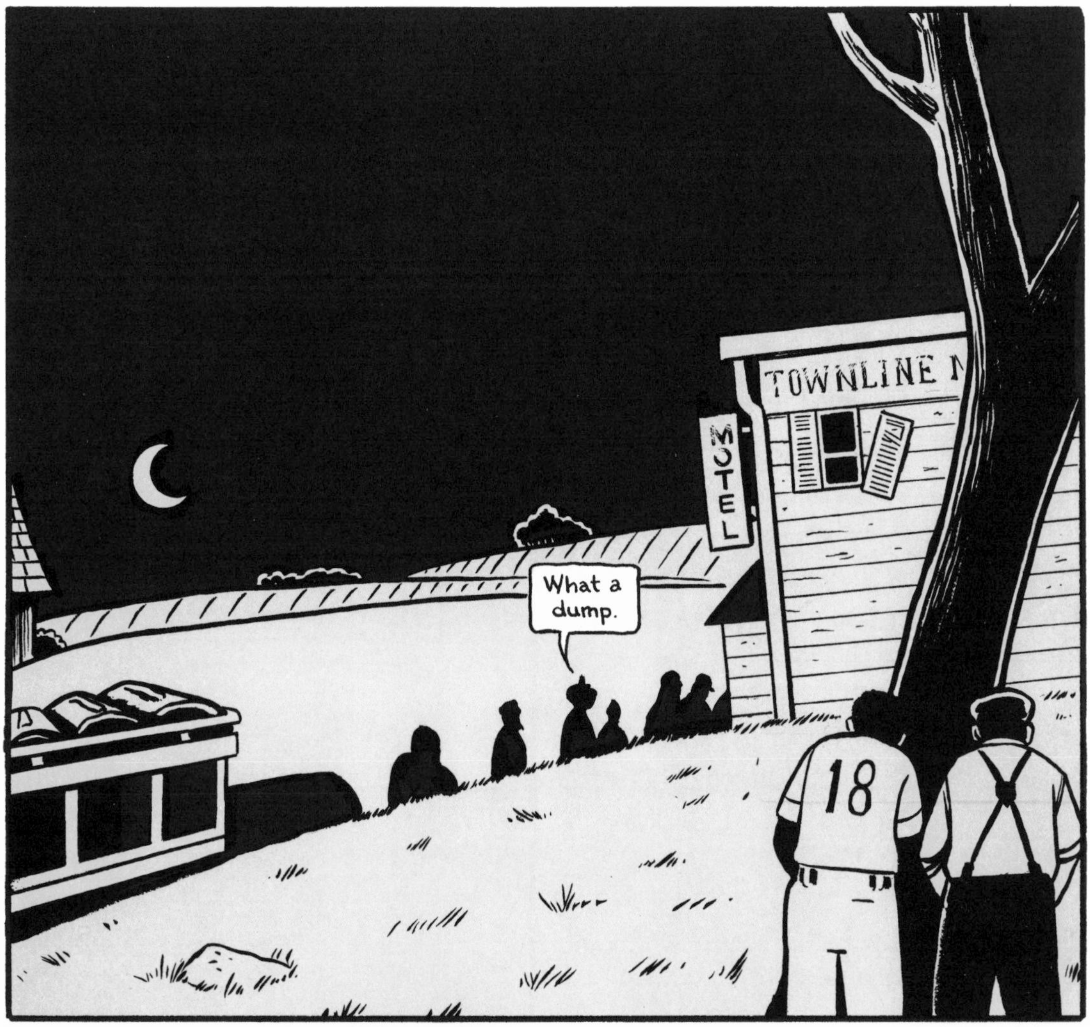
TOWNLINE M
MOTEL
What a dump.
18

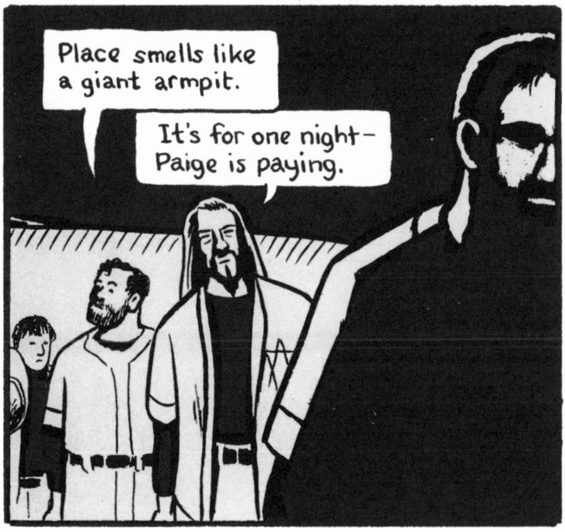
Place smells like a giant armpit.
It's for one night- Paige is paying.

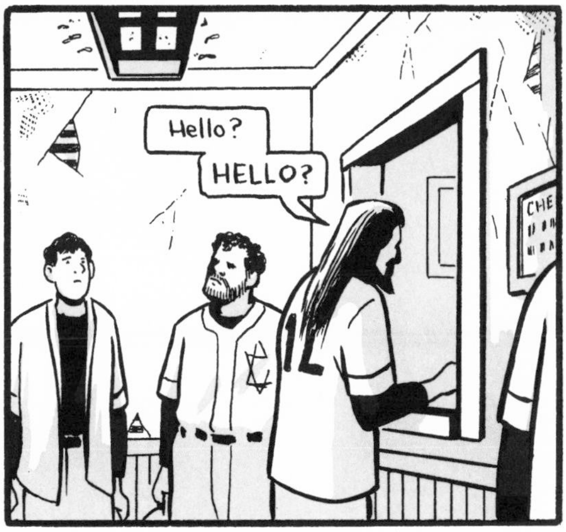
Hello?
HELLO?
12

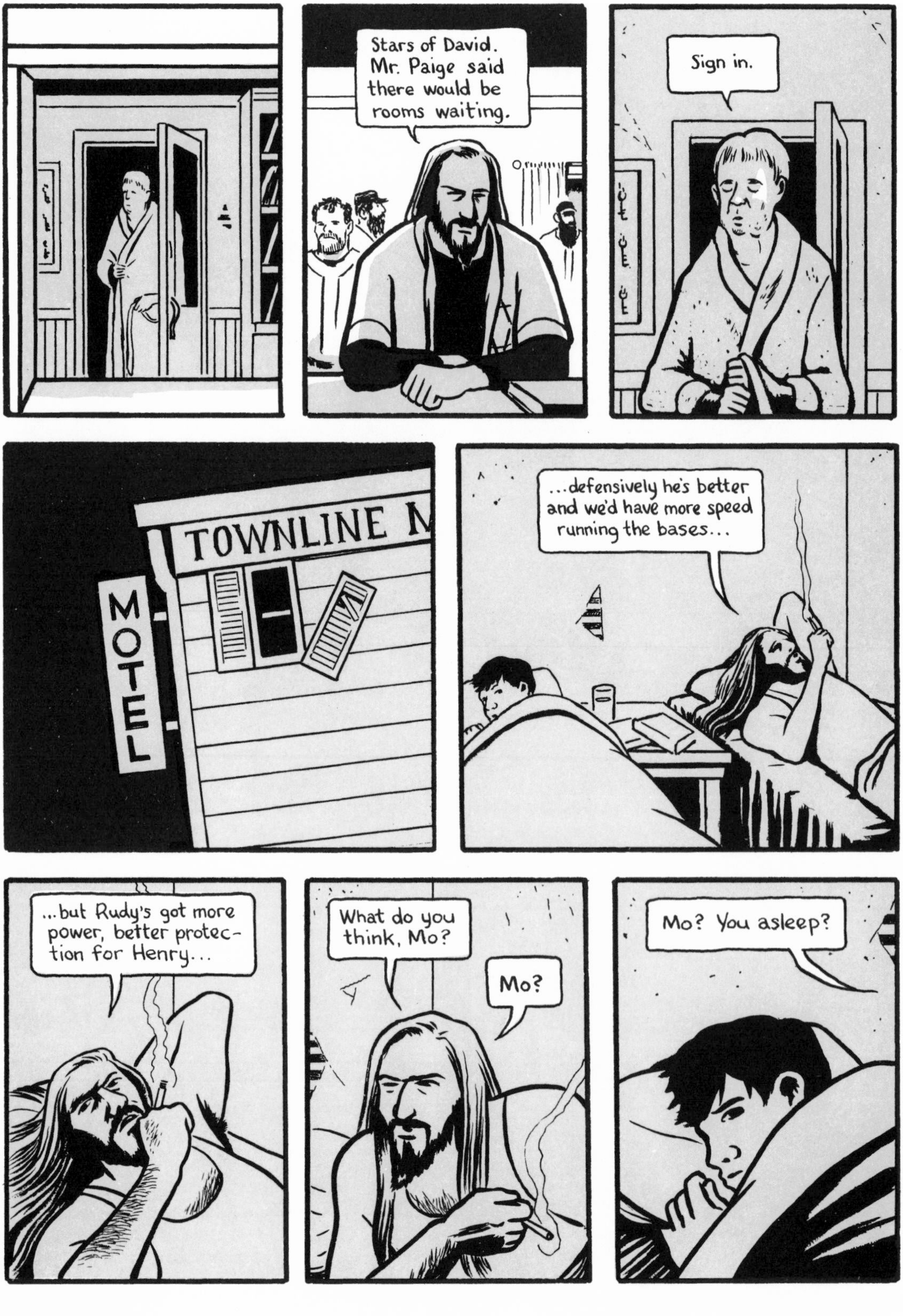
Stars of David. Mr. Paige said there would be rooms waiting.
Sign in.
TOWNLINE M
MOTEL
...defensively he's better and we'd have more speed running the bases...
...but Rudy's got more power, better protection for Henry...
What do you think, Mo?
Mo?
Mo? You asleep?

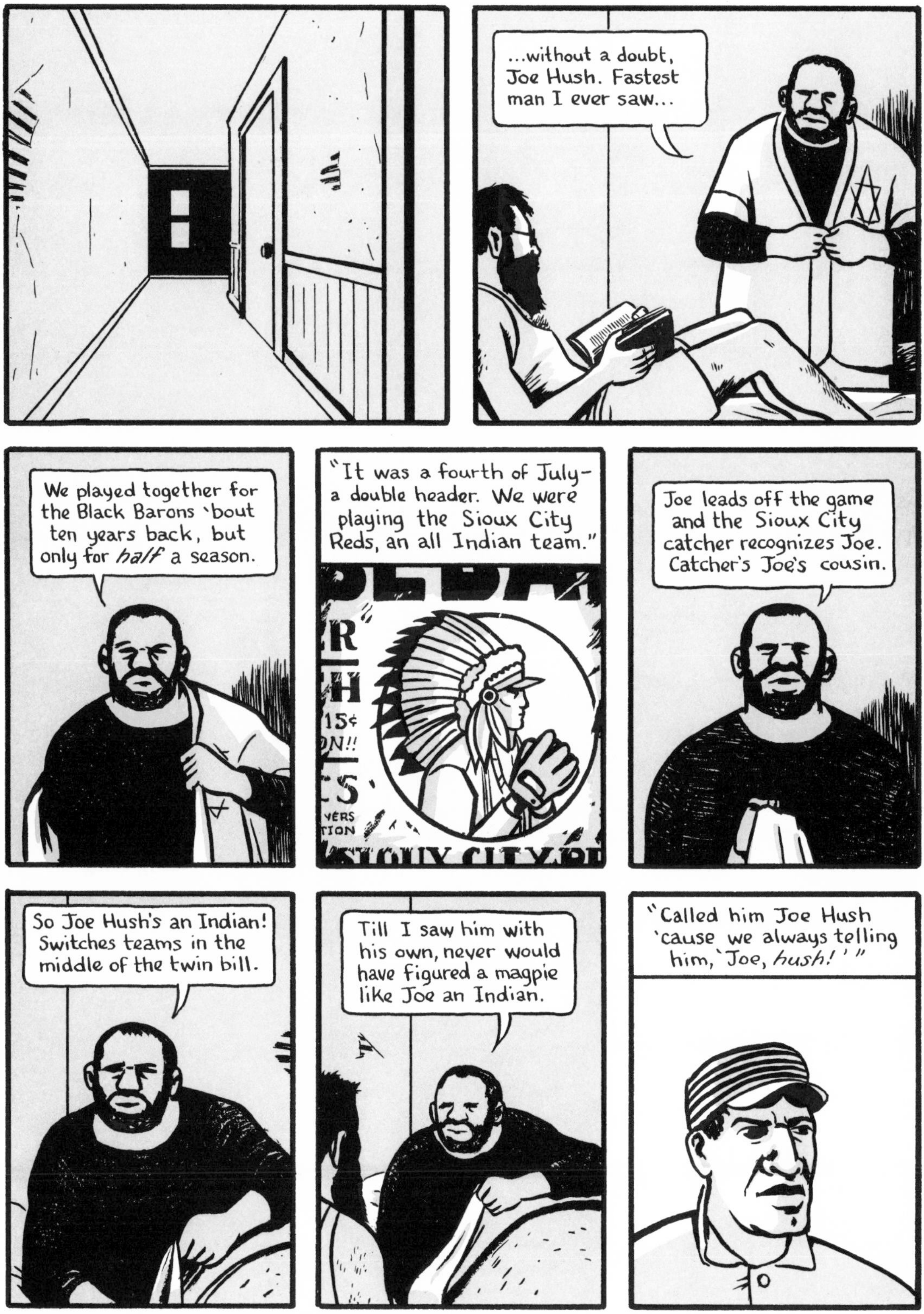
...without a doubt, Joe Hush. Fastest man I ever saw...
We played together for the Black Barons 'bout ten years back, but only for *half* a season.
"It was a fourth of July-a double header. We were playing the Sioux City Reds, an all Indian team."
Joe leads off the game and the Sioux City catcher recognizes Joe. Catcher's Joe's cousin.
So Joe Hush's an Indian! Switches teams in the middle of the twin bill.
Till I saw him with his own, never would have figured a magpie like Joe an Indian.
"Called him Joe Hush 'cause we always telling him, 'Joe, *hush!*' "

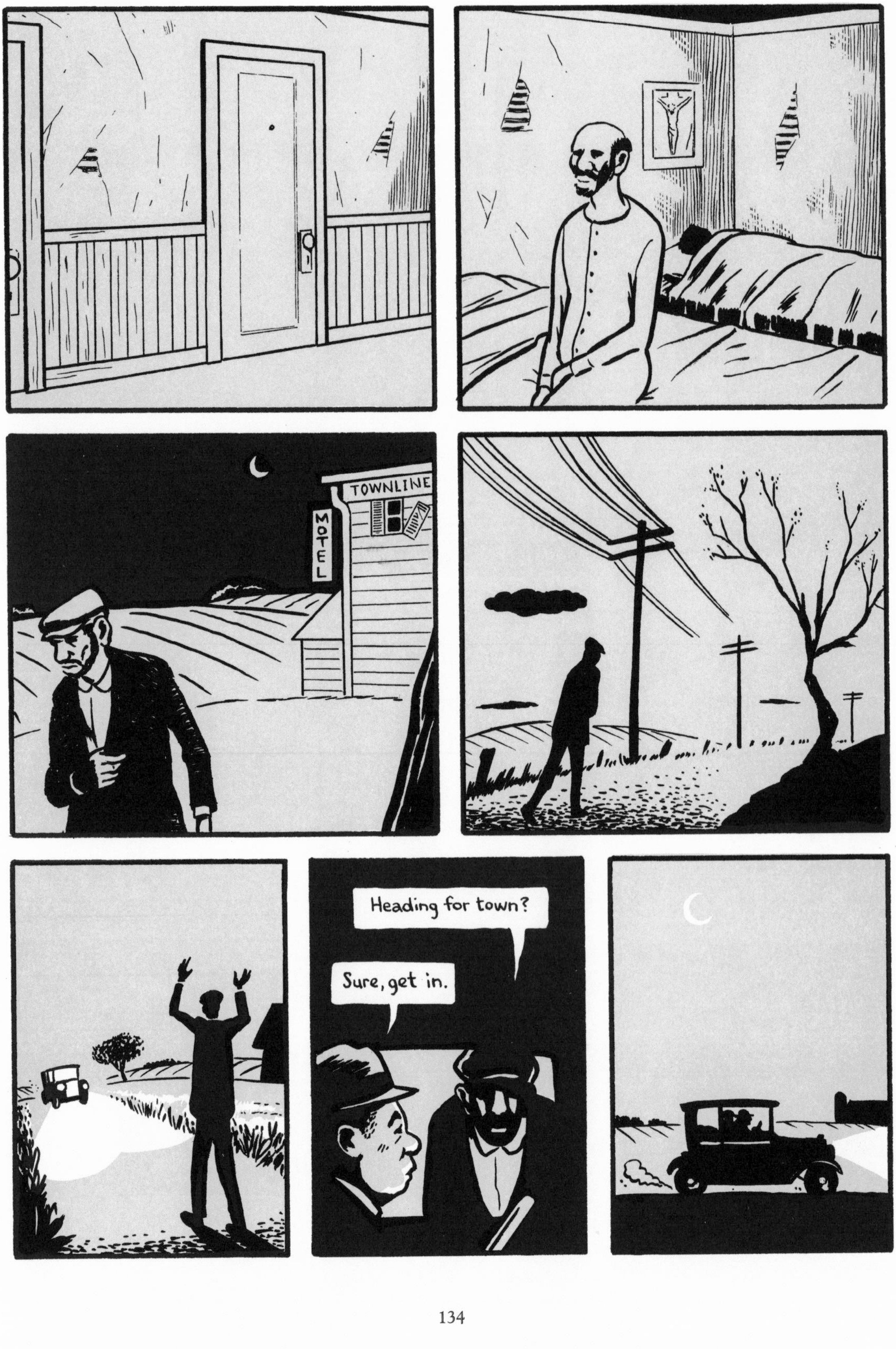
TOWNLINE
MOTEL
Heading for town?
Sure, get in.

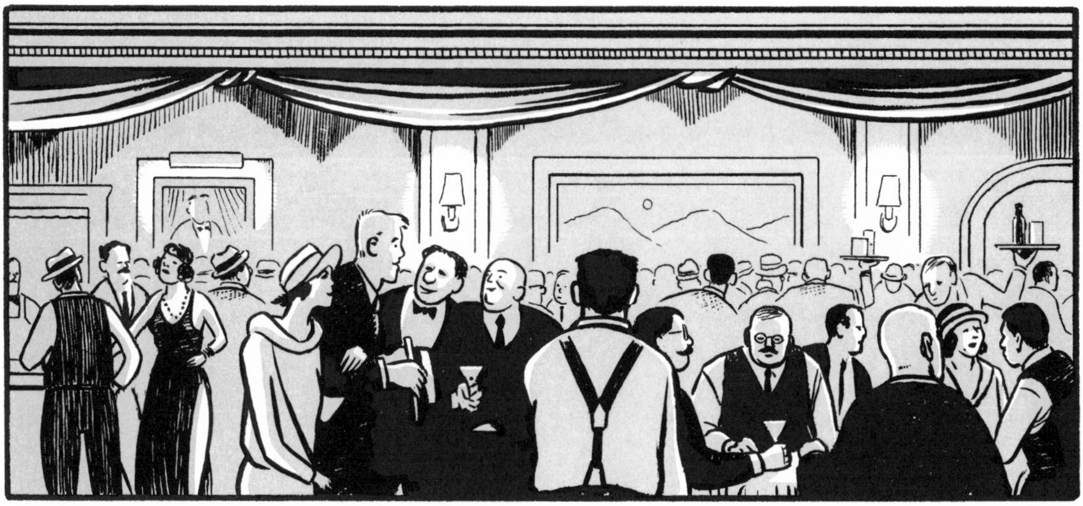

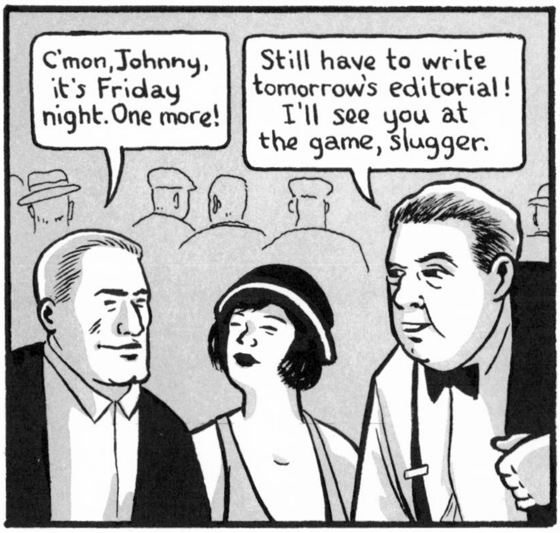
C'mon, Johnny, it's Friday night. One more!
Still have to write tomorrow's editorial! I'll see you at the game, slugger.

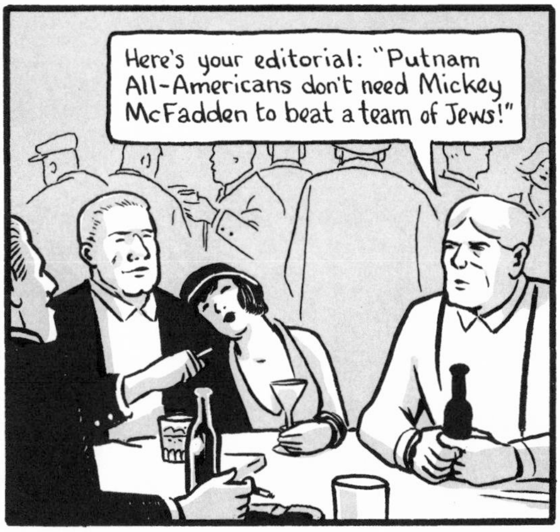
Here's your editorial: "Putnam All-Americans don't need Mickey McFadden to beat a team of Jews!"

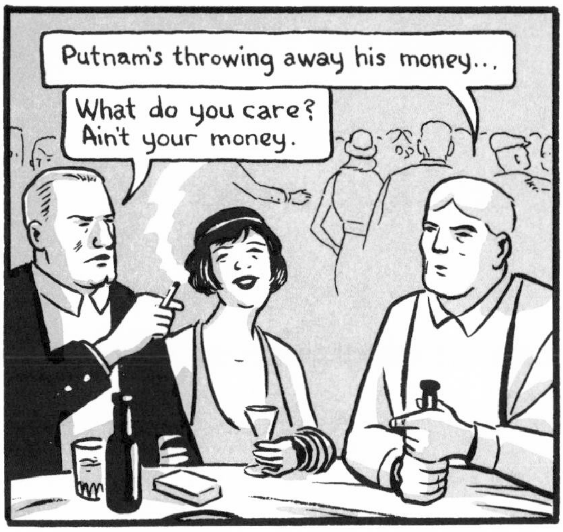
Putnam's throwing away his money...
What do you care? Ain't your money.

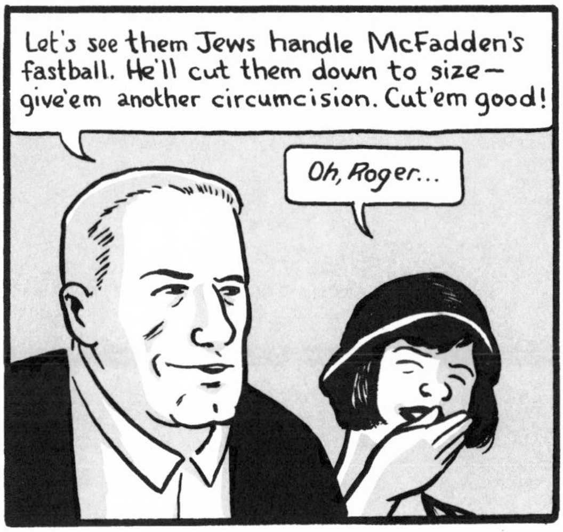
Let's see them Jews handle McFadden's fastball. He'll cut them down to size—give'em another circumcision. Cut'em good!
Oh, Roger...

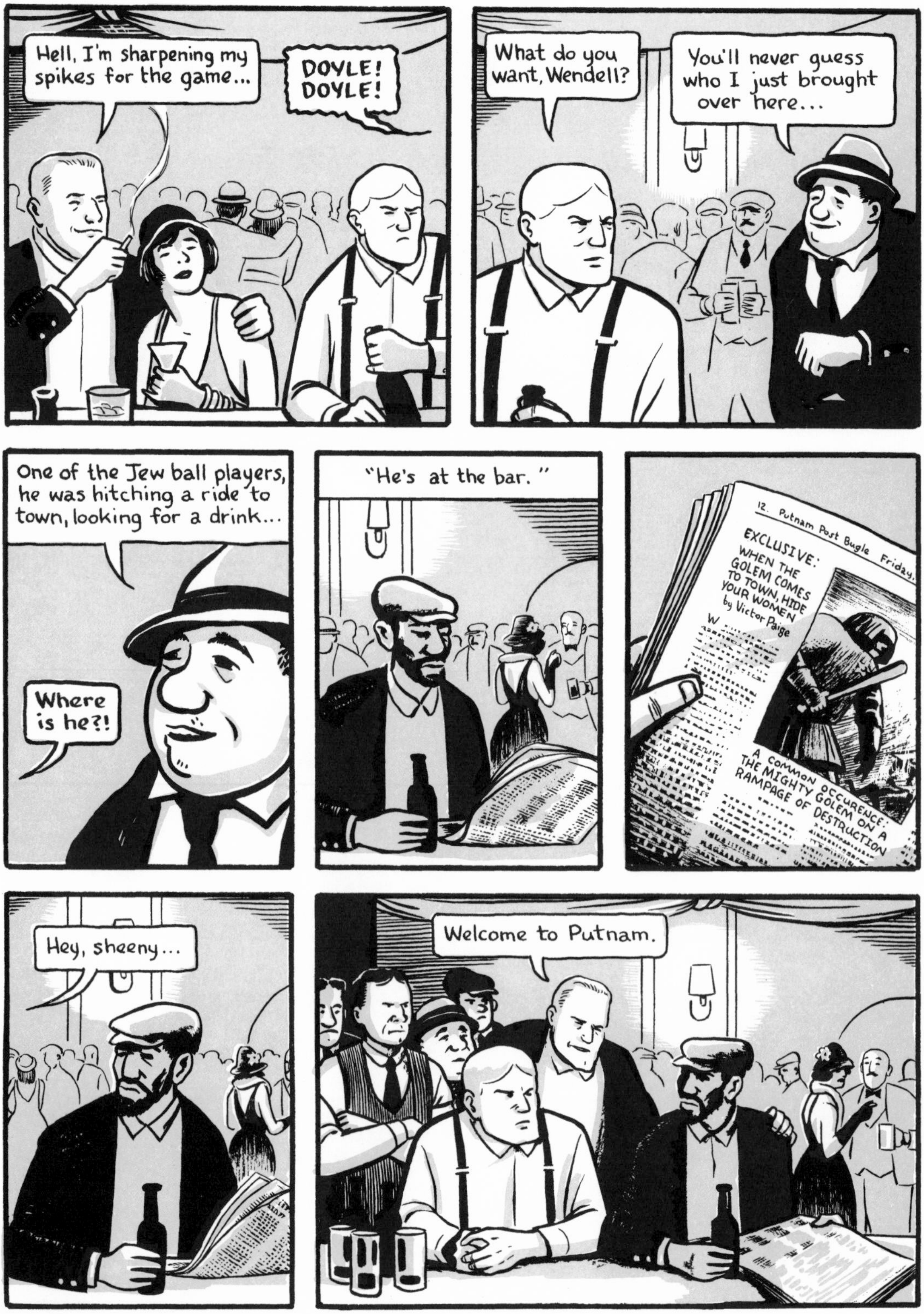
Hell, I'm sharpening my spikes for the game...
DOYLE! DOYLE!
What do you want, Wendell?
You'll never guess who I just brought over here...
One of the Jew ball players, he was hitching a ride to town, looking for a drink...
Where is he?!
"He's at the bar."
12. Putnam Post Bugle Friday.
EXCLUSIVE: WHEN THE GOLEM COMES TO TOWN, HIDE YOUR WOMEN
by Victor Paige
A COMMON OCCURENCE: THE MIGHTY GOLEM ON A RAMPAGE OF DESTRUCTION
Hey, sheeny...
Welcome to Putnam.

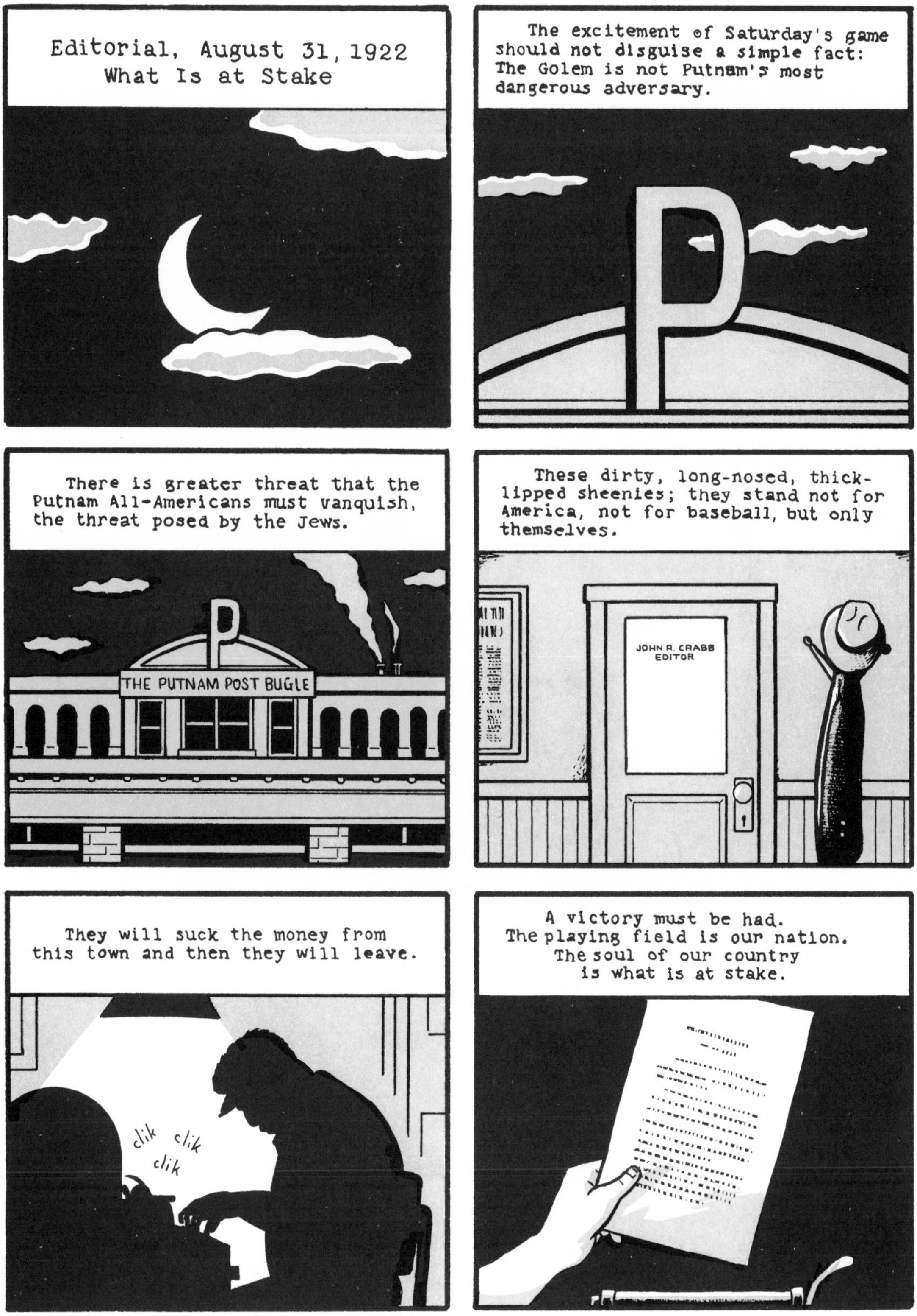
Editorial, August 31, 1922
What Is at Stake
The excitement of Saturday's game should not disguise a simple fact: The Golem is not Putnam's most dangerous adversary.
There is greater threat that the Putnam All-Americans must vanquish, the threat posed by the Jews.
THE PUTNAM POST BUGLE
These dirty, long-nosed, thick-lipped sheenies; they stand not for America, not for baseball, but only themselves.
JOHN R. CRABB
EDITOR
They will suck the money from this town and then they will leave.
clik
clik
clik
A victory must be had.
The playing field is our nation.
The soul of our country
is what is at stake.

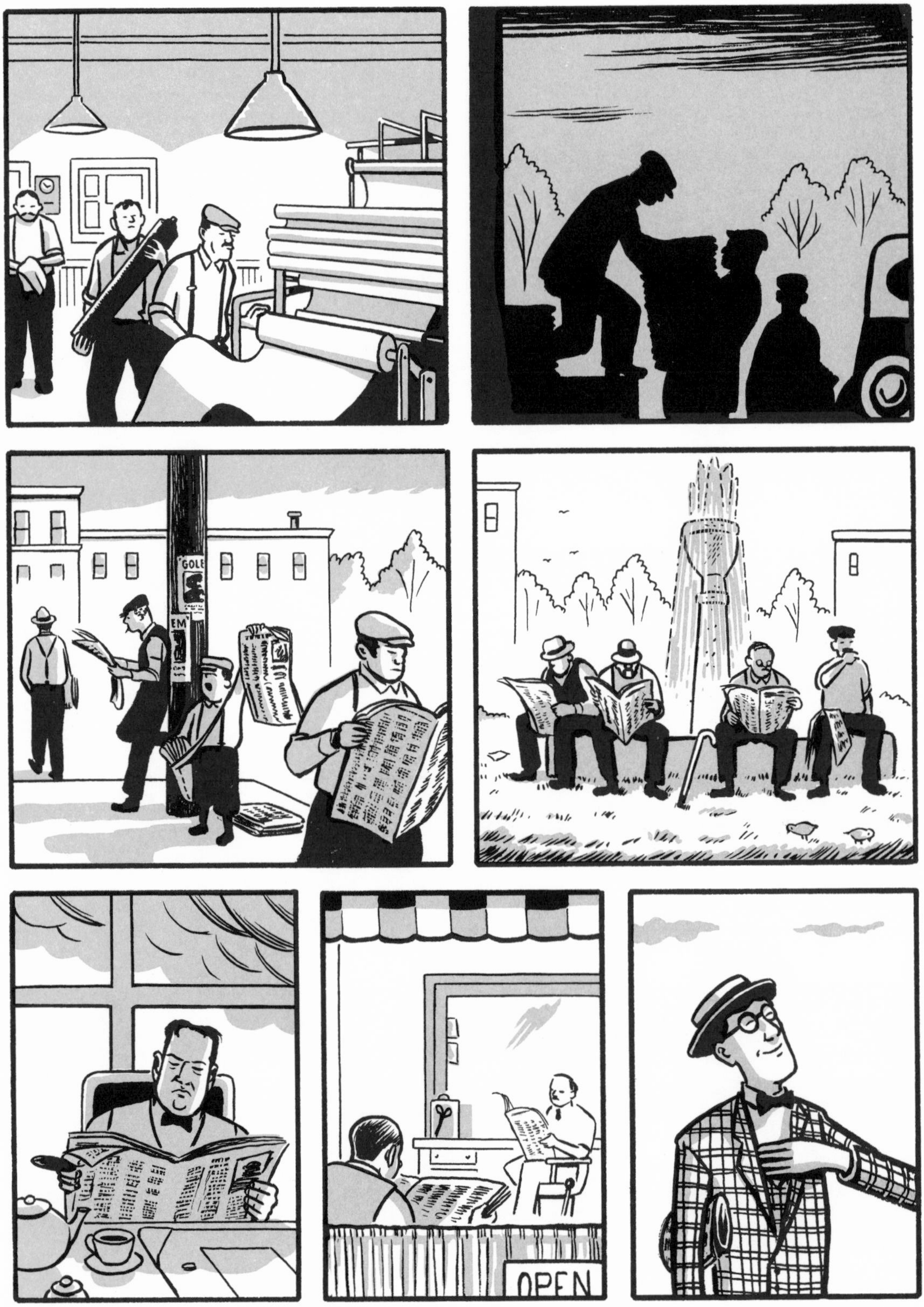
OPEN

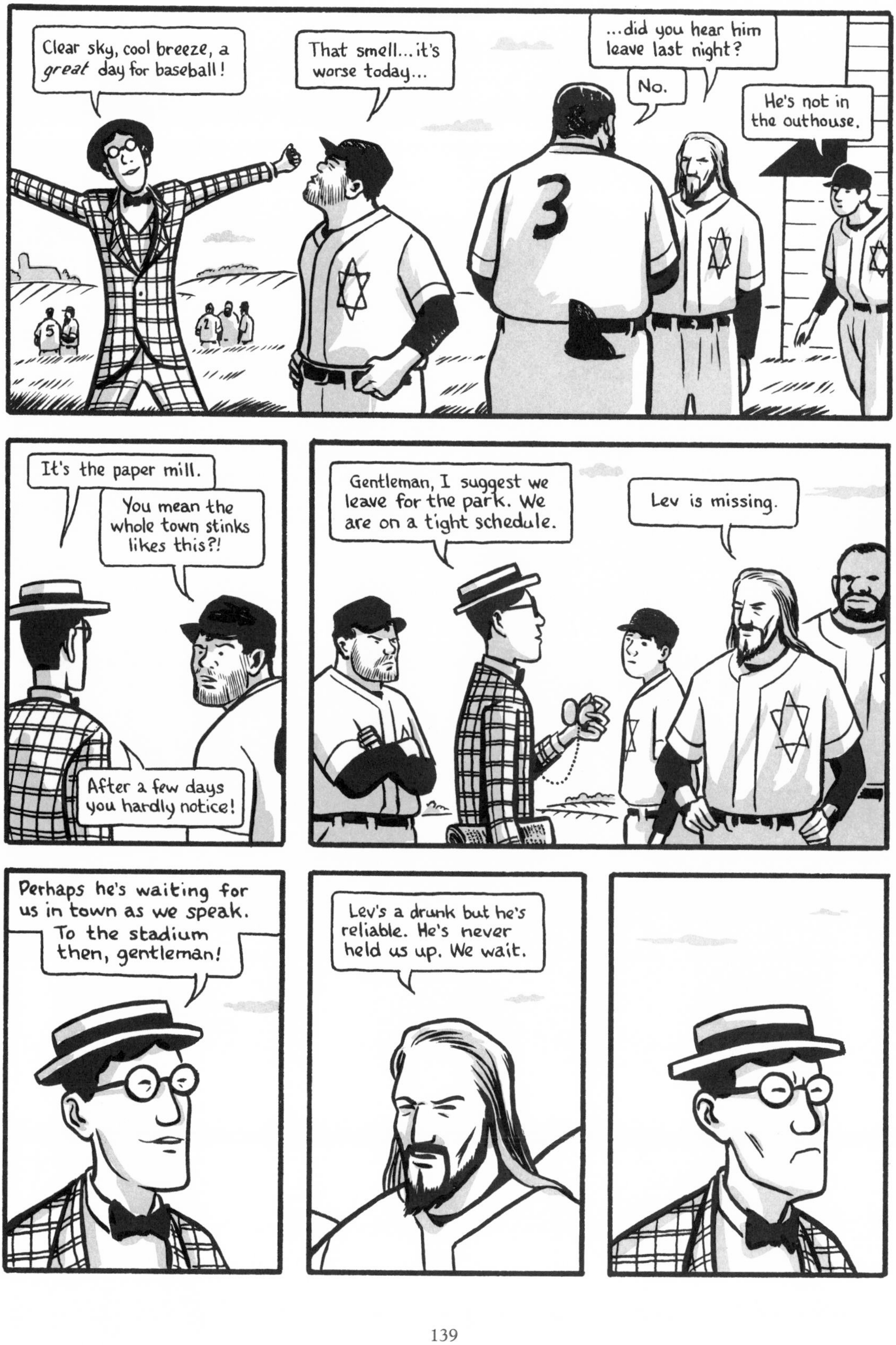

Clear sky, cool breeze, a *great* day for baseball!
That smell... it's worse today...
...did you hear him leave last night?
No.
He's not in the outhouse.
It's the paper mill.
You mean the whole town stinks likes this?!
After a few days you hardly notice!
Gentleman, I suggest we leave for the park. We are on a tight schedule.
Lev is missing.
Perhaps he's waiting for us in town as we speak. To the stadium then, gentleman!
Lev's a drunk but he's reliable. He's never held us up. We wait.

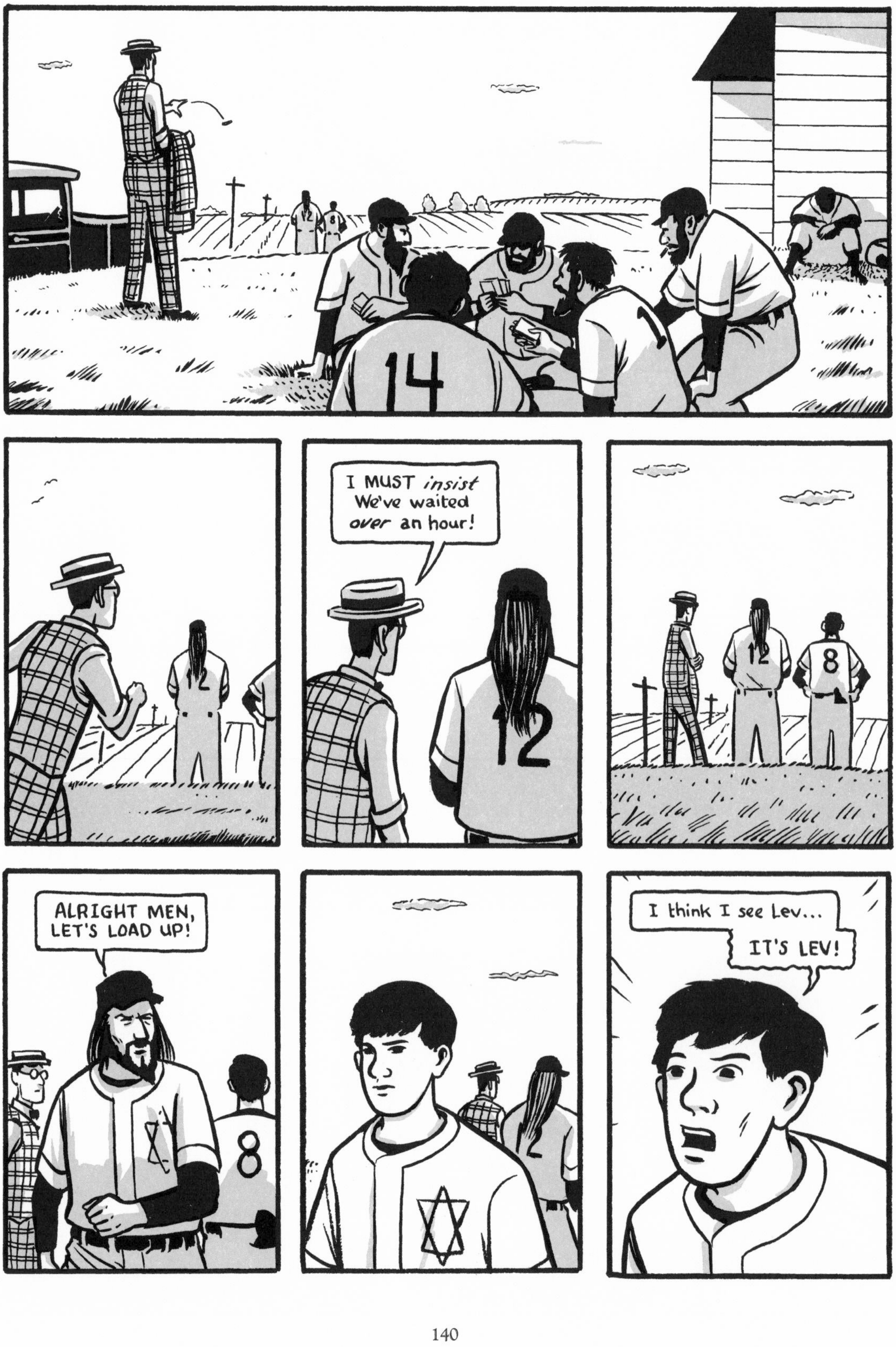
I MUST *insist* We've waited *over* an hour!
ALRIGHT MEN, LET'S LOAD UP!
I think I see Lev...
IT'S LEV!

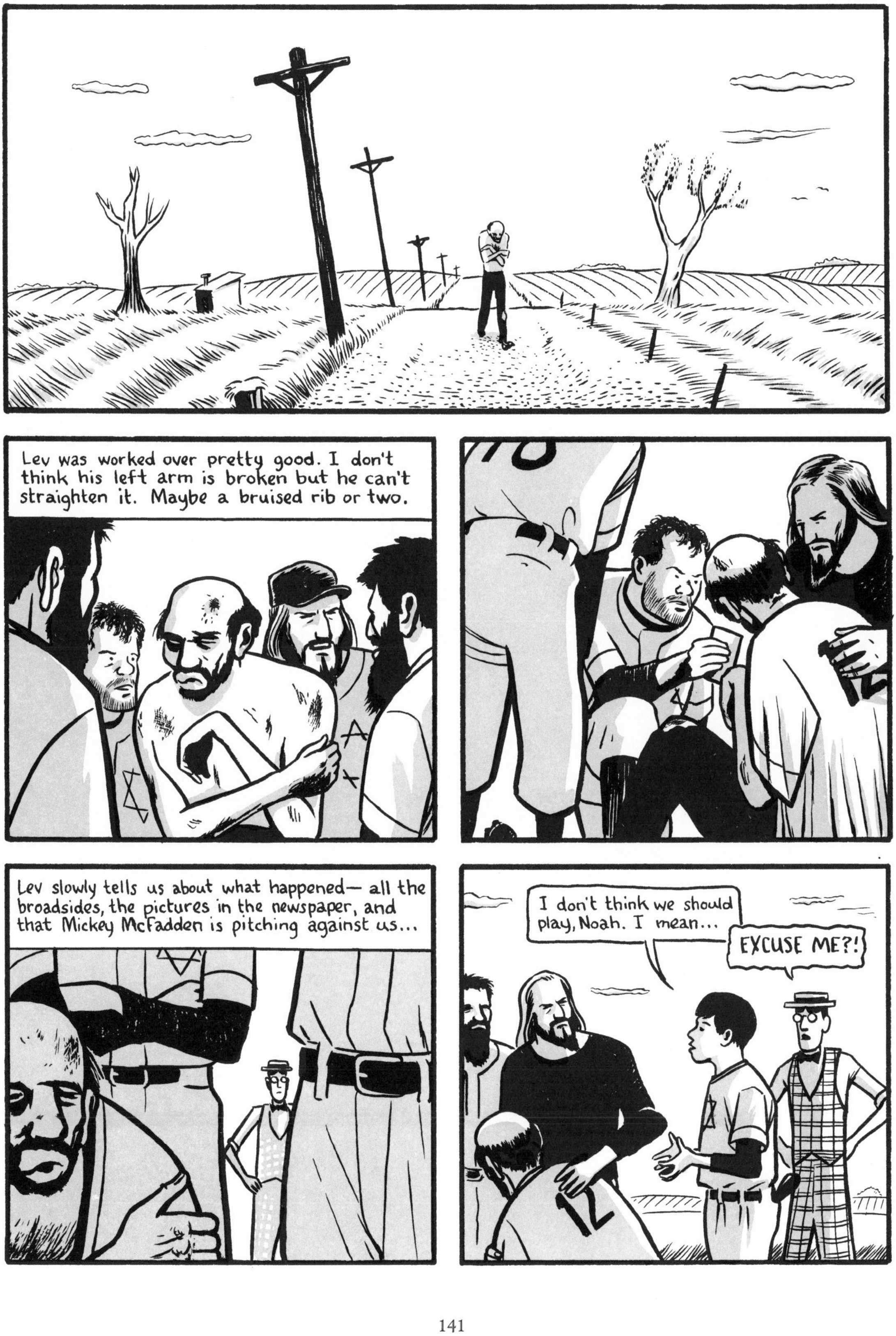
Lev was worked over pretty good. I don't think his left arm is broken but he can't straighten it. Maybe a bruised rib or two.
Lev slowly tells us about what happened— all the broadsides, the pictures in the newspaper, and that Mickey McFadden is pitching against us...
I don't think we should play, Noah. I mean...
EXCUSE ME?!

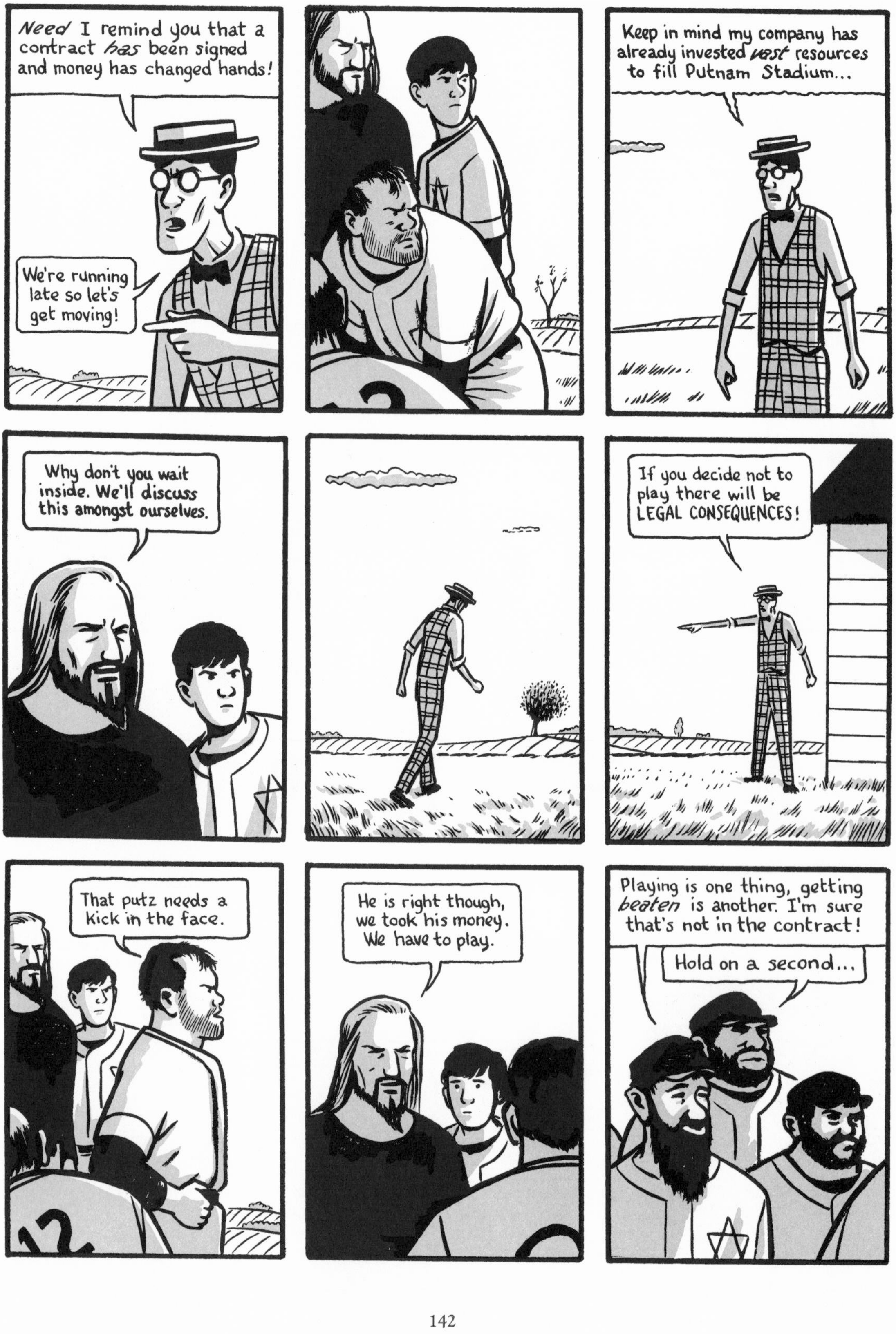
Need I remind you that a contract has been signed and money has changed hands!
We're running late so let's get moving!
Keep in mind my company has already invested vast resources to fill Putnam Stadium...
Why don't you wait inside. We'll discuss this amongst ourselves.
If you decide not to play there will be LEGAL CONSEQUENCES!
That putz needs a kick in the face.
He is right though, we took his money. We have to play.
Playing is one thing, getting beaten is another. I'm sure that's not in the contract!
Hold on a second...

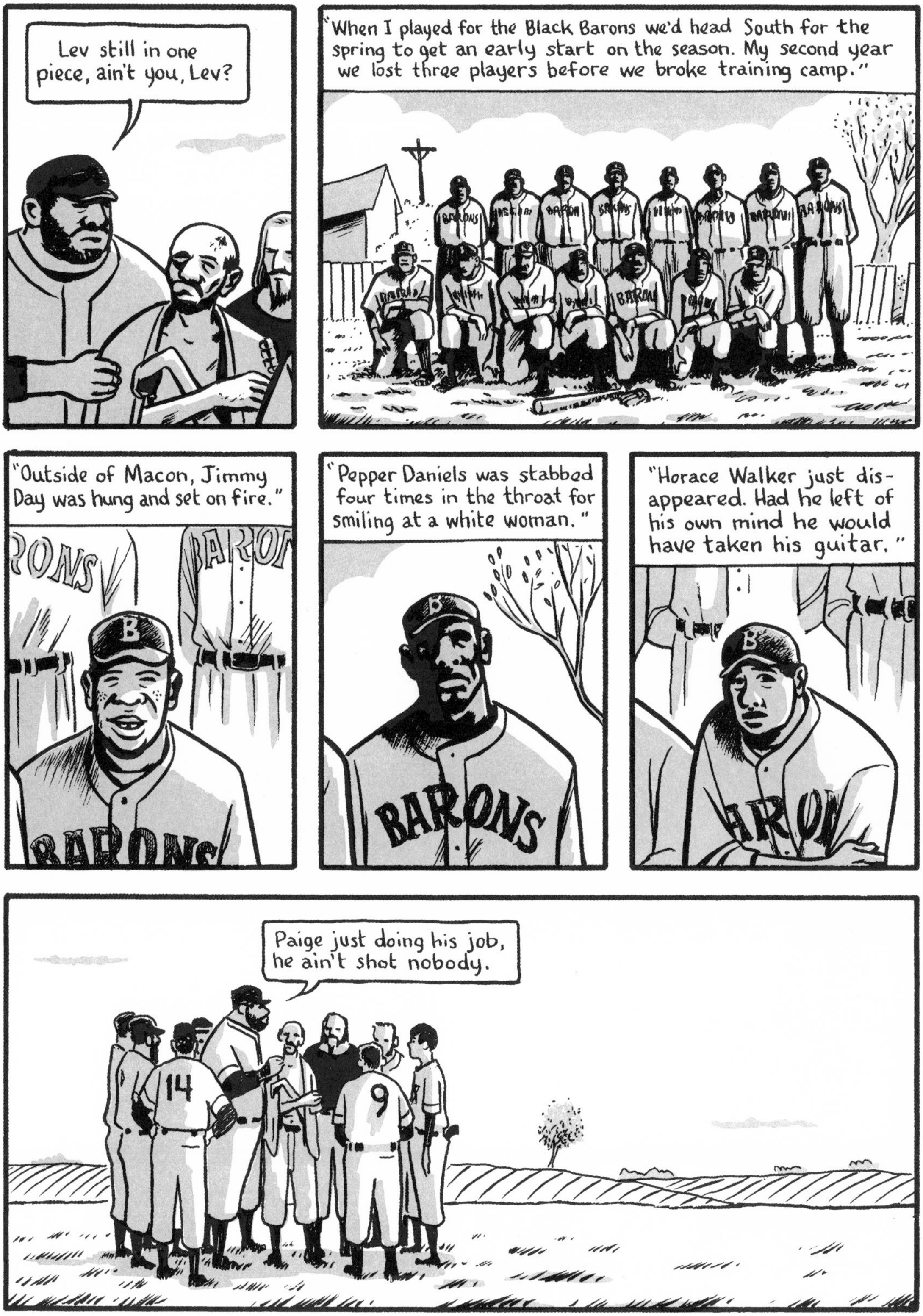
Lev still in one piece, ain't you, Lev?
"When I played for the Black Barons we'd head South for the spring to get an early start on the season. My second year we lost three players before we broke training camp."
BARONS
"Outside of Macon, Jimmy Day was hung and set on fire."
"Pepper Daniels was stabbed four times in the throat for smiling at a white woman."
BARONS
"Horace Walker just disappeared. Had he left of his own mind he would have taken his guitar."
Paige just doing his job, he ain't shot nobody.
14
9

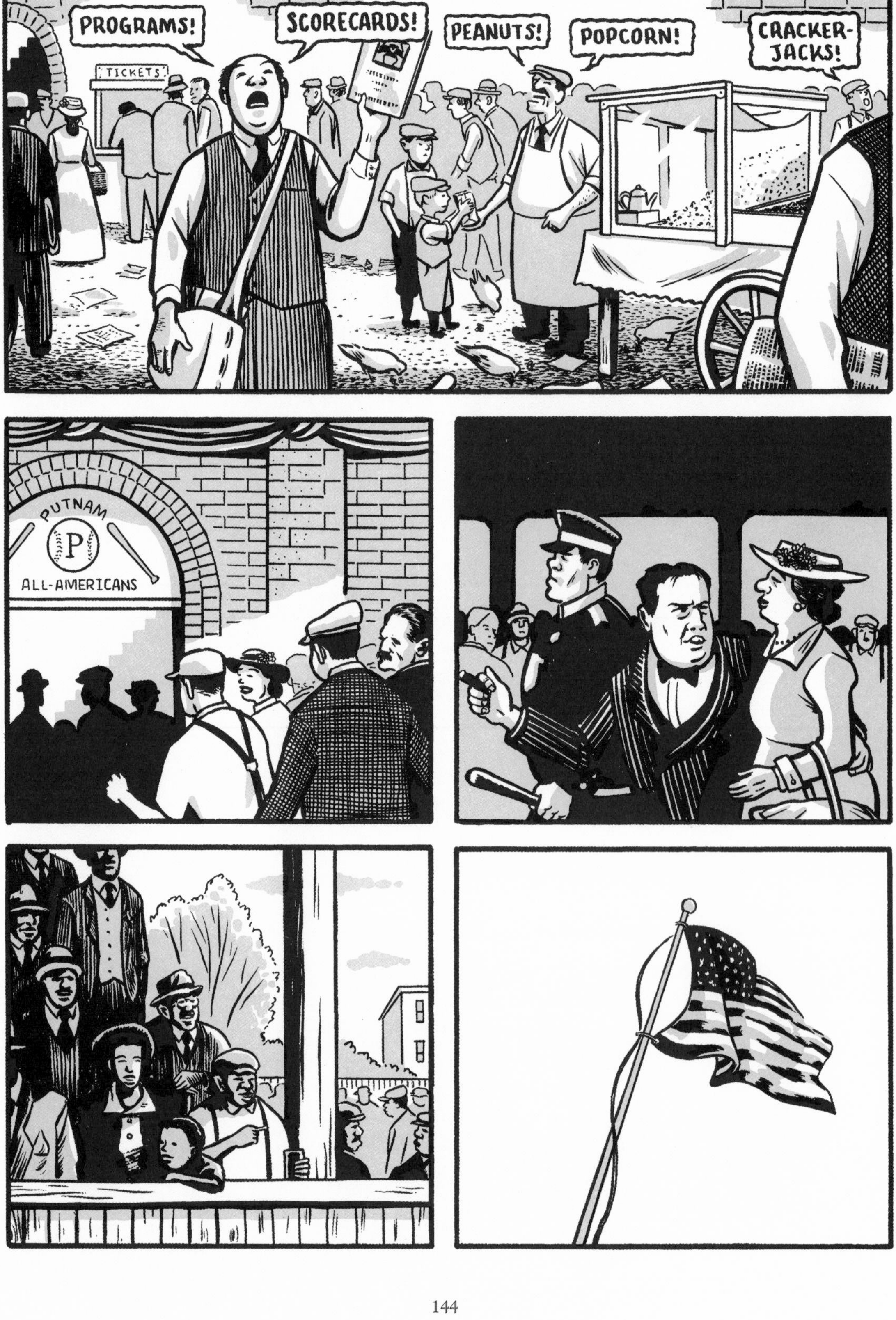
PROGRAMS!
SCORECARDS!
PEANUTS!
POPCORN!
CRACKER-JACKS!
TICKETS
PUTNAM
P
ALL-AMERICANS

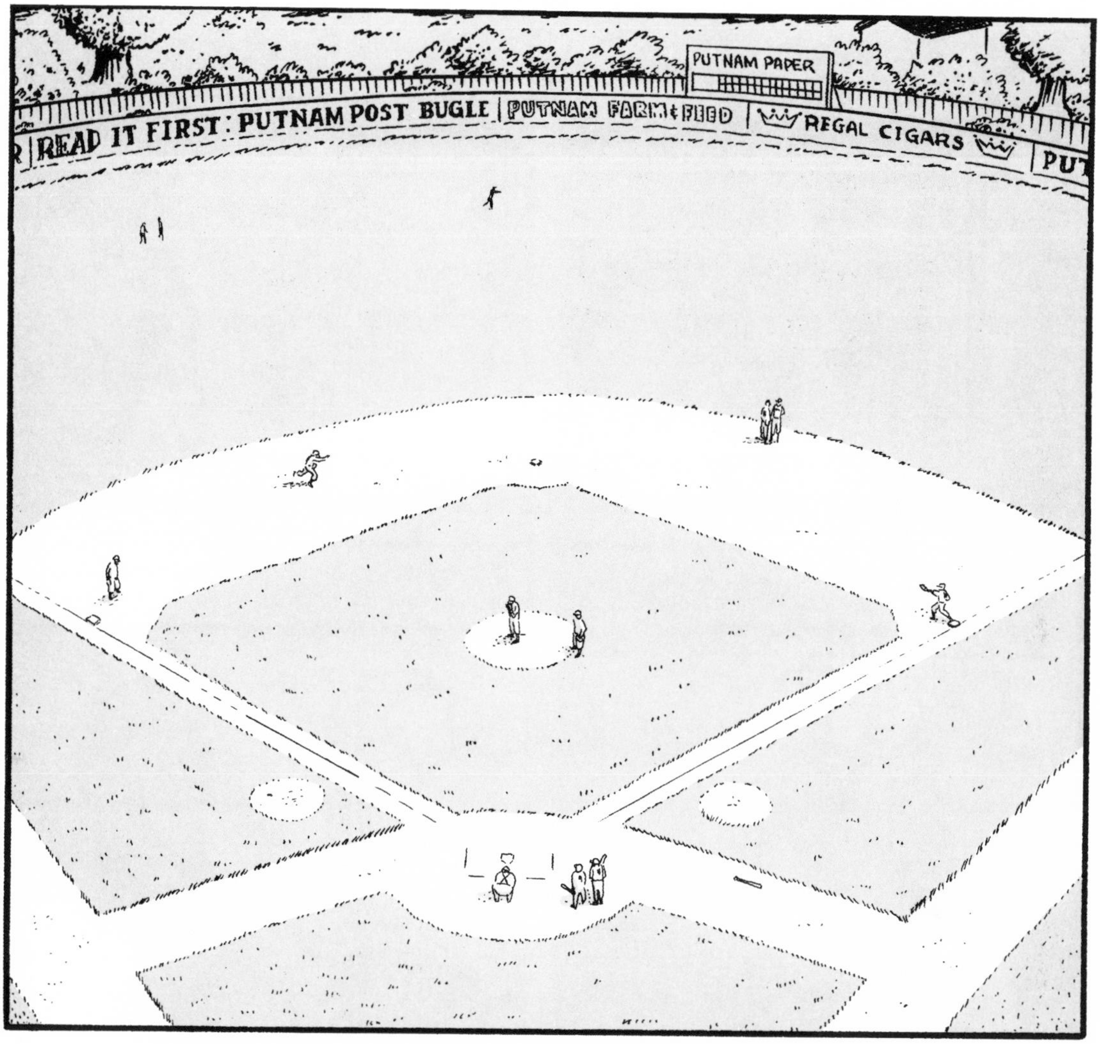
PUTNAM PAPER
READ IT FIRST: PUTNAM POST BUGLE
PUTNAM FARM & FEED
REGAL CIGARS

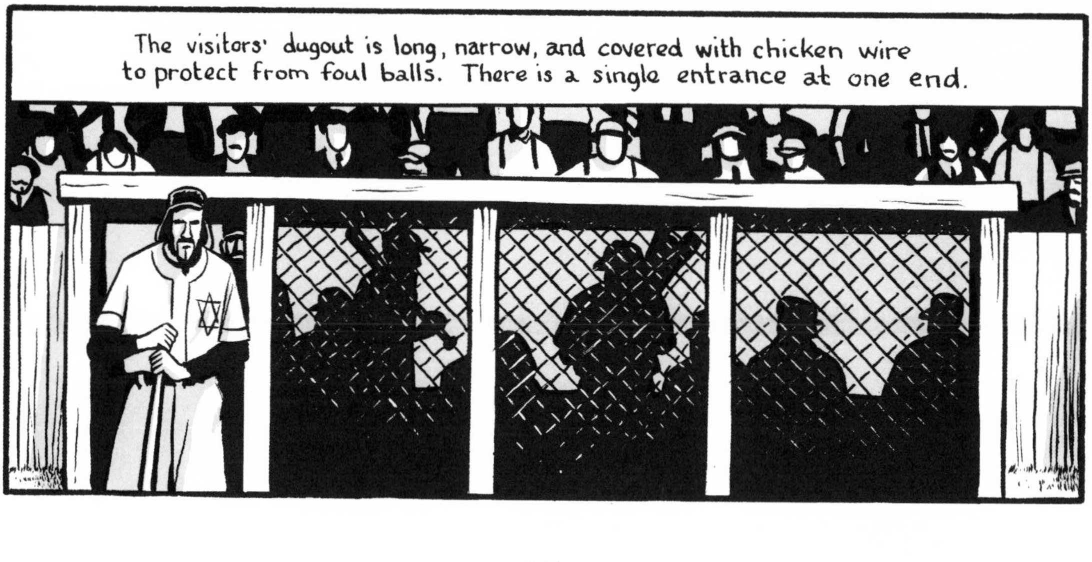
The visitors' dugout is long, narrow, and covered with chicken wire to protect from foul balls. There is a single entrance at one end.

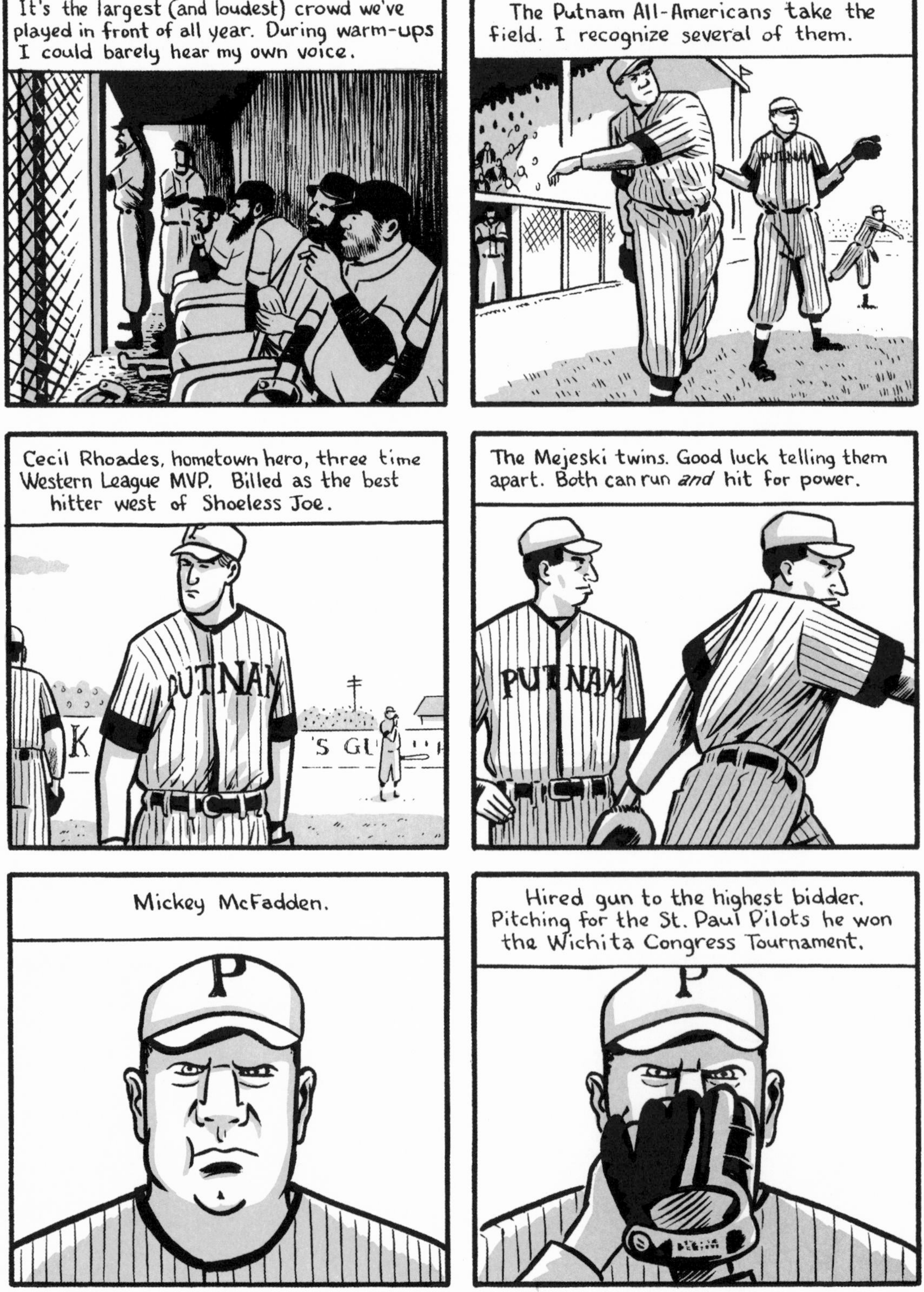
It's the largest (and loudest) crowd we've played in front of all year. During warm-ups I could barely hear my own voice.
The Putnam All-Americans take the field. I recognize several of them.
Cecil Rhoades, hometown hero, three time Western League MVP. Billed as the best hitter west of Shoeless Joe.
The Mejeski twins. Good luck telling them apart. Both can run *and* hit for power.
Mickey McFadden.
Hired gun to the highest bidder. Pitching for the St. Paul Pilots he won the Wichita Congress Tournament.

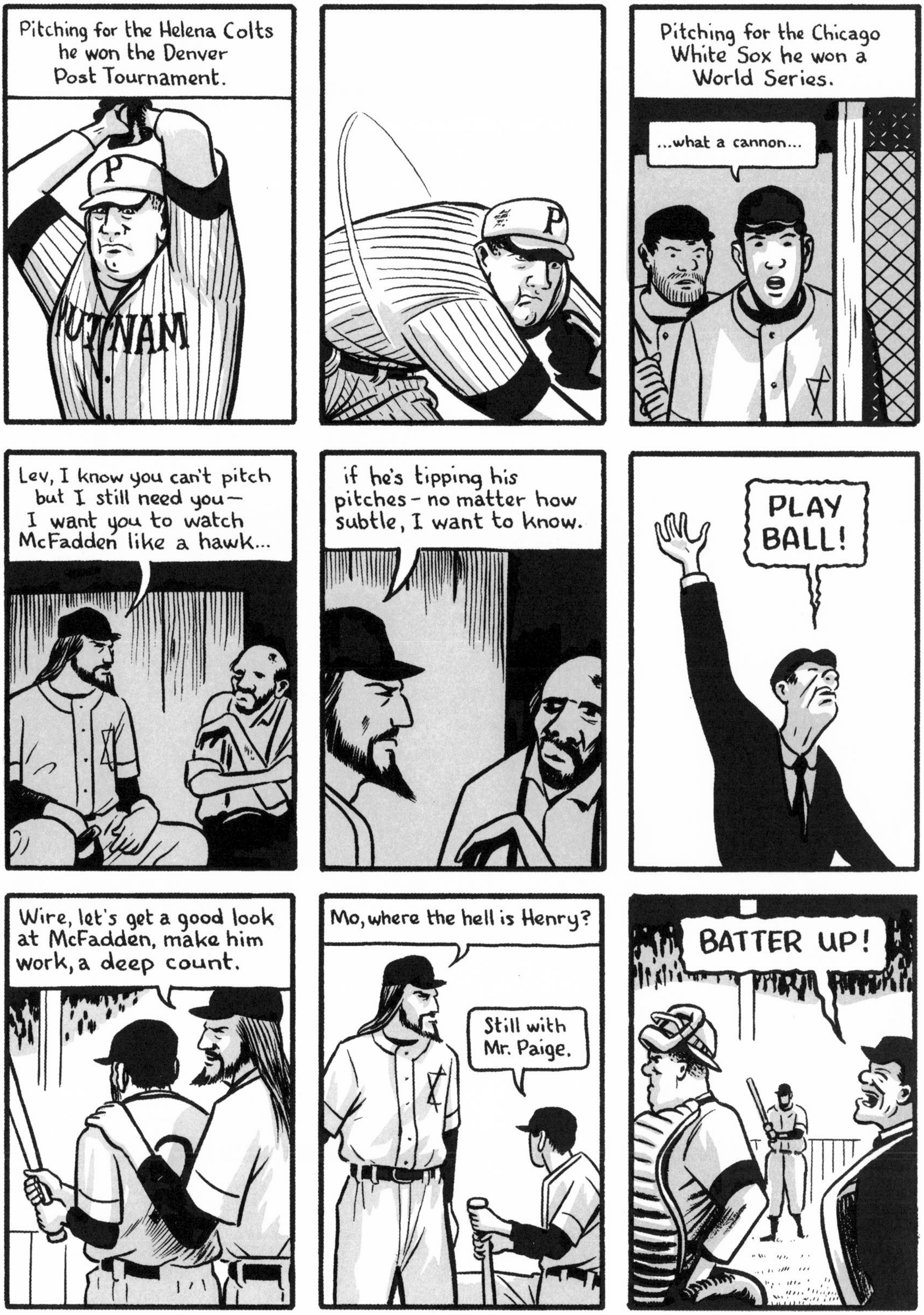
Pitching for the Helena Colts he won the Denver Post Tournament.
PUTNAM
Pitching for the Chicago White Sox he won a World Series.
...what a cannon...
Lev, I know you can't pitch but I still need you— I want you to watch McFadden like a hawk...
if he's tipping his pitches - no matter how subtle, I want to know.
PLAY BALL!
Wire, let's get a good look at McFadden, make him work, a deep count.
Mo, where the hell is Henry?
Still with Mr. Paige.
BATTER UP!

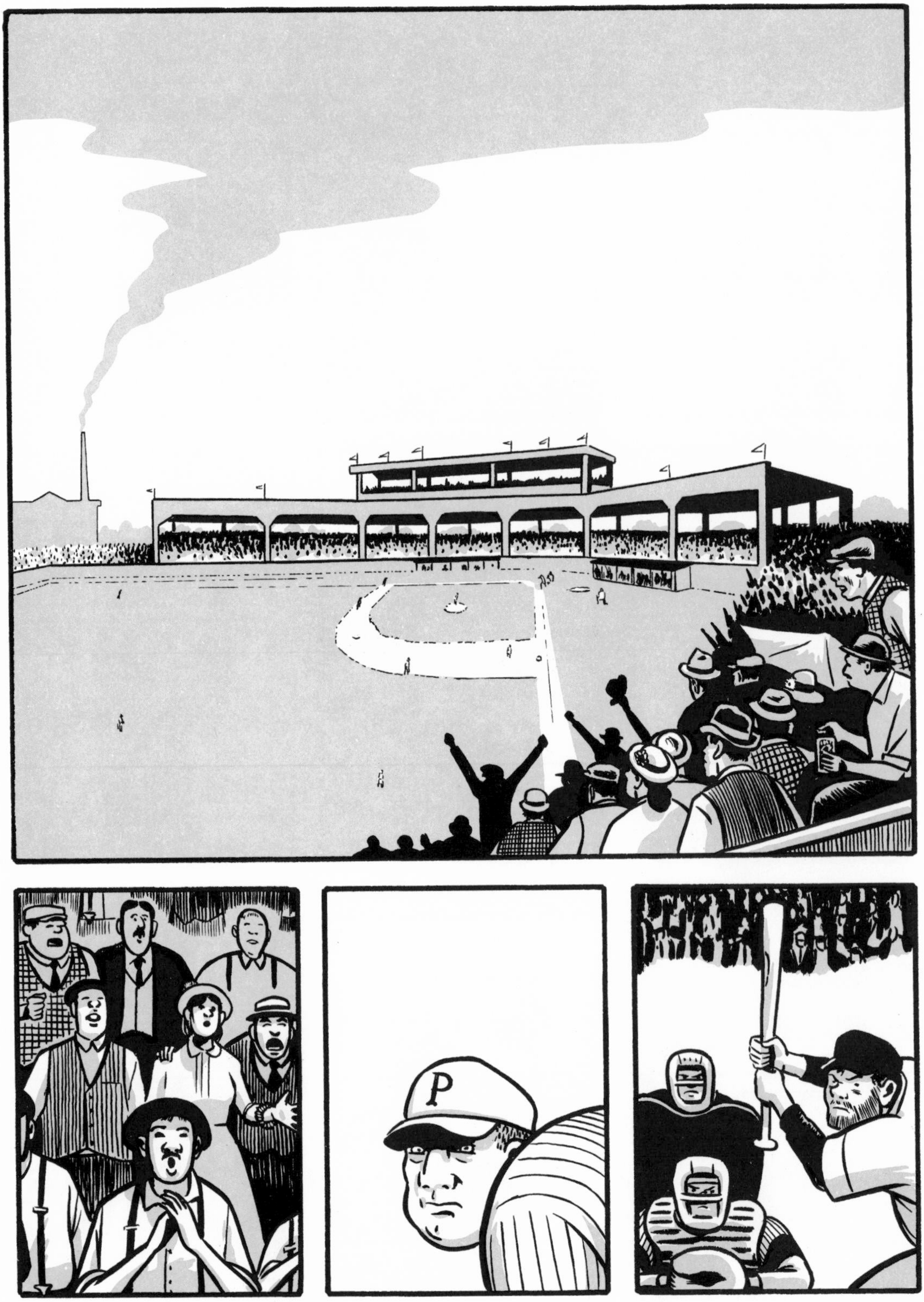

STRIKE ONE!

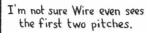
I'm not sure Wire even sees the first two pitches.

STRIKE TWO!

Wire steps out of the box as the crowd grows louder, anticipating a strikeout.

McFadden wastes a pitch high. Wire doesn't chase. 1 and 2.

Next pitch is inside heat. Wire fouls it off (barely).

Fooled badly on a vicious breaking ball. Strike three.

So much for a deep count. Mo steps tentatively towards the batter's box.

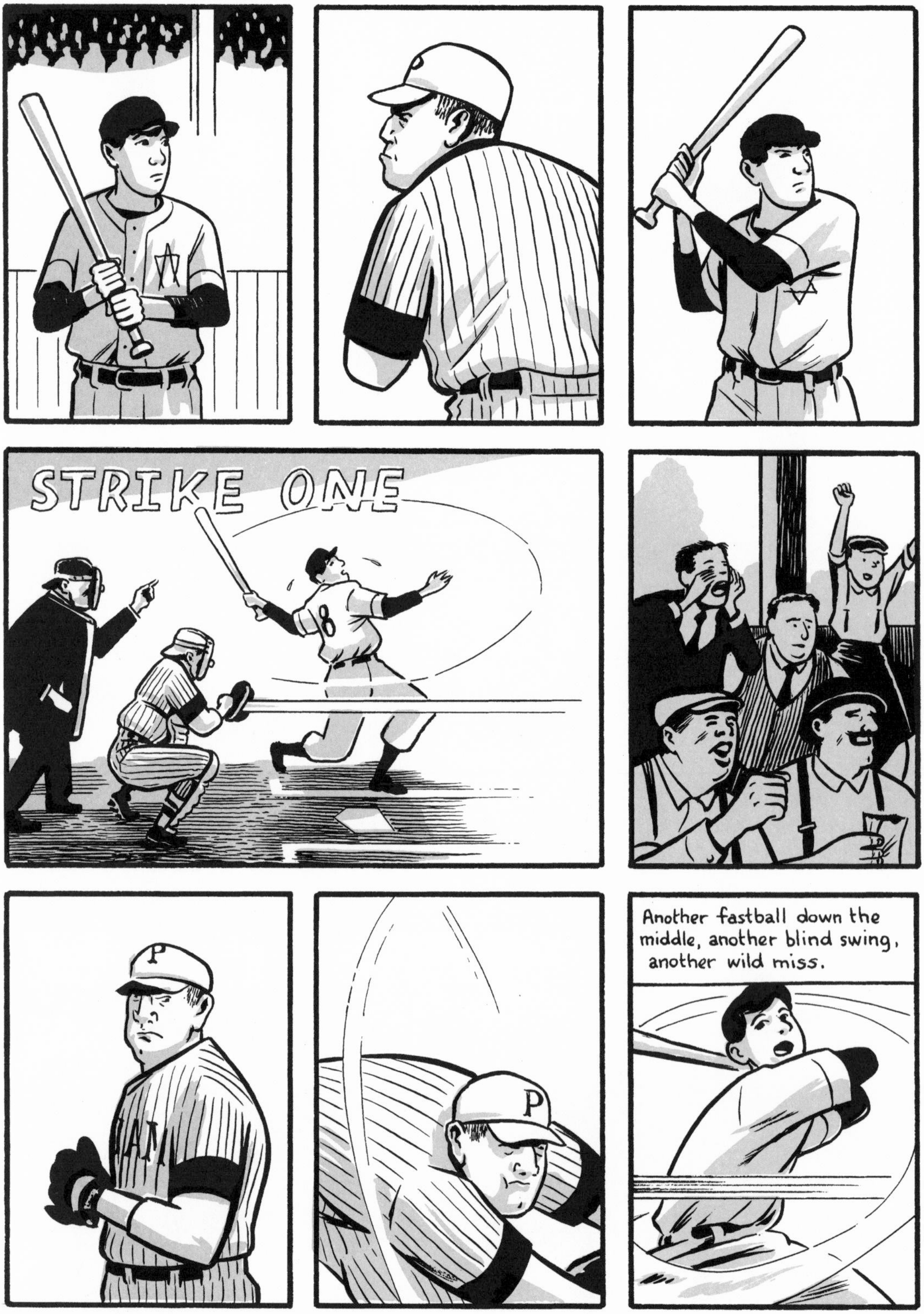
STRIKE ONE
Another fastball down the middle, another blind swing, another wild miss.

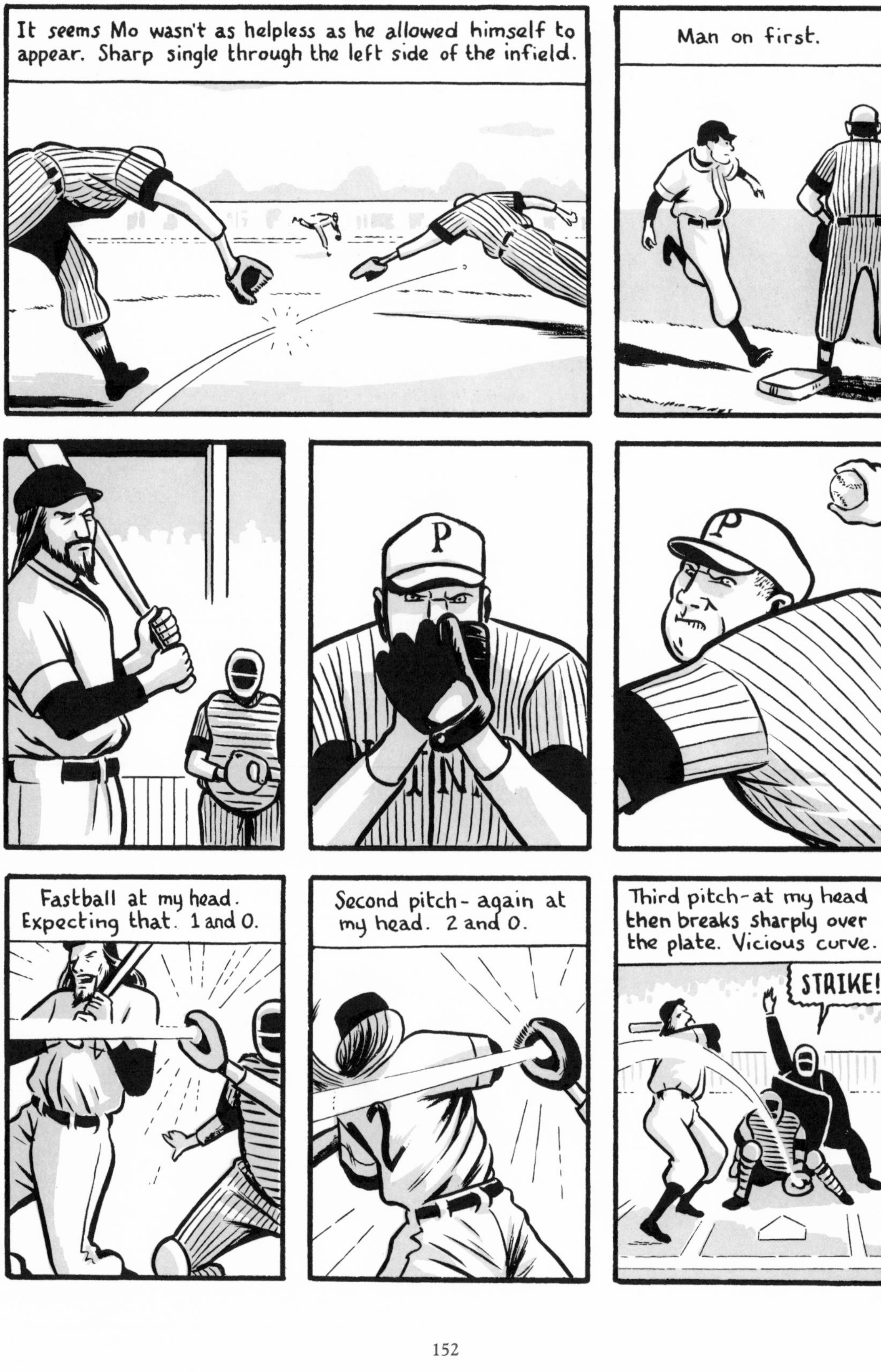
It seems Mo wasn't as helpless as he allowed himself to appear. Sharp single through the left side of the infield.
Man on first.
Fastball at my head. Expecting that. 1 and 0.
Second pitch - again at my head. 2 and 0.
Third pitch - at my head then breaks sharply over the plate. Vicious curve.
STRIKE!

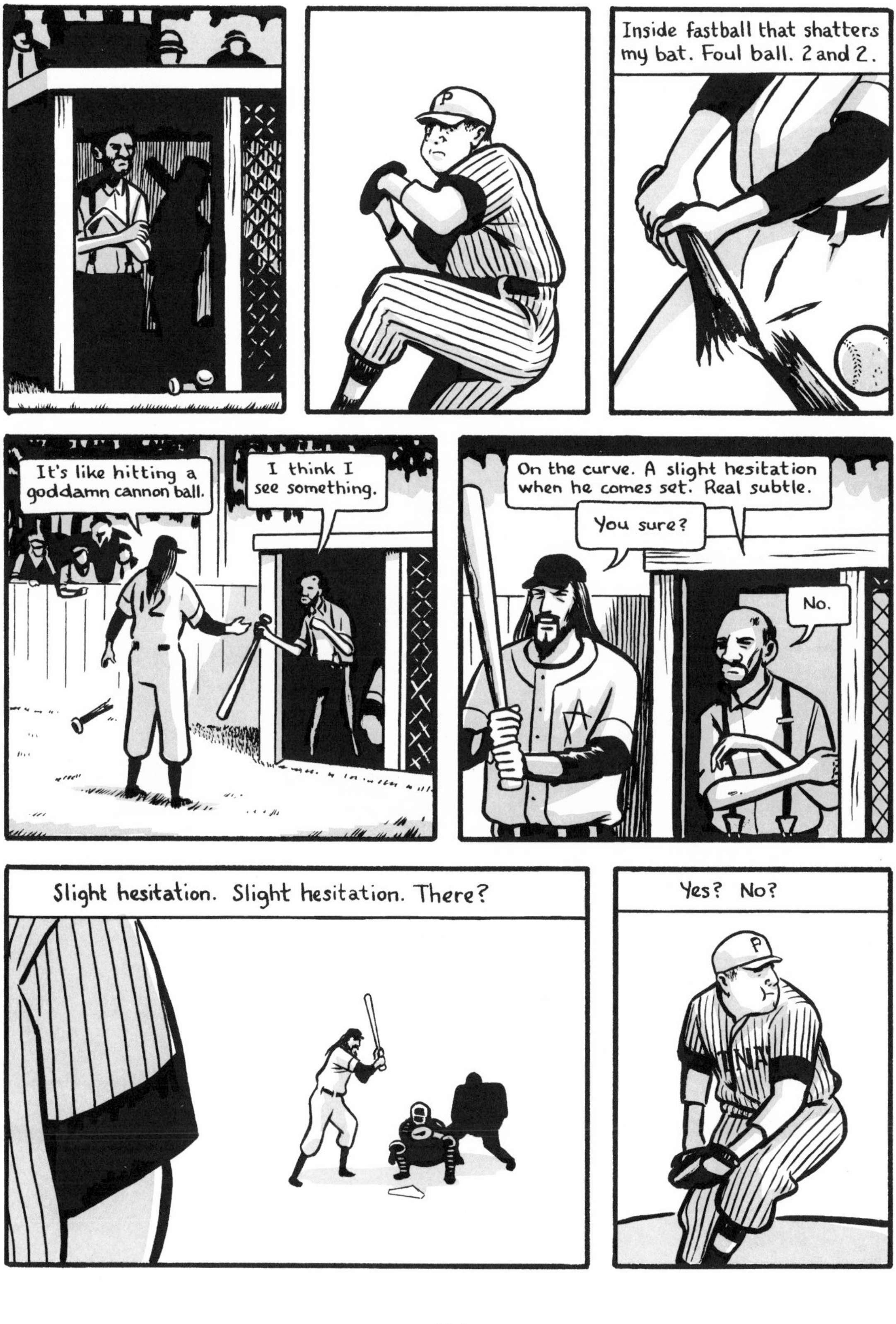
Inside fastball that shatters my bat. Foul ball. 2 and 2.
It's like hitting a goddamn cannon ball.
I think I see something.
On the curve. A slight hesitation when he comes set. Real subtle.
You sure?
No.
Slight hesitation. Slight hesitation. There?
Yes? No?

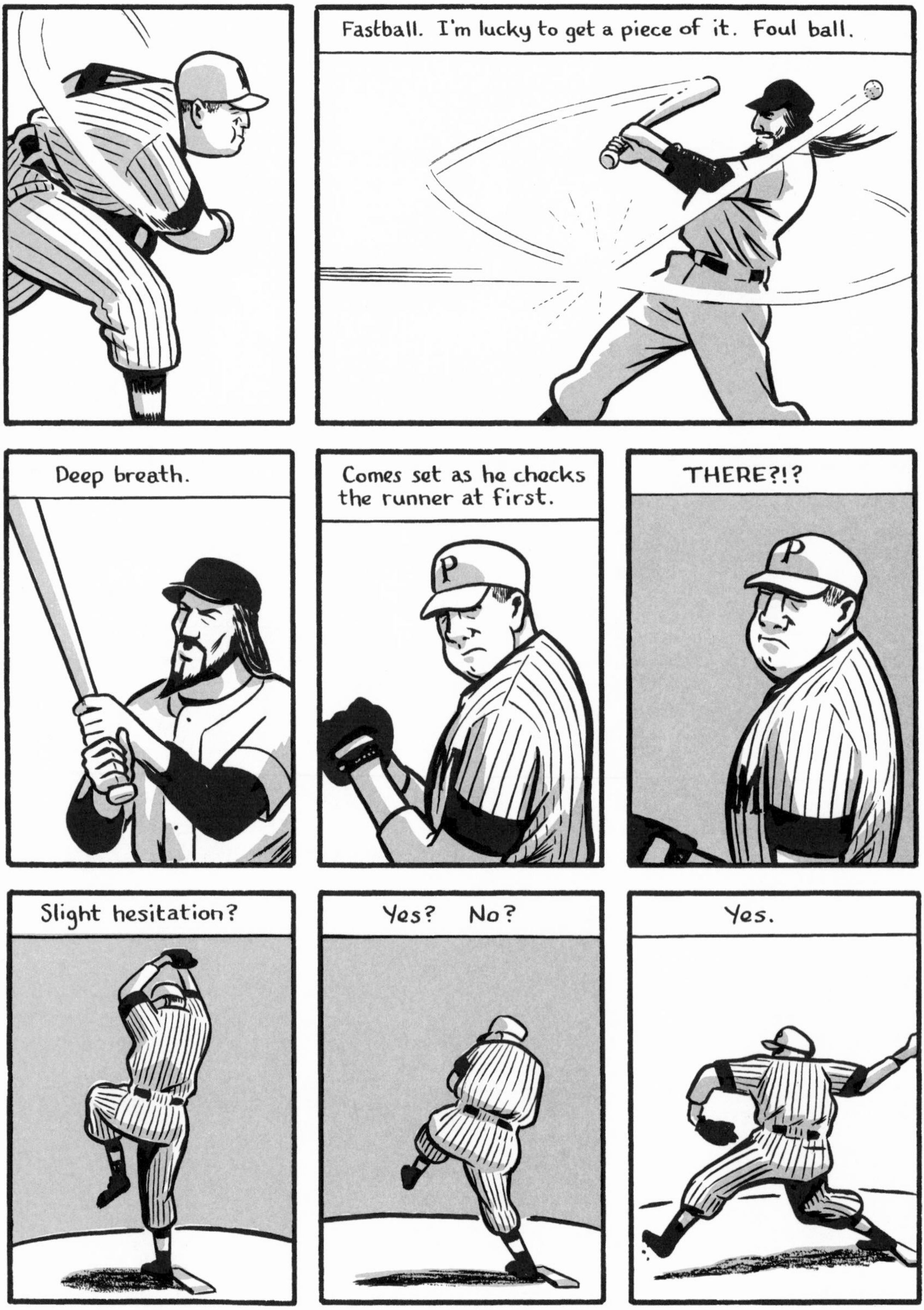
Fastball. I'm lucky to get a piece of it. Foul ball.
Deep breath.
Comes set as he checks the runner at first.
THERE?!?
Slight hesitation?
Yes? No?
Yes.

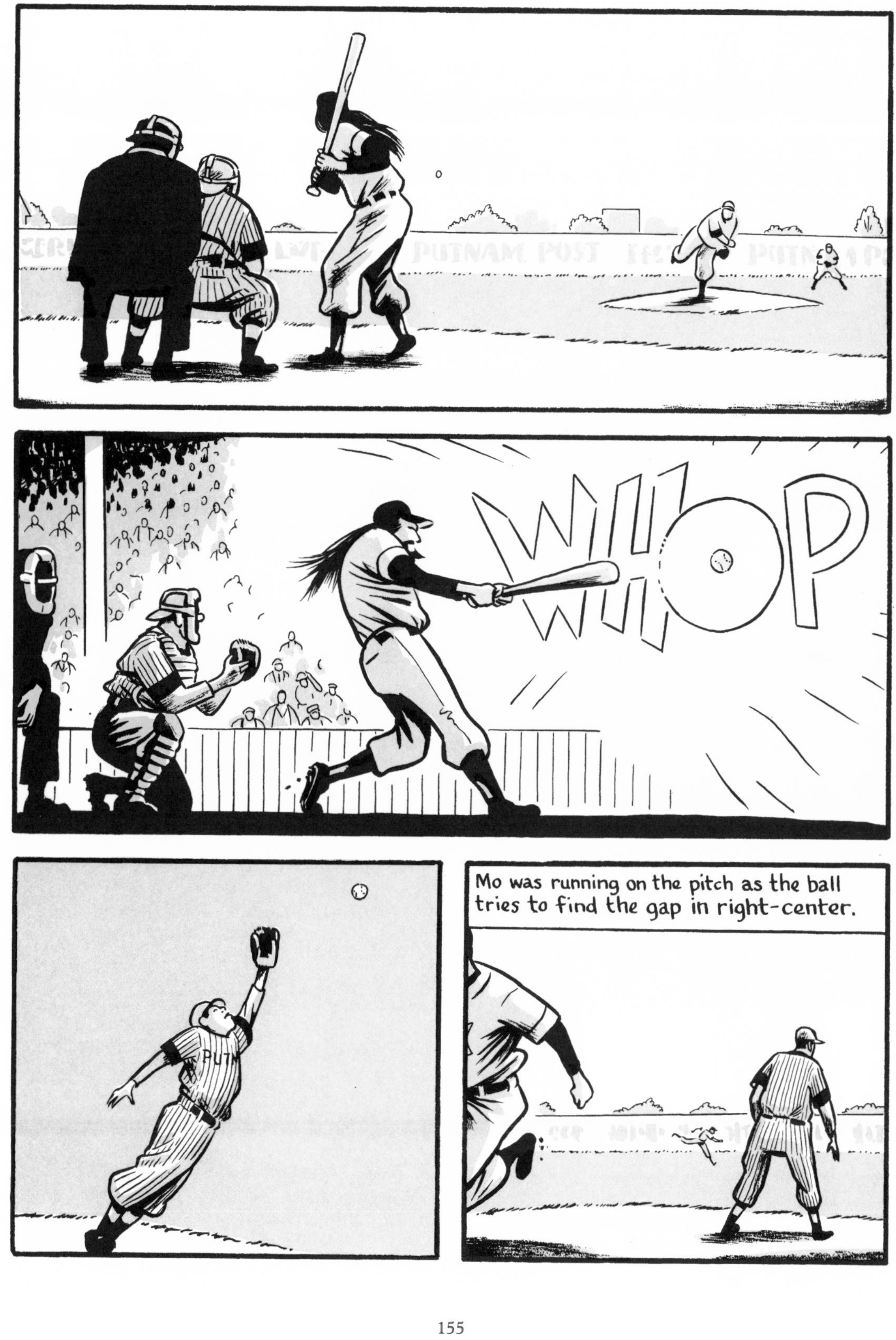
PUTNAM POST
WHOP
Mo was running on the pitch as the ball tries to find the gap in right-center.

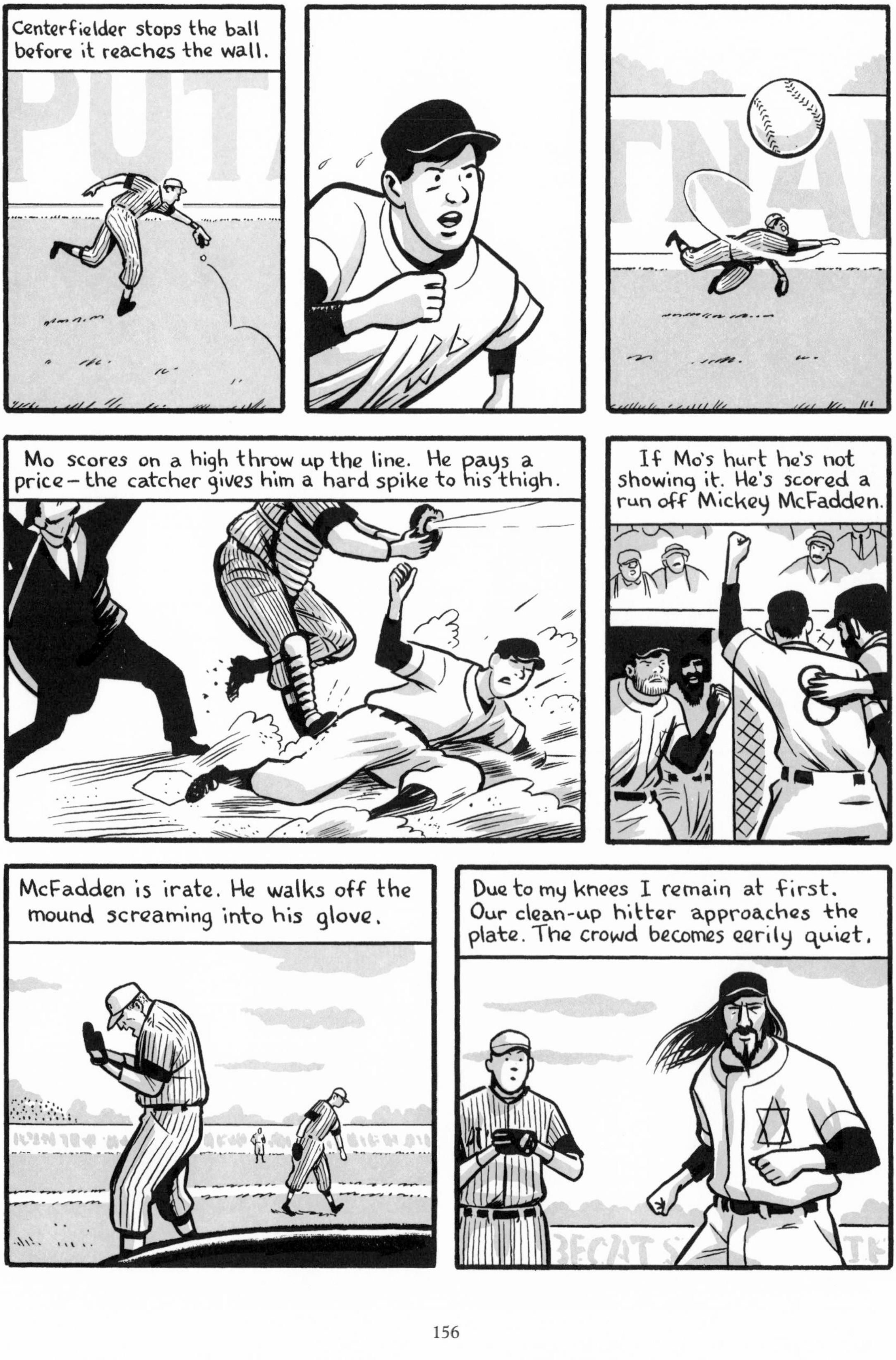

Centerfielder stops the ball before it reaches the wall.
Mo scores on a high throw up the line. He pays a price — the catcher gives him a hard spike to his thigh.
If Mo's hurt he's not showing it. He's scored a run off Mickey McFadden.
McFadden is irate. He walks off the mound screaming into his glove.
Due to my knees I remain at first. Our clean-up hitter approaches the plate. The crowd becomes eerily quiet.

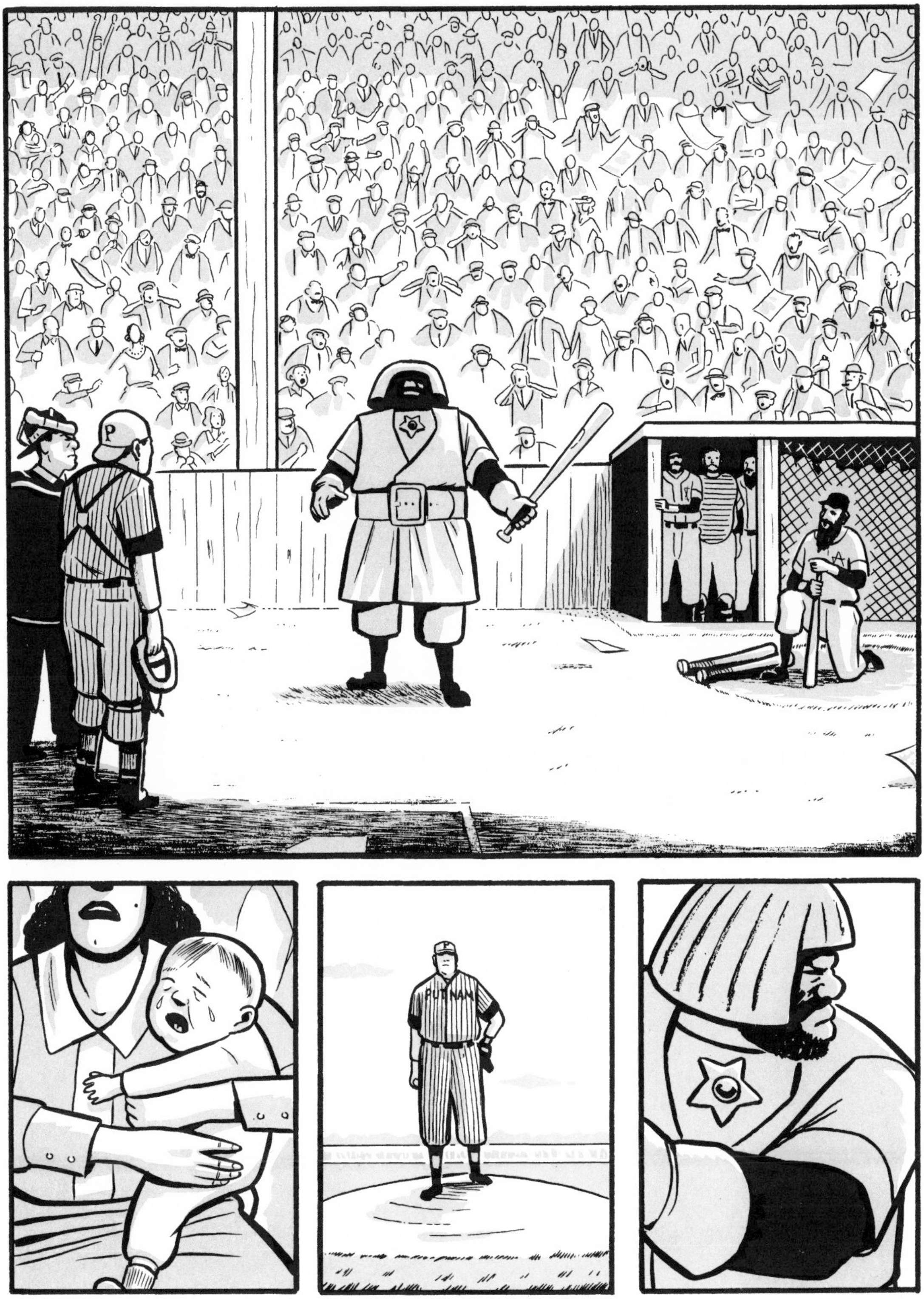

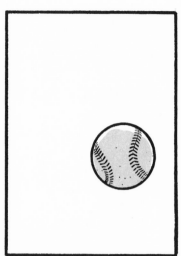

A squib, right
back to the mound.

McFadden fires to second.

Second to first.

Double play. Inning over.

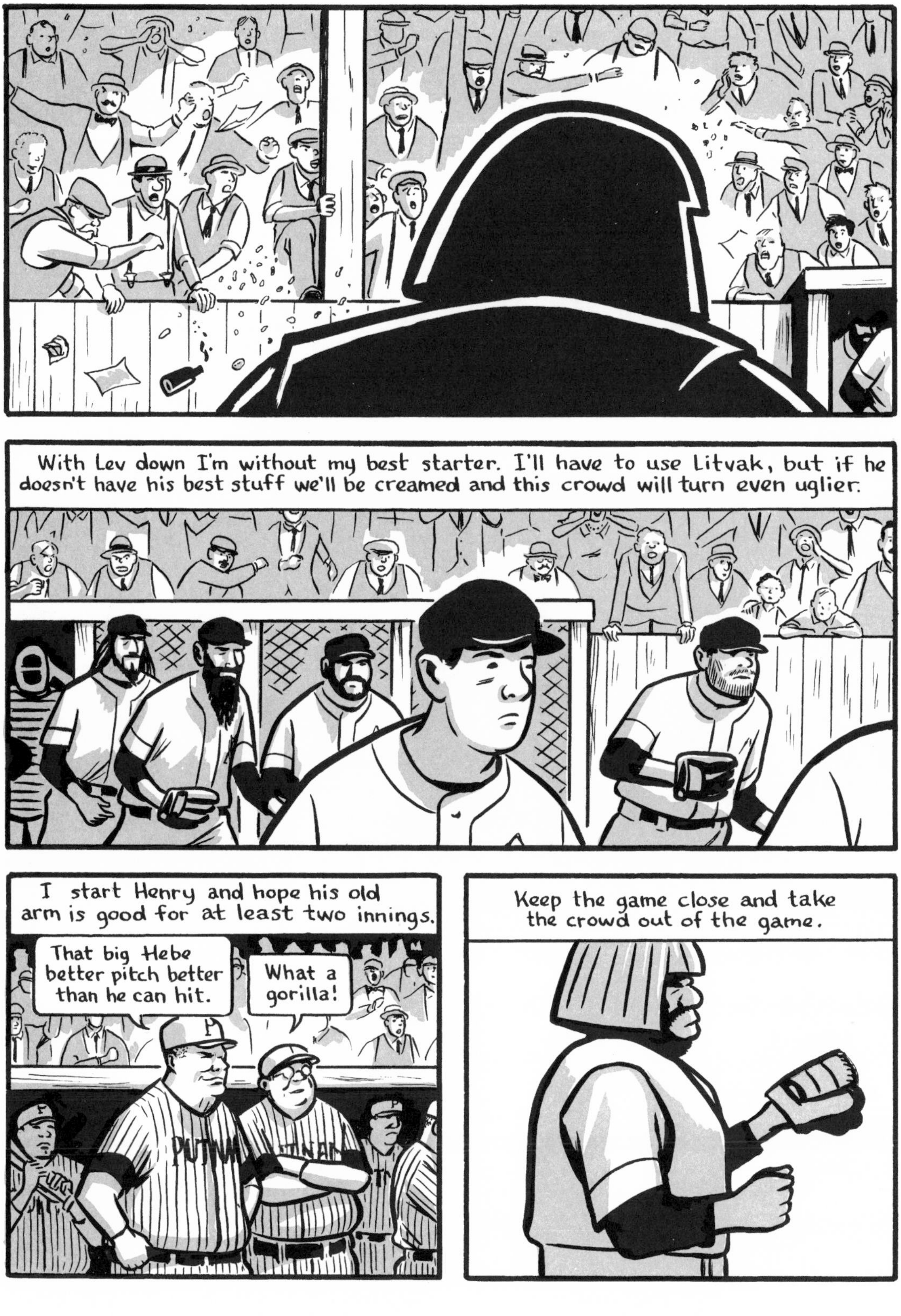

With Lev down I'm without my best starter. I'll have to use Litvak, but if he doesn't have his best stuff we'll be creamed and this crowd will turn even uglier.
I start Henry and hope his old arm is good for at least two innings.
That big Hebe better pitch better than he can hit.
What a gorilla!
Keep the game close and take the crowd out of the game.

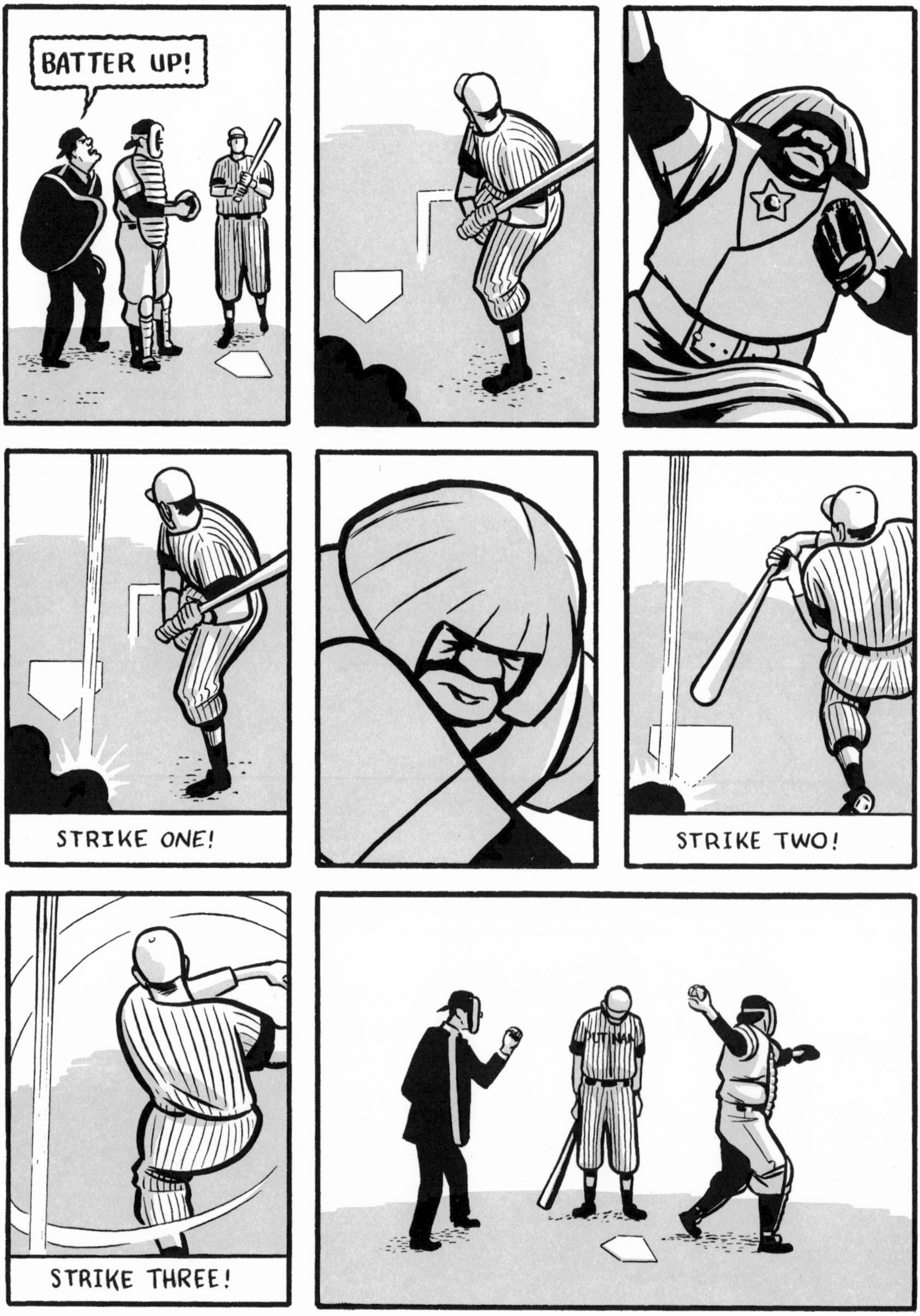

BATTER UP!
STRIKE ONE!
STRIKE TWO!
STRIKE THREE!

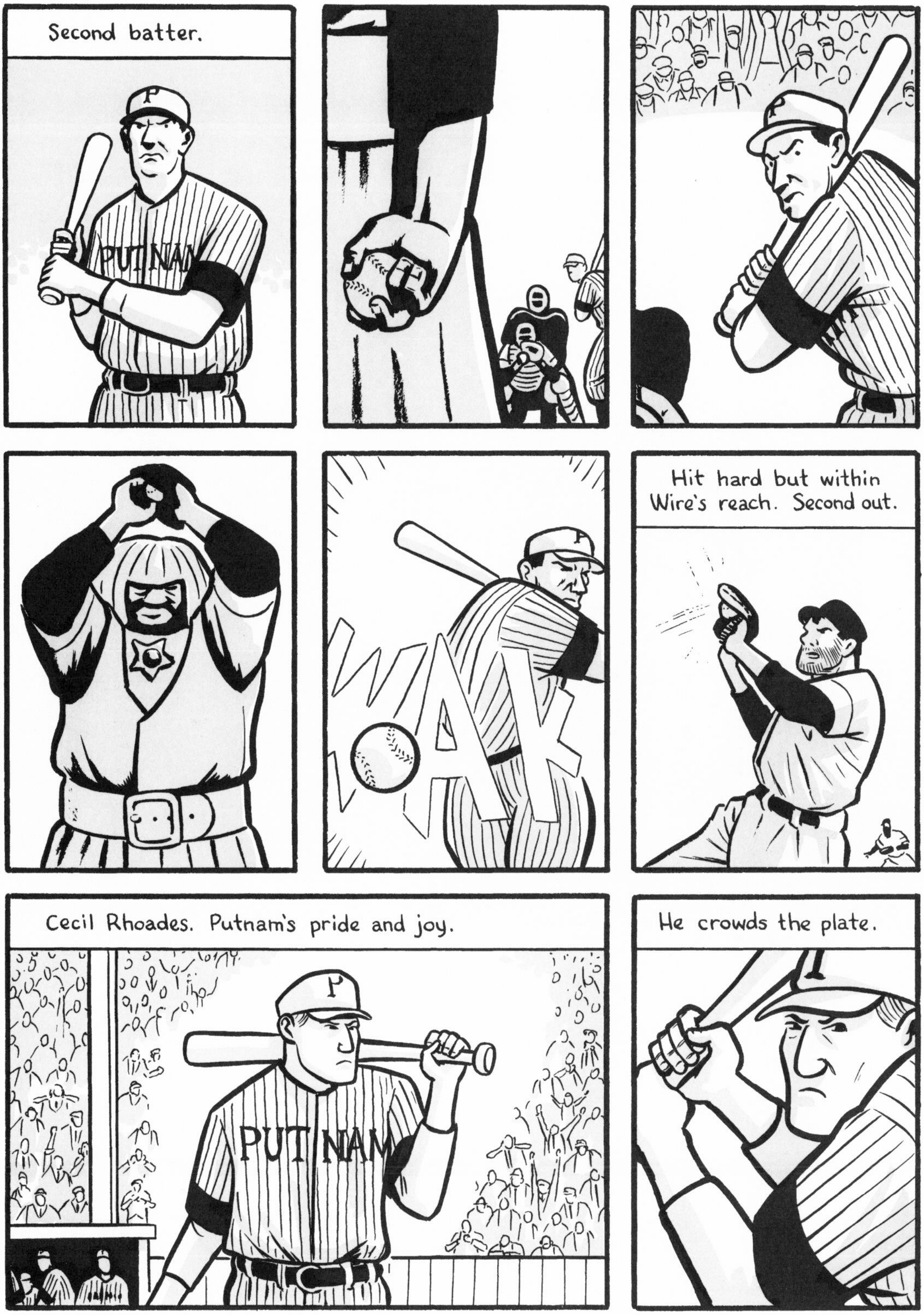
Second batter.
PUTNAM
WAK
Hit hard but within Wire's reach. Second out.
Cecil Rhoades. Putnam's pride and joy.
PUTNAM
He crowds the plate.

The first pitch-in tight, inches from Rhoades's chin. Doesn't even flinch. 1 and 0.

Another inside fastball is called for.

Go on, get out of here...

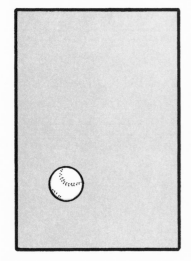

Four hundred footer, but pulled foul. 1 and 1.

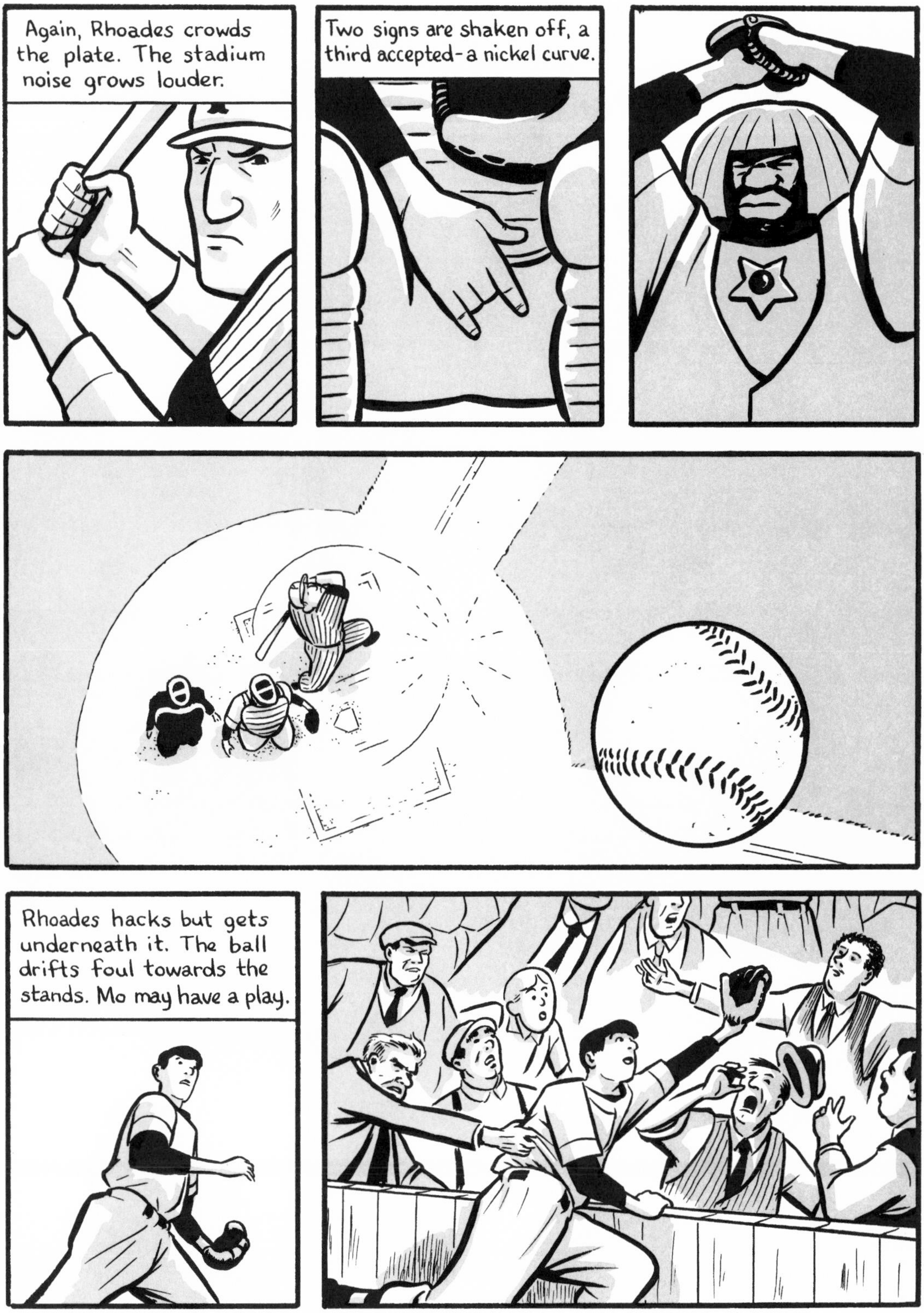
Again, Rhoades crowds the plate. The stadium noise grows louder.
Two signs are shaken off, a third accepted-a nickel curve.
Rhoades hacks but gets underneath it. The ball drifts foul towards the stands. Mo may have a play.

GO HOME, JEWS!

GET T[...]
OUT O[...]

They took my damn glove...

You alright, Mo? You hurt?!

I WANT MY DAMN MITT!

HE WAS PULLED INTO THE CROWD! THAT'S INTERFERENCE!

HE JUMPED INTO THE STANDS!

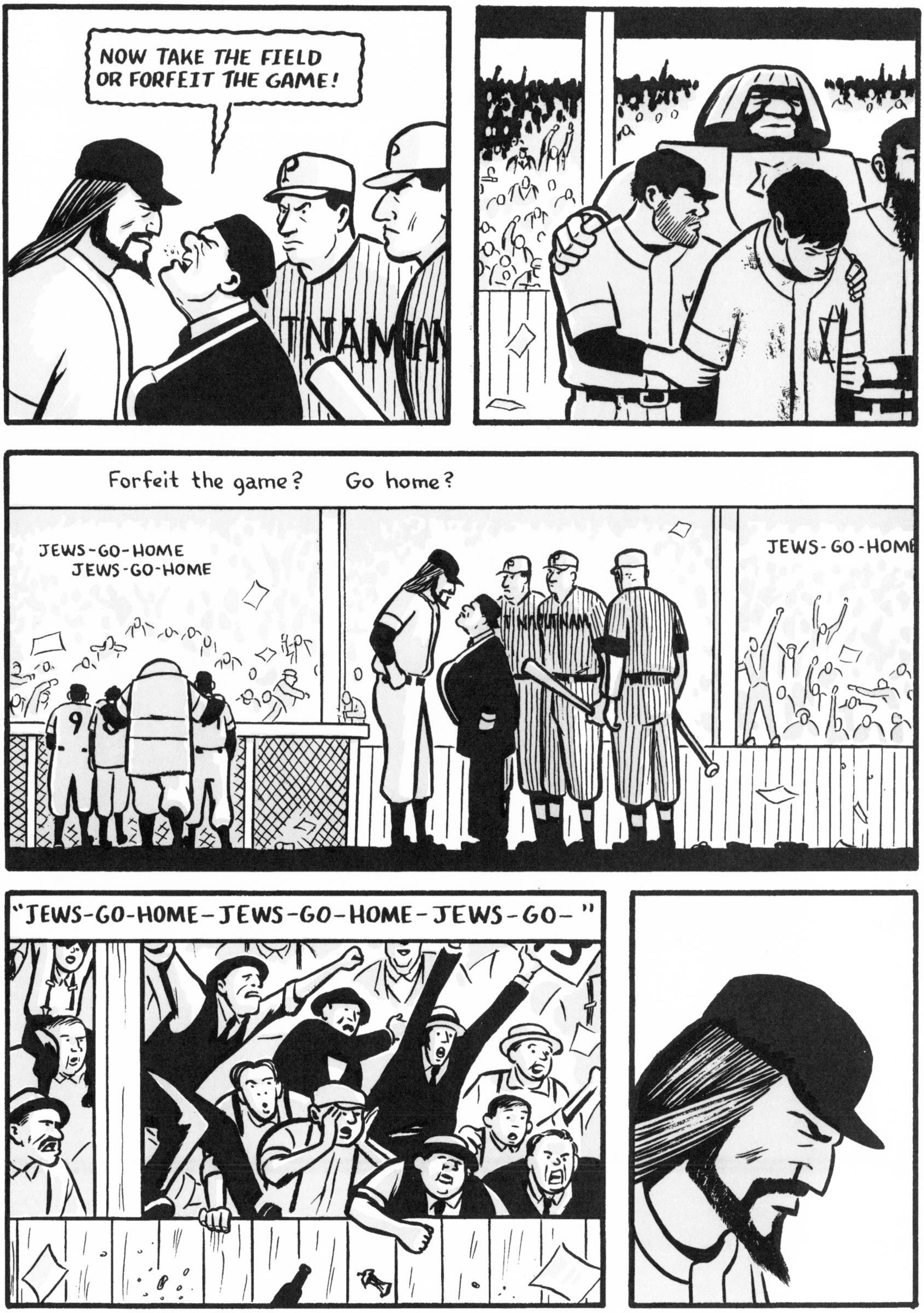
NOW TAKE THE FIELD OR FORFEIT THE GAME!
Forfeit the game? Go home?
JEWS-GO-HOME
JEWS-GO-HOME
JEWS-GO-HOME
"JEWS-GO-HOME-JEWS-GO-HOME-JEWS-GO-"

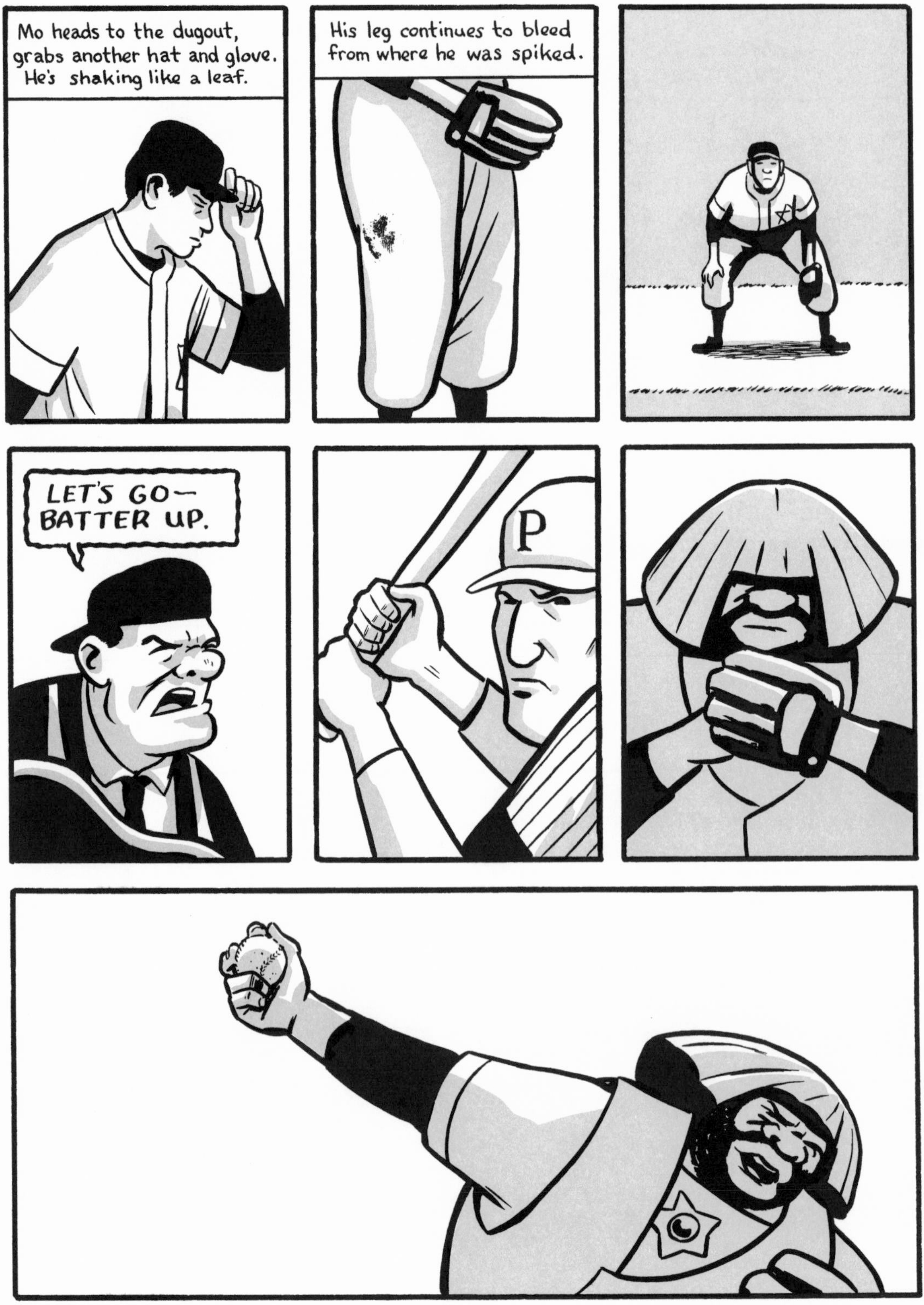
Mo heads to the dugout, grabs another hat and glove. He's shaking like a leaf.
His leg continues to bleed from where he was spiked.
LET'S GO— BATTER UP.
P

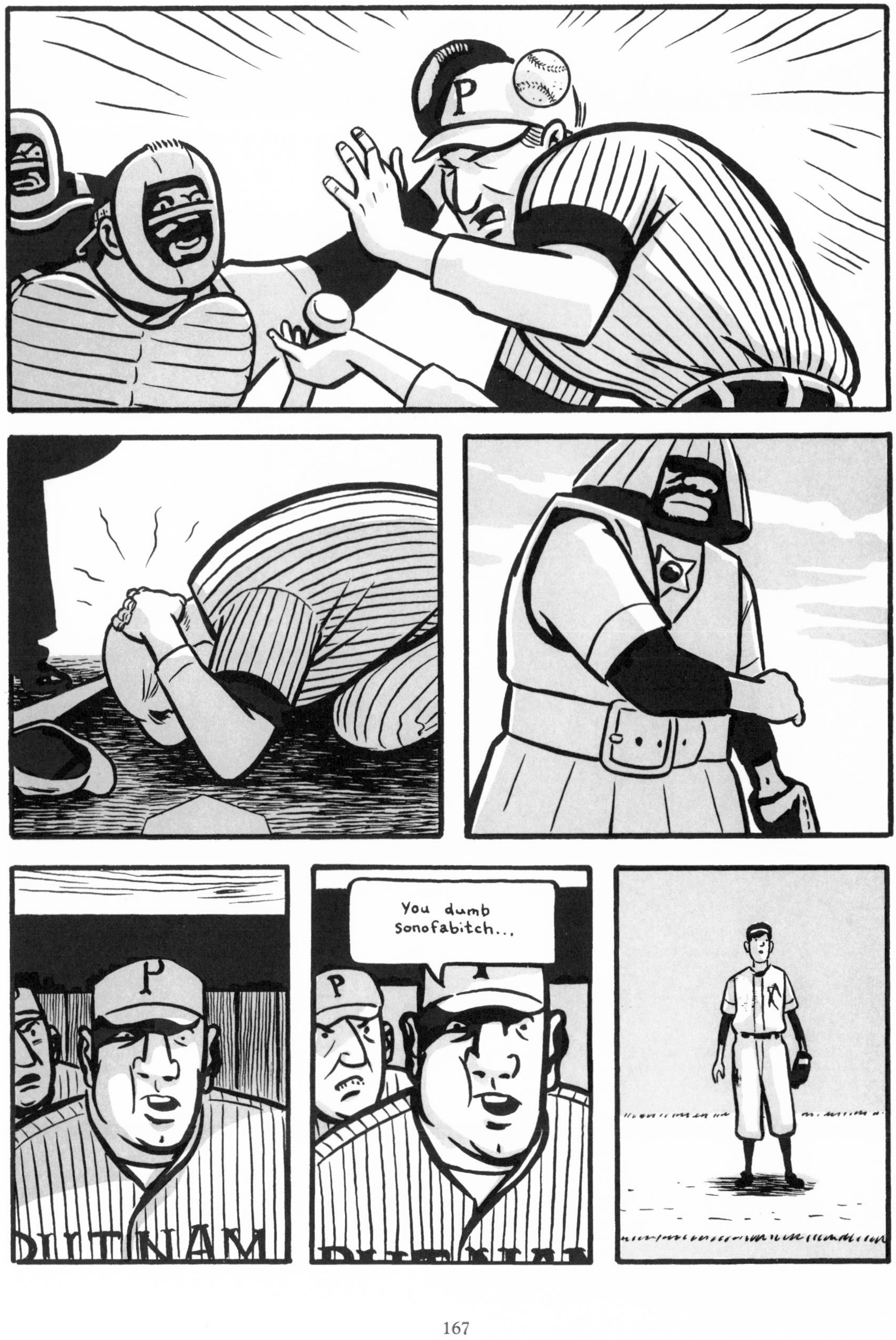
You dumb sonofabitch...

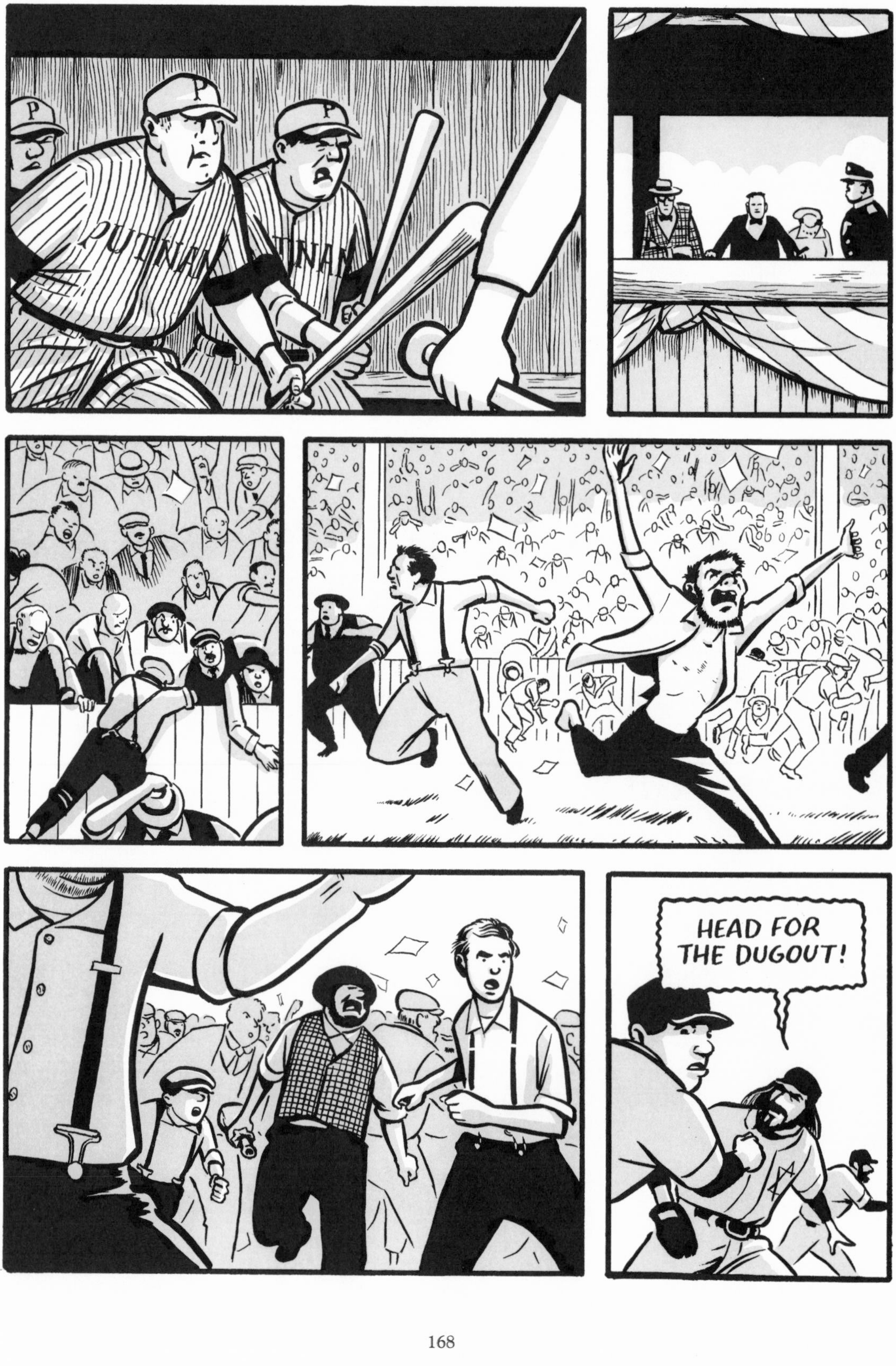
PUTNAM
HEAD FOR THE DUGOUT!

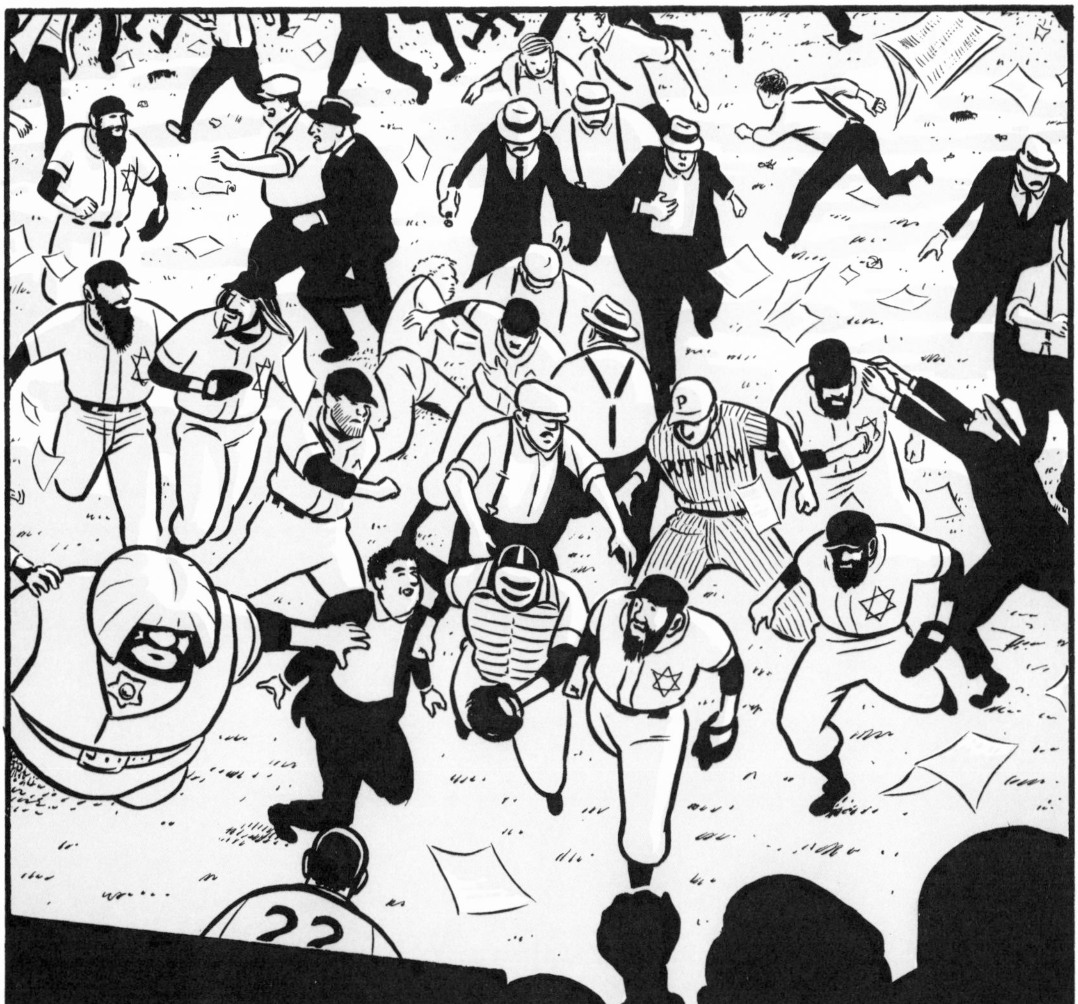

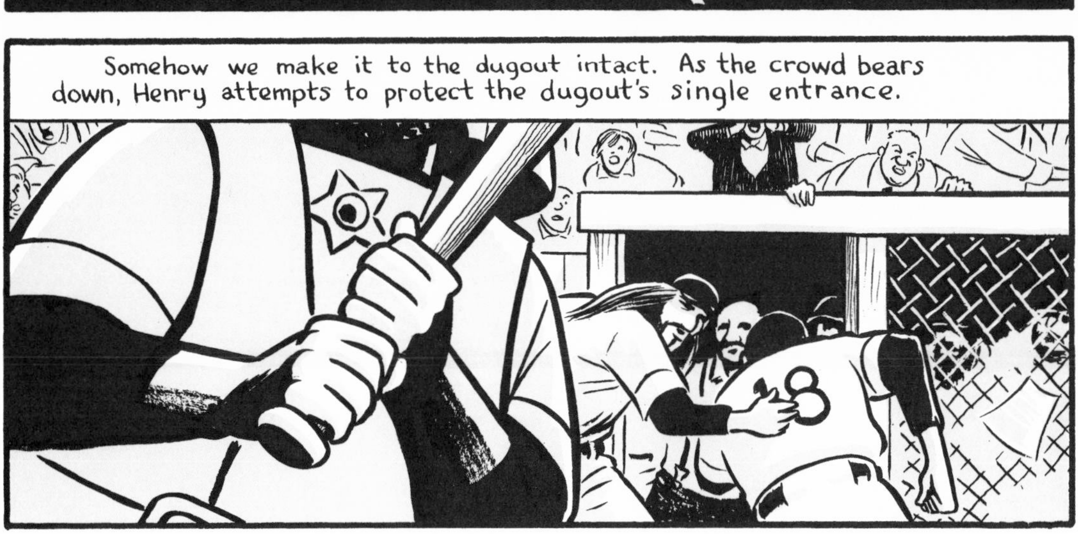
Somehow we make it to the dugout intact. As the crowd bears down, Henry attempts to protect the dugout's single entrance.

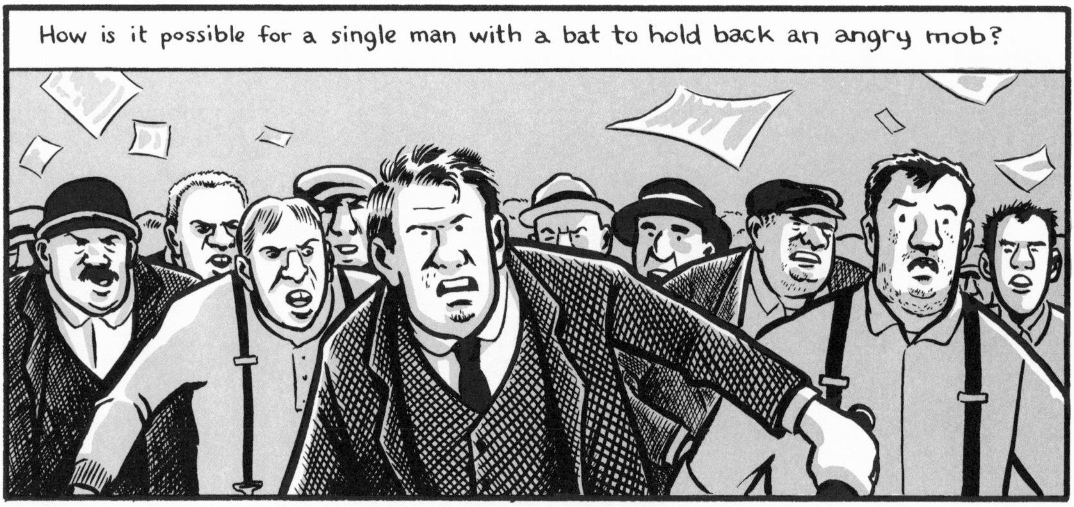
How is it possible for a single man with a bat to hold back an angry mob?

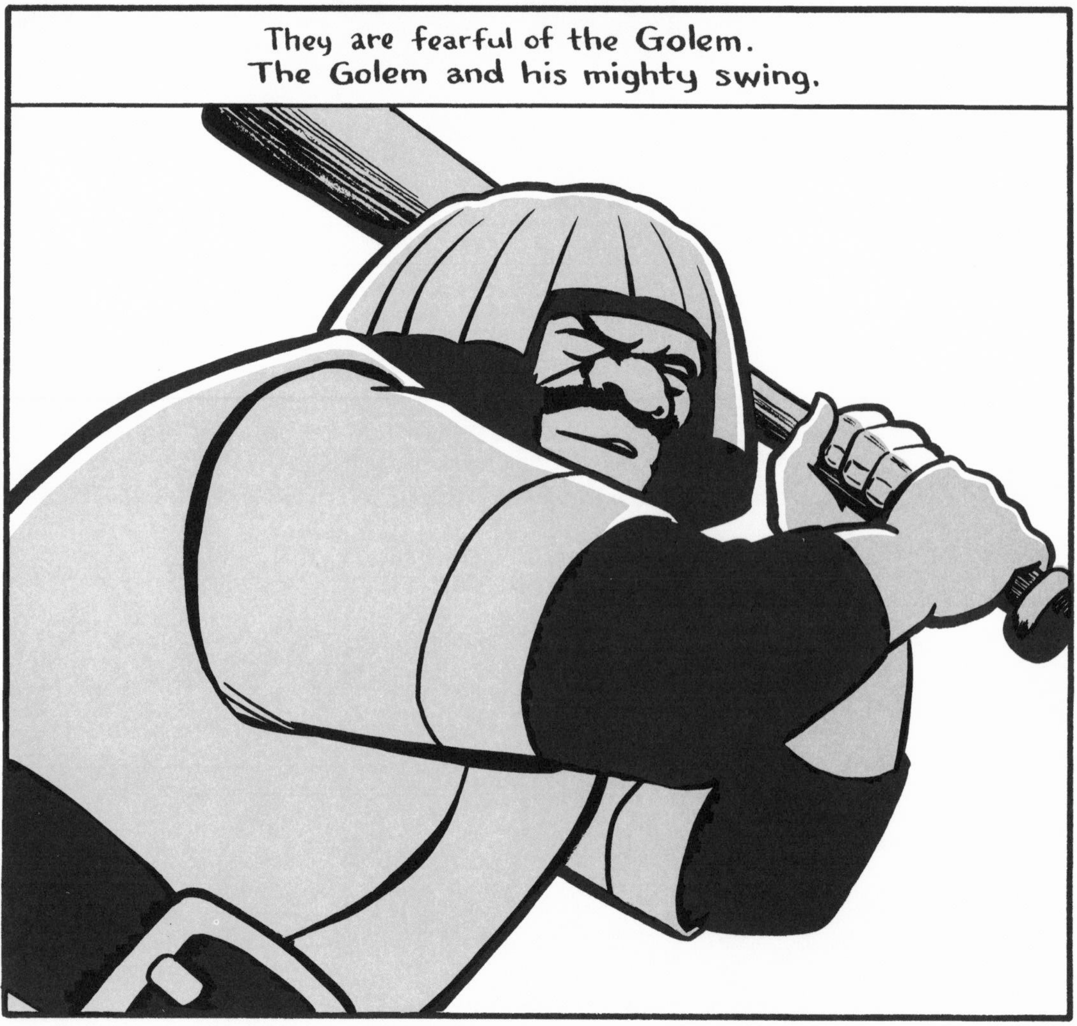
They are fearful of the Golem.
The Golem and his mighty swing.

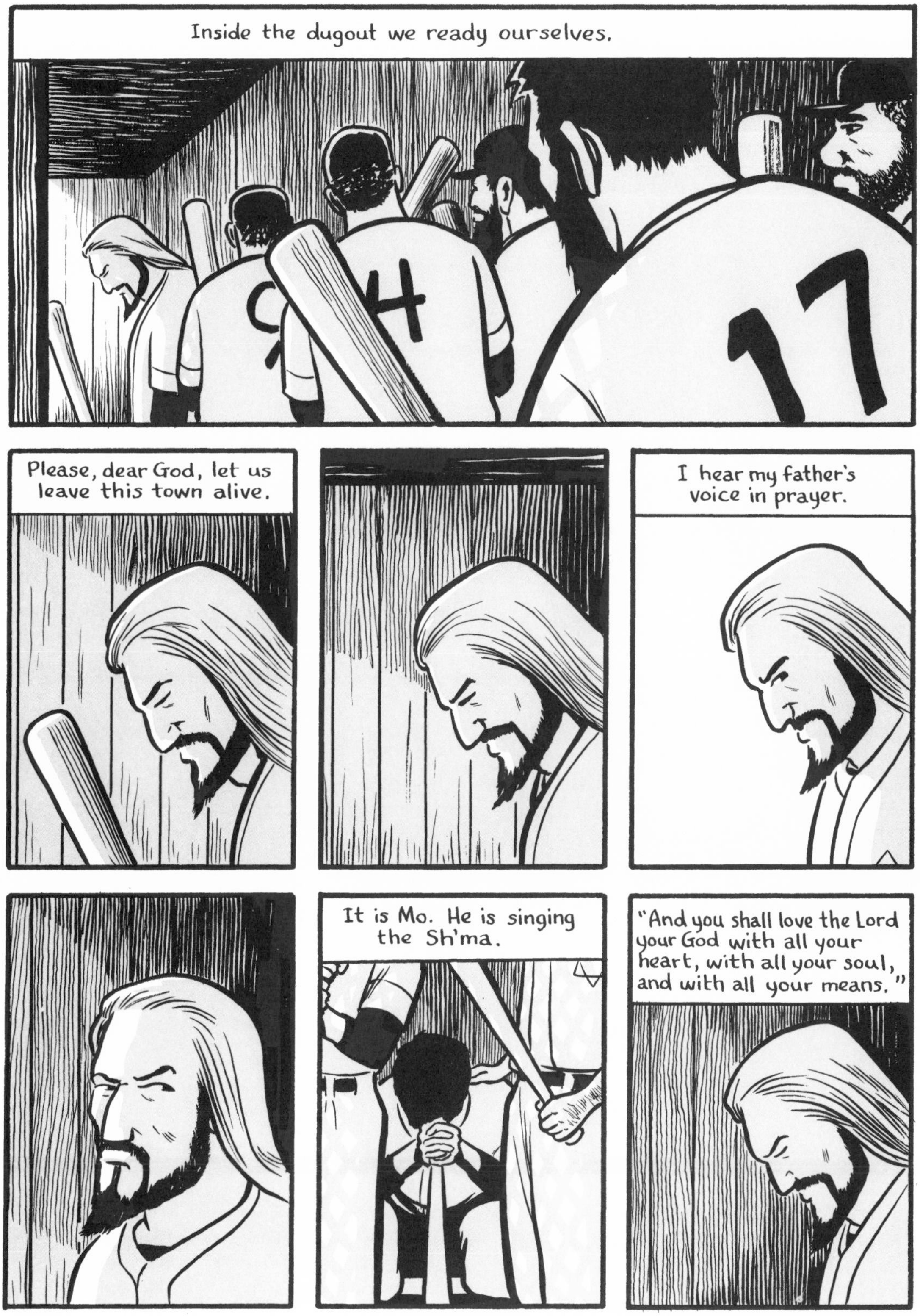
Inside the dugout we ready ourselves.
Please, dear God, let us leave this town alive.
I hear my father's voice in prayer.
It is Mo. He is singing the Sh'ma.
"And you shall love the Lord your God with all your heart, with all your soul, and with all your means."

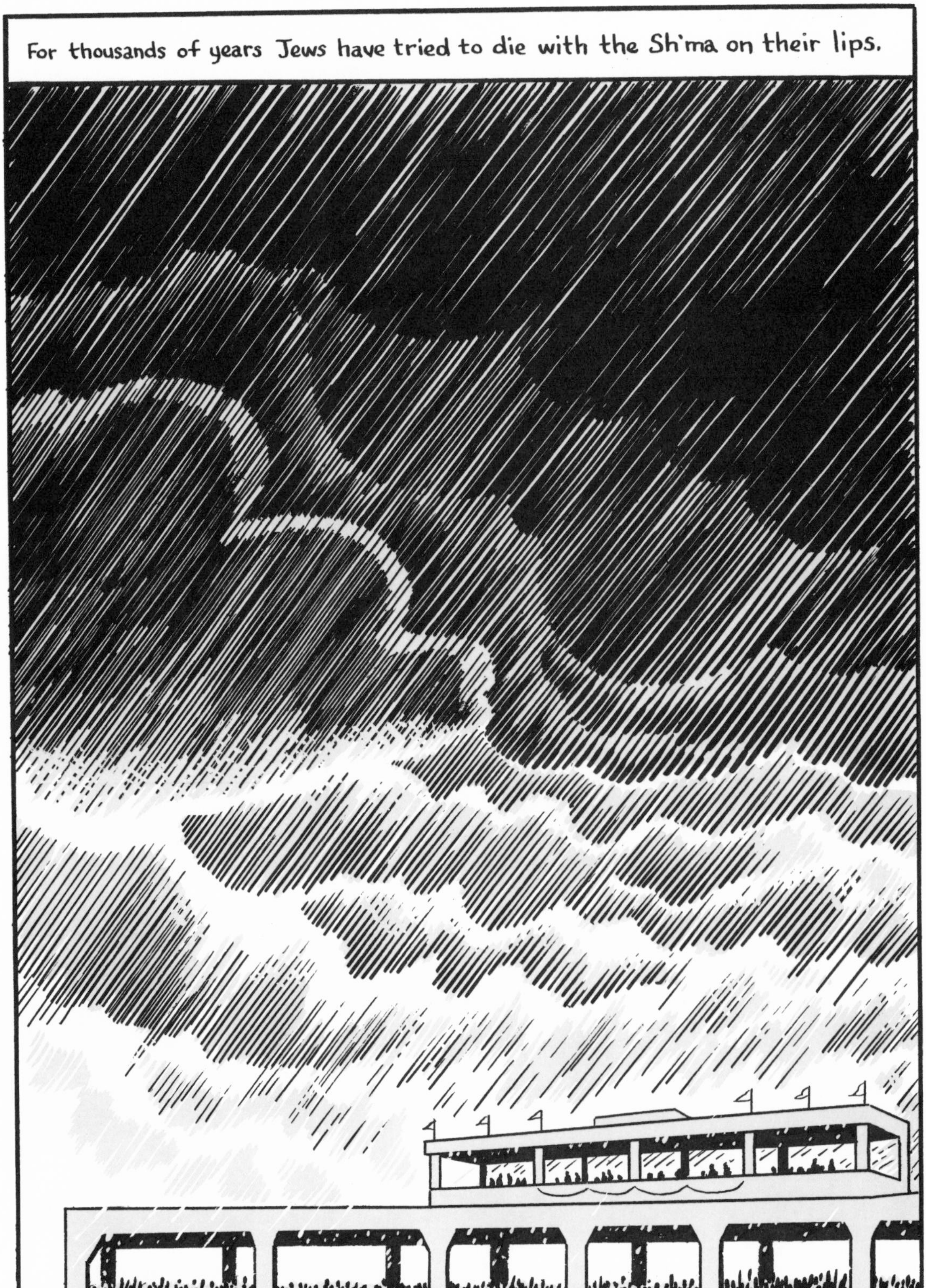
For thousands of years Jews have tried to die with the Sh'ma on their lips.

The Putnam police force pour onto the field. Mr. Putnam has spent a considerable sum for his team. I'm sure he'll feel robbed unless he sees them thoroughly beat us.

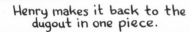
Henry makes it back to the dugout in one piece.

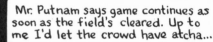
Mr. Putnam says game continues as soon as the field's cleared. Up to me I'd let the crowd have atcha...

This is no passing summer shower.

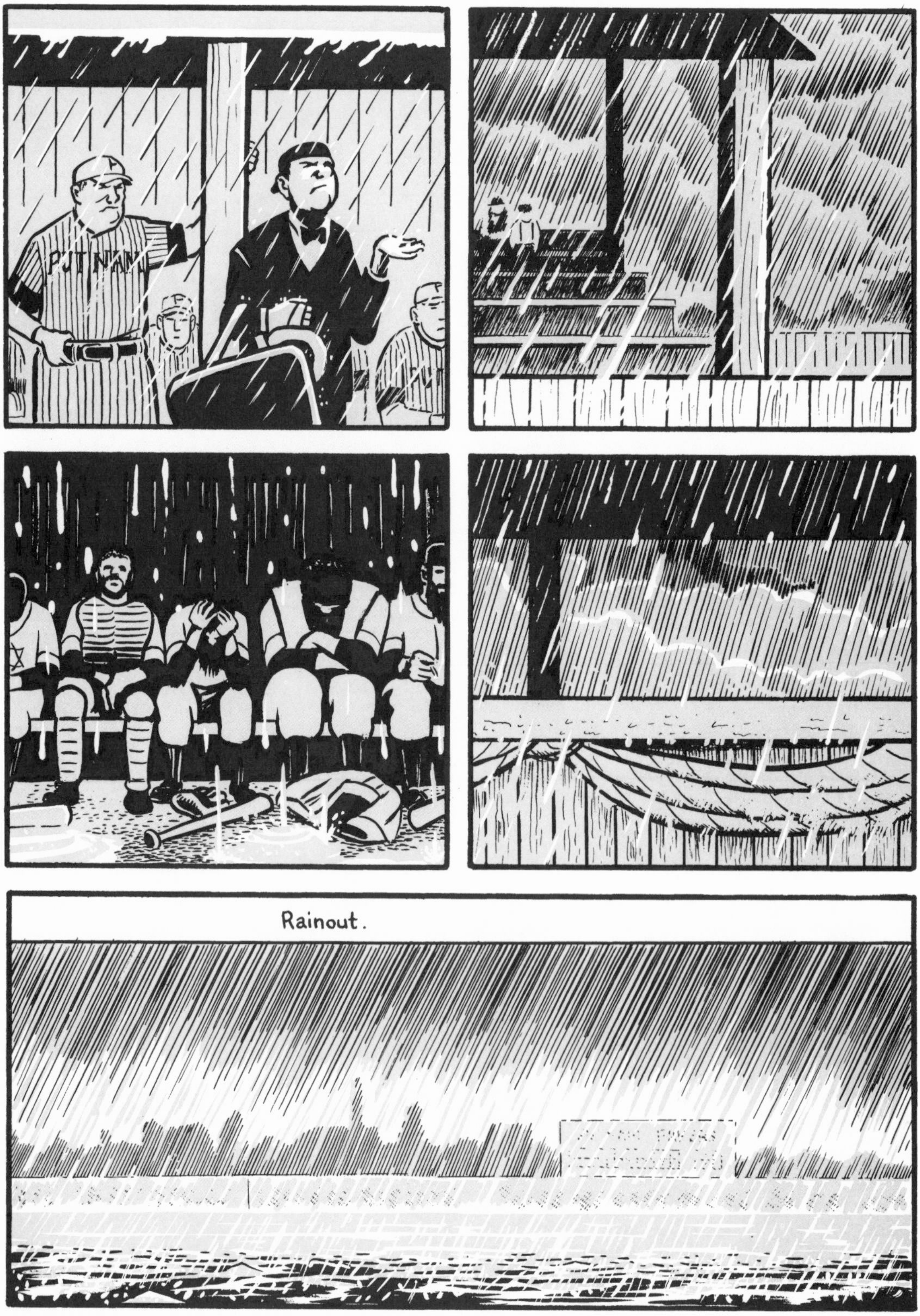
Rainout.

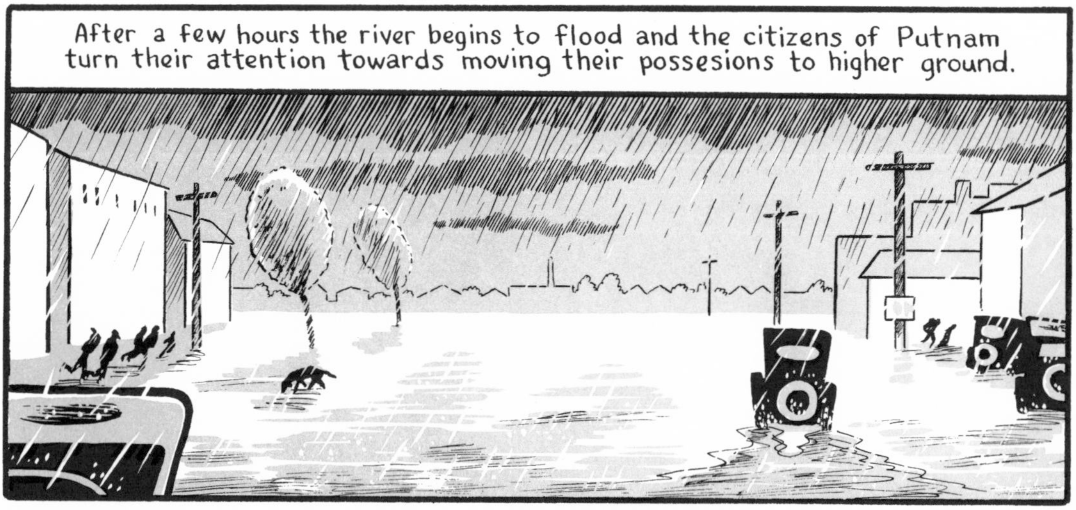
After a few hours the river begins to flood and the citizens of Putnam turn their attention towards moving their possesions to higher ground.

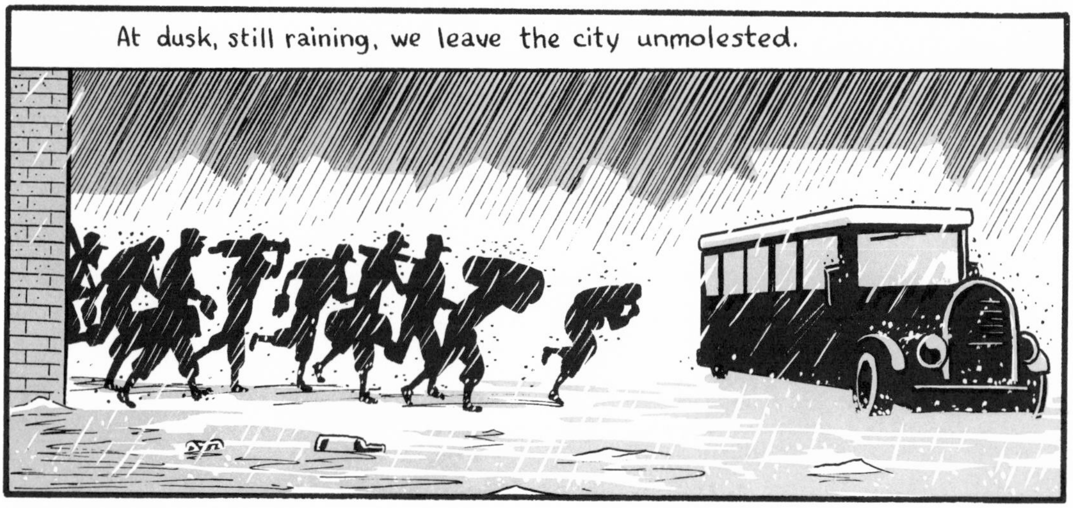
At dusk, still raining, we leave the city unmolested.

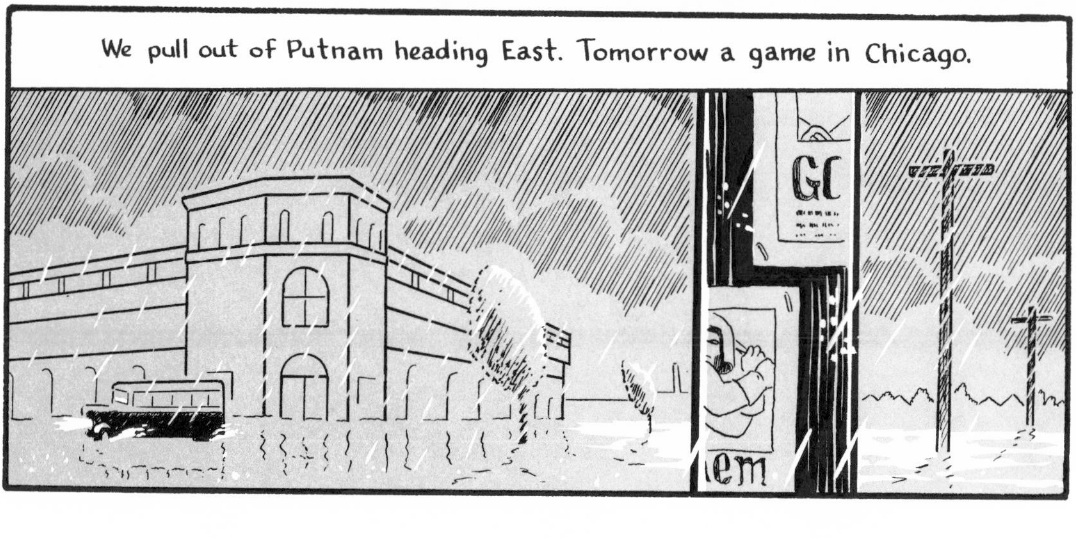
We pull out of Putnam heading East. Tomorrow a game in Chicago.

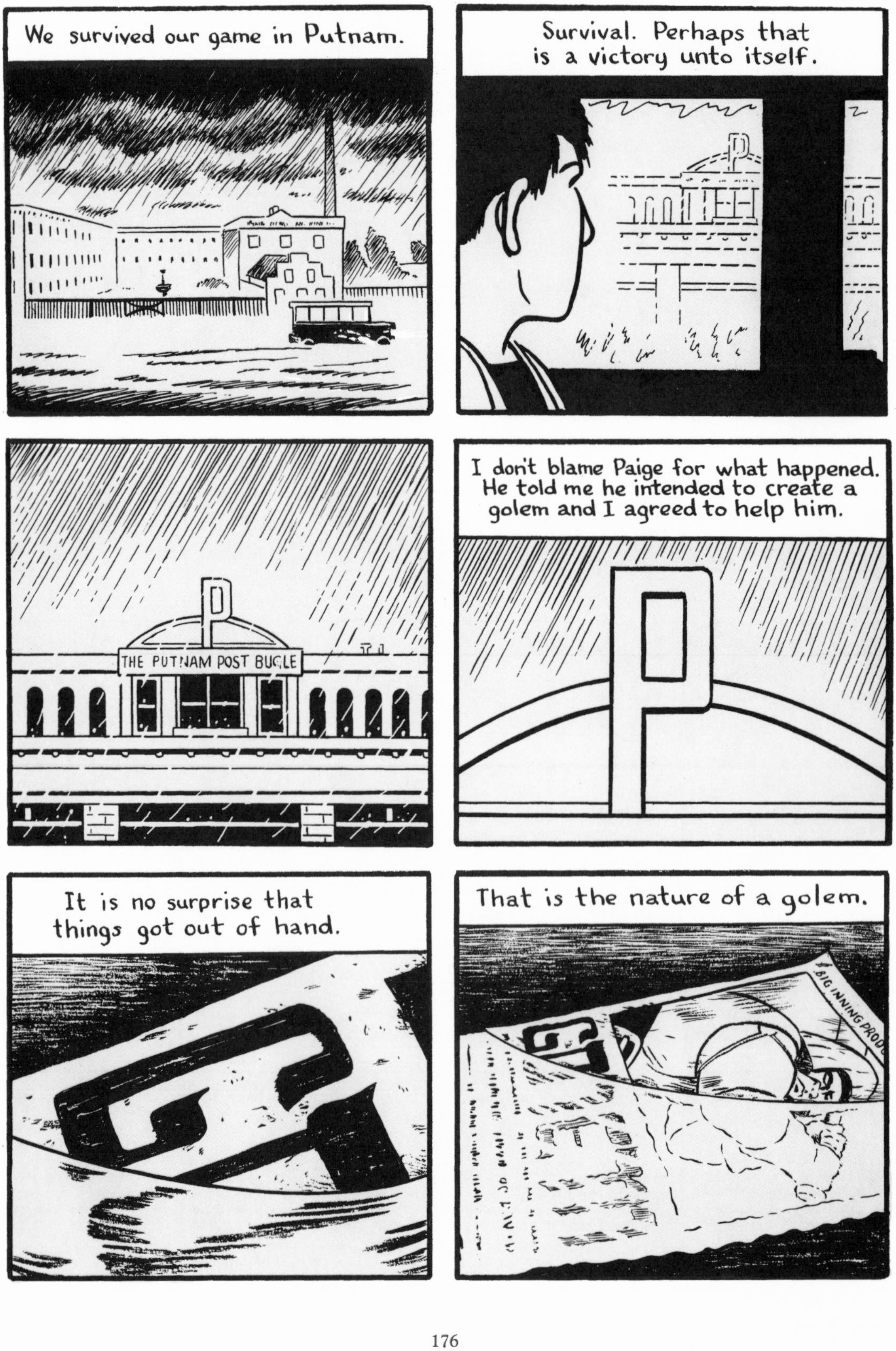

We survived our game in Putnam.
Survival. Perhaps that is a victory unto itself.
THE PUTNAM POST BUGLE
I don't blame Paige for what happened. He told me he intended to create a golem and I agreed to help him.
It is no surprise that things got out of hand.
That is the nature of a golem.
BIG INNING PROD

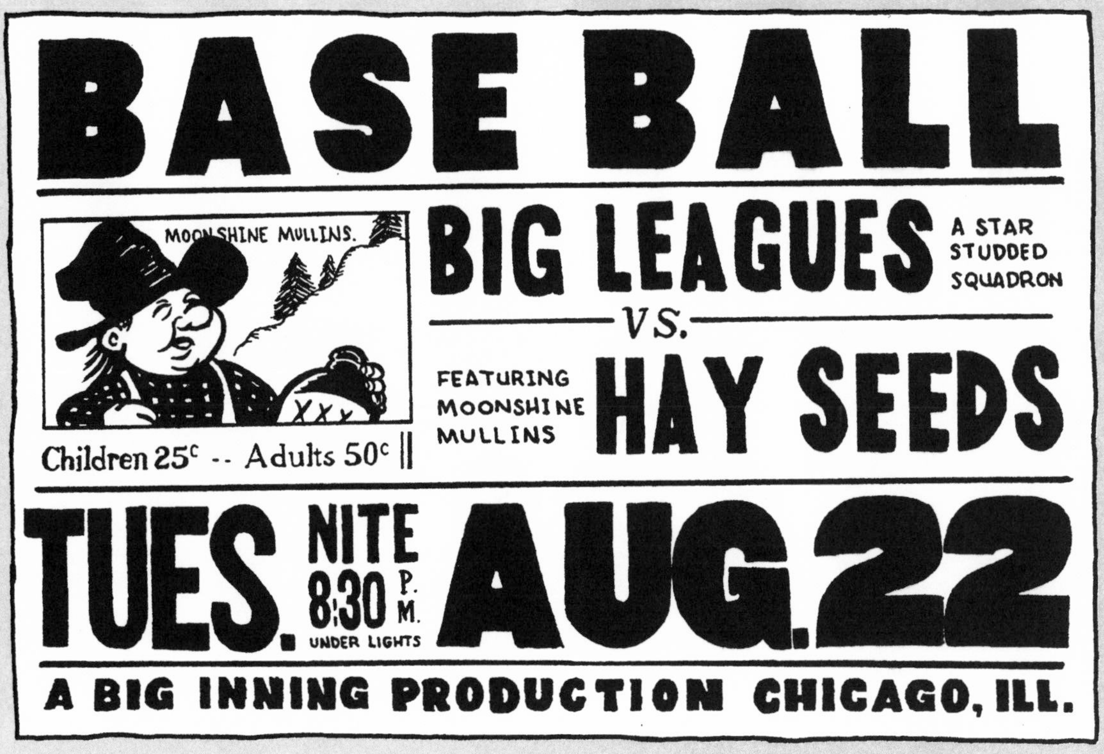
BASE BALL
MOONSHINE MULLINS.
XXX
BIG LEAGUES
A STAR STUDDED SQUADRON
VS.
FEATURING MOONSHINE MULLINS
HAY SEEDS
Children 25c -- Adults 50c
TUES.
NITE 8:30 P.M.
UNDER LIGHTS
AUG.22
A BIG INNING PRODUCTION CHICAGO, ILL.

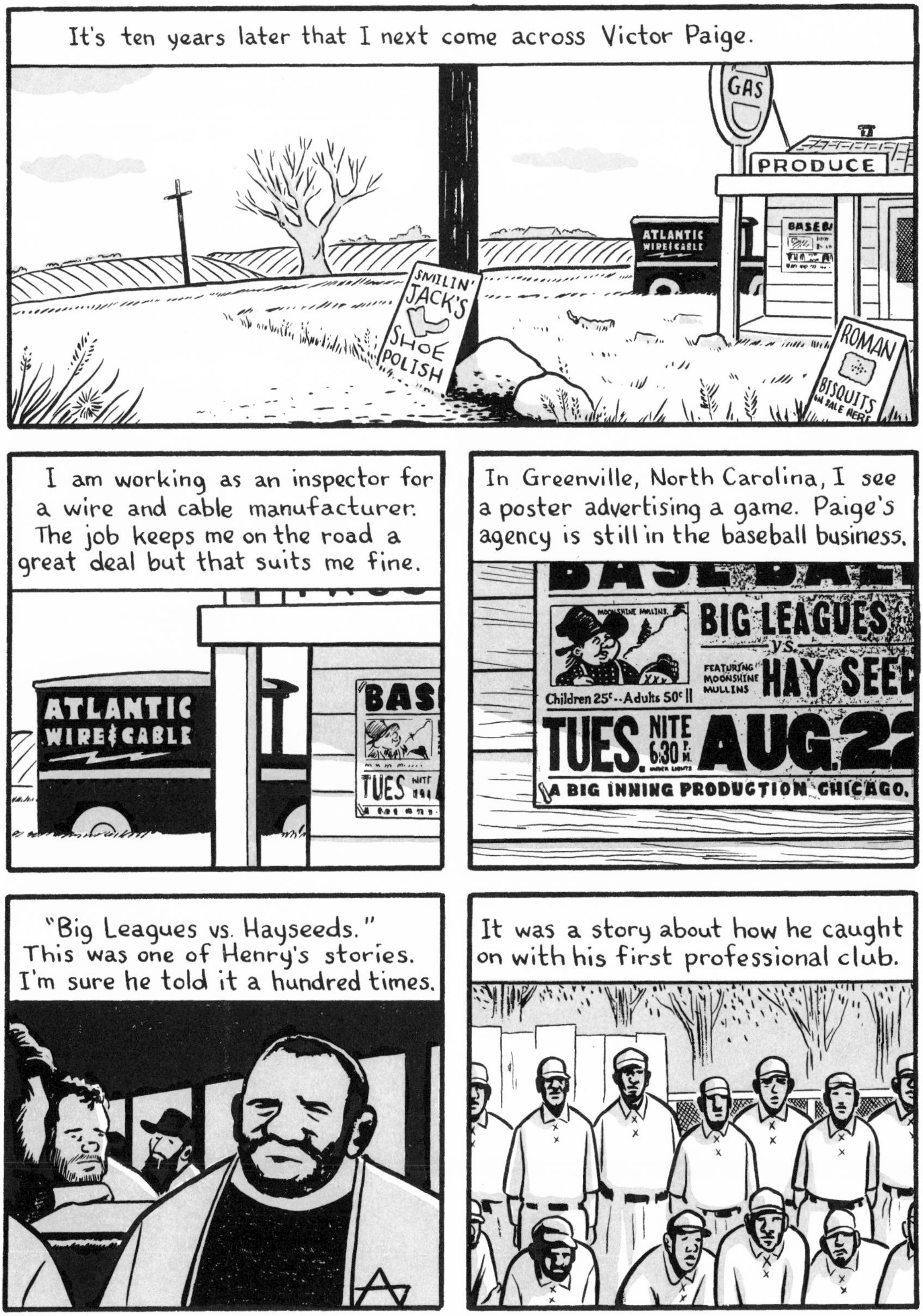
It's ten years later that I next come across Victor Paige.
GAS
PRODUCE
ATLANTIC WIRE & CABLE
SMILIN' JACK'S SHOE POLISH
ROMAN BISQUITS ON SALE HERE
I am working as an inspector for a wire and cable manufacturer. The job keeps me on the road a great deal but that suits me fine.
ATLANTIC WIRE & CABLE
In Greenville, North Carolina, I see a poster advertising a game. Paige's agency is still in the baseball business.
MOONSHINE MULLINS
BIG LEAGUES vs. HAY SEED
FEATURING MOONSHINE MULLINS
Children 25¢ - Adults 50¢
TUES. NITE 6:30 P.M. AUG. 22
UNDER LIGHTS
A BIG INNING PRODUCTION CHICAGO,
"Big Leagues vs. Hayseeds." This was one of Henry's stories. I'm sure he told it a hundred times.
It was a story about how he caught on with his first professional club.

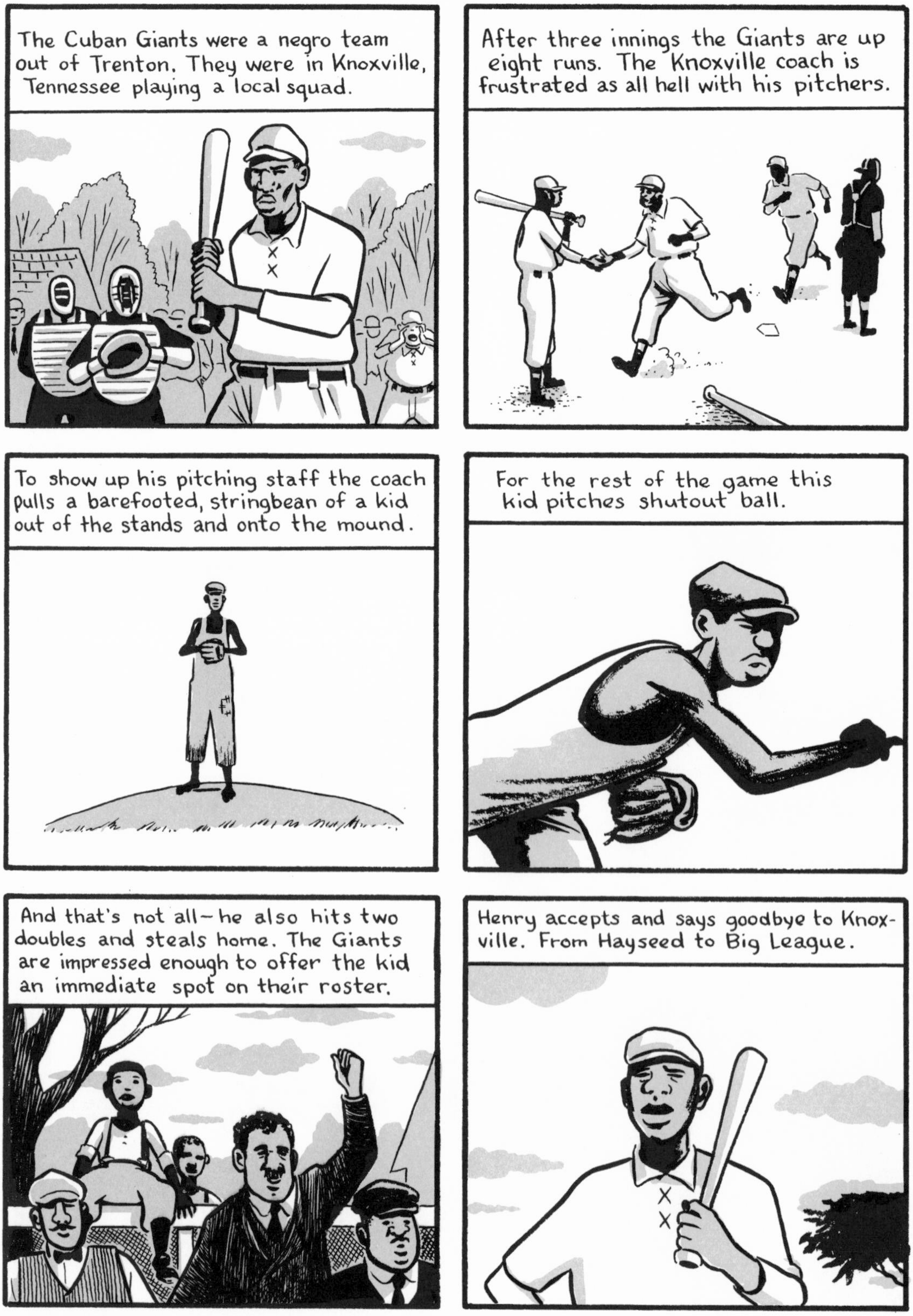
The Cuban Giants were a negro team out of Trenton. They were in Knoxville, Tennessee playing a local squad.
After three innings the Giants are up eight runs. The Knoxville coach is frustrated as all hell with his pitchers.
To show up his pitching staff the coach pulls a barefooted, stringbean of a kid out of the stands and onto the mound.
For the rest of the game this kid pitches shutout ball.
And that's not all—he also hits two doubles and steals home. The Giants are impressed enough to offer the kid an immediate spot on their roster.
Henry accepts and says goodbye to Knoxville. From Hayseed to Big League.

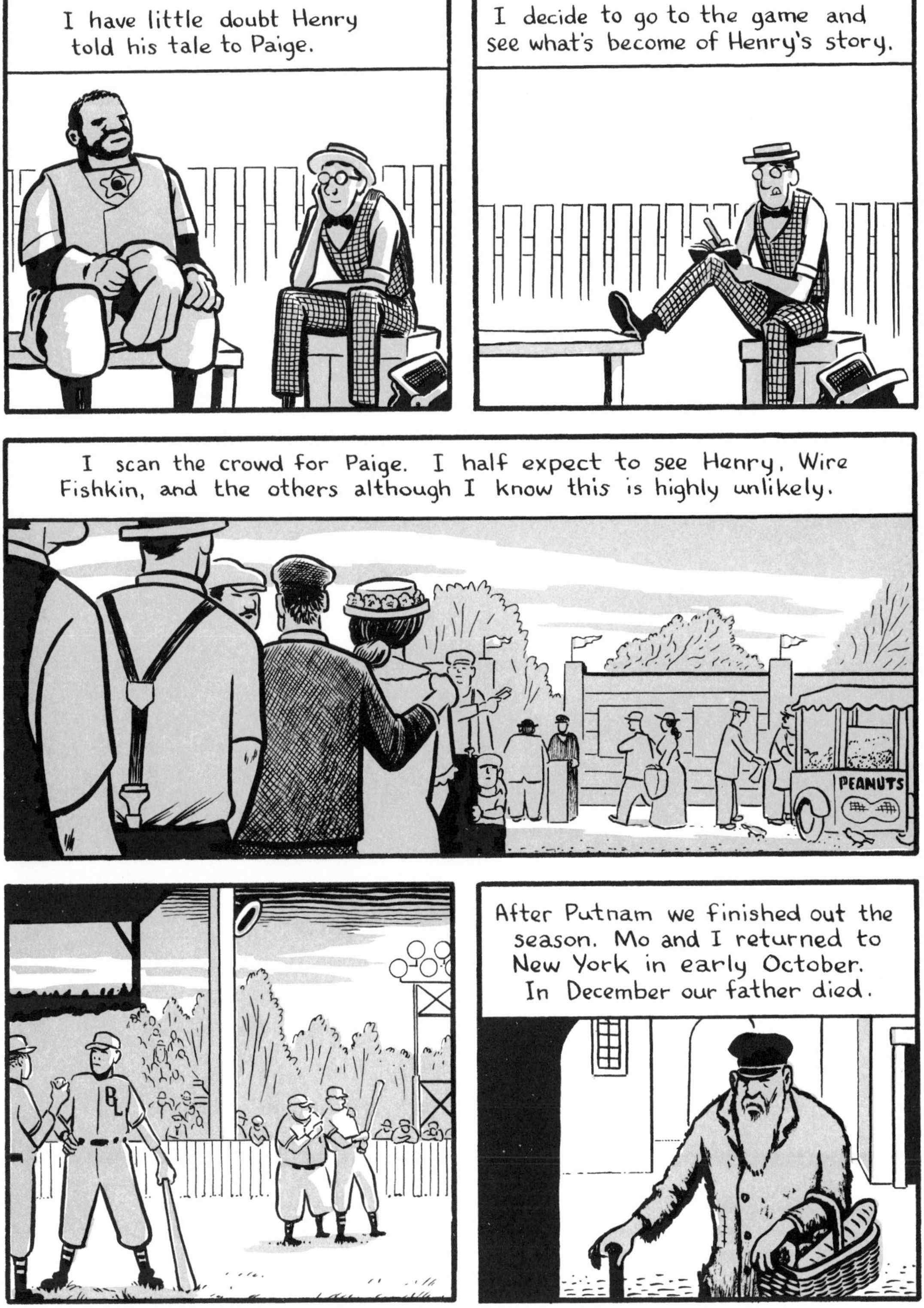
I have little doubt Henry told his tale to Paige.
I decide to go to the game and see what's become of Henry's story.
I scan the crowd for Paige. I half expect to see Henry, Wire Fishkin, and the others although I know this is highly unlikely.
PEANUTS
After Putnam we finished out the season. Mo and I returned to New York in early October. In December our father died.

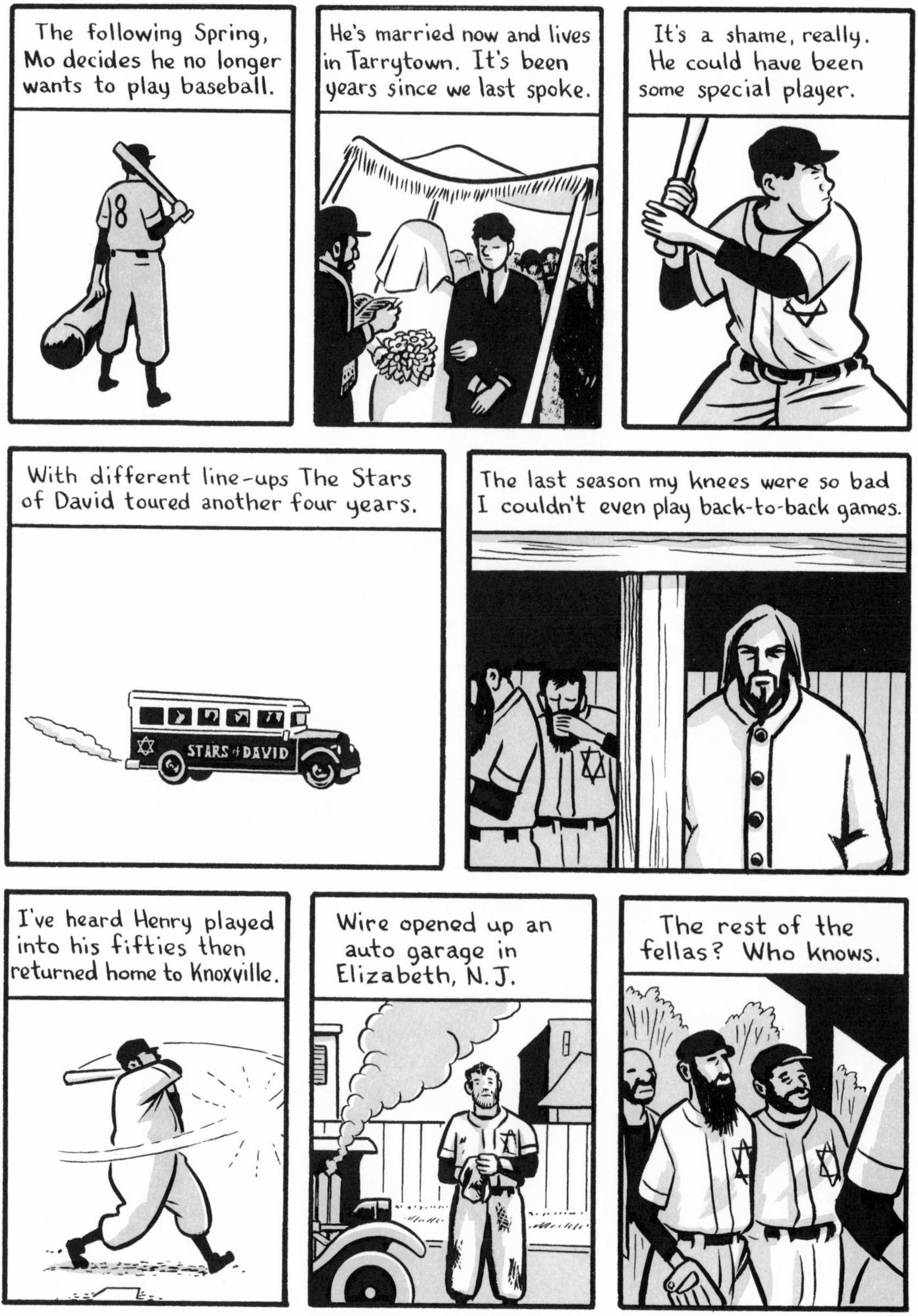
The following Spring, Mo decides he no longer wants to play baseball.
8
He's married now and lives in Tarrytown. It's been years since we last spoke.
It's a shame, really. He could have been some special player.
With different line-ups The Stars of David toured another four years.
STARS of DAVID
The last season my knees were so bad I couldn't even play back-to-back games.
I've heard Henry played into his fifties then returned home to Knoxville.
Wire opened up an auto garage in Elizabeth, N.J.
The rest of the fellas? Who knows.

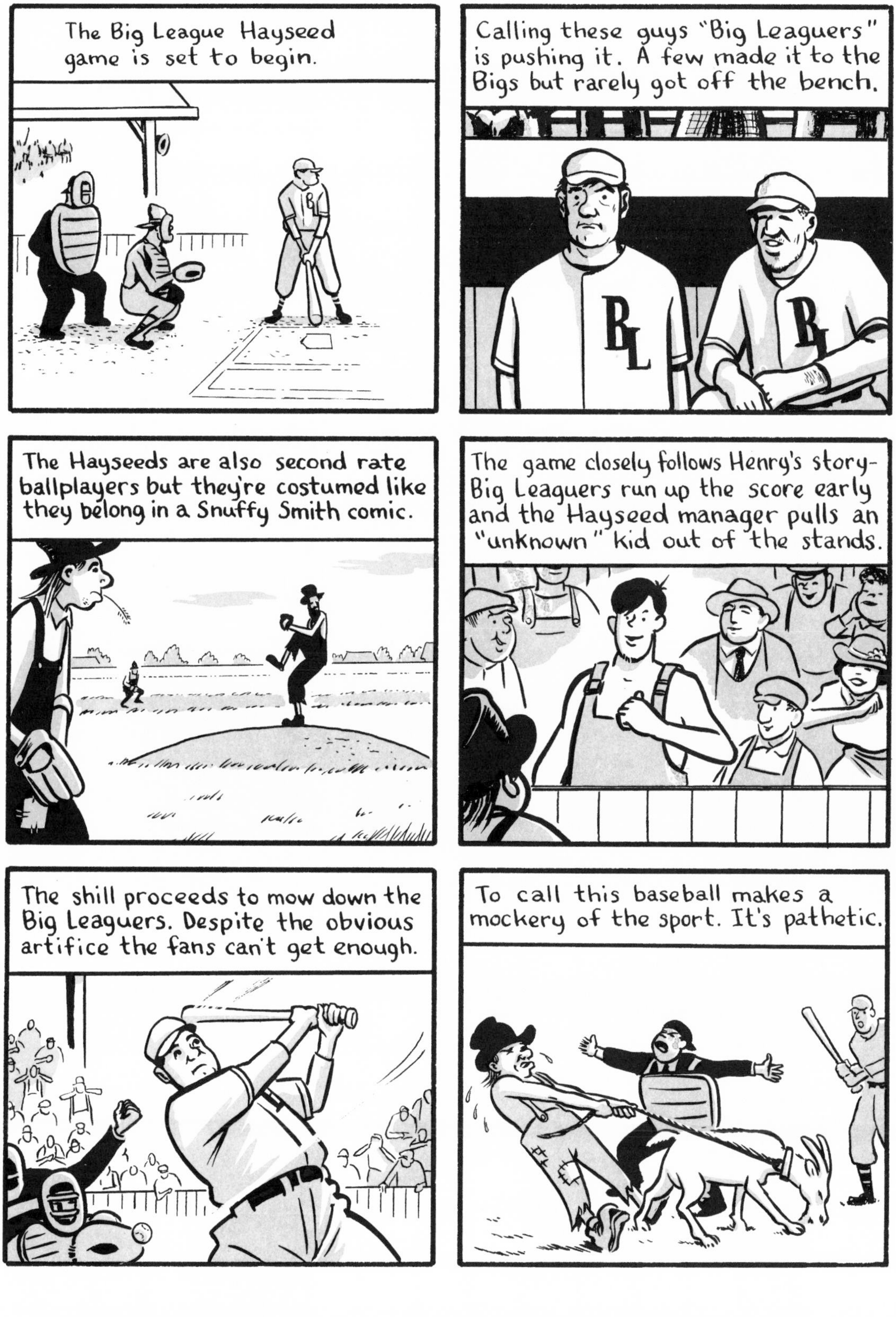
The Big League Hayseed game is set to begin.
Calling these guys "Big Leaguers" is pushing it. A few made it to the Bigs but rarely got off the bench.
The Hayseeds are also second rate ballplayers but they're costumed like they belong in a Snuffy Smith comic.
The game closely follows Henry's story- Big Leaguers run up the score early and the Hayseed manager pulls an "unknown" kid out of the stands.
The shill proceeds to mow down the Big Leaguers. Despite the obvious artifice the fans can't get enough.
To call this baseball makes a mockery of the sport. It's pathetic.

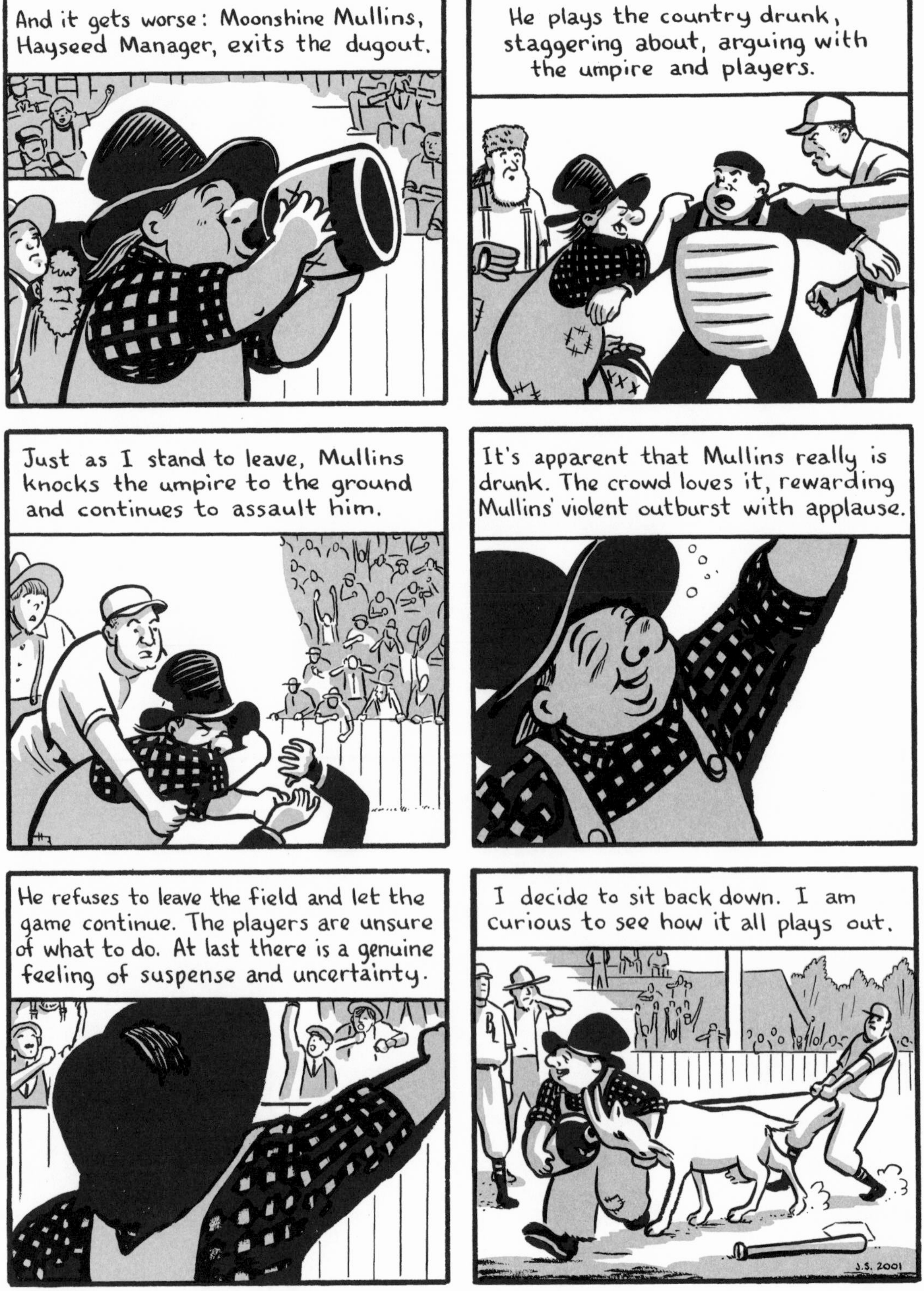
And it gets worse: Moonshine Mullins, Hayseed Manager, exits the dugout.
He plays the country drunk, staggering about, arguing with the umpire and players.
Just as I stand to leave, Mullins knocks the umpire to the ground and continues to assault him.
It's apparent that Mullins really is drunk. The crowd loves it, rewarding Mullins' violent outburst with applause.
He refuses to leave the field and let the game continue. The players are unsure of what to do. At last there is a genuine feeling of suspense and uncertainty.
I decide to sit back down. I am curious to see how it all plays out.
J.S. 2001

# NOTES

## THE REVIVAL

### Background of Events

The American frontier of the late 18th century moved quickly. In 1782 not one permanent settlement existed in the whole of Ohio. Fifteen years later 70,000 called Ohio home. By the early 19th century religious sects and societies flourished in a way unrivaled in the history of American religions: Sabbatarians, Congregationalists, Mennonites, Millerites, Jerkers, Adventists, Shakers, Swedenborgians, Universalists, Friends, Restorationists, Convenanters, School Presbyterians, United Brethren, Methodists, Lutherans, Baptists, and many more, spread their gospels and sought converts.

Spreading their gospels and seeking converts they held outdoor camp meetings where hundreds and sometimes thousands would gather to praise the Lord and revel in His power. In 1801, at Cane Ridge Kentucky, located in the central part of the state, the largest camp meeting this country had ever seen took place. Estimates of attendance ranged from 10,000 to 25,000 with people coming from across Kentucky, Tennessee, and even the territory north of the Ohio River.

### Testimonials of Those That Bore Witness

The impression that Cane Ridge left upon its participants was powerful. However, many accounts were dismissed as too unworldly, outlandish, or blasphemous by those not present.

*"…the mighty power of God was displayed in a very extraordinary manner; many were moved to tears, and bitter and loud crying for mercy…Hundreds fell prostrate under the mighty power of God, as men slain in battle. Stands were erected in the woods from which preachers of different Churches proclaimed repentance toward God and faith in our Lord Jesus Christ."*

*"…no one wanted to go home. Hunger*

and sleep seemed to affect nobody—eternal things were of the vast concern. The eyes of the crowd were blazed with the glory of heaven, seeing only the divine and celestial…"

"…the scene was awful beyond description. The roar of the vast crowd sounded like the roar of Niagara. A strange supernatural power seemed to pervade the entire mass of mind there collected. At one time I saw at least 500 swept down in a moment as if a battery of 1,000 guns had been opened upon them, and then immediately followed shrieks and shouts that rent the very heavens."

"…the first jerk or so you would see their bonnets, caps, and combs fly; and so sudden was the jerking of the head that their long loose hair would crack almost as loud as a wagoner's whip…to gain relief from their jerks they would dance hysterically; they shouted, sobbed, leaped in the air, writhed on the ground, fell down like dead men, then lay insensible, or in grotesque contortions on the ground. They laughed senseless holy laughs, were seized with barks, then jumped around like dogs on all fours and, still barking, treed the devil like dogs chasing a squirrel. When all else failed, they spoke in a jibberish they believed to be other tongues used by the apostles in the Bible…"

"…everyone was crying out for mercy. The anguished screams caused trees to sway…mother, she was fell and breathing hard, like a sheep down on a hot day…little Peter was sobbing and crying out, but his cries sounded not like a six-year-old boy, but of a coarse-voiced older man…"

### HUNDREDS OF FEET BELOW DAYLIGHT

The above image was an often-reproduced drawing by Frank Marryat that depicts a miner's funeral where gold was discovered in his grave. "The preacher stopped and inquiringly asked: 'Boys, what's that?,' took a view of the ground himself, and shouted, 'Gold! Gold! And the richest kind of diggings! The congregation is dismissed!' The dead miner was buried elsewhere and the funeral party, the minister at its head, lost no time in prospecting and staking out new digging!"

## The Golem's Mighty Swing

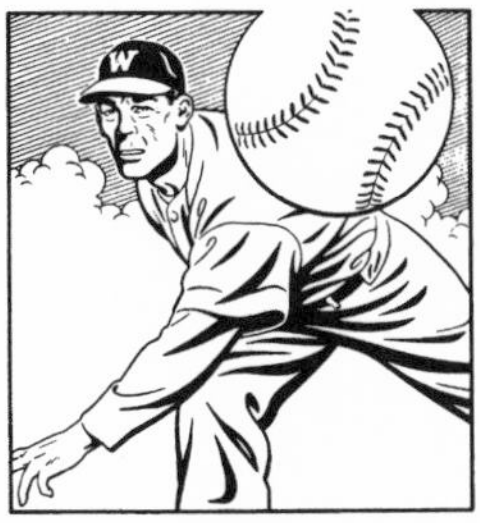

The work of baseball historian Donald Honig, cartoonist Ray Gotto (left), and the baseball manga of Shinji Mizushima (right) were valuable reference in the production of *The Golem's Mighty Swing*. Donald Honig edited many superb volumes of classic baseball photography. Ray Gotto's mid–1950s run on the comic strip *Cotton Woods* were the best American baseball comics that I came across. Shinji Mizushima's *Shonen Champion Manga* are the gold standard of sports comics. Mizushima expertly captures both baseball's grand moments and subtle nuances.

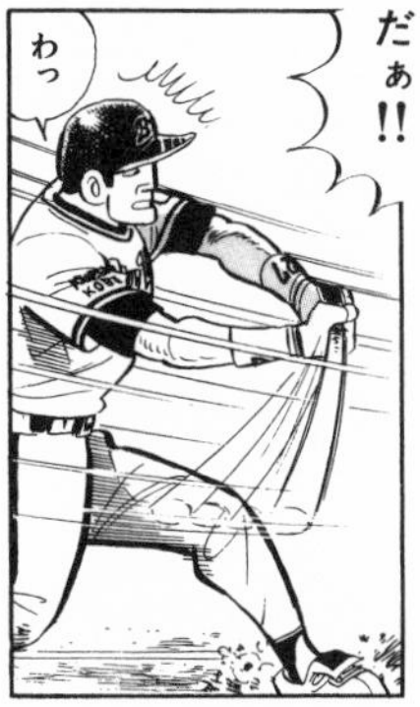
だぁ!!
わっ

### *Acknowledgements*

An intoxicating brew of historical documents and ephemera, history books, fiction, photographs, and, of course, comics were pored over during the years that these stories were crafted. I feel indebted to every author, painter, cartoonist, and historian that I stole from.

Thanks to my good friend R. Sikoryak for providing crucial feedback and generous, steadfast encouragement. Thank you Chris Oliveros, whose early faith in my work provided me a measure of confidence and fortitude that was desperately needed during those days when I was convinced that every line I drew was dead and every idea derivative.

And deepest gratitude to Rachel Gross, who traveled with me every step of the way.

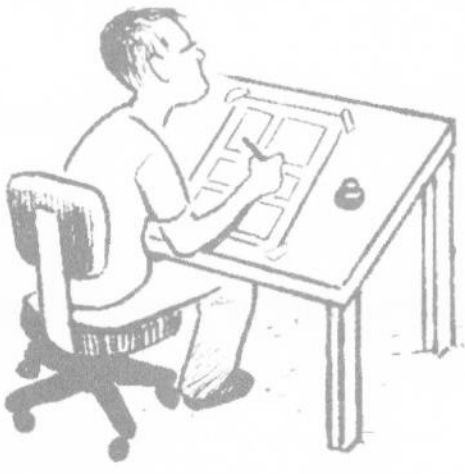

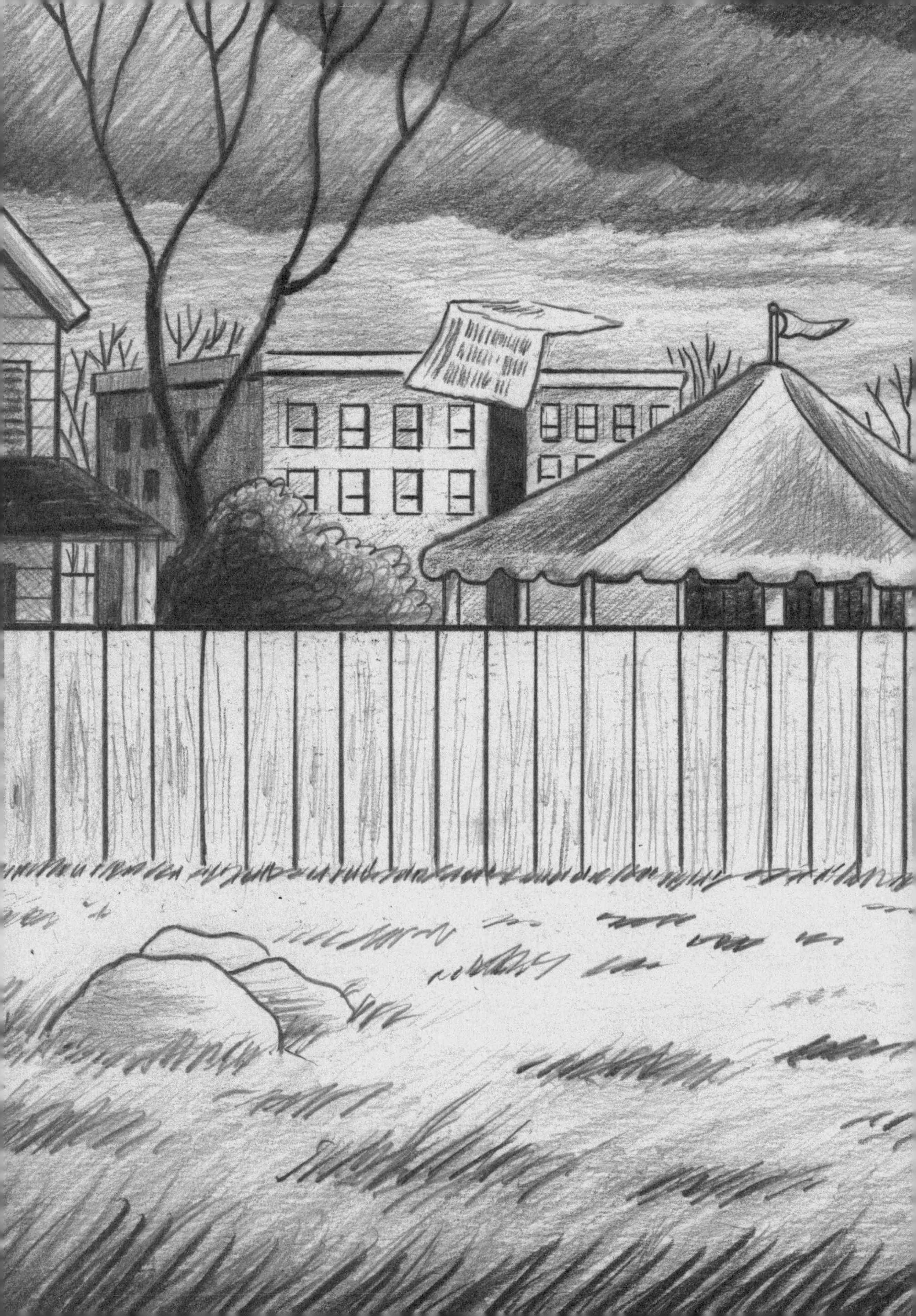